Acclaim for NATHAN McCALL'S
MAKES ME WANNA HOLLER

"So honest, so well-written, so powerful that it will leave you shaken and educated. The book belongs in every prison library and affluent country club. No one—black or white, rich or poor—will come away unrewarded."
—*USA Today*

"Not since Claude Brown's *Manchild in the Promised Land* has there been such an honest and searching look at the perils of growing up a black male in urban America . . . a compelling depiction of the toll that racism and misguided notions of manhood have taken in the life of one black man—and, by implication, many others."
—*San Francisco Chronicle*

"Soul-searing . . . an unsettling account of the human consequences of an American tragedy."
—*Time*

"Both poignant and disturbing . . . *Makes Me Wanna Holler* has the feel of a classic. . . . There is value and depth to what [McCall] reveals. And, above all, there is a two-fisted honesty, unflinching in its recognition of the multifaceted dynamic of America's unmitigated neurosis. . . . Obscene, fiery, in-your-face [and] utterly believable."
—*St Louis Post-Dispatch*

"With great technical skill and insight, McCall . . . shows the humanity of a population commonly perceived as menacing. . . . And he offers sane, well-reasoned explanations for why that group seems to be at the center of so much urban distress. . . . Required reading for anyone interested in American race relations."
—*Philadelphia Inquirer*

"*Makes Me Wanna Holler* will become a modern classic. It is *Manchild in the Promised Land* for a new generation."
—Claude Brown

NATHAN McCALL
MAKES ME WANNA HOLLER

Nathan McCall grew up in Portsmouth, Virginia. He studied journalism at Norfolk State University after serving three years in prison. He reported for the *Virginian Pilot-Ledger Star* and the *Atlanta Journal-Constitution* before moving to *The Washington Post* in 1989.

MAKES ME WANNA HOLLER

MAKES ME WANNA HOLLER

A Young Black
Man in America

NATHAN McCALL

VINTAGE BOOKS

A Division of Random House, Inc.

New York

FIRST VINTAGE BOOKS EDITION, FEBRUARY 1995

Library of Congress Cataloging-in-Publication Data
McCall, Nathan.
Makes me wanna holler : a young black man in America / Nathan
McCall.
p. cm.
ISBN 0-679-41268-9
1. McCall, Nathan.   2. Afro-Americans—Biography.
3. Journalists—United States—Biography.   4. Afro-American youth.
5. Afro-American men.   I. Title.
E185.97.M12A3   1994
305.38'96073'092—dc20
[B]   93-30654
Vintage ISBN: 0-679-74070-8

Manufactured in the United States of America
79C8

"I have ridden the shoulders of my mother and my father
    to arrive at my today.
"I hold their hands as I test the strength of my legs
    to climb into my tomorrow."

(taken from an African rite-of-passage ceremony)

To my parents, Lenora and Bonnie Alvin

CONTENTS

PART THREE

PART ONE

PART ONE

Chapter 1 GET-BACK

he fellas and I were hanging out on our corner one afternoon when the strangest thing happened. A white boy, who appeared to be about eighteen or nineteen years old, came pedaling a bicycle casually through the neighborhood. I don't know if he was lost or just confused, but he was definitely in the wrong place to be doing the tourist bit. Somebody spotted him and pointed him out to the rest of us. "Look! What's that motherfucka doin' ridin' through here?! Is he *crraaaazy*?!"

It was automatic. We all took off after him. We caught him on Cavalier Boulevard and knocked him off the bike. He fell to the ground and it was all over. We were on him like white on rice. Ignoring the passing cars, we stomped him and kicked him. My stick partners kicked him in the head and face and watched the blood gush from his mouth. I kicked him in the stomach and nuts, where I knew it would hurt. Every time I drove my foot into his balls, I felt better; with each blow delivered, I gritted my teeth as I remembered some recent racial slight:

THIS is for all the times you followed me round in stores. . . .
And THIS is for the times you treated me like a nigger. . . .
And THIS is for G.P.—General Principle—just 'cause you white.

While we kicked, he lay there, curled up in the fetal position, trying to use his hands to cover his head. We bloodied him so badly that I got a little scared and backed off. The others, seeing how badly he was messed up, moved away too. But one dude kept stomping, like he'd gone berserk. He seemed crazed and consumed in the pleasure of kicking that white boy's ass. When he finished, he reached down and picked up the white dude's bike, lifted it as high as he could above his head, and slammed it down on him hard. The white guy didn't even flinch. He was out cold. I feared he might be dead until I saw him breathing.

We walked away, laughing, boasting, competing for bragging rights about who'd done the most damage. "Man, did you see how red that cracker's face turned when I busted his lip? I almost broke my hand on that ugly motherfucka!"

Fucking up white boys like that made us feel *good* inside. I guess we must have been fourteen or fifteen by then, and it felt so good that we stumbled over each other sometimes trying to get in extra kicks and punches. When we bum-rushed white boys, it made me feel like we were beating all white people on behalf of all blacks. We called it "gettin' some get-back," securing revenge for all the shit they'd heaped on blacks all these years. They were still heaping hell on us, and especially on our parents. The difference was, cats in my generation weren't taking it lying down.

After my older brother Dwight got his driver's license, a group of us would pile into my stepfather's car some evenings and cruise through a nearby white neighborhood, searching for people walking the streets. We'd spot some whites, get out, rush over, and, using sticks and fists, try to beat them to within an inch of their lives.

Sometimes, when I sit back and think about the crazy things the fellas and I did and remember the hate and violence that we unleashed, it's hard to believe I was once part of all that—I feel so removed from it now that I've left the streets. Yet when I consider white America and the way it's treated blacks, our random rage in the old days makes perfect sense to me. Looking back, it's easy to understand how it all got started. . . .

Chapter 2 CAVALIER MANOR

For as long as I can remember, it seems that there was no aspect of my family's reality that wasn't affected by whites, right on down to the creation of the neighborhood I grew up in. Known as Cavalier Manor, it was located in Portsmouth, Virginia. Most of Cavalier Manor was built in the early 1960s by a local construction bigwig named George T. McClean. Neighborhood lore had it that he was a white liberal do-gooder who felt blacks in Portsmouth needed a community that would inspire pride and help improve their lot. But just as many people thought McClean was a racist who got alarmed by the civil rights movement and built Cavalier Manor to encourage blacks to move there rather than into white neighborhoods.

McClean started building from the edge of an older, low-income black neighborhood and went southward, making the houses larger and more elegant with each successive phase. He named the streets after U.S. presidents and prominent blacks, particularly entertainers. The streets had names such as Belafonte Drive, Basie Crescent, Eckstine Drive, and Horne Avenue. To add to the sense of optimism that the neighborhood was supposed to reflect, they even named one street Freedom Avenue.

Although some folks there liked to think of themselves as middle-class, Cavalier Manor was a working-class neighborhood. Most of those who moved there were active or retired military personnel. Few had completed high school or gone to college. The retirees usually found blue-collar jobs at one of the massive military installations in the area, which is home to some of the world's largest shipyards. Many others who moved there were uneducated working-class folks who had scrimped and saved enough money to move from public housing.

By the time the bulk of it was finished, Cavalier Manor had come to be one of the largest black neighborhoods in the Southeast. In terms of political power, this meant that our neighborhood emerged as a potentially influential voting bloc. In terms of street power, it meant that Cavalier Manor surfaced as a helluva gang force throughout the

Tidewater area, which spans several Virginia cities. The neighborhood was so big that dudes formed distinct gangs in different sections of the community. These gangs fought each other sometimes and united when fighting downtown boys.

But I was unaware of all that street action when we first came to Cavalier Manor. I was only nine years old then, in 1964, the year my family moved to Portsmouth from Key West, Florida, where my stepfather had served a three-year tour of duty in the Navy. We'd also lived in Morocco and Norfolk, Virginia, and Portsmouth was to be my stepfather's last duty station before he retired after giving Uncle Sam twenty years.

I still remember how excited my brothers and I were about moving into our first real house. When we drove into our new neighborhood, our eyes and mouths flew wide open. We saw impressive homes with freshly sprouted lawns, broad sidewalks, and newly paved streets. On each side of the street that led to our section of the community were two sets of stately white brick pillars with black cast-iron bars flowing regally through their tops. A huge sign printed in Old English lettering was mounted on each set of pillars: "Welcome to Cavalier Manor." My brothers and I thought we had died and gone to heaven.

It wasn't the kind of neighborhood I associated with black people then. We'd always lived in drab apartment buildings that looked like public housing. All the black people we knew had lived that way.

In Cavalier Manor, we pulled into our very own driveway, which led to a garage where we could park our ride. When we walked into the house, the sun shone brightly through the windows, bringing out every wonderful detail of the place. It was a single-story structure with three bedrooms, a living room, a kitchen, and a formal dining room.

I could feel its newness and smell the freshness of the recently painted walls and ceilings. The hardwood floors had been sanded and buffed. Tiny mounds of sawdust remained in corners, as if construction workers had left only hours before we arrived.

My brothers and I ran outside to inspect our front and back yards. The air was filled with the steady hum of lawn mowers and the sweet smell of freshly cut grass. Pine needles that had fallen from the many tall trees out back were scattered everywhere. We learned to hate raking those pine needles, but our initial reaction to our new home and neighborhood was that we loved everything.

Located in a cul-de-sac named Vaughn Court, ours was one of

several streets that the white folks misspelled in their haste. There were twelve homes in the court. We lived in number 6. Several blocks away, a large lake, Crystal Lake, wound through a portion of the neighborhood.

We got that house just in time to accommodate the expansion of our family. Along with my parents, there were my two brothers, Dwight and Billy, who were two and four years older than me respectively. A short time after we arrived, my mother gave birth to another boy, the first child born to her and my stepfather. They named him Bryan Keith Alvin, after Brian Keith, the white actor. As she had in the past, my maternal grandmother, whom we called Bampoose, came to live with us. Then my stepfather took in Junnie, a son of his from a previous marriage who was three years older than me. So within the first year we were living there, our family nearly doubled in size. It was crowded and we were broke as hell, but it felt like we were livin' large.

■ ■ ■

In those first few years, Cavalier Manor offered a Huck Finn kind of existence for my brothers and me. I hung with Dwight and Greg, an only child who lived across the street. They were my initial tickets into the world beyond our street. They were both two years older than me and were often forced by my parents to let me hang with them. (Billy and Junnie, who considered themselves bona fide teenagers, developed their own circles of friends.)

We did everything, mostly innocent mischief. We skipped Sunday services at the neighborhood Presbyterian church to explore construction sites, climb on house frames, and throw dirt bombs at each other until construction supervisors came and chased us off. We went on expeditions into the nearby woods and played cowboys and Indians with cherry poppers, reeds that we hollowed and used to shoot berries at each other. We even ventured to Crystal Lake and skinny-dipped whenever we could evade grown-ups scouting there to keep children away. We delivered newspapers and mowed neighbors' lawns for spending change, rode our bicycles through the streets, and fought and made up at least twice a week. On weekends, we went to the movies or took turns spending the night at each other's homes.

And we massacred frogs. Because Cavalier Manor had once been a mass of woods and marsh, the place was crawling with them. We tossed frogs as high in the air as we could and watched them descend, spreading their limbs as though parachuting from an airplane. Then they'd splatter in the street and cough up their guts. We'd walk over to see how a splattered frog's intestines look.

We used those frogs for informal biology experiments. What would happen if you put a black widow spider or twenty red ants in a jar with a frog? How long can a frog float in a jar filled with Kool-Aid without drowning? What would happen if you put a frog in a jar, poured in gasoline, and torched it? We answered all those questions, and more.

We also hopped the back of the candy truck. In those days, every southern black neighborhood had a candy man and a candy lady. The candy lady was usually a housewife who lived in the neighborhood and sold sweets, potato chips, sodas, and other stuff out of her house to earn extra cash. The candy man was a traveling salesman who packed a truck with everything from collard greens, fish, and grocery items to candy, cakes, potato chips, and other children's delights, and drove slowly through neighborhoods, ringing a bell. The candy man came through the neighborhood most evenings or nights. We'd wait until he pulled away from the curb after making a stop, then we'd run and hop onto the back or running board as he picked up speed. It reminded me of TV westerns, where courageous cowboys hopped from their white horses onto the running boards of runaway stagecoaches and rescued screaming white ladies inside.

At first, we rode for a block or so before leaping off. Then we chanced longer distances, dangling off the back of the truck and holding on for dear life. Once, we rode all the way across town. It hadn't occurred to us that the candy man didn't live in Cavalier Manor until he pulled up to a house and turned off the engine. We hopped off the truck and had to walk miles to get back home.

■ ■ ■

There was only so much trouble we could get into in those early days. Cavalier Manor was a neighborhood filled with surrogate parents, people who would punish you like your mama and daddy if they caught you doing wrong. The worst among them were Grace, an ornery old woman who always fussed at us about walking on her grass, and Mrs. Patterson, who seemed to live at her front picture window, where she always peered out and caught us throwing rocks on Roosevelt Boulevard. By the time we got home, she would have already called Mama and given her a full report.

School was also part of that surrogate system. Most of the teachers at Cavalier Manor Elementary, where I went to fourth and fifth grades, lived in the neighborhood. Those teachers spanked us like we were their own when we acted up in class. If a disciplinary note didn't reach home, teachers were sure to update parents in church or while standing in the checkout line at Earle's supermarket on Victory Boulevard. Some of the parents even took it upon themselves to patrol the neighborhood on school days to make sure we were where we were supposed to be.

We kids hated that surrogate system. It seemed that everybody was so nosy and bent on making sure we didn't get away with anything. It was only years later, when black communities as we knew them started falling apart, that I came to understand the system for the hidden blessings it contained: It had built-in mechanisms for reinforcing values and trying to prevent us from becoming the hellions some of us turned out to be.

■ ■ ■

Despite our sense of well-being in Cavalier Manor, there were two things that reminded us of our shaky place in the world. One was the poor whites who lived nearby in Academy Park. Cavalier Manor was separated from Academy Park by the commercial strip of Victory Boulevard. Blacks in Cavalier Manor lived on one side of Victory Boulevard, and whites in Academy Park lived on the other. It was a poetic twist of fate that well-off blacks lived so close to the poorest, scruffiest-looking whites in the city. It looked like there was something wrong with that picture, seeing blacks turn their dark, wide noses up at the whites the way they did.

Academy Park whites were mad as hell about that, and they made it known. It was rumored that white squadrons sometimes stole into Cavalier Manor at night to terrorize. It was fact that they hurled bottles and bricks when we drove through their neighborhood. The main street through Academy Park offered the shortest route to other parts of the city. Sometimes blacks gave in to the temptation to take the shortcut through there to get downtown. Shortly after we moved in, a neighbor warned my parents, "Be careful not to drive through Academy Park. Them is some *mean* crackers over there. They'll stone your car and shoot at you for driving through there."

One night, when I was about ten years old, a little girl my age was shot to death while sitting near a picture window in her living room on Freedom Avenue. Nobody was arrested, but people in the neighborhood said they were sure it was the work of one of the "jealous crackers" from Academy Park. The killing brought home the fact that, nice neighborhood or not, we still weren't safe in Cavalier Manor. My mother had trained my brothers and me to be leery of white folks, but she stepped up precautions after the murder. Mama told us not to answer the front door for white folks or Jehovah's Witnesses when she and my stepfather were away. Whenever either came to the door, we just peeked through the curtains and kept quiet until they left.

Our friends and neighbors were cautious, too. We all regarded the sight of white people in the neighborhood as an ominous sign, like rain clouds forming overhead. Whenever a white man came into the cul-de-sac and got out of his car, people who were outdoors working in their yards stopped what they were doing and watched to see which house he'd go to. They watched when he left, too, then looked at the house he had visited for signs of bad news.

Another reminder of the tenuousness of our lives was a big, ugly ditch. It stood prominently in the main thoroughfare as an embarrassing monument to our blackness. That weedy eyesore, which bred snakes and all kinds of rodents, cut straight through the middle of the neighborhood, on Cavalier Boulevard. That ditch stood out like a grotesque open wound. The city never completely closed it, despite vigorous campaigns by homeowners to get it covered. It was as if the city fathers purposely left it open to make a statement, to remind blacks that the community would be only so nice and that, no matter how uppity we got in Cavalier Manor, the white folks downtown still called the shots.

Chapter 3 NIGGER

The folks in my neighborhood were resolute about trying to protect our physical safety, but seemed confused when confronted with more subtle racial hazards, such as our fixation on color. I was a product of that confusion.

My enchantment with whiteness dated at least as far back as Key West, where our family got our first television set. I'd spend hours in front of that black-and-white set, gazing spellbound at whites on TV, drinking in the beauty of their ivory skin, which seemed purer, cleaner, than my own. I was no more than seven or eight years old, but I still recall the Clairol hair-coloring commercial where they zoomed the camera in for a close-up on some saucy white broad who sensually tossed her blond mane backward and forward all over her face. Near the end of the commercial, a throaty voice chimed in and asked, "Is it true blondes have more fun?"

I thought of that ad every time I saw a blonde in real life or on TV. It also came to mind one day when I noticed a group of young whites riding down the street in a convertible ahead of our family car. The convertible's top was down, and the white people's long hair fluttered in the wind, like the TV blonde's. I thought, *White people have more fun.*

One sunny afternoon around that time, I was playing at the beach with my brothers when a little white girl standing nearby began covering her body with the pale, paste-like clay that blankets the Key West ocean floor. I imitated her, rubbing clay on my upper body. The girl looked at me and said, kindly, "If you let the clay dry, maybe you'll be white like me." For a moment, I considered that it might just work. It seemed a grand idea to let the clay dry on my body and turn me chalky white: After all, *White people have more fun.*

It's funny how the memory works. You can forget the name of someone you were introduced to yesterday, yet recall minor details of incidents that took place in your life years ago. For some reason, I always remembered that exchange. When I reflected on it years later, it occurred to me that even at that young age a little black boy and a little white girl had already begun to learn their place in this race-obsessed country. The girl knew she was a member of the favored race, and I understood that my color would be a burden to me.

In Cavalier Manor, I sensed that other blacks struggled with variations of my racial affliction (though I didn't recognize it as such). Even some of the grown-ups who set out to arm their young with racial pride seemed haunted by contradictions, which their children absorbed. Whenever we were going to restaurants or other public places where a lot of white folks would be around, my mother insisted that we get meticulously groomed and pressed beforehand, and when we got there she reminded us (it was more of a threat) to sit, stiff as soldiers, and be quiet. Every now and then, if one of us dared to cut up in public, Mama would yank him firmly by one arm, pull him to within an inch of her face, and whisper through clenched teeth, "Stop showing your color. Stop acting like a *nigger*!"

My brothers and I would sit solemnly and watch as rowdy white kids entered those same public places, shirtless, barefoot, and grimy. Their parents gave them the run of the joint, allowing them to stomp, shout, scream, do virtually anything they wanted, including tear up the place. I envied their freedom and craved the specialness that excluded them from our self-defeating burden: It seemed we were niggers by birthright and destined to spend our entire lives striving in vain to shed that rap. But white people could never be niggers, even when they acted like niggers with a capital *N*.

■ ■ ■

Without knowing what they were doing, a lot of adults in black families passed along notions to their young about white folks' superiority. Even Bampoose, my grandmother, did her part to condition us. Her husband—my grandfather—died of mysterious causes before I was born. Bampoose lived with our family for most of the time after that and worked as a domestic for white folks, cleaning their homes, cooking their meals, and raising their children. When we moved to Cavalier Manor, Bampoose began working for an affluent Jewish family, the Diamondsteins, who lived in Norfolk. Every morning, she rose before daybreak and caught several city buses to get to their house, ten miles away.

The daily trips to the Diamondsteins provided Bampoose her only diversion away from our home. She was shy and never socialized outside the family. About the most exciting thing going in Bampoose's life was the fierce games of checkers she played with my brothers and me; during those games, Bampoose often told us what the Diamondsteins' children had done that day.

The two Diamondstein children, Richard and Jamie, were about my age. Bampoose told us every detail about them—their habits, their likes and dislikes, and how well they were doing in school. She also told us about the fine dinner parties their parents threw and the elaborate vacations the family took. It was our first glimpse into the world of white people beyond *My Three Sons* and *Leave It to Beaver* on TV.

To me, Richard and Jamie took on the flawless, larger-than-life quality of storybook characters. I decided I wanted to be just like them. When Bampoose brought us clothes that Richard and Jamie's parents were throwing away, I relished those threads like they were store-bought, and nourished a secret pride that they made me look like their former owners. Once, when Bampoose was helping me get dressed, she said, "Richard and Jamie tuck their T-shirts inside their underwear." I began tucking my T-shirt inside my Fruit of the Loom briefs, just like them.

Bampoose saw how much I admired Richard and Jamie, and used it to gain advantage when she was unable to catch me to lay on a spanking for some misdeed of mine. All she needed to do to regain control of me was mention my white child idols. "Boy, why don't you stop actin' up like that! I don't have to tell Richard and Jamie more than once to stop doin' something. They are *nice* boys. They do everything I tell them to." It worked, too. I'd straighten up and try to behave like the gentlemen I imagined Richard and Jamie to be.

I had often tried to imagine how that family looked. One evening, when my brothers and I were sitting in the den, watching TV, Bampoose brought home a picture of herself taken at the Diamondsteins' home. When she handed me the picture, I studied long and hard the faces of the white people I'd heard so much about. In the picture, Bampoose, dressed in a maid's uniform, stood in the Diamondsteins' kitchen with an apron tied around her waist. Jamie, the younger boy, stood directly in front of her, clasping her wrinkled, caramel-colored hands. Richard stood beside his brother, in front of Bampoose. The boys had a scrubbed, well-attended look about them. They were dressed in fine clothes, and their hair was neatly combed. Bampoose, a short, petite woman who usually maintained a poker face, stood there smiling, like she was the proud mother of those two white boys.

Looking at that picture, I couldn't help but feel jealous. It seemed Richard and Jamie had laid claim to attentions and affections from my grandmother that should have been reserved for me.

I also noticed in the picture that Jamie had dark, straight hair, which he parted and combed sideways on top, like Beaver Cleaver's. I wondered why my thick, unyielding naps couldn't be straight and supple so I could jerk my head back to sling my hair out of my eyes the way white folks constantly did. One day, I got a can of my stepfather's pomade and set out to change my steel wool into "good" hair. I packed the thick, heavy grease into my hair and brushed it until the naps began to unfurl and lie down on my head in perfect submission, just like Jamie's. Minutes later, my hair started to shrivel. It went from straight, to curly, and back to nappy. Nappy and greasy.

My parents were preparing to take us to church that morning. Just as I was about to climb into the car, my mother took one look at my glistening head and got mad as hell. "Boy, *what* did you do to your hair?!"

"I only put some grease in it, Mama!"

Mama yanked me away from the car and slapped me in the back of the head. *Whack!* "Get your butt back in that house and wash that mess outta your head, boy!"

I went inside, wailing, grabbed a bar of soap, and began scouring my greasy head in the bathroom sink, like dirty clothes on a washboard. I nearly scalded my scalp trying to rinse out that gummy pomade. Worse than the blistering water was the painful realization that no matter how hard I tried I could never make my hair straight like white people's hair.

■ ■ ■

After retiring from the Navy in 1966, my stepfather held two jobs to make ends meet. He worked in the shipyard, and on weekends he went to do gardening work for white people in a neighborhood called Sterling Point.

Initially, my parents decided I was too young to go to Sterling Point, but Billy, Dwight, and Junnie went almost from the start. They hated it and bitched all the time. It wasn't clear to me what they were so annoyed about. Our stepfather paid them by the hour for working with him, so I figured they should feel grateful. My brothers used the money they earned to buy school clothes. They always had spending change in their pockets. What more did they want? I had big-time dreams of what I'd do with the money I made when I got old enough to go to Sterling Point. Finally, when I turned thirteen, I got my chance.

Sterling Point was the most affluent neighborhood in Portsmouth. Not only were its white residents set apart from everybody else in the city by their wealth and status, they were physically separated from the rest by the James River and the Churchland Bridge. I remember that when we cruised down High Street toward the bridge, my stepfather slowed the car at the incline to avoid rattling the garden tools sticking out from the back of the opened trunk. I sat in the backseat, sandwiched between Dwight and Billy, who were staring quietly out their windows. We reached the top of the high-arcing bridge and I looked over into the river and saw hordes of colorful sailboats drifting lazily along in the water. I nudged Billy. "Look at all those sailboats in the river!"

He yanked his elbow away from my hand, gritted his teeth, and growled in a whisper, "Leave me alone, boy!"

Dwight, likewise, and Junnie, who was sitting up front, ignored the dazzling sight of the boats with their brilliantly colored sails. I didn't know specifically why my brothers had an attitude that Saturday morning, but it was clear that our destination had a lot to do with it.

When we reached the other side of the bridge, Dad turned left into the elegant neighborhood and I saw shady streets and sprawling, two-story brick estates with antebellum-style columns, expansive yards, and wrought-iron fences. Despite its elegance, the neighborhood had a ghostly, antiseptic air about it. People didn't socialize outdoors or walk down the streets like they did in Cavalier Manor. The only people visible in the placid streets were groups of black women who trudged slowly up the curbless lanes into winding driveways and stately mansions. I nudged Dwight and asked, "Who are they?"

"They work for white people out here. They do the same kind of work Bampoose does for the Diamondsteins."

In those first few weekends, I learned to mow the grounds of the large estates, trim the hedges, prune the shrubs, and tend the flower beds. We gave the places the manicured look that you see in *House and Garden* magazine. It seemed just like working at home—until, that is, three white boys about my age reminded me one day where I was. My stepfather and I were down on our knees, pulling up crabgrass, when they bolted out the front door of the house we were tending to and began bouncing a ball in the spiraling driveway, a few feet away from where we were working. Every now and then, I looked up and waited for them to acknowledge my stepfather's presence in the way that my parents had taught my brothers and me to speak to grown-ups when entering their company. But the boys never said a word. They didn't even look his way. They kept on bouncing the ball and ran around us as if we were trees, shrubs, or some other inanimate part of the scenery. Any other time, my stepfather would've gotten on the children's cases for forgetting their manners. But this day, he looked up whenever the ball bounced close by, flashed the three boys a fixed smile, and kept working.

Those kids' arrogance made me self-conscious. It occurred to me how docile my stepfather and I must have looked there on our knees, working on their yard while they played, carefreely, about. They were as self-assured about their exalted place in the world as my stepfather was certain of how contained his life was. To them, he was no more than a fucking utility, a faceless gardener. To him, they were important people, children of some of the most powerful white folks in Portsmouth.

One of these powerful white folks—and one of my father's best clients—was Richard Davis, who eventually became mayor of Portsmouth. We saw him occasionally, buttoned down in suit and tie, rushing to his car. Always, he dashed out, waved, then hurriedly drove off. I saw more of his wife, an attractive young blonde who busied herself supervising domestic matters. One hot day, she came outside to talk with my stepfather. "Bonnie, I brought you and your boys some lemonade to help cool you off. It sure is hot out here!"

"Yeah, it really is hot," he said, straining to make small talk.

We took a break and gulped down the lemonade. Mrs. Davis looked at us and smiled a contented smile, then issued more instructions for the day. "Bonnie, I want you to do the flower beds for me today, and pull up the grass around the back of the house. I don't want it to build up too much because it might attract snakes."

When she had finished, Mrs. Davis pranced back into her spacious, air-conditioned house and closed the door. My stepfather glanced uneasily at me. I turned away, embarrassed that I had seen the humiliating exchange. I set down my unfinished drink, returned to work, and thought about what I'd just heard. *Bonnie?* That was the first time I'd heard anybody, including my mother, call my stepfather by his first name. He disliked the name anyway because it was a girl's name, but most important was the issue of respect. He addressed Mrs. Davis by her last name, but she called him *Bonnie*. The sound of the name rolling so casually off that white woman's lips stabbed me like a knife in the chest. It sounded like she was talking to a child. A boy.

At school, it was commonly understood that white folks considered grown black men to be boys. "Boy" was a fighting word, one of the most detested, disrespectful things somebody could call someone else. More fights started over one person calling another "boy" than over anything else. To counter that indignity, we addressed each other respectfully as "man," even though we were not adults:

"Hey, man, you goin' to play basketball today?"

"Naw, man, I got too much homework to do."

In the following weeks, I began to pay close attention to other racial nuances in my stepfather's interactions with people in Sterling Point. I didn't like what I saw. I didn't like the way he humbled himself and smiled when white folks were around. I grew to hate the sight of his big six-foot two-inch frame kneeling, with a wide-brimmed straw hat on his head, pulling up crabgrass while one of those privileged white people stood over him, supervising the menial work. It looked too much like pictures of downtrodden sharecroppers and field slaves I'd seen in books.

It is difficult sometimes to pinpoint defining moments in a life. But I'm certain that that period marked my realization of something it seemed white folks had been trying to get across to me for most of my young life—that there were two distinct worlds in America, and a different set of rules for each: The white one was full of the possibilities of life. The dark one was just that—dark and limited.

Over time, I shared my brothers' resentment when my stepfather made us go with him to Sterling Point, even though I knew our family badly needed the extra money. When we drove through Cavalier Manor during our rides to Sterling Point, I slumped down in the seat so my friends wouldn't see me riding in a car with a lawn mower and gardening tools sticking out of the trunk. I joined my brothers' silent brooding during the rides back home and, like them, became sullen, even when we crossed the scenic Churchland Bridge overlooking the colorful sailboats below.

■ ■ ■

My harshest introduction to the world of white folks came in September 1966, when my parents sent me to Alford J. Mapp, a white school across town. It was the beginning of my sixth-grade school year, and I was walking down the hall, searching for my new class, when a white boy timed my steps, extended his foot, and tripped me. The boy and his friends nudged each other and laughed as I stumbled into a locker, spilling books and papers everywhere. "Hey, nigger," the boy said. "You dropped something."

The word sounded vile coming from his white mouth. When I regained my footing, I tore into that cat and tried to take his head off. Pinning him against a locker, I punched him in the face and kept on punching him until his two buddies jumped in to help him out. While other white students crowded around and cheered them on, we scuffled there in the hall until the bell rang, signaling the start of the next class period. Like combatants in a prizefight, we automatically stopped throwing punches and separated at the sound of the bell. The white boys went their way down the hall, calling me names along the way and threatening to retaliate. I gathered my papers, straightened my clothes, and reeled toward my next class, dazed, trying to figure out what had just happened to me.

My parents sent me to Mapp in 1966 because that was the first year that blacks in Portsmouth were able to attend school wherever they wanted. The U.S. Supreme Court had long before ruled against the notion of separate but equal schools; still, Virginia, one of the states that had resisted desegregation, was slow in putting together a busing plan. Without a plan to ship black students to schools across town, over the years blacks and whites in Portsmouth had simply remained in separate schools. I could have gone to W. E. Waters, a junior high school that had just been built in our neighborhood, but, like many blacks then, my parents figured I could get a better education at the white school across town.

I was proud of their decision and held it out teasingly to my brothers as proof that I was the smart one in the family, that I held more academic promise than them. Billy had flunked the second grade, and Dwight and Junnie never showed much interest in books. My less studious brothers would attend their regular, all-black high school, but I was going to a *white* school, which made me feel special.

My parents didn't talk with me beforehand about the challenge I would face as one in the first wave of blacks to integrate Mapp. We had all seen TV news footage of police in riot gear escorting black students through hostile, jeering crowds to enroll in all-white high schools and colleges across the country, but for various reasons my parents saw no cause for alarm at Mapp. It was only a junior high school, which seemed far less menacing than the racially torn high schools and college campuses we heard about. Besides, there were no warning signals in Portsmouth to tip off my parents, no public protests by white citizens or high-profile white supremacist politicians like Alabama governor George Wallace threatening to buck the school integration plan.

At Mapp, I was the only African American in most of my classes. When I walked into one room and sat down, the students near me would get up and move away, as if my dark skin were dirty and hideous to them. Nobody talked directly to me. Instead, they shot daggers to each other that were intended for me. "You know, I hate niggers," they would say. "I don't understand why they're always following white people everywhere. We can't seem to get away from them. Why don't they just stay in their own schools?"

It wasn't much better dealing with white teachers. They avoided eye contact with me as much as possible and pretended not to see or hear white student hecklers. It was too much for an eleven-year-old to challenge, and I didn't try. Instead, I tried to become invisible. I kept to myself, remained quiet during class discussions, and never asked questions in or after class. I kept my eyes glued to my desk or looked straight ahead to avoid drawing attention to myself. I staggered, numb and withdrawn, through each school day and hurried from my last class, gym, without showering so that I wouldn't miss the only bus headed home. Students who missed the first school bus had to walk through the white neighborhood to the main street to catch the city bus. Mapp was located in a middle-class section of town called Craddock, where the whites were as hateful as the poor whites in Academy Park.

The daily bus ride home brought its own set of fears. A group of white boys got on our bus regularly for the sole purpose, it seemed, of picking fights. I was scared to death of them. With older brothers to fight at home, I was confident I could whip any white boy my age and size, but many of the white guys who got on that bus were eighth graders, and they looked like giants to me. Others were older, white, leather-jacket-wearing hoods who I was certain were high school dropouts.

When we boarded the bus, blacks automatically moved to the rear, as if Jim Crow laws were still in effect. The white boys would board last, crowd into the aisles, and start making racial slurs when the bus pulled away from school. "I hate the smell of niggers. They sure do stink. Don't you think niggers stink, Larry?"

"They sure do, man. They smell bad."

Before long, fists flew, girls screamed, and people tussled in the aisles. Few of the black guys on the bus were big and bad enough to beat the tough white boys, who outnumbered us seven to one. I never joined in to help the black guys out. I huddled in the far corner at the rear of the bus, tense, scared as hell, hoping the fighting wouldn't reach that far before the driver broke it up.

Children have an enormous capacity to adapt to insanity. I took my lumps in school and tried as much as possible to shrug it off when I went home. Billy, Dwight, and Junnie came home most days full of stories about the fun they were having at pep rallies and football games at their all-black high school. I envied them because I couldn't match their stories with tales of my own about fun times at Mapp. I savored every minute of my weeknights at home and used weekends to gather the heart to face Mapp again. Monday mornings, I rose and dutifully caught the school bus back to hell.

The harassment never let up. Once, when my English teacher left the room, a girl sitting near me drew a picture of a stickman on a piece of paper, colored it black, scribbled my name below it, and passed it around the classroom for others to see. I lost my temper, snatched it from her, and ripped it up. She hit me. I hit her back, then the whole class jumped in. When the teacher returned, I was standing up, punching one guy while another one was riding my back and hitting me in the head. The teacher demanded, "What's going on here?"

The white kids cried out in unison, "That *black* boy started a fight with us!"

Without another word, the teacher sent me to the principal's office and I was dismissed from school. The weeklong suspension alerted my parents that something was wrong. Mama sat me down and tried to talk to me about it. "Why were you fighting in school?"

"It wasn't my fault, Mama. That girl drew a picture of me and colored it black."

"That's no reason to fight. What's the matter with you? Your grades are falling and now you get into a fight. Don't you like your school?"

I tried to explain, then choked up and broke down in tears. Seeing that, my parents sought and got approval to transfer me to the neighborhood school, W. E. Waters.

But it wasn't over yet. One day, before the transfer went through, I was sitting on the gym floor with the rest of the student body, watching a school assembly program, when a group of rowdy white upperclassmen began plucking my head and ridiculing me. I got confused. *What should I do?* To turn around and say something to them would start another fight. To get up and leave would require me to wade through a sea of hostile white students to reach the nearest exit. With nowhere to go, I sat there and took the humiliation until I broke. Tears welled in my eyes and started running, uncontrollably, down my face. I sat silently through the remainder of the assembly program with my vision blurred and my spirit broken. That was the only time, then or since, that I've been crushed so completely. When it was over, I collected myself, went to the boys' bathroom, and boohooed some more.

■ ■ ■

There was no greater joy than that last bus ride home from Mapp. I sat near a window and stared out, trying to make sense of those past few months. Everything that had happened to me was so contrary to all I'd been taught about right and wrong. Before Mapp, every grudge I had ever held against a person could be traced to some specific deed. I couldn't understand someone hating me simply for being black and alive. I wondered, *Where did those white people learn to hate so deeply at such a young age?* I didn't know. But, over time, I learned to hate as blindly and viciously as any of them.

Chapter 4 — W. E. WATERS

Before going to that white school, I'd never considered the beauty and solace of being around my own people. Nor had I realized the danger in being away from them. Now, rather than catch a school bus across town to a hostile land, I could safely make the eight-block walk from my home to W. E. Waters, where I transferred.

At Waters, I found myself once again in the awkward position of being a new kid, an outsider in school. That discomfort stayed with me a few months. It seemed everybody there knew everybody else and I was the only stranger among them. In truth, many of the students had met only a few months earlier, when the school first opened. Before then, there was no junior high school in Cavalier Manor. The city built Waters, which taught grades six through eight, to accommodate the increasing number of school-age children moving into the rapidly expanding neighborhood. There were probably other motives involved. By building a school in the neighborhood, the city discouraged some black folks from wanting to go to white schools such as the one I'd attended.

I remained low-key and shy in those first months, partly because of my new-kid status, but mostly because I was still dazed from the trauma of what I'd gone through at the white school. Eventually, the shock thawed and I warmed to the comfort of a friendly environment with friendly faces. Friendly black faces.

The sights and sounds at the school had a distinctly black feel that I'd missed in those months at the white school. During break periods outside, students' transistor radios blared with the booming voice of Hot Dog, a popular, hip-talking deejay who always led into his music sessions with this outrageous chant:

> *I'm ou' c'here!*
> *On welfare!*
> *And don't bit mo' care!*
> *I got my big toe stickin' in the wind!*

Waters posed social challenges that didn't exist at the white school, where blacks were alienated from student life. At Waters, I became more attuned to the charged, incessant hum of students laughing, teasing, flirting, posturing, and chattering loudly while standing at hall lockers and changing classes. Suddenly, I was surrounded by giggling girls in my class who wanted to know who I was and where I came from. I felt caught off guard, unprepared for the clumsy dating rituals going on around me. The girls seemed so worldly and so much more mature than me. I felt like a bashful nerd. It seemed my shyness only encouraged them to come on stronger. They sent me notes in class asking me if I thought so-and-so was cute. They called me on the telephone some evenings and launched into conversations about dating and dances and other things I knew nothing about. Those girls kept me on edge.

Part of my nervousness was the awkwardness of early adolescence, that period of self-discovery when kids are introduced to all their imperfections. At Waters, I began to look in the mirror and see a whole new series of physical defects beyond those I'd already noticed. God, I thought, had created a terribly flawed human being: one who was too skinny, whose forehead was too big, whose hairline was too high, and whose eyebrows were too thick. Furthermore, as one of my female classmates pointed out, many of my clothes didn't fit right. She walked over to me one morning in class and said, "Gee, that's a big pocket on your shirt." That was one of my favorite shirts until she cracked on me. After that, I never wore that shirt again.

■ ■ ■

I spent that first year at Waters on the sidelines, getting acclimated, checking out the social scene, and trying to avoid the critical eyes of the jokers whose favorite pastime was picking people apart from head to toe. Guys sat in the school cafeteria and milled around their lockers in clusters, waiting for people to walk by so they could make fun of their looks and dress. It was a widely practiced art they called "jonin'," a spin-off from the older art of "playing the dozens." Good jonin' required a brutal wit, a sharp tongue, and a thick skin. It usually started with a challenge, an offhand comment about somebody's looks or clothes, followed by a retaliatory response. Once a jonin' session got started, everybody crowded around, listened, and instigated to keep it going.

Clearly, there were some underlying issues of self-esteem tied into the obsessive putting down of others, but it wasn't viewed that way at Waters. Guys built respectable reps in the community if they could jone hard. They made fun of each other's tacky clothes, berated each other's ugly mamas, talked about each other's shabby houses—highlighted any flaw they could find while competing to put each other down. If a dude came to school in high-water pants, they joned him hard. If somebody's shoes looked funny, they'd swear they saw him buy them at Pickway, the cheapest shoe store in town. And Lord knows, a funny-looking haircut was an open invitation to being joned out of school. "Look a' dat niggah's head! His mama must a' put a cereal bowl on his head and cut his hair!"

A lot of guys got tagged with nicknames during jonin' sessions: Gruesome, Spook Dust, Dirty Stink, Sack Eye, Roach, Tweety Bird, Itchy Booty, Butter Ball. Dudes such as White Mouse, Turkey Buzzard, and Rat Man had been joned so hard about their resemblance to animals that the names just stuck with them. In the course of fierce jonin' sessions, guys also created nicknames for others based on something silly or stupid they'd done. A dude who showed up for school one day with a sandwich made of grits and bread had to live with being called Grit Man for the rest of his life. A girl whose arm was contorted from a handicap was dubbed Crowbar. It got cruel and vicious sometimes.

It didn't take long after I got to Waters for somebody to find a reason to jone on me. I stepped into school one morning wearing some bright red hand-me-down pants and brought *hell* on myself. A short dude named Cardell Patillio nudged some of his buddies, pointed at me, and said, loud enough for all the world to hear, "Look a' dat dude's pants! He must think he Superman or somebody with them bright red pants on."

Before the other dudes could start weighing in, I turned and scooted off. I walked hurriedly down the hall and went straight out of the building. When I got off the school grounds and out of view, I broke into a sprint that would have put track star Carl Lewis to shame. I ran all the way home. When I reached the house, my mother said, "Boy, what you doin' home?"

Panting, trying to catch my breath, I said, "Mama, they were jonin' me about my pants."

She seemed to understand the seriousness of the situation. She didn't go upside my head or bless me out. She let me change pants and sent me back to school with a signed note explaining why I was tardy.

A few years later, when I became part of the hip [...]
to jone hard enough to keep cats like Cardell Patil [...]
never forgot how that little sawed-off, blockheaded, j[...]
sin' baby panda humiliated me.

I think the fear of being singled out and joned was [...]
reasons everybody at Waters placed so much empha[...]
looked and carried themselves. You could be emotion[...]
life if you got joned hard enough. To avoid being cracked [...]
to learn what was hip and how to dress. We called it "gettin' cl[...]
When dudes got clean, they wore the latest styles: starched, high-
collar shirts, sharkskin pants, and Stacy-Adams wing-tip shoes. The
tags on their clothes revealed that they were shopping in all the hip
places. Everybody who was cool shopped at Arthur's Men's Shop on
High Street downtown or at Fine's Men's Shop at the Mid-City
Shopping Center.

One of the sharpest dressers at Waters, a guy named Kenny Banks,
who was a few grades above me, had the best of everything. He had
sharkskins in every color, nice knit shirts, and several pairs of Stacy-
Adamses. When Kenny Banks got clean, he wore suits, matching knit
shirts, and wide-brimmed hats to school. He could also dance, shoot
hoops well, and fight. The girls in my class gossiped about him all the
time and shrieked like groupies when he came near. I scrutinized
Kenny Banks and wondered why God favored some people over
others.

Watching guys like him made me painfully aware of how plain I
dressed. I hadn't cared about gettin' clean at Alford J. Mapp, where
fashion wasn't a major issue with the white kids. My wardrobe con-
sisted of hand-me-down clothes my brothers had outgrown, and three
pair of pants, which I rotated through the week. My mother bought
our pants at the Navy Exchange and ordered our other clothes from
the Spiegel catalog. I wore buckled Buster Brown–looking shoes that
she bought me and prayed that nobody at Waters joned on my feet.

There was one style that everybody was able to get with. Waves.
By then, waves had replaced the straight-haired look of the old conks
as the men's hairstyle of the day. Guys got waves by applying a lot of
grease to their hair, brushing it a lot every day, and putting on a
stocking cap at bedtime. If you did it right, the waves looked like
breakers in the ocean. Some guys wore waves just on top of their head.
Others, like Kenny Banks, found ways to send their waves swirling in
different directions around their entire head. We called that a "round-
house."

rse, all the slick dudes at Waters wore the right kind of
s. Nothing but Chuck Taylor Converse All Stars would do.
rse All Stars were to us what Air Jordans are to kids today. In
the arrival of All Stars on the 1960s teenage fashion scene may
ve marked the beginning of young black kids' obsession with sneak-
rs. If a guy wore P. F. Flyers or some other cheap, off-brand shit his
mama bought at some discount store, he was dismissed as a lame.

I studied every detail about All Stars. They came in high-tops and
low. They came in two colors, black and white. The white ones had
thin red and blue stripes around them. The high-top whites had a
large blue star on a round patch attached to the inside ankle. The black
high-tops also had a blue star on the patch. I even liked the design of
the soles and the track they left in the dirt.

Everybody who was anybody had All Stars. My older brothers,
Billy, Junnie, and Dwight, got newspaper routes and saved their
money to buy some, but I had to wait because they cost too much and
my foot size was too small. All Stars only came in certain sizes.
Companies then didn't have the good sense to manipulate the children's market the way they do today. Since Dwight's foot size was
only slightly larger than mine, I tried on his All Stars a lot and
admired myself in the mirror at home.

The hip dudes profiled in their All Stars and pimped down the
hallway at school like they *owned* this white man's world. The pimp
was a proud, defiant, bouncy stride. You take a regular step with one
leg, then sort of hop or drag the other on the second step. At Waters,
the best pimpers twisted their torsos slightly and swung their arms in
unison with that hop. It made guys look cool and tough. Kenny Banks
pimped so hard he looked crippled when he walked. Instead of hop-
ping upward on the second step, like most guys, Kenny sort of jerked
to the side, like his leg was hurt.

The pimp was essential, even to Li'l Man, whose family moved in
across the street from us. One of Li'l Man's legs was much shorter
than the other. Sometimes he wore a special shoe with an extra-thick
sole to even the short leg with the long one. He didn't like wearing the
special shoe because it made him look handicapped. Most of the time,
he just wore regular shoes and converted his hobble into a serious
pimp. The only problem was, when Li'l Man stood still, he had to
tiptoe on the short leg or rest it on the elevated curb with the long leg
in the street. Likewise, guys who had bad feet could pimp in a way
that made their deformity look halfway cool.

My Aunt Iris in New York once told me a theory about the origin of the pimp. She said it was handed down through the generations from the slavery days. As she explained it, some slaves were forced to walk with a ball and chain attached to one ankle. When they walked, they took a regular step with the free leg and sort of hopped on the other to drag the heavy ball and chain. I have no idea if this is true. I just know the pimp has always been around and accepted as something every dude learns to do, like riding a bicycle and playing basketball.

■ ■ ■

I eventually realized that there were only two types of dudes at Waters: solitary lames like me and those who got into the slick incrowd. The slickest among these guys were the older dudes, the thugs, who ran the school and hung in the streets. They were the most popular. They got all the attention from the fly girls. They set the standards for hip and cool at Waters, and everybody else followed suit. They dragged long and hard on cigarettes in the boys' bathroom and ceremoniously passed them among themselves like it was no big thing. When they were standing around in there, they constantly cuffed their crotches, as if they were clutching organs so heavy they might bust through their pants. They often fought in school and cut classes.

I learned a lot by watching them. They were lovers. They had strong rap games, the studied ability to talk smooth and persuasive to get their way with the ladies. Most of the time they were jivin', lying to girls about how much they liked them, repeating romantic lyrics from songs they'd heard on the radio. As phony as it sounded, it worked. They got the finest babes in school just by telling them what they thought the girls wanted to hear. One guy followed girls through the halls all the time, begging for their telephone numbers. "Baby, you know I'm for reeeaal! When you gonna gimme that phone number? Why don't you lemme come over and see you sometimes, huh, huh, huh?!"

I was captivated by these guys. They seemed to have all the self-confidence I lacked. I was into honor rolls and spelling bees. They were into sock hops and talent shows. I looked all neat and boring, like my mama dressed me for school. They looked—exciting. They wore their hats backward and left their belt buckles unfastened and shoelaces untied. I stood around the school yard sometimes after classes, studying them, listening to their lyrical slang, which they spiced heavily with cuss words. I learned all their nicknames: Li'l Lo, Joe Ham, Skinny Pimp, Baby Joe.

The most popular among the thugs was a guy named Jerome Gary. His buddies nicknamed him Scobie-D and called him Scobe for short. He lived with his family in one of the older sections of the neighborhood. My brother Dwight had told me about Scobe a few years before I first saw him. I could tell from the sense of awe and wonder when Dwight talked about Scobe that he revered the guy. Without even seeing him, I admired him, too, and envied Dwight for having the chance to see him, live and in person, every day in school.

Scobe stood out from the other hoods because he was super-baad, meaning he took flak from no man, white or black. He had a medium build, bronze skin, flaming red hair, and a sizzling hot temper to match. When I transferred to Waters, Scobe was a ninth grader there—three years ahead of me. He practically ran the school. Everybody, teachers and girls included, feared and respected him. Scobe was no hell-raiser with his hands, but he had more heart than anybody I'd seen. When he lost his temper, he'd take on anybody and will himself to win. He eventually became known among blacks throughout Portsmouth as the baaddest cat to come out of Cavalier Manor.

Scobe had an older brother, Arnold, a stocky knockout artist. The two of them double-banked guys when they got into fights. Arnold was as cool as Scobe was baad. He had a pair of black high-top All Stars, which he laced with two pair of shoestrings, one black, one white. He wore his All Stars with thick sweat socks that pushed his pant legs up, giving them a disheveled look. He left the laces untied, and let the tongue of his sneakers droop, just so. It was the coolest thing I'd ever seen. Arnold had a unique pimp, too: He took the first short step, then paused longer than the normal pause for a pimp, then took his hop real slow. It was a brazen pimp that said, *"I know I'm baad."*

Scobe and Arnold set the standard for manliness in Cavalier Manor. Guys talked about their street exploits and their persuasive charm with girls. Dudes studied them like schoolbooks and imitated their walks and the lispy way they talked. Whenever I saw Scobe in the hallways at school, I'd stand off to the side and watch, drinking in every detail about him.

I remember the first time Scobe spoke to me. One day, when my grandmother Bampoose sent me to the 7-Eleven, I saw his buddies and him hanging around in front of the store. After I came out, I hung around nearby, listening to them talk. Scobe saw me gazing admiringly at him and infused in me the fear of God. He walked over, looked deep into my eyes, and asked sincerely: "Don't you think pussy stinks?"

I was shocked that *he* had said something to *me;* I was dazed, like the fan who's touched the hem of a rock star's garment. I tried to come up with a way to respond without revealing myself as a no-name lame, but the words stuck in my throat like a chicken bone. So I just stood there, wide-eyed, tongue-tied, and paralyzed. I went away that day, bewildered still by the question he'd asked, but proud to have been acknowledged by a hero.

■ ■ ■

After watching the older cats, I knew I *had* to work on getting my act together. Shyness or not, I had to break into the social scene or risk being victimized in some way by it. My coming out—of sorts—was sparked by a simple summertime birthday party I was invited to at the home of one of my classmates. I wouldn't have gone were it not for Denise Wilson, who was a bronze-skinned cutie with pretty green eyes and long, sandy hair. She and I had started sending each other heart-shaped love notes in class before the school year ended. With much prodding from other classmates, I had sent her a note asking if I could "have a chance." I had no idea what I wanted a chance to do. That was what people at Waters said when they wanted to date someone, so I said it, too. Denise had said yes, and we started our summer vacation as boyfriend and girlfriend and dated mostly on the telephone.

I had had no intention of going to the party until Denise pressured me. Going to that party would be risky. Many of my classmates would be there, and everybody would be watching everybody else to see who could or couldn't dance. If I danced and didn't do well, I'd get joned hard. All that school year, I'd avoided the Friday sock hops in the gym for that very reason. I'd peek in, then dash for fear that one of the girls from my class might see me and ask me to dance.

Dancing was a big thing at Waters, and everywhere else. The Temptations, the Supremes, and the Four Tops were hot, and the dances done to their tunes—the Shing-a-ling, the Turtle, the Horse—were smooth. When Marvin Gaye came out with his hit tune "I Heard It Through the Grapevine," everybody was doing a dance called the Dump. You'd take three steps, then lean down low and pause. It was real slick.

My brother Billy was the dancer in our family. He could watch a dance one time, catch on, and modify it so smoothly that people would crowd around and watch when he did his thing. I studied Billy when his teenage friends came to the house and played 45s and danced in the den. Then I'd practice alone in the bedroom when nobody was looking. I learned to do the Dump, but was too shy to try it in public with a girl.

I was most afraid of being asked to slow-grind. That required grabbing a girl, holding her close, and moving your two entangled bodies in harmony with the music. I had never held a girl before. I was scared that if I tried, my dancing partner might see that I didn't know what I was doing or some dude might see my clumsiness and start jonin' me in the middle of the floor.

The most popular slow song of the day was a love ballad by the Dells called "Stay in My Corner," one of the longest slow songs recorded up to that point. People who knew how to slow-grind loved that song because it gave them an excuse to hold each other real close for a long time.

On the day of the party, I got dressed in an orange Ban-Lon shirt and my favorite plaid pants. Although the midsummer heat was scorching outside, I put on an extra pair of pants beneath the plaid ones to make me look bigger. When I got there, the sounds of the Temptations filled the living room. My classmates ambled about, talking and sipping soda from paper party cups. I spotted Denise and stood alone with her, pinned to the wall near the punch bowl, scared to death.

As the music blared and people gigged out on the dance floor, I pretended to get so deep into conversation with Denise that I didn't have time to groove. Several times, she popped her fingers and said, "C'mon, let's dance?"

Each time I begged off and headed for the punch bowl. "Not right now."

At some point during the party, the birthday girl's older brother and some of his friends—they all seemed gigantic—came into the house and started loud-talking the wallflowers. "Why ain't you li'l niggahs dancing with these girls? We gon' pry all the wallflowers off the walls and force 'em to dance!"

That threat inspired everybody. A slow record was played. One by one, guys paired off with girls and took them onto the dance floor. Denise glanced at me. I waited until the dance floor was nearly filled, then, in an act of sheer will and faith, popped the question. "Denise, you wanna dance?"

"Yeah. I'll dance with you."

I pulled her into the middle of the floor in the thick of the crowd so that no one would be able to see us clearly. Not knowing quite where to put my hands, I held her loosely and tried to follow her body movements. I was sweating like crazy. I was nervous, and the heat from the two pairs of pants I was wearing had set my butt on fire. My lips grew parched and my palms got moist. I was stiff as a board, but my knees quivered so much I thought I might collapse. I'm sure Denise felt me trembling.

As we swayed to the music, I looked around the dance floor and saw other guys talking easily with their partners as they danced. A few others seemed uptight like me.

The Dells were crooning, "Stay in my cooorner . . ."

As the song played on, I focused on the two-step rhythm of the slow-grind and followed the movements of Denise's body, concentrating hard to make sure I didn't mess up. After I caught on, it was fun and I was surprised to find that it felt so good. When the song ended, I walked with Denise back to the punch bowl and breathed a deep, deep sigh of relief. I felt like I had accomplished something major, and I'd done it without once stepping on Denise's feet. As I headed back toward the wall I thought, *That was nice*. It made me realize that maybe a lot of the social situations that had intimidated me before might not be so bad after all.

I survived that party, and went on months later to learn to slow-grind like a champ. Once I learned, you couldn't get me off the dance floor, especially when they played "Stay in My Corner."

Chapter 5 HANGING

I hung around my locker, stalling, until the morning late bell rang. The hallway cleared as students went into their homeroom classes. I ducked into the boys' bathroom near the main hallway exit door at the back of the building and waited for Chip, Cooder, and the others who were supposed to meet me there. We'd planned to leave school and go to Turkey Buzzard's house a few blocks away to shoot pool while his parents were at work.

After a few minutes, Cooder hurried in, looking panicked, and said, "Where is everybody?!"

I hunched my shoulders. "I dunno. I didn't see anybody at the door when I came back this way."

Cooder grew even more nervous. "We gotta hurry up and get outta here. *Mr. Blair* is walking the halls!"

I got scared. Mr. Blair often patrolled the hallways to make sure students went to classes on time. Tall, heavyset, and stern, he was intimidating. He didn't play. He'd just as soon paddle your ass as take you to the principal's office.

Minutes later, Chip hurried into the bathroom, waved his arm at Cooder and me, and said, "C'mon. We gotta get outta here! Mr. Blair is coming!"

We must've looked like the Three Stooges bumping into each other, trying to rush out of there. I'd stepped out of the bathroom and pushed against the rear exit door to make my dash when I heard a booming voice behind me. "Stop right there! Don't you *dare* go through that door."

I froze, glanced at Cooder and Chip, then turned around and looked sheepishly at Mr. Blair, who was bearing down on us from about twenty feet up the hall. We were busted cold. Mr. Blair took us to the principal's office, scolding us along the way. The principal suspended us for two days and sent us home with notes for our parents to sign.

Walking home, I got scared when I thought about what my parents would say and do. A suspension would bring a guaranteed whipping from my stepfather and probably confinement to the house for a week or two. The other dudes would probably get the same. Cooder, the idea man in the group, came up with a way to save our lives. "Shit, why worry about what your folks gonna say? Why you gotta tell 'em? We can simply do what we were planning to do in the first place: Hook school and go shoot some pool. All we gotta do is wait till Turkey's parents go to work, then go over there and shoot pool and hang out for the next two days."

Somebody said, "What about the notes we gotta get signed?"

"Man, *we* can sign the fuckin' notes for each other."

It seemed like a good idea. It was one of the things that made me glad I had hooked up with dudes like Cooder.

During those two suspension days, we met on Roosevelt Boulevard, about a block from Waters, and wandered around Cavalier Manor, keeping an eye out for truant officers and nosy neighbors, killing time until we were sure Turkey's parents were gone for the day. Then we went over there, shot pool, watched TV, and plundered Turkey's refrigerator until it was time for school to let out. Then we went home to our parents and pretended we'd come in from school. Just like Cooder predicted, it worked out fine. We had a ball. We were hanging.

By the time I reached the seventh grade, I'd learned that a dude's life had no meaning unless he hung with someone. You had no identity if you didn't belong to a group. When I first got to Waters, I'd asked classmates the names of slick dudes I saw around school and they always identified them by the group they hung with: They'd say, "That's Li'l Blount. He hangs with Kenny Banks and the boys from Taft Drive," or "That's Fat Man. He hangs with Leon Bishop and the boys from Henderson Street."

Now, at age twelve, I was trying my damnedest to hang loose with a group and get with the styles. I'd picked up a few decent rags from my brothers to shed that nerdy look and finally got my first pair of All Stars, a well-worn pair of black high-tops that Dwight gave me. They were still too big for my size-six feet, but I doubled up on the sweat socks to tighten the feel. Imitating Scobie-D's brother, Arnold, I walked around with one pant leg rolled up so the blue star on the sneaker's ankle was in full view. I played those All Stars so hard and washed them so much that the black color turned a faded gray.

I also got waves in my head. I got a pair of my mother's old stockings, cut them, knotted the legs, and put *two* stockings on my head instead of one. Seldom did a night pass without me pulling those stocking caps over my head to work on my waves. It felt like the pressure from those two stockings compressed my skull, but the headaches it gave me seemed worth the results.

I also worked on my pimp—when walking down the halls at school, when walking home, anytime I thought about it—until I got it down so tight it fit my normal walk. My pimp became so much a part of me that years later, when I grew up and tried to get rid of it, I'd stumble sometimes trying to walk straight.

I hung with Cooder and Chip in school because they were in my homeroom class. Chip, who got his nickname because he was jet-black, like the chocolate chips in cookies, had an uncle who hung with Scobie-D. Cooder had an in with the hip crowd because he lived near respected hoods who also hung with Scobe. The first time I met Cooder, I knew he was hip. He had on a pair of ragged, oversized white high-top All Stars and baggy sweat socks that drooped down over them. He was pimping hard down the hallway between classes singing "Expressway to Your Heart." A short, stocky, light-skinned dude with a serious Napoleonic complex, Cooder was game for anything. He seemed hipper than most guys our age. At twelve, he had the older guys' slang and manner down tight and had gotten an early jump on the rest of us as an accomplished thief. A lot of his rags were too big because he stole them off people's clotheslines and wore them to school.

Cooder taught me how to gamble in the boys' bathroom. We pitched pennies with other dudes, and whoever landed his coin closest to the edge of the wall collected the money. Eventually, I got good enough at it to win money to buy my lunch at school. With five boys, four of them in school, my mother couldn't afford to give each of us thirty-five cents to buy lunch every day. She usually packed me a sandwich, cookies, and a piece of fruit and sent me to school with a brown-bag lunch. Dudes joned brown baggers about being too poor to buy school lunches. All the hip folks bought "hot plates." I got a complex and stopped brown-bagging it, so I gambled hard. If I didn't win, I didn't eat. Sometimes, though, I won enough money to buy hot plates all week.

Chip, Cooder, and most of the other guys I fell in with were from the new families moving into my expanding section of the neighborhood. We started out as a loosely knit group of restless adolescents who shared a passion for sandlot sports. The ties we formed playing football, basketball, and baseball evolved into friendships, and we started hanging together away from ball fields.

Hanging with Chip, Cooder, and the others, I grew wilder. As we entered the eighth grade, we threw spitballs and pinched girls' butts in class. We went to Friday-afternoon sock hops and raised hell in the halls. Just for fun, we'd trip people walking down the aisles in class and make them stumble, then we'd burst out laughing. I got suspended from school for tripping one girl who fell over several desks and chipped a bone in her arm.

In general, hanging out solidified the bond among my buddies and me. Everywhere we went, we traveled in packs of seven to fifteen boys. The core group included Frog Dickie (the shortest among us), Beamish, Tony, and Shane (the loudest in the group). There was also Leprechaun, who we called Lep for short, and of course Turkey Buzzard. Turkey had earned his right to hang with us by being able to hurt guys on the football field. Everybody wanted to earn a rep for being able to hit hard and mess somebody up in sandlot football. Turkey was the best. He'd spear dudes and send them flying in the air and crashing hard to the ground. He gave guys broken arms and swollen heads. He tackled me so hard once that I thought I was permanently paralyzed. It was the first time I ever rode in an ambulance.

Through those guys, I discovered the strength and solace in camaraderie. It was a confidence booster, a steady support for my fragile self-esteem. Alone, I was afraid of the world and insecure. But I felt cockier and surer of myself when hanging with my boys. I think we all felt more courageous when we hung together. We did things in groups that we'd never try alone.

The group also gave me a sense of belonging that I'd never known before. With those guys, I could hide in the crowd and feel like the accepted norm. There was no fear of standing out, feeling vulnerable, exiled, and exposed. That was a comfort even my family couldn't provide.

After I started hanging, the purpose of school changed completely for me. It seemed more like a social arena than someplace to learn. The academic rigors lost their luster and the reward of making the honor roll just wasn't the same. Suddenly, I didn't want to be seen carrying an armload of books, and I felt too self-conscious to join in class discussions. I sat in the back of the room with the hard dudes, laughing, playing, and jonin' the nerds.

■   ■   ■

In the summertime, the gang's favorite hangout spot was Bimbo's crib. Bimbo (who got his nickname in a jonin' session when somebody said he looked like a big, dumb elephant) was tall, fat, and insecure. At age thirteen, he was somewhat shy and made friends by giving people whatever he had—money, food, anything. When he told us that both his parents worked days, we turned his crib into Party Central. One by one, the fellas would start showing up there close to noon each day. Ignoring the shrill protests of his younger sister—"I'm gonna tell Mama!"—we made sandwiches and cooked pancakes, propped our feet on Bimbo's mama's best furniture, listened to music, called girls on the phone, and generally enjoyed the soothing cool of their central air until the evening, when it was time for his parents to return. Then we dashed, spilling into the streets in search of adventure.

Like young lions, we staked out our own turf under shade trees on the corner of Roosevelt Boulevard and Bardot Lane and spent endless hours there, lolling, posturing, lying, wrestling, and gambling. That corner became our operations center, the point from which all activities flowed. It became our school, our home away from home, our starting point and checking point.

Our rowdy presence there posed problems for Mr. Miller, the man who owned that lot, which he carefully maintained. Over time, we trampled that corner of his lawn into a hard, bald patch of dirt, which we used as a board for crap games. Often, Mr. Miller would come charging out of his house in Bermuda shorts and slippers, cussing, raising hell, and threatening to shoot us with a gun we never saw. He'd say, "Get off my goddamn grass! If you come by here again, I'll bus' a cap in your ass!"

He ran us off many times, but we paid him back as often, returning at night to egg his picture window and splatter his car. (A few years later, when we got bigger and badder, we didn't even bother to run when Mr. Miller came outdoors. We just stood there and stared him down, forcing him to call the cops to run us off. Eventually, we got so big and so bad that Mr. Miller didn't even bother to come out at all.)

When we weren't retaliating against Mr. Miller, we crept through backyards to the houses of girls we knew and peeked into their bedroom windows. Sometimes, while we were shortcutting through backyards at night like that, people called the cops on us or came out and chased us themselves, pitting their rage against our youthful speed, wind, and knowledge of backyard escape routes and clothesline booby traps. We learned the precise locations of tall fences and savage dogs. We knew where clotheslines hung and remembered when to duck. Police and adult neighbors foolish enough to try to catch us always ran the risk of catching those taut wires right across the Adam's apple. I'd hear a painful groan and, glancing back, see feet fly skyward, followed by the heavy thud of an adult body slamming to the ground. Then there'd be silence, or maybe a muffled curse. After we escaped, the fellas and I would laugh so hard our stomachs ached.

We also made nighttime foraging missions in search of unchained bikes and, in the wintertime, cut through the linings in our coat pockets to make it easier to steal from the 7-Eleven. We'd walk into the store, three and four at a time, and fan out through the aisles. There was no way the store clerk could watch us all at once. As soon as the clerk's eyes focused on people at the counter, we stuffed our pockets with Almond Joys, Clark bars, Reese's cups, and Hershey bars.

One day, when we were walking home from a golf course, where we had tried to earn money tracking balls for white people, we stopped at a Zayre department store. We split up, cruising the aisles where the food was kept. I picked up a pack of peanut brittle, looked around, and stuffed it under my shirt. After I left the aisle, a tall white man dressed like an ordinary customer came up to me. "C'mere, son. Come in the back of the store with me. I want to talk to you."

He grabbed me before I could take off running. When I got caught, the rest of the gang scrambled out of the store. The white man took me to a back room where some other grown-ups were waiting. They kept me back there forever. I waited in that room, crying and wishing I could take back the moments before I was caught. It was a feeling I would come to recognize.

After a while, a policeman came, led me outdoors, and placed me in the backseat of a squad car. Riding toward the police station, I knew I had a marathon whipping coming at home. My mind raced ahead to the telephone call that had probably already been made to my parents.

My mother and stepfather came to the police station and talked to the lawmen about what had gone down. The entire time he spoke, my stepfather kept a straight face, like he was more concerned than mad with me (he never showed his real emotions around white folks). I could tell that my mother was angry also, but I think she was more concerned about the thrashing I had coming from my stepfather than anything else. Tall, dark, and muscular, my stepfather had always looked to me like a charcoal Muhammad Ali, and it seemed he could hit just as hard.

When we got home, he said, "Go to your room and wait for me."

A minute later, he came in and stood over me, carrying a belt so fat it looked like a razor strap from a barbershop. His huge arms brought that belt down with even, slashing strokes that came only seconds apart, sending me running for cover. He beat me forever, then put me on punishment.

I went to juvenile court and was placed on probation. On the way home, Mama made vague references about me being sent to "a home for bad boys" if I continued to steal. I think the whole ordeal was an eye-opener for my parents, who perhaps realized for the first time that my innocence was gone. I had been changing right under their noses and they hadn't known.

Much later, when I thought about it, I realized that my folks were typical of their generation of parents: Their idea of raising children was making sure we were clothed, fed, and protected. They didn't focus much on us unless we were sick or had done something wrong. They didn't hold conversations with us. Love was understood rather than expressed, and values were transmitted by example, not word of mouth.

I could tell that my stealing confused my parents. That wasn't the kind of example they had set for me. It wasn't like I *had* to steal. We weren't dirt-poor. My folks didn't understand what I know now: My stealing had nothing to do with being hungry and poor. It was another hanging rite, a challenge to take something from somebody else and get away clean.

■ ■ ■

My stepfather might not have known all the wild shit that was happening out there, but he had sense enough to know that it wasn't good. That's why, from day one, he did all he could to keep my brothers and me from hanging on the block.

Early on, before I even had an interest in hanging, my stepfather imposed curfews on my brothers and me to keep the leash on us. The curfew was 9:30 on school nights and 11:30 weekends and summers. My old man didn't play with that curfew. If you were five minutes late, you'd broken the curfew and had to answer to him. Several times, he clashed with Billy, Junnie, and Dwight over that issue and won.

In fact, the curfew was partly responsible for Junnie leaving home. He came in late from seeing his girlfriend one night and my stepfather pounced on him. Junnie was seventeen. I must have been about thirteen. I remember being in bed and being awakened by my stepfather's voice, a calm, even tone that never rose more than a decibel or two, even when he was fiery mad. "I thought I told you to be in by eleven-thirty."

Junnie tried to explain. "I thought it was—"

His words were cut off by a noise that sounded like the thud of a boxer throwing body shots against a punching bag. Junnie must have tried to throw a few blows himself because I heard a rumbling sound, like there was a slight tussle in the hallway. But it didn't last long. My old man dusted him off and sent him, wailing and hurting, into the bedroom that he shared with Billy, Dwight, and me. Junnie left home and joined the Army soon afterward.

When I started hanging, my stepfather imposed the curfew to try to reel me in. But that wasn't easy. I was just getting into the party groove and was more defiant than any of my brothers. I launched into what provoked a serious test of wills between my stepfather and me. I went to every party I wanted to and came home on time only when the party was dying or the crowd was dead. If the party was jumping, the dancing was good, and the girls were fine, I'd stay until it was over and take the heat: confinement to the house, or maybe more.

I was determined to do what I wanted, and he was determined to control me, or break me trying. As a result, I spent almost as much time on confinement as outdoors. I hated being confined. Years later, when I went to prison, it nearly drove me crazy being locked up like that.

Eventually, I got tired of him trying to push me around, even if I was only fourteen years old. Like Junnie, I decided to leave home. I had no idea where I was going. I just left and told myself, *I ain't goin' back. I'm tired of takin' orders from him.*

I telephoned Ba-Ba King, a school buddy whose family had moved to Cavalier Manor from Norfolk, where he'd spent most of his life. When Ba-Ba dropped out of school, he returned to Norfolk to live with his grandmother, who was too old and feeble to keep up with him. That's why he liked living with her.

I'd thought life at Ba-Ba's grandmother's house would be all fun and games. I figured we'd chase girls, hang out, and do whatever we wanted as often as we chose. But after a few days, it turned into a different vibe. Ba-Ba was satisfied sitting around the house all day, watching TV, but I was too restless to sit still for that long. Plus, the comforts at Ba-Ba's grandmother's house didn't match the comforts of home. In fact, there *were* no comforts at Ba-Ba's grandmother's house. It was a drafty, one-story frame structure that reeked of kerosene and old folks' medication.

I got homesick after several days and realized I wasn't yet the man I'd thought I was.

One day, I left Ba-Ba watching soaps on TV and showed up at home, unannounced. My stepfather came home from work and promptly took the belt to me. I was so glad to be back that I accepted the beating as his way of saving face. He confined me to my room for a while, but after I served my sentence, I returned to the block contented to hang with the boys.

■ ■ ■

I was hanging on our corner with a bunch of other guys when two cats drove up in a convertible. "Yo, man, y'all wanna ride with us?"

We hopped in and took off down the street. At fifteen, the driver was older than most of us. He and his family had recently moved into Cavalier Manor from Lincoln Park, a public housing project across town. That joyride was his way of introducing himself and getting acquainted with the rest of us.

We pulled into the driveway of a filling station, pitched in money to buy gas, and took off again, joyriding through the city. Cruising down the street, Frog Dickie asked, "Hey, man, is this your folks' car?"

The driver and his friend looked at each other and snickered, like they knew a joke that the rest of us weren't privy to. "Naw, not exactly."

That was all that was said about it, but I knew the deal. We rode downtown to Lincoln Park, where the driver showed off his car to some girls and dudes he knew. We went to the Portsmouth City Park and profiled in front of people strolling through the fields, then the cat drove to other neighborhoods, where we hollered at girls and asked their names. "Hey, girl! Lemme have that phone number so I can call you sometimes!"

We had a good time cruising around, showing off with the convertible top down. It occurred to me that the driver probably didn't even have a learner's permit. But I was having too much fun to be scared. We were hanging, riding around in a stolen car like we owned the world.

Chapter 6

TRAINS

I was hanging on our corner, slap-boxing with another dude, when Nutbrain came through one day. Nutbrain, who was in high school when most of us were still in junior high, often stopped on our block to shoot the breeze and drop morsels of wisdom he'd picked up on the streets. He studied us slap-boxing for a while, then shook his head sadly, as if he pitied us fools. "Why you wanna bruise your hands on some hardhead when you can be somewhere fuckin'? Y'all can fight all you want. I wants me some *pussy*. Tha's the only sweatin' I'm gonna do."

Nutbrain commanded *big* respect on the block by virtue of his status as an established lover, a silver-tongued player who conquered women for sport. A mentor to young bloods who lived around my way, Nutbrain often came through nights after he had "gotten over" on some broad he'd been working on. If he had time and was in a talking mood, he'd sit down on the curb with us and run down the details of his latest score, from start to finish. "When I slipped my hand in that blouse, that bitch got hot as a firecracker. . . ."

The fellas and I listened closely because we were curious about love and sex. I was shedding my shyness with girls, but had never done more than feel on some of them. Looking back, I realize that I knew absolutely nothing about sex when I started chasing girls. When it came to that topic, I was dumb as a brick.

Nutbrain and other old-heads eagerly pulled my coat to everything I wanted to know. They talked about things like "beatin' your meat," "bustin' a nut," and "gettin' some head." Practically everything was described in abusive terms, even the whole intent of sex. They said a dude should try to "knock the bottom out of it and make a bitch scream and stick fingernails in your back."

One day, when I mentioned that I had seen a transparent fluid flowing from the tip of my penis, an older guy schooled me about what was happening to me. "Aw, man, you ain't got nothin' to worry bout! That means your manhood is rising!" He slapped me on the back.

"You a motherfuckin' *man* now! You can get bitches knocked up and shit! . . . Make sure you wear a raincoat when you bone them broads."

I know now that a lot of what those cats told us was dead wrong, but since there was no one around refuting what they said, it was accepted as gospel. A dude once warned the fellas and me, "Don't ever fuck no old bitch. Old bitches give you worms." I believed that right on up to the time I was grown.

Those corner conversations helped shape our views about women, love, and sex. The old-heads said there was no place for love in a *real* man's life. The pursuit of women was a macho game. The object was to "get the pussy" without giving love. If a guy was able to do that, he won the game. If he fell for a babe, developed genuine feelings for her, he lost. Whenever one of the fellas acted like he was down for a heartfelt, monogamous relationship, the old-heads made him feel that he should be ashamed of himself. "Aw, niggah, you fallin' in love! You weak! You pussy-whipped!"

According to street wisdom, there were two types of females: There were women, such as your mother, sister, and teacher, and there were bitches and 'hos, all females who didn't fall into that first category. Bitches and 'hos were good for one thing—boning. It didn't matter that bitches and 'hos were somebody else's mother or sister or daughter. As long as they weren't your relatives or the relatives of a hanging buddy, they were fair game.

On our grading scale, girls' attractiveness was linked closely to their complexion. "Red-bone bitches," light-skinned women who looked almost white, were considered more desirable. Deep dark women got dogged to death. And white women, of course, were viewed as the ultimate catch. It's ironic that as much as we claimed to hate white folks, we lived for the chance to bone a gray broad.

It didn't even cross my mind to talk to my parents about love and sex. Beyond his occasional comments about the virtues of hard work, my stepfather never held facts-of-life conversations with my brothers and me. I doubt he would have known how to approach the topic of sex. My mother would have seemed the person most likely to run it down. Her whole life had been shaped by costly experiences with teenage sex. She met and started dating my blood father in the summer of 1949 in a tiny North Carolina town. She was thirteen, and he was an eighteen-year-old high school dropout. After my mother got pregnant with Billy, she lied about her age and married my father to avoid the disgrace of an out-of-wedlock birth. By the time she turned eighteen, she found herself trapped with three young children and a half a man. Once she and my father split, he faded completely out of our lives. I never saw him again until I was grown.

You would have thought that after all she went through my mother would preach to us about the dangers of moving too fast. But she didn't. I think she was too embarrassed because she was a woman and we were boys.

Once, when I was about ten, I asked her, "Mama, where do babies come from?"

Sweeping her hand from her breast area on down to her thighs, she said, "From down here."

I didn't understand, so I asked again. "Where?"

She swept her hand across the front of her body again. "Down here."

It was clear that the question made her uneasy, so I let it drop. That was the last time Mama and I came even close to talking about sex.

■ ■ ■

By the time I was thirteen, I felt pressured by all the bravado around me to get some conquests literally under my belt. I could tell by the way they talked that the other fellas also felt pressed. Eventually, several of us lucked out—with the same girl. Her name was Sharon, and her family had recently moved into the neighborhood. We discovered her just as her body was shedding that soft girlishness and beginning to take on a womanly shape and form.

Sharon was easy, but no one got anywhere with her if she didn't want them to. She could rumble like a *man,* and she had an older brother who could fight, too. So I went around there when I knew her big brother was away and tried to catch her in a willing mood, which was most of the time. Sharon was as dark as night. I'm convinced to this day that she gave herself up so readily because her dark skin affected her self-esteem.

The fellas and I constantly talked about Sharon when we were together. In our moments apart, we'd slip to her house to try to get in some petting time alone with her. One night, after she had gotten a job baby-sitting for a neighbor, I went there expecting to get in some kisses and grinds and ran into Holt, one of my boys. Holt was the first to score. Then, on another night, she finally broke me in. By the end of that summer, Sharon had turned several of us out and launched us on the way to becoming serious hounds.

■ ■ ■

One night, some dudes from another section of the neighborhood came rushing past our block while we were hanging out. We called out, "Yo, man, where y'all goin'?"

One of them yelled, "There's a train at Crystal Lake!"

I knew what a train was. It was what happened when a bunch of guys got together and jammed the same girl. The white boys called it gang-banging.

The fellas and I went running back there with the other dudes to watch. There, in the dark seclusion of the woods, I saw a parked car with the rear doors opened. A woman's leg was propped up on top of the rear seat, and a pair of man's gyrating legs—held tightly together with the pants rolled down—hung partly out the door. Standing near the car, supervising the lineup, was Scobie-D, the dude I'd worshiped at Waters. I could see that flaming red Afro moving around. About twenty to thirty guys milled about, talking trash, smoking cigarettes, passing a wine bottle, and awaiting their turn.

The fellas and I didn't even think about trying to get in on the train. We were scared of Scobe and were half-grateful he let us stand back there and watch. We just wanted to see what it was all about. Once we got the idea, we knew it was something we had to try.

Scobe and his boys trained anybody they could get their hands on. They even trained Pearl, a neighborhood drunk who was my parents' age. A glassy-eyed, disheveled mess of a woman with no teeth in her mouth, Pearl got wasted all hours of the day and night and staggered through the streets of Cavalier Manor. Scobe and his gang caught her stumbling by one night and trained her in a wooded area behind the 7-Eleven. I heard recently that Pearl died, but I doubt she ever knew she was trained. That's how tore-down, sloppy drunk she'd get. She had two nice, respectable daughters my age. Every time I saw them in school, I wondered what they'd think if they knew their mother had been jammed by teenage boys.

Different groups of guys set up their own trains. Although everybody knew it could lead to trouble with the law, I think few guys thought of it as rape. It was viewed as a social thing among hanging partners, like passing a joint. The dude who set up the train got pats on the back. He was considered a real player whose rap game was strong.

I think most girls gave in when trains were sprung on them because they went into shock. They were so utterly unprepared for anything that wild that it freaked them out. By the time they realized that they'd been set up, they were stripped naked, lying on a bed or in the backseat of a car, with a crowd of crazed-looking dudes hovering overhead. I always wondered what went on inside girls' heads when that was happening to them.

Afterward, most girls were too ashamed and freaked-out to tell. They knew that if they snitched to the cops, the thing would become public news and their name would be mud. But every now and then, some chick squealed, and somebody caught a charge. Then guys got their buddies to go to court and testify that the girl was a footloose 'ho whom they each had boned.

Most girls seemed to lose something vital inside after they'd been trained. Their self-esteem dropped and they didn't care about themselves anymore. That happened to a girl named Shirley, who was once trained by Scobe and so many other guys that she was hospitalized. After that, I guess she figured nobody wanted her as a straight-up girl. So Shirley let guys run trains on her all the time.

■ ■ ■

It was the first day of summer vacation. I was fourteen years old and had just completed the eighth grade, marking the end of my junior high school days. I was sitting at home, watching TV, when the telephone rang. "Hello," I said.

"Yo, Nate, this is Lep!"

"Yo, Lep, what's up?"

"We got one. She phat as a motherfucka! Got nice titties, too! We at Turkey Buzzard's crib. You better come on over and get in on it!"

"See you in a heartbeat."

When I got to Turkey Buzzard's place a few blocks away, Bimbo, Frog Dickie, Shane, Lep, Cooder, almost the whole crew—about twelve guys in all—were already there, grinning and joking like they had stolen something. Actually, they *had* stolen something: They were holding a girl captive in one of the back bedrooms. Turkey Buzzard's parents were away at work. I learned that the girl was Vanessa, a black beauty whose family had recently moved into our neighborhood, less than two blocks from where I lived. She seemed like a nice girl. When I first noticed her walking to and from school, I had wanted to check her out. Now it was too late. She was about to have a train run on her. No way she could be somebody's straight-up girl after going through a train.

Vanessa was thirteen years old and very naive. She thought she had gone to Turkey Buzzard's crib just to talk with somebody she had a crush on. A bunch of the fellas hid in closets and under beds. When she stepped inside and sat down, they sprang from their hiding places and blocked the door so that she couldn't leave. When I got there, two or three dudes were in the back room, trying to persuade her to give it up. The others were pacing about in the living room, joking and arguing about the lineup, about who would go first.

Half of them were frontin', pretending they were more experienced than they really were. Some had never even had sex before, yet they were trying to act like they knew what to do. I fronted, too. I acted like I was eager to get on Vanessa, because that's how everybody else was acting.

I went back to the room and joined the dudes trying to persuade Vanessa to let us jam her. She wouldn't cooperate. She said she was a virgin. That forced us to get somebody to play the crazy-man role, act like he was gonna go off on her if she didn't give it up. That way, she'd get scared and give in. That's how the older boys did it. We figured it would work for us.

Lep played the heavy. He started talking loud enough for her to hear. His eyes got wide, like Muhammad Ali's used to do when he was talking trash. As guys pretended to hold Lep back, he struggled wildly, like he was fighting to get into the room. "If that bitch don't give me some, she ain't never leavin' this house!"

Frog played the good guy, acting like he was fighting to hold Lep off. "Come on, man, let the girl go. She said she don't wanna do nothing, so you can't make her."

In the ruckus, Turkey Buzzard stood over a deathly silent Vanessa as she sat on the bed, horrified, looking at the doorway where the staged struggle was going on. Buzzard talked soothingly to Vanessa, trying to convince her that he, too, was a nice guy who was on her side. "Look, baby, if you let one of us do it, then the rest of them will be satisfied and they'll let you go. But if you don't let at least one of us do it, then them other dudes gon' get mad and they ain't gonna wanna let you leave. . . . Lep is crazy. We can't keep holdin' him off like that. If we let him come in this room, it's gonna be all over for you."

Vanessa seemed in a daze, like she couldn't believe what was happening to her. She looked up at Buzzard, glanced at the doorway, then looked back at Buzzard. I stood off to the side, studying her. I could see the wheels turning in her head. She knew she was cornered. She had never been in a situation like this before and she didn't have a clue how to handle it. I could tell by the way she kept looking at Buzzard, searching his face for something she could trust, that she was on the verge of cracking. She *had* to trust Buzzard. There was really no choice. It was either that or risk having that crazy Lep burst into the room and pounce on her like he was threatening to do. I could see her thinking about it, adding things up in her mind, trying to figure out if there was something she could do or say to get herself out of that jam. Then a look of resignation washed over her face. It was a sad, fearful look.

She looked so sad that I started to feel sorry for her. Something in me wanted to reach out and do what I knew was right—do what we all instinctively knew was right: Lean down, grab Vanessa's hand, and lead her from that room and out of that house; walk her home and apologize for our temporary lapse of sanity; tell her, "Try, as best as possible, to forget any of this ever happened."

But I couldn't do that. It was too late. This was our first train together as a group. All the fellas were there and everybody was anxious to show everybody else how cool and worldly he was. If I jumped in on Vanessa's behalf, they would accuse me of falling in love. They would send word out on the block that when it came to girls, I was a wimp. Everybody would be talking at the basketball court about how I'd caved in and got soft for a bitch. There was no way I was gonna put that pressure on myself. I thought, *Vanessa got her stupid self into this. She gonna have to get herself out.*

Turkey Buzzard put his hand on her shoulder and said, "What you gonna do, girl? You gonna let one of us do it?"

Vanessa's eyes filled with water. Her lips parted momentarily, as if she intended to speak, but no words came out. Instead, she swallowed hard and nodded her head up and down, indicating that she'd give in. Slowly, she lay back on the bed, like Buzzard told her, and closed her eyes tight. Moving quickly, Buzzard slipped her pants off. When he grabbed the waistband of her panties, she rose up suddenly and grabbed his hands, as if she'd changed her mind. She gripped his hands tight for a second, looking pleadingly into his eyes. Then she turned and looked at Frog and me as if she wanted one of us to come and rescue her. I looked away. Buzzard said, almost in a whisper, "C'mon, girl, it's gonna be all right. It'll be over in a minute."

Sitting upright, Vanessa searched his face again, then released his hand, lay back on the bed, and cupped her hands over her eyes.

By then, the fellas in the living room had grown quiet. They knew she was about to give in, and the sense of anticipation—and fear—rose. Some guys, curious, crept to the doorway and kneeled low so that she couldn't see them peeping into the room. Others stayed in the living room, smiling and whispering among themselves. "Buzzard got her pants off. He got the pants."

I don't remember who went first. I think it was Buzzard. When Vanessa tried to get up after the first guy finished, another was there to climb on top. Guys crowded into the room and hovered, wide-eyed, around the bed, like gawkers at a zoo. Then another went, and another, until the line of guys climbing on and off Vanessa became blurred.

After about the fifth guy had gone, I still hadn't taken my turn. I could have gone before then, but I was having a hard time mustering the heart to make a move. I was in no great hurry to have sex in front of a bunch of other dudes.

The whole scene brought to mind a day a few years earlier when I was sitting in the gym bleachers at my junior high school, watching an intramural basketball game. Scobie-D and some older hoods came and sat near me. At one point, Scobe got on another dude's case for failing to make a move on a girl who'd given him some play. I'll never forget it: Scobe stood up and announced loudly to the rest of the guys, "That motherfucka is scared a' pussy!" The other dude hung his head in shame.

While hovering near Vanessa, I remembered how Scobe had disgraced that guy. I wasn't about to let that happen to me. I wasn't about to let it be said that I was scared of pussy. I took a deep breath and tried to relax and free my mind. I knew I couldn't get an erection if I wasn't relaxed. That would be even more embarrassing. I didn't want to pull my meat out unless I had an erection. It would look small. Somebody might see it, shriveled up and tiny, and start laughing. Imitating some of the others in the room, I took one hand and cuffed it between my legs, caressing my meat, trying to coax it to harden so I could pull it out proudly and take my turn. Then Lep said, "Nate, have you gone yet?"

I said, "Naw, man. I'm gettin' ready to go now."

I moved forward. My heart pounded like crazy, so crazy that I feared that if somebody looked closely enough they could see it beating against my frail chest. I thought, *It's my turn. I gotta go now.*

As several other guys hung around nearby, I went and stood over Vanessa. She was stretched out forlornly on the bed with a pool of semen running between her legs. She stayed silent and kept her hands cupped over her eyes, like she was hiding from a bad scene in a horror movie. With my pants still up, I pulled down my zipper, slid on top of her and felt the sticky stuff flowing from between her legs. Half-erect and fumbling nervously, I placed myself into her wetness and moved my body, pretending to grind hard. After a few miserable minutes, I got up and signaled for the next man to take his turn.

While straightening my pants, I walked over to a corner, where two or three dudes stood, grinning proudly. Somebody whispered, "That shit is *good*, ain't it?"

I said, "Yeah, man. That shit is good." Actually, I felt sick and unclean.

After the last man had taken his turn, Vanessa got up, put on her pants, and went into the bathroom, holding her panties balled up in her hands. She came out and stood in the living room, waiting for somebody to open the front door and let her out. By then, the fellas and I were lounging around, stretched out on Buzzard's mother's couch, sitting on the floor or wherever else we could find a spot. Vanessa looked solemnly around the room at each of us. Nobody said a word. Then Lep led her out and walked with her down the street.

I felt sorry for Vanessa, knowing she would never be able to live that down. I think some of the other guys felt sorry, too. But the guilt was short-lived. It was eclipsed in no time by the victory celebration we held after she left. We burst into cheers and slapped five with each other like we'd played on the winning baseball team. We joked about who was scared, whose dick was small, and who didn't know how to put it in. Everybody had a story to tell: "Beamish couldn't even get his dick hard! He had to go in a corner and beat his meat!"

"Did you see the bed sink when Bimbo climbed his big, elephant ass up there?! I thought he was gonna crush the poor girl!"

"She acted like she didn't even wanna grind when I got on it! I had to teach the bitch how to grind. . . ."

That train on Vanessa was definitely a turning point for most of us. We weren't aware of what it symbolized at the time, but that train marked our real coming together as a gang. It certified us as a group of hanging partners who would do anything and everything together. It sealed our bond in the same way some other guys consummated their alliances by rumbling together in gang wars against downtown boys. In so doing, we served notice—mostly to ourselves—that we were a group of up-and-coming young cats with a distinct identity in a specific portion of Cavalier Manor that we intended to stake out as our own.

After that first train, we perfected the art of luring babes into those kinds of traps. We ran a train at my house when my parents were away. We ran many at Bimbo's crib because both his parents worked. And we set up one at Lep's place and even let his little brother get in on it. He couldn't have been more than eight or nine. He probably didn't even have a sex drive yet. He was just imitating what he saw us do, in the same way we copied older hoods we admired.

One night, when I was sitting at home by myself, thinking about it, it occurred to me that the whole notion of running trains was weird. Even though it involved sex, it didn't seem to be about sex at all. Like almost everything else we did, it was a macho thing. Using a member of one of the most vulnerable groups of human beings on the face of the earth—black females—it was another way for a guy to show the other fellas how cold and hard he was.

It wasn't until I became an adult that I figured out how utterly confused we were. I realized that we thought we loved sisters but that we actually hated them. We hated them because they were black and we were black and, on some level much deeper than we realized, we hated the hell out of ourselves.

I didn't understand all that at the time. I don't think any of us understood. But by then, we had started doing a whole lot of crazy things we didn't understand.

■   ■   ■

I began scoring with a lot of girls and built a rep as a lightweight player with a decent rap. It was easy once I learned that all a guy had to do to get his way was sound sincere. A dude was considered really slick if he could score on a virgin or talk the drawers off a chick without a single kiss. I got so good that I started taking bets with the fellas on girls I went after. I had my rap game down tight by the time I ran into Denise Wilson, my old sixth-grade sweetheart. When I think about that meeting, I still wish fate had made me walk the other way.

By this time we'd reached the ninth grade and had been sent to separate high schools; we hadn't talked or seen each other much. Denise knew I was more worldly, but I'm sure she had no idea how jive I'd become. When I ran into her, I started laying on the heavy rap to get her into bed. "Hey, Denise, if you wanna get serious, then we gotta do what serious people do. You know, you gotta show me in a special way how you feel 'bout me. I been knowin' you for a long time, and I've had a thing for you since way back when. But, you know, I wanna be sure you feel the same way 'bout me that I do 'bout you. How 'bout it, baby, what you gonna do?"

After I rapped my heart out, Denise finally agreed to let me be the first, and one of the fellas gave me the okay to use his crib. We went there and went into one of the back bedrooms, where we began kissing and carrying on. Denise took off her clothes and climbed into bed. Before we could get started, about eight guys burst into the bedroom. Shocked, I jumped up from the bed and saw that it was a dude called Plaz and some of his boys. They were hardened hoods, guys three and four years older than me. To this day I don't know who told them we were at that house or how they got inside. They broke into the room like they had a right to be there. I could tell they were planning to run a train.

I stood between them and Denise, who was fumbling around, looking for her underwear. But before she could get fully dressed, Plaz started toward her. I swung at him and we started rumbling in the room. A few of his boys jumped in and tried to break up the fight. In the chaos, I lost sight of Denise. All I knew was that some of the other guys were talking to her, but I couldn't get to her to make sure she was all right. When the fight ended, I looked around and Denise was gone. I assumed she went home, but when I telephoned her house, she wasn't there.

Later that evening, Denise's parents came to my house. I was washing dishes in the kitchen. Mama called me. "Nathan, come in here. We need to talk to you."

I walked in and faced Denise's mother and father, who were sitting down. I could tell from the somber looks on their faces that something was seriously wrong. Denise's mother did all the talking. "Nathan, we need you to tell us what happened earlier today. Denise is at home and she's very upset."

I had to stand there in front of four grown-ups and recount what had gone down. Before I could finish, I broke down in tears. It dawned on me that something terrible had happened to Denise. I found out later that the other guys who had come into the room with Plaz had taken Denise to another house. They had told her she could go there to put on her panties and bra, then they forced her to have sex.

Denise's parents filed rape charges, and several guys went to trial. I was subpoenaed as a witness, but was excused from testifying because at fourteen I was underage and might have incriminated myself. A few of the guys, who were eighteen or older, were convicted and served short sentences for the crime.

The word went out on the streets that I'd set Denise up on a train. For months after that, girls in school wouldn't talk to me because of what they'd heard I'd done. It hurt me to know that someone believed

I would do that to Denise. What was worse, I had no idea what *she* thought of me. I wanted badly to talk to her and apologize. But I didn't speak to her for years after that. I called, but her mother told me not to call there anymore.

That whole ordeal messed up my head pretty bad. Before then, I hadn't considered that a train might be run on somebody I cared about. Now someone I had genuine feelings for had been victimized by the very behavior I had embraced. It made me think long and hard about the stuff in the streets I was getting into. I was struck with the sense that I was deeply involved in some things that were over my head. At the same time, I couldn't conceive of altering my course or turning back.

Chapter 7 RESPECT

Shortly before the end of summer vacation, some guys and I were playing baseball at the Cavalier Manor recreation field. When the game ended, I called out to Shane, who was preparing to leave. "Yo, Shane! Gimme a ride home, man!"

Shane had ridden his bicycle to the rec field, but I'd walked. "I can't! I gotta get home before my parents get mad!"

Shane hopped onto his bike and rode away, pedaling so fast I couldn't catch him. A bunch of other guys were standing around when he pulled off. They looked at me pitifully. "Damn, man. He s'pposed to be one of your hanging buddies and he won't even give you a ride home? Tha's messed up."

Another guy chimed in. "Yeah. He ain't shit."

It really hadn't bothered me at first. But after they made such a big deal about it, I began to think that maybe Shane had disrespected me. No one actually said it, but the tone of those guys' comments suggested that the insult required some macho response. I had to react in front of the boys: "Tha's all right. I'm gonna fuck Shane up when I see him again."

A few days later, Shane came onto my street to join in a baseball game. Everybody was out there—Lep, Turkey Buzzard, Chip, Frog, the whole crew. I stormed over to Shane and went into my Scobie-D macho act. "Niggah, why didn't you give me a ride home the other day?!"

Shane tried to explain again. "I had to be home before dark, Nate!"

"You could've still given me a ride! I had to walk all the way home because of you!" I cuffed him in the collar and punched him in the face.

Everybody stopped playing ball and crowded around to watch the rumble get under way. Seeing he had no choice, Shane prepared to throw down. He climbed off the bike, I punched him in the face again, and we got it on. About two minutes into the rumble, I realized I had made a *major* mistake. I had pretty good boxing skills. But I had no idea Shane was as good with his hands as he turned out to be. That boy could hit! We battled in the street and worked our way into Greg's front yard. With everybody looking on, cheering, shouting, and coaching, we parried and wrestled and fought our way into the flower bed and shrubs. We were about even, blow for blow, when Shane backed me into a tall shrub and shoved me over. I flipped backward and landed facedown. I sprang to my feet and we locked horns again, holding each other with one hand by the collar, pounding each other's faces, rapid-fire, with our free fists.

At some point, my parents were alerted and came outdoors to break it up. Shane and I kept swinging wildly, trying to get in extra licks, even after they pried us apart. My stepfather asked my mother if he should let us continue. "They want to get at each other so bad," he said, "that they'll probably fight again if we don't let them get it over with."

My mother studied me. I was dirty and sweaty and had a bloody nose. Then she looked at Shane, who had a swollen lip. While we awaited her decision, I prayed to the high heavens that she wouldn't let us continue. I didn't know how Shane felt, but I was exhausted. My arms were so weary from swinging that I could barely lift them. My knuckles throbbed from knocking against Shane's cement head. My face ached from the punishing blows I had absorbed. And I was winded. Actually, I was more shocked than tired. I'd busted Shane in the face with my best shots and he'd simply responded with some shots of his own that were just as good. Clearly, my preference was to quit. But pride dictated that if my mother gave the word, I'd have to fight on until one of us dropped. I panted hard, trying to catch my breath in case I had to go another round. Then Mama announced her decision: "Naw. Don't let them fight anymore." She turned to Shane and me and said, "You two shake hands and make up. Shane, you go on home, and Nathan, I want you to come inside the house."

I was so relieved I could have kissed her on the spot. But there was an audience out there. I had an image to project and a role to play. So I acted disappointed, like I was pissed off that my mother kept me from tearing off that nigger's head. When Shane got on his bike and started to ride away, I balled up my fist, pointed it threateningly at him, and yelled: "It ain't over, niggah! I'm gonna finish you off when I see you again!" My mother smacked me in the head and shoved me indoors.

When school started the following week, people were still talking about how hard Shane and I had rumbled. Cooder came over to me in class and said, "Yeah, man, I heard you and Shane were throwing down the other day."

I went into my tough bag again. "Yeah, and I'm gonna dust that niggah off when I catch him."

The truth was, Shane never had to worry about me again. The last thing I wanted to do was tangle with him. He had won my complete respect. He proved he had heart and that he could rumble. I'm sure I won his respect, too. We became good friends after that and never fought each other again.

■ ■ ■

That happened a lot when two dudes locked horns. Each learned what the other could do with his hands, and both developed a mutual respect, especially if they'd nearly taken off each other's heads. The whole emphasis in the streets on being able to rumble was rooted in respect.

For as long as I can remember, black folks have had a serious thing about respect. I guess it's because white people disrespected them so blatantly for so long that blacks viciously protected what little morsels of self-respect they thought they had left. Some of the most brutal battles I saw in the streets stemmed from seemingly petty stuff, such as Shane's unwillingness to give me a ride. But the underlying issue was always respect. You could ask a guy, "Damn, man, why did you bust that dude in the head with a pipe?"

And he might say, "The motherfucka disrespected me!"

That was explanation enough. It wasn't even necessary to explain how the guy had disrespected him. It was universally understood that if a dude got disrespected, he had to do what he had to do.

It's still that way today. Young dudes nowadays call it "dissin'." They'll kill a nigger for dissin' them. Won't touch a white person, but they'll kill a brother in a heartbeat over a perceived slight. The irony was that white folks constantly disrespected us in ways seen and unseen, and we tolerated it. Most blacks understood that the repercussions were severer for retaliating against whites than for doing each other in. It was as if black folks were saying, *"I can't do much to keep whites from dissin' me, but I damn sure can keep black folks from doing it."*

The guys on the street who got the most respect were those who had reps as crazy niggers. A crazy nigger was someone who had an explosive temper, someone who took flak from no one—man, woman, or child. He would shoot, stab, bite, or do whatever he could to hurt somebody who disrespected him. It was a big thing then to be considered a crazy nigger. We regarded craziness as an esteemed quality, something to be admired, like white people admire courage. In fact, to our way of thinking, craziness and courage were one and the same. So most guys in the street tried to establish a rep as a crazy nigger, or a baad nigger.

The epitome of the crazy nigger was Scobie-D. There are crazy niggers, and niggers who *act* crazy to build a rep. Scobe was a crazy nigger. Once, he got into a rumble in the cafeteria at Waters and tried to stab a guy with a fork. It's one thing to pull a blade on somebody, but stabbing somebody with a fork means a dude grabbed the first weapon he could find. That means he went blank. He went crazy. I was impressed when I saw that.

Another time, Scobe went totally off when he and his boys were turned away from a house party in Cavalier Manor. He got so mad he punched his fist through the glass storm door and cut his hand up so bad it was nearly severed from his wrist. After getting it sewn back up, Scobe's hand always dangled, kind of limp-wristed, but nobody dared suggest that it looked like a girl's.

■ ■ ■

Everybody was tradition-bound to learn to shoot hoops. Those who could hawk ball were respected almost as much as those who could dress well, rap, and fight. Shortly after we moved into Cavalier Manor, my brothers and I erected a basketball goal in the backyard. Cats from our section came back there and we played feverishly, often deep into the night, until we could hang on neighborhood courts.

Each week during basketball season, the physical-education teachers at Waters held intramural games in the gym after school. Everybody went to those games because Scobe, Kenny Banks and all the other popular guys played on those teams. Most of the teams were really hoodlum squads, filled with hackers, but nobody cared about the mechanics of the games. It was a popularity thing.

The weekday intramural games were exciting, but the *real* basketball was played weekends on the concrete court behind Waters. In Cavalier Manor, that was *the* stage, the premier place that guys in the neighborhood went to showcase their athletic skills and go against the best among their peers, while throngs of guys looked on from the sidelines. The best players from all over the city came to Waters.

It seemed that every male between the ages of eleven and twenty-five—literally hundreds of them—went to the recreation field behind Waters to play or watch. I started going out there, too, for the same reason many other dudes my age went: to look, learn, and be where the excitement was. The older guys stepped out there profiling in their super-clean All Stars. By then, everybody was wearing imitation silk underwear in matching colors. On a hot day in the summertime, a dude could wear a red silk sleeveless undershirt, leave his belt buckle unfastened, and let his pants droop low on his butt to show his matching boxer shorts. The older dudes looked slick in those because they had physiques.

Some, the pure athletes, ran full-court games from sunup till sundown. Others, the pure hoods, stood on the sidelines all day and talked trash to each other, passed around cheap wine, rolled dice, or harassed awestruck lames, who had come out there to hero-worship. Some guys wanted so badly to see what was going on with the old-heads that they got too close to the action sometimes. Every now and then, one of the younger guys would get kicked in the butt or slapped in the head or body-slammed by some fool hood showing off or trying to build a rep.

Those pickup games at Waters were fierce. Often, arguments got started during heated games, and fights broke out. The older guys fought over the least little thing—one guy checking another too tight, or somebody calling foul.

"How you gon' call foul, man?!"

"Because, motherfucka, you hacked me!"

"I didn't hack you, man! You just mad 'cause you losin'!"

"I'll tell you what, hack me again, goddammit!"

If the hack came, fists flew, and often, onlookers were treated to brutal spectacles even more thrilling than the fabulous games being played.

When guys from other parts of the city came to Waters to hawk ball, it was almost assured that there would be a good scrap before the day's end. I'd risk missing lunch and dinner waiting for some action to jump off when downtown boys came out there. The same scenario played itself out over and over again: Somebody from downtown would get into an argument on or off the court with somebody from Cavalier Manor. Somebody from either side would strike the first blow, then all hell would break loose. Scobe and his boys would be right there in the thick of it.

■ ■ ■

The best way to guarantee respect was simply to be able to thump. Then, nobody disrespected you. If they did, they paid a price. Once a guy made somebody pay for disrespecting him, the word went out that he "don't take no shit." Everybody else got the message, and it stuck. One dude who hung with Scobe and his boys earned his rep by breaking another guy's nose in a fight at Waters. I thought about that fight every time I saw him after that. Guys would say, "Don't fuck with him. He broke a niggah's nose." There was respect and admiration in their tone when they said things like that.

I wanted that kind of respect. Everybody I knew wanted it. So we all worked on our knuck games to earn our reps. We tried to learn various ways to hurt people, to fuck somebody up so bad it was remembered in the streets for a long, long time. We wrestled and slap-boxed each other all the time, like gladiators preparing for some future war.

I learned how to shoot cuffs—to tackle a man and bring him down. A deceptive move, it's done by faking a swing at the opponent's face, then diving to his ankles to snatch his legs from under him. No matter how big he was or how much he weighed, he'd go down if his cuffs were shot right. Then you could pin him on the ground and punch him in the face, or stomp him six feet under. I learned how to jock-slap a man, grab him by the head and ram a knee into his face. That virtually guaranteed a bloody nose or a busted lip. Some of the serious thumpers found ways to literally use their heads. They cold-cocked dudes that they tangled with. They'd grab their man's head and butt him a few times. I saw a few guys get cold-cocked in fights and knocked unconscious.

The best way to guarantee winning a rumble was to double-bank someone, get several guys and gang up on him. Scobe and his boys were notorious for double-banking. The fellas and I started doing it, too, especially to white boys. One guy would shoot his cuffs, and another would hit him high. He'd fall like a tree, then we'd dust him off.

In my eighth-grade school year, I also learned indirectly from Shane the importance of sneaking a man. One day after school, the fellas and I were watching a rumble near the intersection of Roosevelt and Cavalier boulevards when we saw Shane coming up the street, surrounded by a group of people. As he got closer, I noticed red coloring around his mouth. It looked like he was eating a candy apple. When he reached us, I realized the red stuff was blood. We ran over to him. "Shane, what happened, man?!"

Before he spoke, he spit out a mouthful of blood. It turned out Shane had been selling wolf tickets, running off at the mouth to Dwan Moore, this guy at school, and gotten four of his front teeth knocked through the back of his head. Folks who had seen it told us later that Dwan got somebody to distract Shane, then blindsided him, knocking him cold. I realized from Shane's experience that it was critical to sneak a man, to find some way to catch him off guard. Because they had snuck Shane so well, he never got a chance to use his exceptional boxing skills.

The concept of sneaking a man went against the grain of everything I'd been taught as a youngster about the honor of fighting fair. As I got older, though, fairness, honor, and all that other virtuous bullshit went right out the window. The object was to *win* and to do serious damage, like Dwan Moore did to Shane.

That fight became legend in Cavalier Manor. It turned Shane into a tougher, smarter brawler and earned Dwan Moore a rep as an up-and-coming knockout artist. Respect dictated that Shane should get some get-back, but he didn't even try. Everybody understood why: Dwan Moore was a crazy nigger, and it's hard to prevail against bona fide crazy niggers because they keep coming back until they win.

■ ■ ■

I was sitting on the curb, shooting the breeze with the rest of my boys, when an old, scarred warrior named Horace Perry came bopping around the corner. Horace was nineteen, five years older than me, and widely respected on our block. He loved to fight, and it seemed that he got a special thrill out of going upside my head. As he approached, he fixed his evil, beady eyes dead on me. Seeing what was coming, the fellas sitting near me got up and moved off to the side. I stiffened, stood up, and prepared to throw down. Without saying a word, Horace walked up to me and swung wildly at my head. I threw up my guard, leaned to the side, and swung back, barely missing his face. Horace ducked, charged low into me, and shot for my cuffs. I backpedaled, throwing punches all the while, trying to keep that bull from grabbing me. Too late. Short, squat, and strong as an ox, Horace locked his huge hands around my skinny thighs, took my legs from under me, and rode me down. We struggled, tussled, and rolled around on the ground until Horace wormed his way on top. After he pinned me, Horace smiled devilishly, reached down with his free hand, and pulled up a fistful of grass and dirt. Then, as all the fellas looked on, he stuffed it into my mouth. I clenched my teeth, spat, and bobbed my head, trying to avoid the grass and dirt he ground into my face. I shoved and heaved, but he was too heavy for me to push him off.

Finally, when he was satisfied that he'd humiliated me, Horace Perry jumped up from the ground and ran playfully off to a safe distance, taunting and teasing. "Ah, ha, ha, ha. . . . I kicked your ass, you li'l motherfucka! Now what you gonna do?!"

There wasn't a whole lot I could do. I stood there with dirt on my face and blood in my eyes, spitting grass out of my mouth and wishing I was bigger, stronger—strong enough to put my foot up Horace Perry's ass. Instead, I just huffed and cursed at him: "Fuck you, Horace Perry!"

Horace turned and headed up the street, still laughing and making fun of me.

As much as I hated chewing grass, I didn't get too mad with Horace Perry. In a weird way, I knew he had my best interests at heart. He actually liked me a lot. Older guys such as him often tried to toughen up young bloods they liked by beating up on them. They knew we needed to be hard in order to hang. They knew what we might face down the road, and they understood that if we couldn't take a jive beating every now and then, we'd never survive the serious thumpings that would come in time. We understood it, too. So every time Horace Perry saw me, he forced me to fight him on sight. And every time I saw him coming, I prepared to throw down and give it my best. If I fought hard, I ate less grass. If I didn't fight hard, he'd continue stuffing grass and dirt until my mouth was full.

Later, when I got bigger and older, there was no wrestling, and certainly no grass eating, when Horace Perry came onto our corner. We talked man to man. He gave up respect. He knew instinctively that school was out; the time for all that wrestling and carrying on had passed. That was a rite of passage that all the old thugs understood because they had once been young, too.

■ ■ ■

I could usually measure the strength of my knuck game by how well I fared in battle with Greg and my brother Dwight. Greg was tall and lanky and had long arms and quick moves. I was short and wiry and relied on fast hands to keep him at bay. We'd start off slap-boxing playfully until, invariably, he'd slap me silly with one of his quick moves. Then I'd get mad and want to fight for real. Greg, good spirit that he was, would run and laugh rather than knock me out. It was about the same with Dwight, only we fought for real more than we played. (My brothers Billy and Junnie refused to fight me. There was such a big age difference between them and me that they swatted me away whenever I pestered them.) Dwight wasn't much bigger than me, but he was the better athlete—he was stronger and more skilled with his hands. Usually, whenever we fought, it didn't last long. I could never seem to take him, even when I snuck him or hit him with a stick.

A kind of turning point for Dwight and me came one day when we started arguing about something in the house. There was nobody inside but him and me. When the argument reached a pitch, I hit him. We locked horns in the dining room and threw down, hard. We battled our way into the living room. He popped me in the eye, like he normally did. What was different was the furor in which I fought back. I landed a couple of shots to his face that were so hard and clean they surprised me, so much so that I paused a moment to admire my work and left myself open to a barrage of punches that knocked me into the front door. It was summertime. The wood door was opened wide. The storm door was closed, but we'd left the glass panes in rather than install the screens. I fell through the door, sending shards of glass flying everywhere. My mother happened to be sitting on the front porch, talking with neighbors. When she saw me come flying through that glass door, all hell broke loose. She jumped up from her seat, came indoors, and TKO'd both of us. She confined us to the house.

Although I lost that and every other rumble I had with Dwight, that particular fight was a symbolic victory for me. It served notice to him that the days of pitty-pat with little brother were over. There would be no easy wins from there on out.

■ ■ ■

It was a cardinal rule on the block that a brother couldn't let himself be beaten by three groups of people: gays, girls, and white boys. Of the three, defeat at the hands of a white boy brought the most disgrace. If a dude let himself be beaten by a white boy, he was forever afterward identified by that dishonor: "That's So-and-so. He let a *white boy* beat him." Everybody within earshot would sadly shake their head, as if So-and-so were the sorriest motherfucka on the face of the earth.

I guess that's why I never told the fellas about what happened to me at Alford J. Mapp, that white junior high school I briefly attended.

Even though those white boys double- and triple-banked me, it didn't seem likely that the brothers would sympathize. So as far as the public record was concerned, I was undefeated when it came to fighting white boys. I was about 30–0. All the fellas went undefeated because we double-banked.

We all hated white people. The fellas and I never talked about specific things they'd done to us, but we instinctively knew that each of us had been through bad scenes with white folks before. So we took it out on white boys.

After we reached the ninth grade and were sent to the mostly white Woodrow Wilson High School across town, we fucked up white boys more than we went to class. We walked through secluded areas of the building after classes on Fridays. When we came upon a white boy, somebody would light into him, then everybody else sprang and we'd do him in.

One day, we double-banked a guy standing at his locker in the area where the wood-shop classes were held. We walked as if we were going to pass him, then Lep hauled off and punched him in the face. Then I popped him in the mouth. He fell back and slammed his head into the lockers. Before I could hit him again, somebody else hit him with a barrage of punches that sent him crashing to the floor. We kicked him in the face and stomped him until blood squirted everywhere. After we finished, we ran out a side door and went home.

I saw that white boy in school about a week later. Walking down the hall, Lep nudged me and pointed him out. He had his arm in a sling and bandages taped to the bridge of his nose. I snickered and told Lep, "We fucked him up *good*."

I knew my heart was hardening. In fact, I *wanted* it to harden so I wouldn't get scared or feel weird inside when we did crazy things like that. I didn't want anybody to see me equivocate. I think some of the other guys felt the same way, but no one said anything. No one wanted to be called a chump.

When we couldn't get to white boys, we gang-wrestled among ourselves or took on dudes from other parts of the neighborhood. If a group of guys our age happened to walk past our corner, we'd challenge them to match their force against ours: "Naw, man, y'all can't just walk past our corner any old kinda way. This is *our* block! You got to give up some *respect* when you walk by here!"

They might say, "Fuck you *and* your corner!" Then we'd get it on, pretending to be gang-bangers fighting a war.

All that rumbling we did in those early days was dress rehearsal for things to come. Respect was incomplete until we had proven ourselves in the serious throwdowns with downtown boys. Scobe and his buddies were always battling downtown boys, and we expected to pick up the mantle when our time came. We prepared by honing our skills and rumbling hard. But it wasn't long before we gave up fistfighting for guns.

Chapter 8 POWER

I witnessed the power of the gun, close-up, one night when I saw Scobe shoot a guy. I was fifteen, and I'd gone to a pool party at the Cavalier Manor recreation center and was standing around outside when a major fight broke out between Scobe's boys and a group of guys who didn't live in our neighborhood. The other guys broke out running, but Scobe and his boys caught up with one of them before he reached the bus stop at Greenwood Drive, about a hundred yards away. I'd run along with the crowd to watch the rumble and was standing less than ten feet away when they caught the dude. Scobe ran up to him, pointed a gun barrel at his stomach, and shot him at point-blank range. The guy slumped to the ground. As everybody scrambled to get away, I stood there a moment and stared at him lying motionless in the dirt. Then I took off running, along with everybody else.

For much of that night, I lay awake in bed, thinking about what I'd seen and wondering if the guy would live or die. It bothered me that I'd left somebody like that who might be dying, but I wasn't about to snitch on Scobe, or anybody else. The next day, when the fellas and I met at our corner, we talked admiringly about Scobe, about how wild he was, how he would shoot anybody for looking at him the wrong way. We said, over and over, "That niggah is crazy!"

Scobe eventually was arrested and charged with the shooting. The man he shot survived, and I think Scobe got off with probation. That was the amazing thing about Scobe. He always seemed to get away with the wild things he did. Nobody ever associated consequences with him.

Scobe had a reputation for being trigger-happy long before most dudes on the block even thought about carrying guns. He was notorious for flashing all kinds of guns at the basketball court. Whenever he got into arguments on the court, guys began gathering their coats, because they knew he was packing. The disputes often ended with him running to get a gun from his coat, or storming off to his house a few blocks away and returning with one of the many pieces he owned. He'd return, cussing, foam forming in the corners of his mouth, the veins in his neck bulging like they were about to snap, and that flaming red Afro would look like it was on fire like the rest of him. He'd open fire, *tat, tat, tat, tat, tat,* sending everybody scattering. Guys would leap over the tall fence or dive to the ground when he started shooting. It was some sight to see one dude make hundreds of people scramble for cover in all directions like that. That was power.

■ ■ ■

We were lounging around in a friend's living room one day when he stood up and announced, "I got something to show you."

The friend, a guy named Bobby, was a goofy dude, more soft-edged than most of us. He wanted to hang with the fellas and me and was trying to impress us any way he could. He went into his parents' bedroom and returned, gloating, with his father's gun. "Check this out."

He proudly passed the unloaded piece around the room for us to hold and examine. Awestruck, dudes caressed it, squeezed the trigger several times, and talked about its power. They even took turns stuffing the piece under their belts to see how easily it could be concealed.

When it was my turn to hold it, I gently cradled it in the palm of my hand and turned it at various angles, carefully examining its features. I marveled at its size. I'd never held a gun that small before.

Occasionally, when my parents were away, I toyed with my stepfather's gun, a .38 service revolver that he used on his job as a security guard at the shipyard. He kept it in his dresser drawer when he was off duty. But it was bulky, nothing like the pearl-handled, black-and-chrome .22 Bobby showed me. A lightweight piece, it could fit snugly in your pants with barely a bulge. A dude could stick it in his pocket and walk along a crowded downtown street and no one would even suspect he was packing a piece.

It was beautiful. I fantasized about owning it. I even inspected the cone-shaped bullets that came with it and considered that each one carried within its shell the power to take a human life.

I felt that sense of power even more after we pitched in and bought a box of bullets of our own to try it out. Bobby sneaked the gun out of the house and we went into the woods near Crystal Lake and took turns shooting it. When my turn came, I held it tightly with two hands, closed my eyes, and squeezed the trigger. I can't describe the exhilaration I felt when I fired that gun. I was smitten by its power and what it symbolized. Instantly, I understood why Scobe was hooked on guns.

■ ■ ■

In many ways, high school marked a turning point for me. Most important, it marked the end of school days insulated in the neighborhood. When we started going to Woodrow Wilson High School across town, we got to a place where the tensions flowed in many directions: between blacks and whites; between Cavalier Manor guys and downtown boys who also went to school there; even between my gang and other young groups from different parts of Cavalier Manor.

Those tensions heightened during football season, when groups of guys ran into each other at games. By the time I was fifteen, the fellas and I had solidly established ourselves as a combative bunch of young hoods. We often went to school dressed alike, sat together, and raised hell during Friday-morning pep rallies. Pumped up with the testy rumbling spirit of Cavalier Manor, we'd pile into cars and go to nighttime football games, armed with assorted knives and Bobby's father's .22. At halftime, we'd pimp around to the visitors' side of the field, profiling and rapping to girls from competing schools. Other groups of dudes did the same thing. I saw them eyeing us, and we returned the hostile glares: "Look at them punk motherfuckas. They think they baad."

Tension also flowed heavy at school-related parties, especially those outside of Cavalier Manor. I loved those parties, as much for the danger they posed as the fun we had. When the music slowed, you could find me standing in the middle of the floor, slow-dragging hard with some babe I'd honed in on. Frog Dickie, with his short self, might be dancing nearby with his head barely reaching up to some chick's breasts. Lep, who always kept a towel slung over his shoulder to wipe the sweat, would lean his slow-dance partners against a wall to get better leverage to grind on them. And Shane, who never could dance well, would be doing his fucked-up version of the two-step slow-grind. Instead of shifting from one leg to the other in time with the tune, he'd stay locked on one leg, like he was dancing to a scratched record. The other fellas would be somewhere nearby, talking trash, jonin', and waiting for trouble to jump off with dudes from other groups.

The specter of a rumble after football games and parties always hung heavy. Often all it took was a minor excuse—an accidental brush against some dude's coat sleeve or a misunderstood look—to trigger a brawl or a shooting.

Our first rumble involved rival groups in my own neighborhood. It was sparked partly by an old friend of mine from the fifth grade, a guy we called Shell Shock, who started swinging with the fellas and me when we got to high school. He had a brown belt in karate and had earned a strong rep in Cavalier Manor by kicking out the front teeth of an established old hood who hung with Scobe. That was some feat since the hood, known as Joe Ham, was no chump and since he was a full four years older than Shell Shock. After that, people thought Shell Shock was a bona fide crazy nigger with a strong knuck game. Shell Shock and I grew tight. He was kinda slow in school, but he seemed to know more than the rest of us about the streets. He showed me how to take a spent bullet shell and shape it to fit around my tooth so that it looked like I had a shiny gold cap.

One night, a bunch of us were standing on our corner, drinking wine, when Shell Shock said he had a beef with a group of dudes known as the Cherry Boys. We played football against them some-times and ran into them at parties. The Cherry Boys began coming to our bus stop some mornings to rap to girls who lived around our way. Shell Shock said we should "fuck 'em up" and put a stop to that.

It was a dumb excuse to fight, but we were so pumped up and anxious to fight somebody—anybody—that we went along. Bobby sneaked his old man's gun out of the house one morning, and we headed to the bus stop to put the Cherry Boys in check. I made sure I was the one carrying the piece. I tucked it into my belt and bopped in front of the crowd, feeling like I was the baaddest nigger on the East Coast. We reached the bus stop and started throwing down. We had them outnumbered and clearly were beating them when I drew the piece. I shoved it to the temple of a guy named Jimmy and went into my Scobie-D macho act. "Make a move, motherfucka, and I'm gonna blow you away!"

I hadn't thought beforehand how far I'd go with the crazy-nigger act—you don't think like that when you're in that frame of mind. I do know that I had no intention of killing anybody. But for a minute, I got so caught up in the excitement of the moment that I started to pull the trigger to blow the guy away. It was nothing personal; actu-ally, he was a likable guy. But for that moment, in my head, I was Scobie-D, a crazy nigger, and my audience was the fifty or so mesmer-ized schoolkids watching. As I stood there, holding that pistol barrel

flush against the side of Jimmy's head, everybody grew silent. That
was my moment. On some level, I felt pressured by the expectations
I'd created to complete the scene and thrill the crowd. If I offed
Jimmy, it would be talked about in the streets for years after that. I'd
claim my minute of glory and people would pay me the ultimate
tribute: "Nate McCall blew that niggah's head off! He's a crazy
motherfucka!"

I don't know why I didn't shoot. It's likely that Jimmy's total
surrender sobered me. He stood there, his eyes bulging and his body
stark still, with his hands raised skyward as far as they would go.
"Don't shoot, man. Don't shoot!" I calmed down and pulled the gun
away, satisfied that I'd publicly chumped him down.

I can never forget that moment. Whenever I hear about shootings
now, I try to imagine what happened in the gunman's head. I try to
imagine what he was thinking, because I know the feeling of standing
there with all that power literally at one's fingertips. For someone who
has felt powerless and ignored all his life, that's one hell of an adrenaline rush.

After the fellas and I were content that we'd whipped the Cherry
Boys, we let them go. They limped away, battered and bruised, and
we celebrated the triumph of our first real throwdown. "Did you see
that niggah's face when I hit him? I cold-cocked his ass!"

"Yeah, I saw him. Them pussies ain't got no heart."

But that wasn't the end of it. The Cherry Boys regrouped to
retaliate. They found allies in some of the older hoods, many of whom
didn't like Shell Shock and me. They questioned my loyalty to Cavalier Manor, because I had pierced my ear and gotten a gold tooth,
fashions that were popular among downtown boys. They considered
me the ringleader in the rumble and made it clear that I was tops on
their hit list.

■ ■ ■

When I saw the Cherry Boys again, I was alone and unarmed. They
jumped me outside a party on a Sunday night. They were closing in,
rushing me from all sides, when an older, well-respected hood stepped
in and saved me—because the odds were so uneven. I survived that
lightweight clash with only a few scratches to my face.

When I got home, I telephoned all the fellas to talk about getting
some get-back. I didn't hear the same cockiness in some of my guys'
voices that had been there before. They didn't sound like they were
into the rumble for the long haul. I sensed then that I was doomed.

I called Bobby. "I need the piece. We gonna rumble again tomorrow at the bus stop."

He said, "I can't get it, man. I think my old man is gonna be home."

By then, I was desperate. "You gotta get it! I *gotta* get some get-back."

He said, "I'll see what I can do. I'll meet you out there tomorrow."

The next morning, I woke up feeling nervous as hell. My intuition was on fire, telling me that only a faithful few of the fellas would show. Before walking out the door, I hesitated near the kitchen, where my mother was cooking. I considered telling her that I expected big trouble at the bus stop. I thought about asking her to drive me to school. But I couldn't bring myself to do it. How could I turn punk after having been so baad before? How could I face all the people I'd tried to impress at the bus stop the previous week? I *had* to go.

I went out into the backyard and broke a broom handle against the side of the concrete porch. Then I left with my makeshift club and went down the block to meet the fellas. When I got there, nobody had shown up but Shane and Shell Shock. Bobby was nowhere in sight. We waited awhile, then gave up. I said, "C'mon, man, let's go on out there. Them motherfuckas ain't runnin' me off *my* block."

We walked slowly toward the bus stop. I could see off in the distance that there was a larger than usual gathering at the corner of Roosevelt and Cavalier boulevards. Word had spread that there was going to be another big rumble, and people had come from everywhere to watch. The Cherry Boys, as well as some older hoods, were out there in full force, waiting to do battle.

I don't know how Shane and Shell Shock felt—we walked in silence—but I was scared to death. All of a sudden, I didn't want to be rock hard anymore. I would have given anything to be a regular schoolboy, a no-name lame with no rep to defend; to go to school and do my classwork; to have the freedom to be scared, unbound by false bravado. But I'd crossed the line and was compelled by teenage illogic to go all the way. So I walked on toward my crucifixion.

As we approached the corner, about thirty guys, led by the Cherry Boys, met us in the middle of the street. Some had lead pipes and others carried clubs. I suspected there was a concealed gun or two in the crowd. Most of them also were wearing heavy brogans. In those days, one of the fashions for serious thumpers was baggy khakis and spit-shined, steel-toed brogans. The "bros," as we called them, were good fighting shoes, used for landing a hard kick to the nuts or delivering a severe stomping to a fallen foe.

When we met in the street, I held up my hand to call a truce. Before I could speak, somebody snuck me and punched me in the face. I swung back and kept swinging until there were so many of them swarming around me, throwing punches, that I couldn't move my arms. I felt myself being knocked off balance. I tried desperately to stay on my feet, fearing what would happen if I hit that ground. And it did happen. I fell and felt the force and number of blows multiply as they kicked me with their bros and beat me with pipes and clubs. The pain ricocheted like a pinball from my head to my toes and back again. I curled up in the fetal position and tried to cover my head to cushion the blows. I felt myself fading and remember thinking that I *had* to hold on, that eventually they would have to stop. But it seemed an eternity passed and the beating went on. Then my fear turned to horror; the horror that comes the instant you realize that they have no way of knowing when they've gone too far; they don't know how many blows to the head will bring permanent damage or death.

I wanted to scream, as much in fear as in pain. But I held back. *Only punks cry out. Men take their lumps.* Eventually, though, an involuntary wail worked its way up from the pit of my throbbing gut to my aching throat and shoved its way through my bleeding mouth. It wasn't a manly sound. It was more like a pleading cry. I'd never heard that sound come from me before. It competed against the ring of pipe against my body and the thud of bros against my head. I kept thinking, *They gotta stop! They gonna kill me! They gonna kill me!* Then, almost as suddenly as it started, it ended. There was silence. I was so fucked up I felt high, paralyzed, like all of time was suspended, as I lay there in the street, writhing in pain.

Somebody, I don't know to this day who it was, lifted me off the ground. There was one person on each side of me. They threw my arms over their shoulders and lugged me toward my house, which was less than two blocks away. My mouth bled so much that I almost gagged on my own blood. My vision was blurred, but I could make out the images of concerned neighbors, who had run out of their houses and were standing around, staring. I saw Shane lying on the ground inside a neighbor's fence, where he had been beaten and tossed over. I didn't see Shell Shock anywhere.

As I was being carried toward my house, a group of little kids approached. They were leaving the cul-de-sac, headed for school. My seven-year-old brother, Bryan, was among them. I saw the shock on his face when he saw me, bloodied and limp. Somebody screamed, "Get him away from here! He don't need to see this!"

They took me inside the house and laid me down on the living-room floor. My mother, shocked, ran and got her coat and car keys and instructed my helpers to lift me into the backseat of the car. She sped me to the Portsmouth Naval Hospital emergency room.

White doctors placed me on an examining-room table and began asking questions in the slow, deliberate manner that doctors have. "Where does it hurt?" "Can you lift your arm?" "Are you allergic to any medication?"

I grew impatient. *How can I tell them where it hurts? It hurts all over.* I just wanted the doctors to shut up and stop the pain. My body felt like a battered heap of broken bones.

I spent the day at the hospital and eventually learned where the damage was done. The doctors said there had been injuries to my vertebrae. They put my neck in a brace. They put my arm in a sling and treated me for bruised ribs. My face was swollen. Several of my teeth had been knocked loose. The tip of the fake gold bullet cap fitted over one of my teeth had been knocked up into my gums, cutting them badly. Assorted other pains roamed my body.

I stayed home in bed more than a week, recuperating. In that time, I relived the fight in my mind a thousand times. Friends called and came by to visit and tell me other details about what had happened. Shane, I learned, took a pretty bad beating, but he was all right. Shell Shock got jumped, too, but he also survived. I heard that Frog Dickie and some of the other fellas had arrived late at our meeting spot. When they came up the street and saw us being double-banked, they turned around and ran home. As far as I know, Bobby never showed up with his father's gun.

When Shell Shock came over, he suggested that we retaliate against some of our guys for punking out, then get some get-back from the Cherry Boys. But I was in no mood to talk about fighting. "Fuck it, man. It don't matter."

That fight proved some things to me that I'd sensed all along but never acknowledged: I was too puny to be a heavy thumper. My frail body could never take another beating like that. I also realized that I couldn't depend on other people to come through for me. When we were hanging, the fellas and I had pledged to go down together, if and whenever necessary. Now I saw that that was mostly talk. If I was going to hang, I needed somebody—or something—I could depend on, always. I needed a piece.

■ ■ ■

Initially, I used Shell Shock's mother's gun, a neat little two-shot derringer that fitted nicely into my shirt pocket or pants. A widowed hospital clerk who worked nights, Shell Shock's mother carried it in her purse. He started "borrowing" the derringer around the same time he began stealing her car keys to take joyrides and chase girls.

Meanwhile, I put the word out on the streets that I was looking for a piece, and somebody came up with exactly what I wanted, a compact .25 automatic.

Scobe was always known for carrying big guns, .44 Magnums and .357s. Over time, as the gun craze caught on, other dudes began going for bigger, more impressive-looking pieces, too. Eventually, the fellas and I built an arsenal that included a mix of lightweight and powerful stuff: several handguns, a sawed-off shotgun, and a high-powered 30-30 rifle.

We worshiped those guns. We practiced shooting at targets in the woods, and took aim in the streets at barking dogs. We sat around some nights, polishing and doting over them, like they were fine ladies we loved. One night, when a bunch of us were sitting around in Shell Shock's dining room, cleaning our weapons and talking, I accidentally almost shot a dude we called Whiskey Bottle. I thought I'd unloaded all the bullets from my gun when I pointed it his way to make a conversational point. Whiskey was standing at the kitchen sink, drinking water, when the gun fired, *Bam!* For a full minute, the world stood still. Everybody in the room, including me, closed their eyes, too scared to look and afraid to speak. Somebody shouted, "Nate!" They just knew I'd killed Whiskey.

When I opened my eyes, I was relieved. Whiskey was still standing. He was shocked and speechless, but alive and well. We all got up from our seats and went over to where he stood and saw that the bullet had struck a cabinet directly beside his head. It missed him by a few inches.

■ ■ ■

Carrying a gun did strange things to my head. Suddenly I became very much aware that I had the power to alter the fate of anybody I saw. The greatest power on earth is the ability to give life. The next greatest power is the ability to take one. When carrying a gun, I was full of the sense of that power. I felt confident, invincible, like Scobie-D.

For me, guns were life's great equalizer. When I was armed, the older hoods who had once seemed so intimidating didn't faze me anymore. And I no longer feared going across town or being double-banked by two, or even twenty, guys, because I had the equalizer. Even grown-ups like my stepfather began to look more vulnerable to me when I had that piece nestled in my belt.

My faith in the power of guns shot up a few notches more one night, a few months after I was jumped. I was walking home by myself from a girl's house when the Cherry Boys and some others spotted me and came charging my way.

Normally, I would have had to dash or take another head-thumping. But I had the loaded .25 tucked into my coat. I had the equalizer, and I wasn't scared. I waited until they got within twenty yards of me, drew the gun, aimed, and fired several shots into the crowd, *bam! bam! bam! bam!* They dove to the ground and then scattered like flies. It made me feel powerful to be able to scatter a crowd like that. I stood there for a moment, full of the sense of what I'd done. I just stood there and took it in. Then I turned and calmly walked home.

I didn't consider the potential consequences of what I'd done until I stepped into the house. Then I got scared and had to force myself to be cool. Mama met me in the living room, pointed a finger, and said, "You better stop coming in this house so late on school nights!"

I stopped, looked at her like she was crazy, and shook my head. "Okay, Ma."

I wanted to say more. I wanted to tell her what had happened, in case the police came to the house. I wanted to say, "Ma, I think I may have shot somebody." Instead, I kept quiet and went to bed.

I heard talk the next day that a bullet had grazed a dude's hand. The police never came, but that was no surprise. The Cherry Boys weren't the kind of dudes who would snitch to the cops. I knew that if one of them had been shot, they'd try to get some get-back. So I waited, determined not to let them or anybody else catch me unarmed. As long as I had a piece on me, I would fear no man, not even Scobie-D.

Chapter 9 WAR

The feud with the Cherry Boys probably would have resumed until somebody got seriously hurt or killed, but it was interrupted by a more pressing matter: Cavalier Manor went to war against downtown. I didn't know what sparked the battle. That was irrelevant. All I knew was that the word went out that our neighborhood was at war, and that meant every able-bodied hood with heart was expected to do his part.

Cats in Portsmouth treated such urban combat with the utmost seriousness, building arsenals and planning tactical strikes like armies in a real war. The word on the grapevine was that Scobe and his boys had broken into the local National Guard armory compound and stolen gobs of weapons to use in their attacks. Downtown guys, led by a dude called Black Sam, routinely stoned and shot at city buses headed for Cavalier Manor, forcing passengers, young and old, to hit the floor and remain there until the driver got them out of harm's way. The battles, of course, intensified during the school year, when football season started.

I'd heard a lot about such wars when I went to Waters Junior High. I was thrilled when I became old enough to take part. I was about sixteen then. Like everybody else, I was motivated by turf loyalty, driven by the sense that as a resident of "the Manor" I was bound by some unwritten code to help defend its honor.

I saw my first real action with downtown boys when Shell Shock and I went to a crowded dance at the Douglas Park recreation center near downtown. As music played, guys from the Manor and downtown milled about on separate sides of the room, glaring at each other. The tension was so thick that nobody dared slow-drag for fear of getting blindsided if something jumped off. I had my piece, and I remember walking through the crowd, thinking, *More than half the dudes in here are probably packin'.*

Before the party ended, dudes from Newtown, Truxton, and various public housing projects downtown filtered out of the room, leaving guys from the Manor inside. I assumed initially that they had left because they knew they were outnumbered. But when the party ended and I stepped outdoors into the drizzling rain, gunshots creased the air. Hiding behind trees, houses, and cars, downtown boys opened fire from all directions, ambushing us. Guys from the Manor drew and fired back, panicking innocent partygoers, who got caught in the middle of the gun battle. Some ran, screaming, and dived for cover. Shrieking girls crawled in the mud under parked cars. Others, terrified, lunged to the wet ground and tried to cover their heads. It was wild. I'd never seen anything like it. For a moment, I just stood there, taking it all in.

My excitement overshadowed any concerns about safety. I was so thrilled to be in the thick of the action that I didn't have sense enough to be scared. War meant that there would be bloodshed, carnage, but I was caught up in the street glory. Besides, like many young people, I felt invincible. As far as I was concerned, none of those bullets bore my name. Tragedies happened only to other guys.

Gripping my piece, I looked for my stickman, Shell Shock. I spotted him bopping through the crowd like he thought he was God. When we connected, we chilled along the edge of the recreation-center wall and watched the shoot-out in amazement. It looked like TV footage of Vietnam. I could see sparks spitting from guns everywhere, lighting up the place like the Fourth of July.

About fifteen minutes after the shooting started, the downtown boys started pulling back. A lone guy from downtown, a short, cocky dude apparently trying to earn a rep, defiantly strolled up the sidewalk toward a group of us who were milling about. Waving a sawed-off shotgun, he shouted: "Punk-ass motherfuckas from Cavalier Manor!"

As he cursed, he lifted the gun barrel and pointed it toward a guy standing about five feet from me. Another dude from the Manor crept up behind him, broke a wine bottle over his head, and slung him to the ground. The shotgun went off into the air, *boooom!* The downtown dude jumped up and bolted across the baseball field, with about twelve guys from Cavalier Manor, including Shell Shock and me, hot on his ass. While he sprinted, he tried to reload his shotgun to get off another blast. But Shell Shock, who had run track one season, caught him, tackled him, and wrestled the shotgun from his hands. When the others and I caught up, we pounced on the dude and stomped him into the ground.

Shell Shock probably saved somebody's life that night. I'm sure several of us would've been struck by scatter shot if that crazy dude had gotten a chance to reload and fire another blast.

■ ■ ■

Eventually, the war between downtown and Cavalier Manor expanded into a three-way battle. After several shoot-outs between the initial two factions threatened public safety, the cops jumped into the mix. It seemed the rollers in Portsmouth knew as much about what was going on in the streets as the guys hanging out. They knew there was a war raging and that it involved lots of guns. They were determined to break it up.

I found out the rollers were hip to the happenings when they turned up the heat on our block at Roosevelt Boulevard and Bardot Lane. Several times a week, they pulled up to our corner in unmarked cars, screeched to a halt, jumped out, and shook us down. "All right, everybody, up against the wall! Spread-eagle! Nobody move!"

They took a knife off me once, but let me go. Unless they found guns, they simply ordered us off the block. Riding four-deep to a car, they'd return a few days later and assault our block again.

I grew accustomed to being confronted by lawmen wherever I went. It fed my already deep hatred for them. All but a few on the force then were white. Their skin color and arrogance with blacks boiled my blood. They acted like their job was to protect white people and control blacks. I couldn't stand their bossy tone when they talked to us, and hated the way they got right up in my face, with their white noses almost touching mine. Sometimes, when they ordered you to move on, they'd reach out and shove you, even while you were trying to do what they said.

I knew what that was all about. There is a forbidden zone that exists among men. If a man invades that zone, if he gets too close in another man's face, it's considered a challenge to his manliness and an invitation to tangle. I suspected that those cops got in my face like that to provoke me to attack so they could blow me away.

I hated cops so much I fantasized sometimes about ambushing one. But I wouldn't dare try because I feared them, too. Those cops were trained to kill, and I could tell sometimes by the look in their eyes that they wanted badly to use that training, especially on blacks. For me, then, the choice was clear: Shoot at downtown boys and avoid the cops.

Of course, there were some cats who were so bodacious that they even took on cops. Like the dude who beat a cop to the ground and took his gun. And, of course, there was a cop story about Scobie-D. Neighborhood lore had it that Scobe chumped down a state trooper once. The trooper pulled him aside for speeding on Interstate 264. When the trooper approached Scobe's car and leaned over, he looked right down the barrel of a sawed-off shotgun. According to the story, the shocked trooper turned, walked slowly back to his cruiser, and drove away.

At first, that story struck me as a little too wild to be true, but I hated cops so much that I wanted to believe that one of them had been chumped down for a change.

■ ■ ■

One of the downsides of war was that it screwed up everybody's love life. Downtown boys couldn't safely come into our neighborhood and rap to girls, and we couldn't go downtown rapping without risking repercussions. When the war got under way, I was seeing a girl named Nita, who lived in the Lincoln Park public housing project downtown. One night, Bimbo, Lep, Frog Dickie, and I caught the city bus, on the spur of the moment, to Lincoln Park to see Nita and meet some of her girlfriends. (It was a big thrill then to cut into crosstown girls.) When word spread that we were there, one of Nita's friends rushed into the apartment and warned, "You better get outta here. Guys out here are gettin' ready to come after you."

Nita told us, "Go out the back door!"

We stepped outside and saw a mob of guys coming down the sidewalk, carrying sticks, pipes, bricks, and broken bottles. None of us was armed because we hadn't planned on going to Lincoln Park. We had to think fast. I told the fellas, "Look, man, we gotta make it to Portsmouth Boulevard and catch the bus. We gotta make a dash for it. When I give the signal, make your break."

We took a few steps toward the approaching mob, then I said, "Now!" We bolted across the street and they took off after us, throwing rocks and hurling bottles. Then I heard the gunshots, *tat, tat, tat, tat*.

Anybody with common sense knows it's impossible to dodge bullets, but common sense fades in the face of terror. My mind told me to zigzag, to dodge the bullets, so I zigzagged in the street, making sure no one could get a steady aim to cut me down. Instinctively, the fellas and I split and ran apart from each other. When we reached Portsmouth Boulevard, we spotted a motorcycle cop riding by and flagged him down. I have never been so glad to see a lawman in all my life. Breathless, we told him, "Some guys back there are shootin' at us!"

He called for reinforcements. That's when we realized Bimbo was missing. Bimbo was the fattest and slowest runner in our bunch. That made him the most likely to be caught by downtown boys or, worse, struck by a stray bullet. We backtracked with the rollers to search for him. They flashed searchlights high and low, but found no sign of Bimbo. I had images of poor Bimbo lying under a car or in a dark yard somewhere, wounded, bleeding to death. After a while, the police told us, "Go on home. There's not much we can do to find him in the darkness. We'll check around here some more tomorrow."

On the bus ride home, we were somber. I felt guilty because I'd taken the fellas, unarmed, into a rough, hostile neighborhood where we'd been ambushed. One of my partners was missing in action because of me. Lep asked, "Should we call Bimbo's moms and tell her what happened?"

"I don't know," I said. I didn't want to think about talking to adults.

Lep pushed the issue. "We *have* to call, man. Bimbo could be somewhere dead by now."

"You gonna call his moms?"

"Naw, we shouldn't tell her this on the phone," Lep said. "We gotta go over there and tell her."

We reached Cavalier Manor after midnight, walked wearily to Bimbo's house, and rang the doorbell. A minute passed, then the door opened. Standing there, in the darkness of the doorway, was Bimbo, looking relaxed, refreshed, and, of course, well fed. I shouted, "What the fuck you doin' at home, man?! We thought you were dead!"

Bimbo laughed. "Naw, man. I ain't dead. When the shootin' started, I hauled ass through some backyards and caught a cab. I been here a long time. I was wonderin' what happened to y'all."

Bimbo, the fattest and slowest dude among us, had beaten us home. We laughed about that one for a long time.

■　■　■

The war between downtown and Cavalier Manor went on for a while, with each side winning battles here and there. The fellas and I got our chance to strike back for being chased from Lincoln Park. A group of us was hanging out at the bus stop one night when two guys hurried past us down Cavalier Boulevard. Lep recognized one of them. "Hey, man, them niggahs from downtown!"

The guys, one of whom dated a girl in our neighborhood, apparently were trying to catch the late bus leaving Cavalier Manor. They never made it. We caught them several blocks down the street, beat them like they stole something, and threw them, battered and bleeding, into the muddy ditch on Cavalier Boulevard.

Weeks later, downtown boys came back with a stronger strike. I'd left the fellas on the block about 10 P.M. that night, gone home, and fallen asleep. Later, I was awakened by a faint noise that sounded like firecrackers, followed minutes later by the sound of people crying out. "Help! Help! Help!"

I got up, looked out my bedroom window, and saw someone lying in the front yard. I got hold of my stepfather and we went together to the front door. There, we saw Bimbo lying on the ground, bleeding. He'd been shot in the side. Another guy, Tony, who had also been shot, was lying about thirty feet away. The downtown boys had struck; the fellas had seen them pull up and start shooting.

We telephoned my buddies' parents, who came and helped us load them into separate cars, and we sped toward the hospital. Bimbo was placed in the backseat of my father's car. He lay stretched out, moaning and groaning and holding his side. I rode back there with him. I kept saying, "Hold on, man. We gonna get there in a few minutes."

Bimbo kept his eyes closed, breathing deeply, trying to blow it off. I remember thinking, *He's gonna die! Oh, God, he's gonna die!* I was so overcome with emotion that tears welled in my eyes. It was the first time that I realized I loved my swinging partners. Sometimes, when we were hanging on the corner, jonin', drinking wine, and harmonizing songs, I felt warmed by the camaraderie we shared. But never had I allowed myself even to *think* in terms of loving them. Love was a weakness. When it dawned on me that that was what I might be feeling, I caught myself. I was so uncomfortable with the emotion that I quickly wiped my face and pushed the feeling aside.

Bimbo and Tony survived the shooting, but spent weeks mending in the hospital. That incident made me realize that war was serious business and that I could get killed—I had missed being on that corner by half an hour.

■ ■ ■

A popular expression in the streets of Cavalier Manor says: "Payback is a motherfucka." That's really what our war was about, and after the Lincoln Park incident and the shooting attack in our neighborhood, Shell Shock and I were eager to get some get-back.

One night, we waited until Shell Shock's mother fell asleep, then went out to her Chevrolet Caprice and pulled our usual stunt. We released the emergency brake and let the car glide gently from the slanted driveway into the street. There, Shell Shock produced his extra set of keys and started the car. I had my .25 automatic, fully loaded and ready to go. It was less than five miles to Lincoln Park.

It wasn't hard to find marks in the compact community of attached brick apartments. There were only about eight buildings, set in a semi-courtyard, comprising Lincoln Park. We spotted a crowd of dudes hanging on an apartment porch. Shell Shock drove slowly up the dimly lit street and angled the car so that the passenger side, where I sat, faced the porch. When I gave the word, he stopped the car and turned off the lights. I took dead aim at the moving figures on the crowded porch and opened fire. *Tat, tat, tat, tat, tat.*

Today, I can't remember whether my gun was a six- or a nine-shot. All I know is, I kept my finger on the trigger until it emptied, shattering windows and sending people on the porch diving for cover. When I finished, Shell Shock burned rubber out of there, keeping the car lights off so that nobody could see the license number. I had no idea whether somebody was struck by a bullet. For a few days afterward, I held my breath, hoping no police cruiser crept onto my street full of cops bearing an arrest warrant. I didn't hear anything about the shooting being in the newspapers or on the evening news. After a few weeks, I relaxed, feeling comfortable that we'd gotten away. Then I gloated over our successful strike.

■   ■   ■

It was a Friday the thirteenth, and my stepfather had said I could use the car. I got dressed and left home, headed on a hot date. As I passed our corner, Shane, Bimbo, and Chip waved me down. "Yo, man, Lep just called from a party in Douglas Park! He said some downtown boys are waiting outside to double-bank him!"

After healing from his shooting wounds, Bimbo was back in circulation and eager to get some get-back for himself. We pulled together our arsenal, packed into my stepfather's car, and headed toward Douglas Park to rescue our swinging partner. When we got there, we saw that the rumble had already gone down and the party was over. I saw people walking away from the area in groups. Just as I began to drive off, somebody in the car said, "Yo, man, be cool. The rollers are scopin' us."

A police cruiser pulled behind my stepfather's black Mercury Comet and began trailing us. I got that strange, intuitive feeling I get when something heavy is about to go down. I drove cautiously at the speed limit until the rollers turned on their flashing red lights. Then I sped up, trying to decide what to do about the guns. Everybody panicked. They all began shouting at once. "Hide the guns under the seat!"

"No, throw them out the window!"

"No, be cool!"

One by one, they flung weapons out the passenger-side windows into a weedy lot. Eventually, other cop cars joined in the chase and forced me off the road. Police, with guns drawn, ordered us out of the car, handcuffed us, and loaded us into a waiting paddy wagon. Others, using flashlights, searched the grassy area and ransacked my stepfather's car.

When we got to the police headquarters, Shane went crazy. He began kicking over tables and chairs and cursing the policemen. He had to be restrained and locked in a private room. The fellas and I understood. That was typical of Shane. He'd go off sometimes and act like he'd lost his mind.

We were all herded to a room and placed in a police lineup. It was then that I learned why the rollers had given chase. Somebody had been shot only minutes before we got to the party, and the police, seeing my car loaded with people, considered us suspects. We were cleared by a witness, who verified that we weren't the ones who had done the shooting. But still, there was the matter of the guns. Lawmen took us to separate rooms and interrogated us, first allowing us to telephone our parents.

My stepfather was working an overnight shift and wouldn't even hear about what had gone down until the next day. I knew he would go berserk when he found out his car had been confiscated and torn apart.

When my mother got there, a detective told her, "Your son could be facing up to twenty years in prison for possession of a sawed-off shotgun." I figured that was a scare tactic; at seventeen, I was still a juvenile. I figured the courts wouldn't hang the maximum sentence on me unless I had offed somebody.

Then the cops offered to cut a deal in exchange for information. They said they'd recommend leniency in court if we'd give them the names of people who had guns. That gave me an incentive to cooperate. I devised what I thought was a brilliant scheme. I huddled with the other fellas and said, "Look, man, all we gotta do is give 'em the names of all the motherfuckas we hate."

That's what we did. We gave the cops a full list of names and made up the kinds of guns they supposedly owned. I never found out whether the cops followed up on our bogus tips. All that mattered to me was that we were released from jail early the next day.

■ ■ ■

The skirmishing between Cavalier Manor and downtown ended with a tragedy that shifted the focus of the war to issues larger than our neighborhood and Portsmouth. It happened following a Saturday-afternoon football game at Frank D. Lawrence Stadium. Both sides were out there in full force, and when the shooting started, everybody panicked. The scene grew even more chaotic when the rollers showed up and joined in the gun battle. Instinctively, both sides turned and began firing at the police. Like most people out there that day, I took off running for the nearest bus stop. I paused long enough to see a downtown guy called Prairie Dog slump to the ground after being struck down in the middle of the street by a bullet. A popular guy who was no more than a year or two older than me, he later died of that gunshot wound.

It was unclear whether he'd been killed by an enemy bullet or if the police had gunned him down. The outcry that followed Prairie Dog's death generated a lot of press because the country was already dealing with a lot of racial strife. The incident attracted the attention of the Black Panthers, who apparently saw an opportunity to use Prairie Dog's death as a rallying point and recruiting tool. The fellas and I heard that Panther representatives had handed out flyers and called a meeting with all the gangs in Portsmouth. We didn't go, but we heard about a plan that supposedly came out of the meeting. We heard they wanted blacks to unite and strike back at white folks. At the appointed time, there would be strikes at strategic points throughout the city. Fires would be set in some places and there would be shootings in others. It was designed to send a political message to the city fathers and to white folks in general.

Shell Shock and I didn't give a shit about all that political stuff, but the plan to shoot and start fires carried some appeal. I didn't even have to think about whether I'd join in the assault. I hated white folks and the system anyway. It felt so much better striking out at them in the name of a lofty cause.

On the night of the planned assault, Shell Shock and I hooked up with a carload of downtown guys. It felt refreshing to unite with former enemies against a common foe. We went out to shoot up a white neighborhood. We drove to the designated street, stopped the car, and fanned out to separate houses.

Armed with a sawed-off shotgun, I walked to a house that was fronted by a huge, ground-level picture window. When I got up close, I peeked through sheer curtains and saw adults and children sitting in the living room, watching TV. Without allowing myself to think about it, I steadied myself, aimed the barrel at the window, and fired, *booooom!*

The blast shattered the window. As I dashed back to the car, I heard shots fired from my companions' guns and saw lights go out all over the street. We all hopped into the car and sped away.

I was so scared the next day that I avoided television and newspapers. For a long while after that, I wondered if I'd hit someone with the blast. I wondered what would happen if someone had been killed and I was caught. As usual, after I was pretty sure I'd gotten away with it, I allowed myself to brag. I told the fellas on our block, "We fucked up some white folks a few days ago." I felt proud that, for one night, I'd engaged in urban guerrilla warfare. I had fought in the real war and contributed to the Cause.

Chapter 10 WORK

Of all the guys I hung with, Turkey Buzzard, whose family moved to Cavalier Manor from downtown, had the hippest father. Known around Portsmouth as Country, Turkey's old man was so hip that the fellas and I figured that he was a hustler. As far as I could see, the only people in our neighborhood who didn't bow before the white man were preachers and hustlers.

I saw a big difference between Turkey's old man and the fathers of my other friends and me. They looked bent over and defeated. Country stood tall and proud. They seemed depressed and standoffish. Country often stopped in the den when we were shooting pool and laughed and joked with us. They were always dirty and tired. Country drove Cadillac Eldorados, sported a shiny gold tooth, and was always as clean as the Board of Health. I wasn't sure how Country got his money, but that didn't matter. All that mattered to me was that he chose not to earn his living slaving at the shipyard or bowing to white folks on some other gig.

Turkey had an older brother who was definitely a hustler. He and his friends gave me my first inside look at those blacks who live and operate almost completely outside the white man's system. They make money doing business with other blacks and buy almost everything they need—hot appliances, food, jewelry, clothes—from hustlers, who sell the merchandise dirt cheap. The only time they interact with white folks is to buy insurance, vote, and pay their bills.

The fellas and I spent many evenings shooting pool at Turkey's house. Sometimes, other hustlers who made their living on pool tables and crap boards came there to shoot pool, and I stood around and watched.

Following his brother's footsteps, Turkey learned all the tricks of the street trades. He could shoot pool far better than any of us, and by the time we were fourteen, he was hell in the crap games. We played Tonk and 21-Blackjack and got Turkey to teach us how to mark the cards and do the bait and switch with loaded dice.

When hanging on the corner, I tried to imitate the small-time hustlers who came to Turkey's house. I walked around, constantly shaking dice in my hands, waiting for the next crap game to get under way. I didn't know nearly enough about the hustling life to make a living at it, but it seemed glamorous and appealing enough to want to learn.

■ ■ ■

If my stepfather had anything to say about it, there was going to be no hustling, gambling in the streets, or carrying on. Besides the curfews he imposed on my brothers and me to try to rein us in, he tried keeping us off the streets by constantly giving us work to do. My old man had a serious thing about work. My brothers and I would wake up on a Saturday morning and he'd have a *long* list of things for us to do: rake the yard, cut the grass, wash the car, clean the gutters, sweep the walk. . . . Through the years, that got on our nerves and tightened the tension already building between him and us. My oldest brother, Billy, used to complain, "Work, work, work. All he ever thinks about is work."

As long as I can recall, my stepfather's life was controlled by work. It was all he'd ever known. He'd grown up on a farm in Milledgeville, Georgia, where he did backbreaking labor every day and learned to master with his hands skills that most college-educated people never learned. He dropped out of school after the tenth grade, left home to join the Navy, and relied on his strong work ethic to carry him through life.

Although I hated him sometimes for trying to work us to death, I marveled at the things he could do. With our help, he converted our garage into a den and paneled the walls. He bricked the entire pathway around the side of our house, making a cobblestone walkway and patio that led from the front to the back door. He did all his own auto and household repairs. On top of that, he always did part-time work along with his full-time shipyard job. He used to tell my brothers and me, "If you work hard, you can get anything you want in life."

But my brothers and I didn't see it that way, especially after we started going to Sterling Point with him to work in white people's yards. We saw my old man working hard, and he had nothing. The white folks whose gardens we tended seemed to be taking it easy, and they had everything. Tanned and rested, they looked like they were living well. My stepfather stayed so bone tired from constantly working that he slept most of the time when he was home.

It seemed that my brothers and I viewed everything in life differently than our old man. We represented two generations of blacks that had come up in very distinct places and times. Coming from the Deep South, my stepfather believed that you had to ignore all the shit that white people dished out and learn to swallow pride for survival's sake. Cut from the civil rights mold, he believed blacks could overcome racism by slaving hard and making do with what little they had.

But our more militant generation was less inclined to make those kinds of compromises. As we were growing up, all that talk about patience and civil rights played out and gave way to more aggressive Black Power chants, which gave us a whole new look and feeling about ourselves. People had let their hair grow into long, thick Afros. Defiant activists, such as the Muslims and the Black Panthers, appeared on TV, punching their clenched fists into the air and calling for equality *now*. Black singers such as James Brown blasted the radio airwaves with songs that urged us to fight back and build racial pride:

> *Say it loud, I'm black and I'm proud!*
> *Say it loud, I'm black and I'm proud!*

African Americans were undergoing a radical change, and ripples from that change filtered into the heads of my brothers and me. We'd get pissed at our old man for insisting we go with him to Sterling Point. With all that militancy as a backdrop for us, that work seemed strangely out of sync with the times. The Black Power movement signaled an end to the day when blacks bowed humbly to white folks—yet there we were, literally on our hands and knees, working for white folks.

■ ■ ■

In spite of his belief that work was the answer to overcoming racism, I could tell that race-related pressures at his full-time shipyard job were eating my stepfather up inside. He and co-workers who came to the house constantly complained about whites on the shipyard security force being promoted over more qualified blacks. When he wasn't sleeping, my stepfather drank a lot, and he usually got drunkest on the day before it was time for him to go back to work. He'd jump out of bed the next day, hungover and running late, and rush into work to meet the man.

He bought a little, old car, a powder-blue Renault, that he used to drive to his job. Often, when he woke up hungover and late for work, he'd jump into his security-guard uniform like a fireman on emergency call and go speeding out of the cul-de-sac, headed for the shipyard. The wheelbase of that little car was so narrow that, several times, my old man turned it over before he got out of Cavalier Manor. Passersby helped him turn it back on its wheels. Then he'd get back in that car and zoom to work. The following day, he'd pull that Renault into the backyard, take a rubber hammer, and bang out the dents. Over time, that car looked like it had been in a demolition derby.

I saw striking similarities in most of my friends' fathers, who were also heavy drinkers. The fellas and I called them "oilers" because they drank that firewater to loosen their tensions. They slept when they weren't working, and drank when they weren't sleeping. They looked downtrodden and were so burdened and preoccupied with white folks that they seldom talked much with their children. One, Whiskey Bottle's father, always seemed tense, unless he was drunk. Whiskey's real name was Johnny. We started calling him "Whiskey Bottle" and nicknamed his younger brother "Baby Wino" because their father stayed drunk all the time. He'd get drunk and stagger through the streets, or fall down and pass out in his own front yard. Bimbo's old man also drank a lot and stumbled around the streets sometimes, and Shane's dad would get drunk and go berserk in the house.

I never heard my friends say they wanted to be like their fathers when they grew up. Why would we want that when we knew our fathers were catching hell? That would be like saying we wanted to catch hell, too. If anything, we wanted to be the *opposite* of our fathers. We didn't want to work for the white man and end up like them.

That's why I shake my head when I hear so-called social experts harping on the problems of black single-parent households. They don't seem to understand that the problems go deeper than that. A two-parent home is no better off than a single-parent one if the father is fucked up in the head and beaten down. There's nothing more dangerous and destructive in a household than a frustrated, oppressed black man.

■ ■ ■

There was nothing more frustrating to me than looking for work. Whenever I went job hunting, I literally staked out strips of businesses on a given street and walked into each one to ask if they were hiring. Most of the time, the result was the same: They'd say they weren't hiring. Usually, by the time I got home in the evenings I'd be tired and evil as hell. The times I did nail down work, it was toward the end of summer, when it was nearly time to return to school.

I saw that the summer-job experience for my white teenage peers was very different from mine. I saw that wherever I went, whether it was with a friend to get a driver's license, or to some office downtown, young whites my age already had choice summer jobs in air-conditioned offices where they could learn things. They weren't skilled workers. But they got jobs running errands, cleaning up, fetching coffee—anything to keep them from slaving on the back of some truck in the scorching heat.

Whenever I saw white kids working in those places, I filled out applications to work there, too. The people running those offices would look at me like I was crazy. They seemed to be annoyed that I'd even entertain the thought of working in an office with them.

The white kids looked at me with that pompous air, too, like they knew they were *supposed* to be there and I *wasn't*. Their attitude got on my nerves, but everything I saw around me suggested to me that they might be right. They had a serious inside track on the best summer gigs in town. When looking for work, many of them had to look no further than their own neighborhoods, where people owned their own businesses or held influential government or civilian positions and could set aside jobs for young white kids before openings were even posted.

The only job contacts *our* parents had—if they had any contacts at all—were for manual-labor jobs. Even then, they often weren't in a position to make sure that their kids, or other kids in the neighborhood, got the inside track.

■ ■ ■

The summer of 1971, when I was sixteen, a bricklayer named Mr. Daniels, who attended our family's church, told my parents there were openings for construction helpers on the site where a shopping mall was being built near Cavalier Manor. I went there, applied, got the job, and started work. Almost instantly, I clashed with the white construction supervisor, who, I later learned, had wanted the helper's job for somebody else. It was my responsibility to get water and tools for the skilled workers and to supply bricks, mortar, and anything else they needed. I worked hard, but it seemed that nothing I did satisfied my boss. A tall, plump, pale man who hovered over everybody like an overseer, he fussed and cursed at me constantly. "When you gonna bring the water, boy?!"

The older black workers knew the supervisor was giving me hell. But they were too scared to say anything to him about it for fear they might jeopardize their own jobs. Every now and then, when the supervisor wasn't around, Mr. Daniels whispered encouragement and tried to keep me cool. "Young blood, I know he's a tyrant, but don't let him get next to you. Just try to ignore him and do your job."

I was tempted to quit after the first week, but I held on. I wanted the money, and I also wanted to demonstrate that my stepfather was wrong about me. He said my mother coddled me, and he argued with her sometimes about the best way to keep me off the streets. He'd say, "The boy needs a job, but he don't wanna work. He's lazy."

I suspected he was waiting for me to lose the construction job so he could prove a point to Mama. Over the years, his and my relationship had soured to the point where we barely talked directly to each other about anything meaningful. Instead, we vented our complaints through Mama, who became a referee between the two of us.

Working that summer, I felt caught in a vise: I wanted badly to prove with that job that I wasn't scared of work, but it required painful psychic sacrifices to remain employed. It required me to take humiliation daily from a supervisor who seemed to think he'd been a slave master in another life. He'd bark orders at me like we were in the fucking military. "Git over there and take some more bricks to the crew. . . . You gotta move faster than that. You act like you got lead in your britches, boy!"

I'd walk away, mumbling to myself: *Boy? Who the hell is he callin' boy? I oughta slap that motherfucka upside his head.* But I kept my mouth shut and did as I was told.

The construction job forced me to develop two personalities that kept me in conflict with myself: Away from work I was the baad-assed nigger who demanded respect; on the job I was a passive Negro who let the white man push him around. The suppression of my pride tore me up inside and messed with my head in a big way. I wondered what the fellas, or anybody who knew me, would think if they happened by and saw me taking shit off a white man like that.

I never found out because the job didn't last. I lost it soon after my stepfather, driving a shiny new Cadillac, came to the construction site one evening to pick me up from work. I saw the supervisor glaring as I walked over, climbed in, and rode away. After that, he grew even more hostile. One day, during one of his harsh tirades, I exploded: "Who the hell you think you talkin' to! I ain't gotta take this shit from you!" That was all the excuse the supervisor needed to fire me.

I went home and told my parents what happened, and afterward I heard through my mother that my old man cited my being fired as proof that I didn't want to work. That sealed the split between my stepfather and me. It frustrated the hell out of me that he seemed unable to understand that the problems I had had on that job had nothing to do with my not wanting to work. It had to do with my refusal to let arrogant white men humiliate me.

Later, Mr. Daniels, the bricklayer who helped me get the job, told my parents that the construction supervisor admitted why he really fired me. He said that if my stepfather had money to buy a Cadillac, then I didn't need a job.

That wasn't the first or last bad experience I had with working or job hunting, but it was one that turned me off even more to the whole notion of working in the system. After that, I took on the attitude about work that a lot of the brothers I knew had: "If gettin' a job means I gotta work for the white man, then I don't want a motherfuc-kin' job."

■ ■ ■

Hustling seemed like the thing to do. With Shell Shock as my main partner, I tried every nickel-and-dime hustle I ran across, focusing mainly on stealing. We stole everything that wasn't nailed down, from schoolbooks, which we sold at half price, to wallets, which we lifted from guys' rear pockets. We even stole gifts from under the Christmas tree of a girl we visited. She left the room to get something, and we stuffed small gifts into our pants and coat pockets before she returned.

One winter night when we went to a house party in a Norfolk neighborhood, Shell Shock came up with another brainstorm. When we went inside, the host told us to leave our coats in a first-floor bedroom. Hungrily eyeing the pile of leather, cashmere, and other stylish coats on the bed, Shell Shock whispered, "Nate, we can rip these niggahs off."

We partied for a while, then Shell Shock left and went around back. I went into the bedroom, closed the door, opened the window, and handed about thirty overcoats to Shell Shock, who loaded them into his mother's car. After we'd gotten all the coats, I said good night to the hosts, and left. Driving down the highway, we laughed and joked about the rip-off. "It's gonna be a lotta chilly niggahs comin' outta that house when the party is over."

Shell Shock had a creative criminal mind and a knack for finding ways to hustle folks. His cleverness fascinated me, and I picked up from him the habit of constantly being on the alert for opportunities to steal.

One night when we were heading into a nightclub in Norfolk, Shell Shock said, "Nate, hold up for a minute." He started checking car doors in the parking lot. When he found one unlocked, I served as the lookout while he opened it, reached in, and searched inside. He pulled out a key, slipped it into the ignition, and started the car. I hopped in and we drove away.

Riding down the street, I asked him, "Man, where did you find that key and how did you know to look for it in the car?"

He said, "I found it under the floor mat on the driver's side. A lotta babes leave a key there when they go out, just in case their pocketbooks get stolen or they get drunk and lose the main key ring." I never understood where he learned such things.

We kept that stolen car for about two weeks—using it mainly to take girls out on dates—then ditched it at Crystal Lake.

■ ■ ■

A bunch of us were sitting on the curb on our block, shooting the breeze, when the ice cream man drove up the street. It was scorching hot. Bored, we were waiting for the evening to set in, when the temperature cooled and the girls came outside to stroll along the sidewalks. The ice cream man rang his bell and stopped a half block from us as excited young children ran outdoors, flailing their arms. When the ice cream man, who was white, got out of the truck, Frog said, "Let's go fuck with him."

There was no special plan. We just got up, drifted on over, and studied the scene. The ice cream man was so busy serving children that he didn't notice us surrounding him. While the fellas stood in back, watching the man go in and out of the freezer, I walked to the front of the truck and peeked inside the cab, looking for a gun or something valuable to steal. I noticed he'd left the engine running. I quietly opened the door and slid inside, then stomped the accelerator and pulled away. As I drove down the street, I glanced into the big rearview mirror and saw the shocked ice cream man standing in the middle of the street, holding Popsicles in each hand.

Instantly, the fellas took off running behind the truck, and the younger children took off running behind the fellas. I laughed, rang the bell, and waved at people I knew as I cruised down Roosevelt Boulevard in the ice cream truck. After driving about five blocks, I pulled over to the curb and gave the fellas time to catch up. When they reached me, Bimbo shouted, "Take the truck to my house! My mama got a big freezer we can put the ice cream in!"

I drove the few blocks to Bimbo's house. We opened the rear freezer and formed a line, unloading boxes of ice cream and stuffing them into Bimbo's mother's oversized freezer. When it was filled, I took the truck back to an isolated area near Roosevelt Boulevard and let the little kids get all the ice cream they wanted.

We stayed at Bimbo's house the rest of that afternoon, laughing, jonin', and eating ice cream. When I left that evening, I took a backstreet home rather than travel down Roosevelt Boulevard past the crime scene. I hopped fences and came through a neighbor's backyard, entering my cul-de-sac from the rear. My stepfather was outside washing his Cadillac when I walked into the driveway. Just then, a police cruiser pulled up in front of the house. The cop got out and asked, "Does Nathan McCall live here?"

My stepfather pointed at me. "There he is."

I acted surprised when the cop said he needed to ask me some questions.

The three of us went inside the house and sat down, joined by my mother. "Your son is a suspect in the theft of an ice cream truck that was taken on Roosevelt Boulevard a few hours ago. A woman named Mrs. Patterson said she saw your son take the truck."

I feigned complete ignorance. "I don't know what he's talking 'bout! I ain't seen no ice cream truck! I haven't even been on Roosevelt Boulevard! I been down the street at Glen's house all afternoon!"

To my surprise, my stepfather backed me up. "He's gotta be telling the truth. I was out in the front yard for some time, and I saw him when he came home. He didn't come from Roosevelt Boulevard. He came up the court from the direction of Glen's house."

At first, I was shocked. My stepfather would never cover for me if he knew I had broken the law. Then I realized that he really believed I'd been at Glen's house. I guess the cop was convinced that my alibi was solid. He told my parents there would be "an ongoing investigation," then he left. That was the last I heard of it.

That heist boosted my rep in the neighborhood. Everywhere I went, guys said admiringly, "Yeah, man, I heard you ripped off an ice cream truck."

I was proud. Not only had I proven that I had heart, but I'd gotten over like a fat rat on the white man, and my stepfather had unknowingly helped me pull it off.

Chapter 11

B&Es

The ice cream truck rip-off was just part of an extended binge, a reflection of a shiftless mind-set of stealing and hanging out that the fellas and I acquired as we grew older. Sometimes, we spent whole days standing on the side of the 7-Eleven, talking, gambling and begging coins from customers to buy cheap wine. Rather than go home and eat lunch and dinner, we'd steal food from the store, sending one dude inside to rip off bread, another to take bologna, and a third to pick up sodas. We even stole cookies and ice cream for dessert.

Two large steel drums, which were used as trash cans, sat in front of the store. One night, after the 7-Eleven had closed, we lifted the drums and flung them through the big plate-glass window. The cans made perfect man-sized holes, enabling us to rush inside and loot beer, wine, and the cheap watches they kept behind the counter. We drank the brew and sold the other stuff, which brought in a decent take for a five-minute job.

My introduction to white music came about as a result of a rip-off. I was walking through the parking lot of a shopping mall one day and spotted a carrying case and a pair of tennis rackets in a car. Seeing that the car was unlocked, I reached inside and took the shit, hoping to unload it on somebody and get some cash. But when I got home and opened the carrying case, I realized that it was filled with eight-track tapes by white musicians I knew nothing about. At first, it seemed like a wasted hit. I thought, *Ain't nobody gonna wanna buy no damned white music.* Then I got high on some reefer one night and, just for the hell of it, flipped some of the white eight-tracks into the tape player. I listened and discovered a whole new world of music that I'd never known about. They turned out to be some of the hottest tapes by white musicians of the times: Deep Purple, Spooky Tooth, Foghat, Jethro Tull, Cat Stevens, Chicago. The one tape I tripped hardest on was Pink Floyd's classic *Dark Side of the Moon.* Listening to those tapes, I grew to love that music and, for the first time in my life, learned a lot about what was on white folks' minds.

■ ■ ■

The main reason we hustled and stole so hard was to pick up money to buy clothes. Among the cats who hung in the streets, Cavalier Manor had a tradition of slick dressers: Carbo Earl, Count, Kenny Banks, and others. When I was much younger, I'd always watched a particularly smooth-dressing guy who often went to the bus stop near my house. I never learned his name, but every time I saw him, he was dressed seriously sharp, from head to toe, in a perfectly matching outfit. If he wore green pants, he coordinated them with a green shirt, green shoes, and a green fedora with a green feather. He'd do the same with black, red, purple, and other colors. If I saw a guy dressed like that today, he'd look like a clown to me. But back then, I thought that dude was the essence of cool.

I wondered if he didn't own a ride because he spent so much money on his clothes, and I actually debated in my head whether it was more important to have a car to get around town than to look sharp on the bus. I concluded it was more important to look sharp because I felt better about myself when I was clean.

It was important to Shell Shock to be able to dress well, too. Without clothes, he would have gotten *no* play from the ladies. He had an awkward build, thick lips, a large head, and a super-stringy Afro that looked weird running up from his high hairline. Shell Shock was also short on change in the personality department. He cussed girls out all the time.

Personality or not, babes flocked to guys who ragged hard. There was a big difference in how girls responded to Shell Shock and me when we were clean and when we weren't. Often on Friday mornings, we'd catch the city bus to another high school in Portsmouth to rap to new girls. When we were dressed in blue jeans or khakis, babes wouldn't give us the time of day. But when we were clean, we got all the phone numbers we wanted. The different responses convinced us that we had to hustle because we *had* to have lots of nice rags to run our games.

■ ■ ■

My mother suspected I was doing things I shouldn't be doing. She'd see me leaving the house, dressed sharp as a tack in clothes she knew she hadn't bought. One day, as I was preparing to go out, she asked, "Boy, where you gettin' all those clothes?"

I played it off. "I borrow them from friends, Mama." She had no choice but to leave it alone.

Sometimes, though, she'd look me in the eye and warn, "Boy, you better be careful. You gonna learn one day that life out there ain't as easy as you think it is."

I'd look at her as if to say, "Get the fuck outta my face, woman." Years later, though, I saw exactly what Mama meant.

Every now and then, Mama would give me money to buy a knit shirt or to get a pair of pants out of layaway, even though she didn't have that kind of money to blow. I knew that was her subtle way of trying to discourage me from stealing.

Mama and my stepfather also urged me to try to work part-time gigs in high school to earn money to buy what I wanted. During one year, I got a part-time job through the school work-study program. I went to work cleaning boats for a dealer on Airline Boulevard. After taxes, the minimum-wage pay I earned barely covered my bus fare. I stayed on that job for all of a month. Then, without giving the boss advance notice, I disappeared.

■ ■ ■

In light of all that was happening in the streets, school often seemed like a helluva waste of time. I often wondered why I even bothered going when I could be somewhere working on ways to boost the cash flow. I routinely skipped classes, and often on Fridays, we threw "hooky parties" at Bimbo's crib while his parents were at work. We gambled at those parties, danced, and jammed girls like it was going out of style. Mainly I went to school to hang out, profile, and rap to babes. Most of the fellas were even more nonchalant than me about school. I found out just how little school meant to them when we reached the midway point in our tenth-grade year. The morning late bell had sounded and Bimbo, Lep, Frog, and I were walking down the empty hallway, trying to figure out a way to get admitted to our classes.

Lep grew impatient. "Fuck this shit, man! I ain't goin' through all these changes just to get in class. I'm tired a' this hassle anyway. Let's quit school."

In a half dare, he tossed his books, papers, and notepads into a metal trash can near the water fountain. Bimbo and Frog followed suit. Then they looked at me.

I searched my mind to come up with reasons to stay in school.

"Y'all niggahs crazy, man. What you wanna quit for with all these fine babes in here?!"

I thought of my stepfather and added, "I can't quit school without a job."

They said, "We can go in the war, man! We can go in the Marines on the buddy-buddy plan and get stationed together. Maybe in California."

I got indignant. "Fuck the buddy-buddy plan! I'm goin' to class. I'll catch y'all later."

I turned and walked toward my classroom. Before going in, I turned around and looked just in time to see the fellas bopping around the corner, heading out of the building. They left and never came back. They dropped out of school, just like that.

I understood why it was so easy for them to quit. There was little in the classes we took that seemed even remotely relevant to our world. I couldn't figure out how learning all that stuff would translate into helping us form a better life.

It seemed that everybody wanted to make money and escape Portsmouth, and most saw the military as their only sure way out. Frog went into the Job Corps, but Lep joined the Marines, and Bimbo, Greg, Nutbrain, and several others joined the Army. Two of my older brothers, Junnie and Dwight, went into the Army to get away (Billy left college after one year, but he just went to New York to live). I wanted out, too, but I couldn't see myself taking orders and going to war. There was no future in it. When I thought about my life, it seemed there was no future in anything.

The only one among us who appeared to have a hint of a future was Shell Shock's older brother, Ton, who was a year ahead of us at Woodrow Wilson High. A thuggish star halfback who broke the state scoring record, Ton seemed destined to play football at a major university and go to the pros. Because his athletic skills helped Wilson continue its winning tradition, he even had the support of white teachers and administrators who otherwise kept their distance from blacks at school. Beyond their enthusiastic backing of star athletes, many white teachers at Wilson seemed unconcerned whether black students passed or failed. They weren't committed to preparing us for life in the real world like my black junior high school teachers were.

One white lady who taught English literature took a passing interest in me. I enjoyed the short stories we talked about in that teacher's class. I liked her class enough to go fairly regularly, make good grades, and read the stories she assigned to us. I'd leave the block early some nights just to read those stories. I'd be out there, jonin' and drinking wine until about 10 P.M., then I'd go home, put on a pot of coffee, pop a slice of bread into the toaster, and, when no one was around, read that stuff and enjoy myself.

I think the teacher liked me, too. She pulled me aside one day after class and said, "You know, you *really* are a bright student, and I think you could make something of yourself if you took that dangling earring out of your ear, buckled your belt, and applied yourself more."

She might as well have been speaking French. I couldn't relate to what she was talking about. We couldn't connect. There was no common language. I wondered how I could "make something" of myself in the fucking white man's world? But I knew she meant well, and I suppose the occasional encouragement from her and a few others was enough to keep me minimally motivated to stick around.

Teachers like those made me wonder sometimes what I could do if I seriously hit the books. Every now and then, I'd look at the lames carrying armloads of books and think back to when I was one of them. I wondered what kept them interested in all that stuff. Once, I passed through a school science fair in the cafeteria and stopped to look at the miniature volcanoes and other creations in the competition. I remember thinking, *There was a time when I would have had a project on display.* That time was long gone, and the experience of being engaged in school seemed distant to me.

■ ■ ■

With much of the gang gone, I spent many evenings after school hanging with Shell Shock and looking for hustles. The types of hustles guys got into were often determined by the location of their neighborhood. When we first moved into Cavalier Manor, Greg, who used to hang with my brother Dwight and me, lived across the street. By the time we were teenagers, Greg's mother had gotten a divorce and moved with him across town to a public housing project named Washington Park. Since they lived near the naval shipyard, Greg and his downtown friends spent a good bit of time rolling sailors, who often staggered past Greg's neighborhood on their way back to the shipyard after a night on the town.

Greg and his friends' location downtown also put them close to shoppers patronizing stores along the main commercial strip on Effingham and High streets. They often went out at night to snatch pocketbooks. I went cruising with them a few times, but I couldn't get into that. They often preyed on poor old ladies, who reminded me of my hardworking grandmother Bampoose. Every time I thought about it, I considered how I'd feel if somebody snatched Bampoose's purse.

Sometimes I picked up hustling ideas at the 7-Eleven, which was like a criminal union hall: Crapshooters, shoplifters, stickup men, burglars, everybody stopped off at the store from time to time. While hanging up there one day, I ran into Holt, who lived around my way and often swung with the fellas and me. He had a pocketful of cash, even though he had quit school and was unemployed. I asked him, "Yo, man, what you been into?"

"Me and my partner kick in cribs and make a killin'. You oughta come go with us sometimes."

Holt had been hanging with a guy called Hilliard, who did B&Es, breaking and enterings. They did break-ins in Cavalier Manor during the daytime, when people were away at work. I hooked school one day, went with them, and pulled my first B&E. Before we went to the house, Hilliard, a tall, lanky, self-assured guy who kept a .38 pistol tucked into his belt, explained his system: "Look, man, we gonna split up and go to each house on the street. Knock on the door. If somebody answers, make up a name and act like you at the wrong crib. If nobody answers, we mark it for the hit."

I asked, "How we gonna get in?"

"Don't worry 'bout that." It turned out that he had perfected a special way to kick doors off hinges.

We found a house in no time. Hilliard motioned for Holt and me to stand back, then reared back and shot his big foot against the door hinges, knocking the wood door ajar, *boooomm!* He stood back a moment, admiring his work, then we rushed into the house and started plundering. Hilliard said we needed to be in and out of there in ten minutes, in case someone called the cops. He directed each of us to search a separate room and look for small, lightweight items that were easy to sell: television sets, stereos, jewelry, and guns.

It felt weird entering a stranger's home. As I rifled through those people's most private possessions, I felt a peculiar power over them, even though we'd never met. We got our haul and were headed for the door when Holt said, "Hold up! Hold up, man! I gotta take a leak!" He pulled out his meat and sprayed the living-room walls and furniture. After that, he always left some similar destructive signature when he kicked in a crib. I never understood why he did that. I guess it was his way of showing his contempt for the world. We sold our merchandise to Hilliard's fence and split the loot.

After I learned the ropes, Shell Shock and I branched out, doing

B&Es on our own. We learned to get in and out of houses in no time flat. We unloaded much of the merchandise on a prominent Portsmouth dentist, who paid us in cash. During one visit, he promised to put a real gold tooth in my mouth if I brought him a portable TV on our next haul.

We also sold hot items to a group of transvestites, who operated a lavishly furnished prostitution house near the naval shipyard. Even when armed, I always grew slightly nervous when we entered that house. I thought the transvestites, who wore garish makeup and flirtatiously batted their eyes, might try to lure us into their bedrooms. But they were all business. They paid good money for our merchandise, and once even let us hang around and watch while they entertained a bunch of drunken sailors.

Holt and Hilliard continued as a team until they got busted and tagged with a string of burglaries. They both were sent to prison. That made Holt the first dude in our gang to serve serious time. While he was away, I often wondered what life was like for him there, and sometimes I wondered if I might one day take his place.

I didn't fear going to prison as much as I feared getting caught by surprise in somebody's house. Years before I started doing B&Es, a guy in Cavalier Manor named Charles Lee was shot to death by a woman who caught him burglarizing her home. I never forgot that incident, and I thought about it every time I went into a dark house.

I gave up B&Es after a serious scare in a house shook me up. As usual, Shell Shock and I knocked at the door, then went to the side of the house and broke out a bedroom window with the butt of a sawed-off shotgun. (We couldn't figure out how to kick the hinges off doors like Hilliard.) Since I was the smaller of us two, Shell Shock lifted me up through the window and handed me the shotgun. Once in, I was supposed to go to the front door and open it for him. But when I turned around, I thought I saw something move in the far corner of the darkened room. I froze, fearful. Every nerve stood on end. Thoughts of Charles Lee raced through my mind as I aimed the gun barrel at the corner and eased my forefinger around the trigger. I squinted to adjust my eyes to the dark while trying to balance conflicting voices shouting in my panicked head. *Shoot! It's somebody layin' for you! Shoot now! No, don't shoot! It's a baby! It looks like a baby in a crib!* I stood there, terrified and indecisive, for what seemed like forever, waiting for a telling sign from the corner. But nothing happened. It was a standoff between the darkness and me.

I probably would have stood there frozen half the night had Shell

Shock not knocked hard at the front door. I waited to see if the figure would respond to the knocking sound, but it didn't. Keeping my eyes glued to that corner, I eased my way out of the room and let Shell Shock inside. He said, "Damn, man, I thought you had forgot about me out here."

My heart was still pounding. "Naw, man, I thought somebody was in that bedroom."

With guns readied, we walked back to the room and turned on the light. There, in the corner, the one I had feared contained a sniper waiting to ice me, was a pile of rumpled clothes. We gathered as many valuables as we could carry, then split. I never broke into another house after that.

■   ■   ■

I started going with Shell Shock after school to look for other, more lucrative hustles. Several times, we went to the Virginia Beach oceanfront to rip off adventure-hungry white boys hanging on the tourist strip. We'd offer to sell them drugs, then take their money and dash. But Virginia Beach was too far from home, and the police presence there was too strong, to make a regular go on the strip.

Shell Shock came up with the idea of traveling to Norfolk in search of potential victims, who we called "vics." That's when we started sticking up.

We were both seventeen then, and our first hit came late one night on the main drag of a public housing project named Tidewater Park. We'd dated girls there once and knew our way around the 'hood. It was conveniently located near the tunnel leading to Portsmouth. We knew we could make our strike and shoot back through the tunnel and into our hometown. Some guys were walking down the street one night, and we stepped out from the shadows of a tree and confronted them. "Yo, man, you got a cigarette?" Before they could respond, Shell Shock drew a shotgun, held it aloft, and said calmly, "Give it up." They fumbled through their pockets and handed over their wallets. We made them run in one direction, and we dashed in another.

That first hit tripped me out on a lot of levels. First, it was so easy: Two or three minutes, and we were done. Also, the hit marked a kind of crossover for both Shell Shock and me. All the shit we'd done up to then, even the B&Es, seemed more like mischief than anything else. But when we stuck those guys up, we crossed over deep into felony country. It was serious shit, and I knew it. At the same time, I didn't think about the consequences of getting busted. Nobody thinks about consequences because nobody plans to get caught in the first place. So we crossed over, and we did all right.

Several nights a week, after Shell Shock's mother went to sleep, we took her car and went to Norfolk. We did most of our stickups in and around Church Street, then considered one of the roughest areas in Tidewater. Church Street, which was lined with bars, restaurants, pawnshops, and clothing stores that catered to blacks, bustled round the clock with prostitutes, drug dealers, hustlers, and various thrill-seekers. It was easy to catch vics, especially tipsy sailors walking through alleys and backstreets at night. The police presence was so weak that we could usually make several hits in the same community before making our dash for the Portsmouth tunnel.

Sticking up gave me a rush that I never got from B&Es. There was an almost magical transformation in my relationship with the rest of the world when I drew that gun on folks. I always marveled at how the toughest cats on those street corners whimpered and begged for their lives when I stuck the barrel of a sawed-off shotgun into their faces. Adults who ordinarily would have commanded my respect were forced to follow my orders like obedient kids.

After several clean hits, it became clear to me that I'd found my hustle. I was making good money and didn't have to take hassles from whitey while doing it. The only downside to sticking up in black neighborhoods was that the people were so poor we had to rob several of them to get a hundred dollars. Shell Shock came up with an idea to remedy that: "Let's take the niggahs' clothes, too."

One night soon after, we stuck up a corner that was a favorite gambling spot for Tidewater Park hoods. As they stood under a streetlight rolling dice, we walked up, flashed our guns, and cleaned them out. We took their money, their coats, and their shoes, then fired shots in the air and made them dash, barefoot, down the street. We sold the clothes we didn't want and kept those stylish pieces that fit.

After that, we usually drove home after "work" with a backseat filled with expensive shoes and the finest leather coats around. We'd pimp into school the next day, clean as hell, profiling in clothes we'd stolen off somebody's back the night before.

Our sharp clothes and hip style boosted our popularity in school. I saw girls and dudes, especially young underclassmen, gazing admiringly at Shell Shock and me the same way I had admired Scobie-D, Kenny Banks, and other old-heads not very many years before.

Chapter 12 SUPERFLY

I'm your mama, I'm your daddy,
I'm that nigger in the alley
I'm your doctor, when you need.
Want some coke? Have some weed.
You know me, I'm your friend,
Your main boy, thick and thin,
I'm your pusherman. . . .
　　　　—Curtis Mayfield, from the sound track of *Superfly*

■ ■ ■

It seemed those lyrics, from Curtis Mayfield's album *Superfly*, were blasting from every radio and sound system in black America in 1972. In the movie, actor Ron O'Neal played Priest, a high-rolling, slick-dressing drug dealer who was on a mission: to earn a million dollars, enough money so that he wouldn't have to work for the white man for the rest of his life. He built up a sizable "family" of low-level partners, negotiated all the rip-off land mines in the 'hood, and stayed one step ahead of the rollers. In the end, he did what he set out to do. He made his money selling cocaine, kicked whitey's ass, and rode off into the sunset in his shiny Eldorado.

Almost instantly, Priest became a cult figure for brothers everywhere. Here was a film that gave us something rare in movies—a black hero—and expressed the frustrations of a lot of young brothers, who were so fed up with the white man that they were willing to risk prison, and even death, to get away from him. Perhaps for the first time in this country's history, young blacks were searching on a large scale for alternatives to the white mainstream. One option, glamorized by *Superfly*, was the drug trade, the black urban answer to capitalism.

Superfly influenced the style, thinking, and choices that a lot of young black men began making around that time. I know it deeply affected me. I came out of that movie more convinced than ever that the white man and I were like oil and water: We didn't mix. My partner, Shell Shock, was on the same wavelength. He started thinking that maybe there was a future in dealing drugs. A few weeks after we saw the movie, we were sitting around at his place getting wasted when Shell Shock outlined his game plan, which was essentially a scaled-down version of the plan Priest had devised in the movie. "I *know* I can do it, man. Most of the white folks that got money did something illegal to get it. Look at how the Kennedys got started. They bootlegged liquor during the Depression, then went legit. Now they millionaires! All I gotta do is make enough money to start my own business, then I can quit the drug game."

It was shortsighted, far-fetched fantasy for sure. But to our way of thinking, it was no more far-fetched than the civil rights notion that white people would welcome us into their system with open arms if we begged and prayed and marched enough. As for the risks, dealing drugs seemed no more risky than working a thankless job at the shipyard for thirty years, always under the fear of being laid off. It was six of one and half a dozen of the other.

Shell Shock had no problem getting started. Back then, a four-finger O.Z., an ounce of reefer that equaled the height of four fingers, sold for $20. Shell Shock bought a $20 bag and broke it down into five $5 bags, which he then sold for a $5 profit and reinvested. He continued recycling his profits until he eventually was able to buy quarter, half, and full pounds of reefer and sell $5, $10, and $20 bags. He hired a few guys in school, increased his profit margin, and maintained a hefty stash for his personal use. In no time, Shell Shock was on his way.

I had no interest in selling drugs. It was too time-consuming, and I had money and clothes coming in from the stickups Shell Shock and I did. I'd been smoking reefer since I was sixteen, when my brother Dwight turned me on during one of his visits home from Fort Bragg, North Carolina, where he was stationed in the Army. Dwight and I got busted once with some reefer outside a nightclub on a military base. We were sitting inside his car, toking a joint, when some MPs with narc dogs walked up and ordered us out. They shook us down and found the reefer. Instead of arresting us, they took our names and addresses and barred us from the compound, threatening to press charges if we ever showed up there again.

So I smoked a lot, but didn't deal. I left that to Shell Shock, who eventually became a big man around school and in the neighborhood. Guys looking to cop reefer sought him out when they got paid, and girls who loved to smoke herb flocked to him for a free high. He'd get them high, screw them, then put them out of his mother's house.

For a lot of guys, *Superfly* brought home the economic potential in selling cocaine. We never even knew much about snow until we saw that movie. Until then, most of the local dealers in Cavalier Manor sold only reefer. The problem with reefer was that it was bulky and cumbersome to carry around and conceal, and you had to sell large quantities to turn a decent profit. But the tiny, aluminum foil–wrapped packets of cocaine were easier to handle, and small quantities brought higher profits. With cocaine, a dude could make more money with less hassle.

Superfly also inspired a major fashion revolution. Almost overnight, brothers shifted from Black Power chic to gangster buffoon. Suddenly, cats who had been sporting dashikis and monster Afros broke out in platform shoes and crushed-velvet outfits that made them look like clownish imitations of the flamboyant Priest. Shell Shock and I fell right into line. We went out and bought wide-brimmed hats and long midi and maxi coats. We wore turtlenecks and hung gold coke spoons around our necks, just like the one worn by Priest. I thought I was the cat's meow when I got my first pair of platforms. They made me look a full foot taller, and the heels were so high I had to adjust my pimp to keep from breaking my ankle. But I *knew* I was cool.

Dudes coming home from the Vietnam War in the 1970s were worse than that. They tried to be right-on black and Superfly at the same time. Cats like Horace Perry, the older dude who used to stuff dirt into my mouth, came home with a new consciousness, a sense of history and pride that changed the way they viewed this country and their place in it. Horace Perry and other dudes who'd gone into the war vowed to have nothing to do with the white man's system. They came home calling each other "brotherman" and "blood" and treated each other with more respect than they had before they left. When they ran into each other on the street, they performed "dap," a handshake greeting in which they went through a long series of syncopated movements, slapping each other's palms, wrists, and elbows in a colorful show of black solidarity. One guy who used to school the fellas and me about sex now talked instead about how there was going to be a revolution, and that at some as yet undisclosed time the word would be given and a race war would begin. "Pretty soon it's gonna be all over for Mr. Charlie," he said. "Some heads are gonna roll."

At the same time, the military dudes outdid everybody else with outlandish Superfly fashions. Some had traveled to Korea, Germany, and other countries and discovered they could get tailor-made clothes dirt cheap. They came "back to the world" with some of the craziest-looking polyester-knit outfits imaginable.

There were so few movies featuring blacks that we rushed to theaters every time one was released. *The Mack*, a movie about a black pimp, picked up where *Superfly* left off. Lyrics from the sound track became the rallying cry for cats who wanted to be players, cool and confident dudes who lived life on their terms, not the white man's. After seeing *The Mack*, some of the fellas and I even talked dreamily sometimes about the prospect of "puttin' 'hos on the block," or becoming gigolos. I was sitting around talking about it one day when an old-head sobered me up. He looked me up and down and said, "Niggah, you'll starve trying to sell dick." I knew he was right, but I thought that at the very least it seemed worth trying to find a woman to take care of you. That was a sure way to get over.

The irony of the sound tracks to *Superfly* and *The Mack* is that they both contained songs with strong anti-drug, pro-black messages. I was so caught up in the glitz and glamour of the street-smart stars that those messages went right over my head. Also lost on me was the contradiction in the whole notion of getting over. Drug dealers and pimps operate on familiar turf, preying on their own people. But like so many other guys, I reasoned that the end justified the means—any hustle that kept you out of the system was justifiable.

■ ■ ■

I'm sure *Superfly* and *The Mack* helped boost luxury-car sales in America. After seeing those films, dudes everywhere went deep into debt to buy big cars to profile in. They added imitation "gangster" whitewall tires and long, gaudy TV antennas that hung like octopus tentacles from the rear windows. (There wasn't a television set to be found in most of those cars.)

One older, midlevel drug dealer in Cavalier Manor bought a Mack-like car and became the envy of the neighborhood. He cruised around, profiling in a candy-apple-red convertible Cadillac with a silver statuette of a winged goddess perched regally on the tip of the hood. It was tacky-plush inside, with white fur around the steering wheel, white, fur-covered seats, and a pair of oversized foam-rubber dice—the symbol for players—dangling from the rearview mirror.

When toking a joint and soaking up the mobile plushness of a gigantic hog, it was easy to fantasize about being the Mack. Strains from a song that described the pimp's car and the way he rode in it could be heard floating out of pretenders' windows:

Diamond in the back
Sunroof top
Diggin' the scene with a gangster lean. . . .

It became hip to cruise slowly, coolly, down the street with your wrist resting limply on the steering wheel while you leaned to the side. Imitating Goldie, the pimp in the movie, guys cruised down the street gangster-leaning so hard to the right of the steering wheel that it looked like they were actually sitting in the middle of the car rather than in the driver's seat. All pedestrians could make out from the sidewalk was the driver's beady eyes peering from beneath a wide-brimmed hat that shone just above the dashboard. Most of those cats didn't have a pot to piss in or a window to throw it out of, but they had their cars, and that was a start.

In our crowd, few dudes had their own rides. We profiled in our parents' cars. Every now and then, my stepfather let me drive his Cadillac to the store. I'd take the long way home, riding through Cavalier Manor, fantasizing and gangster-leaning like the world was my playground. With the invention of eight-track tape players inside cars, we used rides as much to entertain and socialize as to transport. Gas prices then were so low that five dollars could fill your tank and you could ride around all day. Whenever one of us got our parents' car, we'd go around and pick up the rest of the fellas. We'd pitch in and buy a full tank of gas and ride around the city for hours at a time, profiling and collecting girls' phone numbers. While cruising, we got high, listened to tapes by War, Stevie Wonder, the O'Jays, and Earth, Wind, and Fire, and we talked about such things as the Watergate hearings and rumors that the platform shoes we wore were part of a conspiracy to ruin black men's spines.

The luxury car has always been a big status symbol for black men. It's a mobile status symbol. A dude can ride it around town and show the world that he owns a thing of style, comfort, and beauty. While cruising in an elegant car, he can pretend he's doing well, even if he isn't, and fantasize about making his entire world as plush as his ride.

Even old-heads like my stepfather got into that fantasy. Although he struggled financially, he always made sure he had an old car to beat around in and a nice hog, a Cadillac, to show off. He didn't give a damn about clothes, but a hog was the one extravagance my stepfather allowed himself. He bought his first one in 1971, and hasn't been without one since. My mother used to get nervous as hell every time we rode by a Cadillac dealership. She used to be scared that he'd see something he liked and find a way to buy it. The white men who sold the cars knew they had a potentially good catch whenever my stepfather came on the lot. They'd even let him take a hog home and test-drive it for a few days, knowing that if he was a true Cadillac lover, he'd break down and get one.

The only time I saw my old man really happy was when he bought a new hog. It was his plaything, his reward to himself for all that hard work he did and all the shit he took off white folks. And nobody, not even Mama, got in the way of him enjoying it. Sometimes on weekends, he'd wash and wax his Cadillac, shower, get dressed, and ride slowly around town, even if he had nowhere special to go. He might have been feeling a little low when he left, but I could always tell he felt better when he got back home.

Chapter 13 **MR. MANOR**

In the fall of 1972, I began my senior year at a newly built school called Manor High. I started that year gripped by fear. I suppose every high school senior feels some anxiety, but I was *seriously* scared because of what the year symbolized: my expected entry into the real world. Graduation would mean that I was one step closer to having to deal with the white man.

I was so uptight about it that I couldn't even concentrate on senior-year activities, such as planning announcements, picking class rings, and ordering caps and gowns. I saw no fun in signing yearbooks, taking senior pictures, and preparing for the prom. In fact, I was so cynical about the whole affair that when a yearbook staff member asked me to state for the record my future ambitions, I poked out my chest and spouted the most outrageous, impossible dream that came to mind. I said, "I wanna be the first black president of the United States."

About the best thing that happened to me that year was that I cut into Elisabeth Miller. I was walking down the halls one day, holding a portable radio to my ear, when Liz walked up and asked, "What are you listening to?"

I said, "It's 'Family Affair,' by Sly Stone."

"Sly Stone? Ooooohh! Can I hear it? I like that song!"

I looked at her, really noticing her for the first time. Liz, who had a slender, shapely frame, thick eyebrows, and dark, piercing eyes, was one of the finest red-bones in school. I asked, "You listen to a lotta music?"

She said, "Yeah, I listen to music all the time."

"You wanna get together and listen to some music?"

"Sure, when?"

"How 'bout this evening at my place?"

"O.K."

Liz was an adopted only child, and I'd known her since junior high at Waters. But we hung in different crowds; we'd never socialized or talked at length until that exchange. She lived with her mother, who sent her to charm school in preparation for a modeling career. She had already begun to make a name for herself locally and had gone to New York on modeling jobs. Her father, a retired Army man who opened the first service station in Cavalier Manor, had died when we were in junior high.

Everybody knew Liz was deeply involved with an older guy, a focused, responsible dude who had held part-time jobs throughout school and joined the Army after graduating the year before. I assumed they were going to get married when Liz graduated, but that didn't stop me from responding when she showed interest in me.

We got together that evening in my parents' den, listened to music, and talked late into the night. I knew then that I was attracted to her and she to me. We were both novelties to each other. I viewed her as a special challenge, as someone who had more class than the fast, hard-edged girls I usually hung with. She was intrigued by street life, and I guess she saw in me a chance to learn more about it. Shell Shock and I were sticking up hard by then. We were falling into school, dressed clean as hell and profiling hard at football games. Liz knew nothing about the drugs and the robberies, but she knew we were street dudes who were into a lot of things.

Liz and I began seeing each other regularly after that first night. We went bowling and dancing on weekends, had picnics in the park, and did things I'd never taken the time to do with other girls. Sometimes we just sat around at each other's houses and listened to music and talked. I'd never really spent so much time just talking with a girl. Usually, I hung with girls just long enough to get over, then made my way back to the block. But Liz had a magnetic personality. She made me want to be around her all the time. She was pretty and dressed well, she had a great sense of humor, and I loved to jone and make her laugh. She had a smile that spread clean across her face and ran up to her dark eyes and cheeks. We'd go places together, laughing and playing and teasing each other about everything. She had a temper, but her anger never lasted long. She could get mad about something, and the next day it would be completely forgotten. She wasn't like me. I could hold a grudge forever, and I lived for revenge.

Liz put me in touch with emotions I didn't know I had. Once, I went fishing with her and her mother on a pier in Virginia Beach. That was the first time in my life that I'd been fishing. When night fell, the water and atmosphere seemed so peaceful and calming. The experience was almost spiritual. We stayed out there all night, then Liz and I walked along the beach at sunrise and ate breakfast at a restaurant on the strip. At times like those, I got the vague sense that there was so much to life that I was missing. But it all seemed so remote and out of my reach. Liz and I eventually fell in love, which was really strange for me. I was very much in touch with hatred, but love was a territory I felt unsure about. In a vague kind of way, I knew I loved my mother, my stepfather, my grandmother Bampoose, and my brothers, but none of us said that to each other. It was understood but never, ever expressed. So I knew it but didn't know it. But Liz inspired me to *say* it and to feel good about saying it. And she said it to me, and I knew she meant it. It was unlike anything I had ever experienced. Anything.

Bampoose, my mother, and my stepfather liked Liz a lot, partly, I think, because she kept me out of trouble. Being around her made me feel and act more like a human being. I was so smitten by her that I stopped hanging on the corner so much. The fellas said she had my nose open, but I was feeling so good about what I felt inside that I didn't give a shit what they said. I stopped running women and focused solely on Liz, in school and out. In school, we talked at our lockers most mornings, ate lunch together, and met outside after classes and waited together for the school bus to take us home. Other people could see how much we were into each other. When underclassmen saw us together, they probably viewed us as the perfect fairy-tale couple. It certainly felt like I was living a fairy tale.

■ ■ ■

Early in the school year, the student government association voted to have the student body select a homecoming king along with the traditional homecoming queen. Liz and I were among those nominated for the competition, which was nothing but a popularity contest. The winners were to be announced during halftime ceremonies at the school homecoming football game.

The night of the game, I fell into the football stadium looking like Superfly in the flesh. I wore a long, blue, crushed-velvet maxi overcoat, a white turtleneck, a matching white stingy-brim Kangol hat, white shoes, and blue-and-white elephant-leg pants. I carried a wine flask over my shoulder, and although it was dark outside, I sported sunshades. I'd smoked reefer and drunk wine at Shell Shock's house before the game, and was flying high as a kite by the time I reached the Churchland Stadium. If Barnum and Bailey had seen me that night, they would have kidnapped me for their circus.

During halftime, the nominees for various student offices were ushered onto the football field. The stadium was packed, but when the announcer began speaking over the public-address system, a weird hush fell over the place. Then the speaker announced the runners-up in different categories. Finally, he got around to the main competition, homecoming king and queen. I closed my eyes and heard him say, "And the winner for Mr. Manor is Nathan McCall!" By then, I was so high that I could barely stand up straight and keep my eyes open. I stumbled forward and nodded, and students in the crowded bleachers cheered wildly and applauded. When Liz's name was called, she stepped forward and stood beside me, and someone handed her a bouquet of roses. We were crowned Mr. and Miss Manor. We stood there, side by side, beaming brightly at each other. It was the perfect fantasy come true—Nathan McCall and Elisabeth Miller, Mr. and Miss Manor. It was the first time since the days of spelling-bee competitions that I'd been recognized for anything constructive in school.

Less than a month later, the fairy tale fizzled. Liz came to me one day and said, "I'm pregnant." The meaning of what she'd said didn't immediately sink in. At first, I assumed she was pregnant by her old boyfriend, but then I realized that he was away and that she hadn't been with him in a while.

It was a wonder that I was surprised. In all those years of throwing down in bed with girls, I never took precautions. For the longest time, I thought the only way a woman could get pregnant was if she and a guy had an orgasm at the same time. Now I learned the hard way that that wasn't true. At age seventeen, I had a "crumb-snatcher" on the way.

Shell Shock had gotten a girl pregnant the year before, and during high school I'd had three other girls tell me they were expecting babies by me. One eventually admitted someone else was the father. I ignored the other two; they were quick hits, crosstown girls I'd assumed were as sexually active as I was and who had done a coin toss to come up with a father. But with Liz, I willingly owned up to my responsibility. I told her, "I'll do what I have to do to help out." But I had no idea what that meant.

■   ■   ■

I spent those last few months before graduation in a deep fog. Time was blurred. The graduation calendar was a reminder that my sentencing date was nearing, that sooner or later I would be shoved into the hostile world to sink or swim.

I could see that other students, those who were preparing for college, seemed to have confidence and direction, so I decided, almost without thinking, that I'd go to college, too. I could hide out there for a while and then figure out what I *really* wanted to do. With time running out, I applied to three colleges: Norfolk State, Virginia State, and Howard University. Nobody in our family had gone to college before but Billy, who had dropped out and moved away.

On commencement day, my parents sat proudly in the bleachers of the school auditorium. I glanced up at them, smiled weakly, then turned away. My mother had notified all our relatives in North Carolina and New York, and had even told the minister of the family church. The Reverend Mr. Ramsaugh had me come to a Sunday service to receive a special graduation gift. It was a blue Bible with my name inscribed in gold letters on the cover.

Sitting in that auditorium, I felt deeply depressed. I couldn't see where I'd be any better off with a diploma than the guys who had joined the military or gone to work at the shipyard. Dressed in my cap and gown, I sat there in a trance, as one speaker after another talked glowingly about the challenges and bright futures we faced. During the ceremony, the principal singled out for special recognition the academic achievers who had received noteworthy college scholarship awards. I'll never forget that one guy, a tall, black, goofy dude, had gotten a $50,000 scholarship to study science at a major university. It seemed that the guys who got the biggest scholarships were the very ones the fellas and I had considered lames throughout school. They were the ones we made fun of and harassed. They'd sacrificed popularity to do their work; now this was *their* day.

Watching them walk proudly to the stage, I wondered why they had gotten so much out of school and I had not. Tears welled in my eyes and I struggled hard to hold them back as I watched friends walk forward to get their diplomas. Liz, with her gown bulging, bounced happily down the aisle. I saw Shell Shock, Shane, Chip, Cooder, and a few others who, along with me, were among the elites from our gang who'd made it through school.

When my name was called, the walk down the aisle seemed like a death march. I walked up onto the stage, took my diploma, and shook the principal's hand without looking at him. I turned around, put on a brave face, and walked back to my seat. The carefree days were officially over.

When we launched into the theme song chosen for our graduating class, it didn't help my mood. It was "We've Only Just Begun."

We've only just begun
So many roads to choose
We'll start out walking, then learn to run
We've only just begun . . .

After graduation, everybody gathered in the main auditorium for a reception. People were hugging and crying and taking pictures with family and friends. Shell Shock, seeing me leaning quietly against a wall, came over and asked, "What's the matter with you, stickman? Why ain't you celebratin' with everybody else?"

I snapped, "What's there to celebrate? A diploma ain't nothin' but a piece a' paper."

Shell Shock nodded. "I know. It ain't shit." Unlike me, he didn't seem worried. He had a game plan. He had his Superfly dreams. I had a pregnant girlfriend and the promise of a life in the white man's world with a hard way to go.

A group of students had made plans to meet later that night and hold our own celebration at some beach. Driving my stepfather's car with Liz and a few other friends, I spent half the night riding around, trying to find the place. The outcome of the evening was a fitting symbol of things to come: We got lost and never got there.

Chapter 14 FALLING

Liz went into labor July 19, 1973. I was doing yard work when the call came from her mother. I dropped what I was doing and left for the hospital. It was one of those cloudy experiences where I went through the motions feeling numb inside.

When I reached the waiting room, Liz's mother was sitting there alone, reading a newspaper. I said "hi" and took a seat.

She said "hi" and returned to her reading. In the hours we waited for the delivery, she was cordial but said no more than was required. A big-boned, gray-haired woman in her fifties, she was wary of me. She viewed me as an irresponsible thug and wondered what Liz saw in me.

Determined to bow to no one, I was just as cool toward her as she was toward me. I picked up magazines and flipped nervously through the pages. We sat there quietly, two strangers bound together by a new life.

Liz delivered a boy just after midnight. They named him Monroe, after his paternal grandfather. I had little say in the matter since I hadn't donated time and money to help Liz through the pregnancy. I was unemployed, with no prospects of finding a job. Liz's mother's military benefits covered the hospital costs.

When the nurses brought Monroe out, he looked like a red, wrinkled, seventy-year-old rubber doll. Although I smiled and held him, I felt no real connection to that young life. I didn't feel the joy I thought fathers were supposed to feel. If anything, I felt fear. How was I going to guide a new life when I couldn't even direct my own? What could one child do for another child?

After Monroe was taken back to the infants' ward, I really felt weird. On TV, whenever somebody had a baby, friends and family passed out cigars, and slapped the father heartily on the back and congratulated him. But there was no one there but Liz's mother and me. I felt empty. Liz, who was wheeled back to a recovery room, must have felt the same way. She was eighteen, recently graduated, and stuck with a newborn and with a boyfriend who she might or might not be able to rely on down the stretch.

■ ■ ■

One day, during the summer my son was born, I came home from job hunting and found a letter from the Selective Service, notifying me that I needed to register for the draft. Although Junnie, Dwight, and half my friends had gone into the military, I knew it wasn't for me. I had hated it ever since Muhammad Ali got screwed over for being a conscientious objector. When he made the statement "Ain't no Vietnamese ever called me nigger," he captured exactly what I felt. I thought, *The nerve of them motherfuckas expecting me to fight for them while they mistreat black folks in this country.* I tore the letter up into a thousand pieces and threw that shit into the trash. To this day, I couldn't tell you my Selective Service classification. I didn't look at it. I didn't care. In fact, I cared so little that I didn't mention the letter to my parents or anybody else. I just threw it away and never heard a peep from Uncle Sam.

■ ■ ■

My life by then was getting very complicated. Shell Shock and I had cut back on our stickups after he began dealing drugs full-time, but I was still in the life. I'd become a father. And shortly after Monroe was born, I got accepted at all three of the colleges I'd applied to. I wanted badly to go to Howard University, to break from Portsmouth and try to make a new start. But my parents couldn't afford it. Anyway, it seemed selfish to go away to school and leave Liz to care for the baby alone. I felt there was no choice but to enroll locally at Norfolk State.

Norfolk State was, and still is, one of those historically black colleges that would let anybody in. They call it "open admissions." That means that if you can write your name and read *The Cat in the Hat,* you're in like Flynn. So I was in.

I signed up to study psychology. In the 1970s, everybody was majoring in the social sciences, especially psychology, sociology, and social work. I had no real interest in psychology. I picked that major because it sounded hip.

■ ■ ■

I bopped into this philosophy class a week late, with dark sunshades on, hat on backward, pants hung low, and slumped down into a seat in the back of the room. The professor, a tall, heavyset dude, the Reverend Elward Ellis, was lecturing. Ignoring me, he kept his eyes on the other students and threw out a zinger without missing a beat. "Some of the best philosophers in the world hang on street corners," he said.

Boom. He got my attention then. I immediately sat up straight in my seat. I knew he knew something; I knew he had to have something on his cap to make a statement like that. From then on, he was all right with me. I had somebody I could talk to.

Reverend Ellis supervised the campus ministry and often invited students to his house for dinner and discussions about spiritual things and life in general. Apparently sensing that I had a lot of heavy stuff going on in my head, he invited me there alone a few times to talk and encouraged me to open up. During one of the visits, he gave me a book entitled *As a Man Thinketh*. I took the book home and forgot about it.

Ellis wasn't the only one to reach out to me that year. There was an English teacher who took a liking to me, and even a man from my neighborhood extended a hand. His name was Hugh Jones. He used to chase the fellas and me all the time when we were young. We'd cut through his backyard, cussing and carrying on, on our way to Bimbo's house, and he'd come out, mad as hell, and try to run us down. Mr. Jones had a niece at Norfolk State. I ran into him at a candlelight service for incoming freshmen. He acted so shocked and happy to see me on a college campus that I thought he was going to kiss me right there in front of everybody. "I didn't know you finished high school!" he said. "I saw you hanging on the corner so much that I figured you had dropped out. Now here you are in college. . . . I want you to know that I'm proud of you and I'll do anything I can to help out. You know where I live. Stop by my house and talk sometimes." He patted me on the back and left.

Before then, I'd thought he was just another tight-butt old-head in the neighborhood who didn't want anybody to have any fun. Then I went by his place to chat and saw a different side of him. I saw that he was a deep cat who cared a lot about black people, especially young black people.

It made me feel kind of good knowing there were people like Reverend Ellis and Mr. Jones pulling for me. The combination of all those people offering encouragement inspired me to apply myself that first year. I finished as a freshman with a 3.0 grade point average, the first time I had made the honor roll since junior high school.

Still, all those folks who tried to help out weren't enough to bring me around. I was too steeped in the life to be easily turned around by a starch-collared cleric and a couple of do-gooders. Besides, my head just wasn't in the right place to take advantage of all they had to offer. There were too many things eating at me.

Some of it was just plain immaturity. Like ego-tripping. In high school, I was the *shit*, Mr. Popularity. But in college, I was suddenly a small fish in a very big bowl. Everybody at Norfolk State looked so together, especially the cats coming out of the military. They went to college on the G.I. Bill and used their monthly allotment checks to get apartments and to buy nice cars and fine clothes. My cash flow had dried up. I stayed broke all the time. So there I was, in college, an unemployed nobody, dressing in last year's rags, depending on my parents for funds. It didn't take long for me to get discouraged.

Beyond all that, I didn't feel I fitted in. The college crowd, with their fraternities and sororities, was a different-type crowd than I was used to. I couldn't get into those folks. And then there were the administrative hassles. From registration, with the long lines and runarounds, to choosing classes, the whole process seemed like one continuous headache.

After that first year, my motivation dropped. I'd go to some of my classes high, tripping off acid, then get paranoid and get up and walk out in the middle of the lecture. I didn't even bother to go to class half the time. With nobody to tell me what to do and where to go, I wandered aimlessly about campus and spent a lot of time gambling on the pool table and in card games in the student union building.

I lost interest in college. Soon I was back on the streets.

■   ■   ■

In the summer of 1974, Liz came to me and said she'd had a run-in with Plaz. She and a girlfriend were riding bikes past the 7-Eleven when Plaz, hanging around with some other guys, called her a name. "He called me a white girl, so I gave him the middle finger," she said.

That was bad news. Plaz and I had a history that went back several years, when he and those other cats barged in on Denise Wilson and me and raped her. I never got any get-back, but I never forgot it, either. I hated Plaz for that. If I thought I had half a chance of kicking his ass, I probably would have moved on him long before the run-in with Liz.

But I was in no hurry to lock horns with Plaz. He hung with Scobie-D. I was nineteen, and he was twenty-two and a much harder cat than me. But he'd cracked hard on my lady. He'd disrespected *me*. Something had to give.

One night, shortly after Liz's run-in with Plaz, she and I took Monroe to a carnival near Cavalier Manor. We were walking along, pushing him in a stroller, when Plaz and three of his boys walked up and confronted us. His eyes blazing, Plaz got within an inch of Liz's face, shook his finger at her, and said, "The next time you flash your middle finger at me, I'm gonna break it off. You hear me?!" Then he scowled at me, looked me up and down as if daring me to say something, and turned and walked away.

I just stood there thinking, *This niggah is gonna make me do something I didn't come here to do.* Not only had he disrespected me again, but he'd done it in *front* of my lady. I *had* to do something. That's when I decided to shoot him.

I told Liz, "Take the baby, put him in the car, and you two go on home."

She got scared. "Where are you going?"

"I'm gonna fuck that niggah up."

She pleaded, "Come on, Nate. We don't have to pay attention to him."

I didn't look at her. "Go on home!"

Liz turned and hurriedly pushed the stroller away.

As I walked in the direction Plaz and his boys had headed, I steeled my nerves. Whenever I wanted to do something really crazy like that, something I didn't have the natural heart to do, I had to run a head-game on myself. I had to shut down my mind. I had to block off all thoughts flowing through my brain to prevent me from talking myself out of it. That's the only way I'd be able to go through with it. That's what I did that night. I decided to shoot Plaz and I didn't want to change my mind. I couldn't allow that.

I had a shoulder pouch that I carried with me. In it were some drugs and a .22 pistol. I spotted Plaz and his boys milling around, talking with some other dudes they'd run into. I walked over to the crowd and said to him, "Yo, man. I wanna talk to you."

Flanked by his boys, Plaz really got loud then. He pointed a finger at me and said, "Niggah, you better get outta my face 'fore I stomp your ass! I'm tired a' you and that bitch . . ."

While he talked, I kept my hand inside the pouch, gripping the trigger. Sensing that a rumble was about to jump off, people started crowding around. I saw my buddy Greg in the crowd, looking nervously at Plaz's boys, counting heads. I knew he would go down with me if it came to that.

Moving close enough for me to smell his breath, Plaz poked a finger in my chest and kept on selling wolf tickets. "I'll kick your ass . . . !"

In one swift motion, I drew the gun, aimed it point-blank at his chest, and fired. *Bam!*

A tiny red speck appeared on the dingy white T-shirt he wore. He fell backward. His arms flew skyward and he dropped to the ground, landing on his back. As soon as they heard the blast, his boys scattered. Everybody around us ran for cover. I walked toward Plaz, looked into his eyes, and saw something I had never seen in him before. Gone was the fierceness that made him so intimidating all those years. In its place was shock. And fear. It was more like terror.

In that moment, I felt like God. I felt so good and powerful that I wanted to do it again. I felt like I could pull that trigger, and keep on pulling it until I emptied the gun. Years later, I read an article in a psychology magazine that likened the feeling of shooting a gun to ejaculation. That's what it was like for me. Shooting off.

I stepped closer and raised the gun to shoot Plaz again, when Greg came up from behind me and called my name. "No, Nate! You don't wanna do that, man!" He carefully pulled the gun from my hand.

The distraction gave Plaz enough time to collect himself. Holding a hand to his bleeding chest, he jumped up from the ground, dashed toward the parking lot, and collapsed between two cars.

The carnival grounds, meanwhile, had turned chaotic. People ran screaming everywhere. It was like one of those movies where a monster is trampling through a city and everybody is running, hollering, fleeing for their lives. It made me feel powerful and light-headed, seeing hundreds of people scattering because of something I'd done. I felt like Scobie-D.

Only I was confused about what to do next. I didn't know whether to beat my chest and yell at the top of my voice, or shout some pithy, John Wayne—esque remark to be quoted when the shooting was recounted on the streets. I yelled, to no one in particular, "I hope the motherfucka dies!"

A security guard had been standing nearby when I first approached Plaz. I half expected him to walk over and arrest me. I waited for a moment for him to come and slap on the handcuffs. But the guard, apparently rattled by all the commotion, also scrambled for cover.

Greg asked me, "You got a ride?"

I said, "Naw."

He said, "C'mon."

We hopped into his car and drove off. When we got out on the main street, he said, "Where you wanna go?"

I realized that I hadn't thought about that. *Where do you go after you've shot somebody?* In all the stories I'd heard about Scobe and his boys, it was never clear what they did after they shot or maimed someone. There was nowhere else to go but home. I said, "Take me to the crib, man."

Greg dropped me off and I went into the house. Walking down the hallway to my parents' bedroom, I met my stepfather coming toward me. I said, "I need to talk to you. . . . I just shot somebody."

He was calm. "Is he dead?"

"I don't know."

He thought for a moment, then said, "Let me get dressed. We gotta go to the police station."

During the twenty-minute ride to the station, neither of us spoke a word. The seriousness of what I'd done was dawning on me. Who knows what my stepfather was thinking? After all the run-ins we'd had, he'd known I was headed for something like this. Yet he didn't try to preach to me or say "I told you so." I actually felt glad to have him on my side.

We went downtown, and I turned myself in. It felt strange giving myself up voluntarily to the same people I dodged every day. After interviewing me about the shooting, a detective escorted my stepfather and me into a hallway and told us to wait on a bench. Sitting there in the quiet, I felt so alone. There was no roaring crowd or group of running buddies to pat me on the back and sing my praises. It was just me, sitting there, suddenly powerless again, waiting to face the consequences.

After an hour or so, the detective returned to the hallway, looked at my stepfather, and said, "I'm sorry to keep you waiting out here so long, but Melvin Thompson, the guy your son shot, was rushed to the hospital. They're operating on him. They don't think he's going to make it. If he dies, we're going to have to charge your son with murder."

The word hit me like a sledgehammer. *Murder?!* On TV westerns, when people got shot they just tied a handkerchief around their arm and went on about their business. Whenever Scobe shot somebody, they lived. Plaz wasn't supposed to die. I thought, *Murder! If he dies, then that will mean I have killed someone. Murder?!* I repeated the word silently to myself, over and over, trying to grasp its full meaning.

Then I got a sharp vision of who I really was. I realized I didn't want to be a cold-blooded, baad-assed nigger anymore. I wanted to erase the past few hours, to wipe the slate clean. In desperation, I bowed my head, closed my eyes—tight—and prayed to God to spare Plaz's life. *"Please, God, don't let him die! Please."* I prayed so hard that a listener would have thought Plaz was my dearly beloved brother. My stepfather remained quiet. I don't know if he noticed me praying. At that moment, it didn't matter. I was too busy trying to establish a personal relationship with my Lord and Savior.

After several hours, the detective returned to the hallway. "I've got good news. Thompson pulled through. The doctors said the bullet barely missed his heart. Another fraction of an inch closer and he would've been pushing up daisies." I thanked sweet Jesus.

Oddly, I was released on my own recognizance. I guess it's an indication of how they felt about the value of black life that I wasn't even required to post bond. When I woke up that afternoon, I checked the newspaper and read a brief story about the shooting.

The gravity of what I'd done sank in again, but this time, I looked at it in an entirely different light. Now that I was certain Plaz would live, I felt hard again and I thought about the glory. I had toppled an old-head.

I got dressed, ate, and went outdoors to catch up with some of the fellas. While walking down Roosevelt Boulevard, I saw a car, filled with a bunch of old hoods, approach slowly. As it cruised closer, heads turned sharply and looked at me. It was some of Plaz's boys. The driver pulled over to the curb, and everybody in the car glared. They started talking to each other—debating, I assumed, whether to jump out and do me in.

Feigning confidence, I reached slowly into my pocket, as though gripping a gun, then stood there and met their gaze. My heart pounded hard. I knew that if they got out of that car, they'd stomp me six feet under. But no one budged. They talked some more, then the driver pulled slowly away from the curb and drove off.

For me, that brief, silent exchange was undeniable proof that I had arrived. I was a bona fide crazy nigger. Everywhere I went after that, guys on the street said, reverently, "Yeah, man, I heard you bust a cap in Plaz's ass." My street rep shot up three full notches. Anybody out there who knew me would think twice about moving against me without a piece. Anybody.

■ ■ ■

My parents got me one of the best criminal lawyers in Portsmouth. By the time I went to court a few months later, he'd worked out a deal with the commonwealth's attorney for me to plead guilty to a lesser charge of felonious assault rather than face trial for attempted murder. I went before the judge, claimed that I shot in self-defense, and got off light: thirty days in jail for assault, a $300 fine for possession of a firearm, and one year's probation. It helped that I was enrolled in college. The judge was so impressed with my college grades that he agreed to allow me to do my jail time on four weekends, meaning I had to do only eight days instead of the full thirty. I was thrilled.

The first weekend in the Portsmouth jail was the hardest. When I went in and was placed in a cell, the time hit me. Twenty-four hours takes on a whole new dimension behind bars. I struggled through each minute and suffered every creeping hour.

By the following weekend, and each week after, I came up with a better way to handle the time. About a half hour before Liz dropped me off at the jail, I'd drop a hit of acid. It usually took an hour or so for it to take effect. By then, I was inside a cell, riding high as a kite. I'd trip on the environment for a while, then doze and sleep off the high. Whenever I was awake, I talked through the bars to other guys and watched a black-and-white TV placed on a stand in the hallway. I left jail on Sunday afternoons, refreshed and ready to face life anew.

■ ■ ■

Sometime after the shooting, I saw Plaz on the streets, near the 7-Eleven. I wasn't armed. For a minute, I feared that he might try to get some get-back. But he didn't. He didn't even look me in the eye. He didn't want to try me again because he didn't know what I might do. That was the way I wanted it.

The shooting calmed Plaz down only temporarily. A few years later, he shot and killed a guy at the Cavalier Manor recreation field. The word on the street was that he did it because Scobe told him to. Plaz went away to prison for a long, long time.

Chapter 15 TRAPPED

One thing I've learned: The mind is like the body. If you don't work actively to protect its health, you can lose it, especially if you're a black man, nineteen years old and wondering, as I was, if you were born into the wrong world. The tricky thing about the mind is that when it's deeply troubled, it can shift tracks on you. It keeps working; you *are* thinking, but the mind shifts from logic to illogic without you being aware. Then one day you step outdoors butt-naked, wearing your underwear on your head, thinking that you're fully dressed.

It didn't get that bad for me, but things were falling apart in my head much faster than they were coming together. And I wasn't alone. I saw it happening to most of the fellas around me: Greg, Shane, Cooder, my older brother Dwight. We were bouncing around like pinballs in a machine, wondering if the world was fucked up or if we were; wondering why we were being pushed into the backseat of life and couldn't get at the wheel. If you're the only person riding in a car, and you're not driving, there's nothing to do but crash.

■   ■   ■

Although I got off light on the rap with Plaz, life got no easier to manage. The shooting, the trial, and the time in jail were just a few in a series of troubles that began pouring in. Even the honeymoon with Liz began to dull. The responsibilities that came with parent-hood were a bummer. We used to be able to jump up and do anything at any time. Then all of a sudden it took forty-five minutes to pack Pampers, bottles, and extra baby clothes just to go on a lightweight outing to the park. Being a father seemed like such a huge hassle, and I lacked both the will and desire to deal with it. So I started tipping out every now and then, hanging with chicks who had no children.

I kept Monroe sometimes when Liz had to work, but I still couldn't get into the groove with that fatherhood thing. As the mother, who'd carried the baby for nine months, Liz had no problem connecting from the jump. But I was just too young and immature to extend that kind of love beyond myself. So I focused on practical matters that affected us all: namely money, which I never seemed to have.

■ ■ ■

Compared to me, Shell Shock was Superfly. By the time we'd graduated, he'd bought a real gold tooth and paid cash for a deuce-and-a-quarter, a Buick Electra 225. He put gangster whitewall tires on his ride and cruised through Cavalier Manor hawking drugs and supervising the guys working for him.

One day I went with Shell Shock to a house where he copped his supply. The dude who owned the house was a Vietnam vet who lived in Cavalier Manor. We got there, sat down in the living room, toked a few joints, and talked. When Shell Shock and the dude went into the back room to transact business, I sat there, tripping and gawking at the tough furniture and slick layout of the place. Here was a cat in his late twenties or early thirties, and he had everything: a nice crib, a fine ride, a dynamite stereo system, and a monthly allotment check coming in from Uncle Sam. He had drug money flowing in, too, and, it appeared, no hassles from the man.

Sitting there, I realized that I needed to get smart. I needed to make some money and get back into the flow of things.

Liz and I combined our funds—a couple of hundred dollars—and bought a quarter pound of reefer. I broke it down into smaller bags to put on the street. With that done, I set out to build a clientele. I made the rounds and got the word out that folks could cop from me.

I quickly discovered that dealing wasn't as easy as it seemed. Selling reefer was a round-the-clock hustle that required more time and energy than I wanted to invest. Unloading a single O.Z. sometimes took up to an hour. Half the time, cats wanted to sample the stuff before they bought it, and even then they'd haggle over the weight. "Man, I can get more than *this* over on Henderson Street."

I'd have to be firm. "Well, go on over to Henderson Street and get it, then."

Selling reefer also required more restraint than I could muster. I often got bored waiting for people to cop, and dipped into my manila packets to smoke some here and there. Some nights I wound up getting so high that I didn't feel like selling anymore. Once I got high, I got the serious munchies and couldn't concentrate on anything but food, music, and sex.

I eventually built up a decent clientele but discovered that that, too, had its drawbacks. Guys wanting to score were always looking for me, pulling up by the carload in front of my parents' house and calling there all hours of the day and night. Dudes always wanted me to meet them in out-of-the-way places to deliver the goods. I didn't have the advantage of beepers, phone recorders, and portable telephones, like cats have today. I had to rough it, work the streets and stay there most of the time. I had to hit all the hot corners and make sure I was accessible, especially on shipyard paydays and "Mother's Day," the first of the month, when sisters in the projects got their welfare checks.

Most of the time, I used Liz's car, a 1973 Buick Opel her mother gave her as a graduation gift. When I didn't have the Opel, I worked the streets on foot, trying to be high-profile and, at the same time, avoid undercover narcs.

Among dealers the competition was stiff. I tried to gain an edge by offering more weight than the next man, which cut down on my profits unless I padded the reefer with a little oregano. I'd also try to lure buys by putting out the word that I had some exotic brand of reefer known for its potency. "Yo, man, this shit is straight outta Mexico. This is *monster* herb." Or, "Yo, blood, I got some cess from Jamaica that's outta sight!"

The problem was, most of the reefer on the streets at a given time came from one source. I didn't learn until later that a lot of the top-level dealers from New York and other places controlled whole regions, meaning that all us low-level dealers were selling the same stuff.

I also found that I damned near had to be an accountant to stay in business. I had to save the money I made and invest and manage it properly so that I could reinvest. That didn't go well, either. I was too lax with spending. Hanging out there on the street, I often got hungry and spent a lot of money on food and drink, lost track of who owed me money, and squandered a lot of cash just having fun. Sometimes, when sales were good, Liz and I threw small parties at local hotels or packed up her car and left town for weekend runs to Washington, a four-hour drive away.

Eventually, I realized it was too much work for me to try to hawk herb alone. Frog Dickie, who had returned home from the Job Corps, was unemployed and down and out, so I put him to work. With him dealing for me, I had to keep track of how much dope I gave him to sell and how much money I was due. I often wrote it down and lost the notes when I got high.

My problems dealing drugs didn't help my self-esteem any. I saw guys like Shell Shock managing their money, supervising hardheads, and moving along, and I wondered what they knew about dealing that I didn't know. The bad thing about it was, I was too proud to ask.

The thing about drug dealing that bothered me most was that I had to be ruthless, or act like I was. I had to be prepared to seriously hurt or kill friend, family, or foe if the need arose. I found out I wasn't down for all that when Frog put me to the test. After taking—and probably smoking—the stuff I gave him to sell for me, Frog dropped out of sight, which was a sure sign that he'd messed up my money. When I finally caught up with him, he put on a sad face. "Aw, man, guess what happened?" he told me. "I was up at the 7-Eleven talkin' to some guys, and the lawmen came down on us from nowhere. They chased us through the path behind the store and I had to ditch the stuff in the bushes. I couldn't take a chance on gettin' busted, man. You know how that is."

I looked at him long and hard. "Hey, man, you playin' me for a chump or what?!"

"Naw, Nate, you know I wouldn't do that, man. That's really what happened. Ask some of the guys up at the store. . . . Hey, man, you know we go way back. You know I wouldn't rip you off."

Frog put me in a position where I had to bust his head, as much to send a message to other folks on the street as to punish him. If word got around that one person got away with running a Murphy, everybody would try it and I'd be out of business in no time. That's the nature of the drug game. Everybody is either looking to get a free high, trying to steal drugs, ripping off drug money, or all of the above. Dopeheads dumb enough to let their apartments be used as the get-high spot often learned the hard way. Often, while everybody's getting high, somebody in that group is scoping the furniture and appliances and checking out the locks. A few days later, the host comes home and hears an echo in his house as hollow as the Grand Canyon. The place is empty, and he knows that one of the ten people he entertained and got high with made the hit.

I knew that I had to fuck Frog up if I was going to keep dealing. But we had grown up together, from junior high. I couldn't erase all the fun times and camaraderie over a $100 debt. So against my better judgment I let it slide, hoping I wouldn't regret it.

■ ■ ■

Eventually, I gave up selling reefer, dumped Frog, and tried selling chemical drugs—orange sunshine, mescaline, windowpane, purple microdots, quaaludes—that were easier to unload. Shell Shock's older brother, Ton, who was at college on a football scholarship, shipped home large quantities of quaaludes from Kansas, where he got them cheap. He was breaking rushing records in college, but he was still a thug. I paid him a dollar a hit for the quaaludes and resold them on the block for three dollars each. That went O.K., but I had to unload thousands of those things to make any real cash. That turned out to be a bummer, too.

I finally had to admit that I lacked the discipline to be a good dealer. Dealing drugs is harder than any job I've had, then or since. To this day, I laugh when I hear folks say drug dealers are lazy people who don't want to work. There's no job more demanding than dealing drugs. It's the only thing I've really tried hard to do, and failed at.

■   ■   ■

I preferred to *do* drugs more than sell them. Drugs helped me get away from it all and escape the pain and confusion I felt inside. But sometimes it seemed the drugs were doing me instead of me doing them. Sometimes I had some really bad trips.

Sometimes I'd trip out somewhere in public and damned near lose control. I'd get so high sometimes and stay ripped for so long— sometimes for as much as eight hours—that I'd get down on my knees and pray to God to bring me down.

The craziest part about tripping on acid was the hallucinations. Actually, they were comical at times. Like the night I was driving down the road with Liz and some other folks while tripping on acid. I pulled into a parking lot on Victory Boulevard to take a leak. I walked over and started pissing on the side of a bus tire. Right before my eyes, the bus started melting. It was wild. It was as if the piss was so hot that it burned the bus to a crisp. It melted into one massive glob of steel and rubber.

I finished leaking and ran back to the car and asked Liz, "Did you see that bus melt?"

When everybody assured me that the bus was still intact, I realized I was tripping.

That acid would do that to you. You could be talking to somebody while tripping on acid and their whole face would become distorted, large and rubbery-looking, like a Halloween mask. Or something somebody would say—it could be something simple and innocent— would be received in a different way than it was intended. I'd get paranoid and ask the person, "What the fuck you mean by that?"

I found out through some trips that your reaction to certain drugs is largely a function of your state of mind at the time. Since my state of mind got to be pretty messed up with the passage of time, I had some bad trips that almost cost me plenty. One night, Liz and I were in a hotel room we'd rented to throw a small party. Strobe lights were flashing and the music was pumping. We'd dropped some acid. Monroe was there in a playpen. He started crying. I went over, picked him up, and tried to calm him. But he wouldn't stop. He kept on crying. It seemed that his mouth opened wider and wider. It got so wide that it looked like the mouth of a whale. I soothed and sang and rocked him, tried everything I could think of to quiet him down. But he kept crying, and the wails, the music, and the flashing lights were all coming at me at once. Then I started tripping. *Why won't he stop crying? Why won't he shut the fuck up? . . .*

Then it got worse. I guess all my resentment surfaced and all the pent-up anger I felt about everything gave in to the drug, and suddenly I turned cold on my own son. Something inside of me said, *I'll bet if you slam his ass against that wall he'll shut the hell up . . . Go on! Sling his li'l ass!*

He kept crying as I stood there, holding him, listening to that sinister voice inside my head and trying to decide whether or not to obey. Illogic ruled the moment. I wanted him to shut up, and he wouldn't, so there was only one thing left to do. I felt my arms raising Monroe higher, higher. Reflections from the strobe lights, flashing red, green, blue, were bouncing off the wall and the music was loud. I raised Monroe and looked at the wall. The voice said, *Go on. Slam him.* I could feel myself about to give in to the urge. *Go on! Do it! Do it!* Then someone gently grabbed my arm. It was Liz. She stood beside me, calmly reached for Monroe, and took him away.

■ ■ ■

My temperament got worse with time, so much so that I got into a beef with my main man, Bimbo. He'd returned home from the Army and, like the rest of us, wasn't doing much of anything with his life. For some strange reason, he crossed me. He told Liz I went to see another babe. It was true, but he was supposed to be my boy. Stick partners don't do that.

Liz confronted me and asked if it was true. I lied harder than a white man and swore up and down that Bimbo didn't know what he was talking about. I think she knew I was talking out the side of my face, but she wanted to believe me. It was part of her own denial about how crazy life was getting for both of us.

Meanwhile, I put the word out in the street that I was looking for Bimbo. I'd decided that I was going to bust him up. Bimbo was much bigger and stronger than me. I knew I probably couldn't beat him in a heads-up rumble. I'd have to bum-rush him, pounce on him and beat him with a stick or something without giving him a chance to recover.

Sitting at home one day, I looked out the front window and saw Bimbo's green Monte Carlo pull up in front of the house. Frog Dickie was riding shotgun. This was my chance. I rushed into my room, grabbed a walking stick, and went outdoors to meet them. When we met in the street, I pointed the cane at Bimbo and said, "You ain't shit!"

He tried to look surprised. "What you talkin' 'bout, man?!"

"You know what I'm talkin' 'bout, niggah!" Then I raised the cane and cracked it over his head. *Whack!*

Bimbo fell back against his car. Before he could stand up straight again, I lunged at him, busting him in the head with the remaining half of the cane. Blood squirted everywhere. My mother, who must have been watching through the window, came to the front door screaming. "Nathan, stop that! Stop! Somebody stop him!"

Frog, who had been standing nearby when the fight started, hung back and stayed away, a shocked expression on his face.

Desperate, my mother telephoned Greg's father across the street. He came running outside and reached for the cane. I looked at him, pointed the cane, and warned: "Mr. Sonny, don't try to take this stick from me." He backed off and tried to reason. "Nathan, give me the cane. You know you don't want to do that."

Bimbo took advantage of the distraction to stumble to his car. He climbed inside and locked the doors. His head was bleeding badly. When I couldn't get the door unlocked, I started whacking his car, hitting the windshield and the hood and kicking the tires. In the background, I heard my mother screaming, "Call the police! That boy's gone crazy! Call the police!"

Lost in what I was doing, I kept whacking Bimbo's car with the cane. I whacked and whacked until he started the engine and drove away.

■ ■ ■

Several days after the run-in with Bimbo, I stepped out of the wintry cold into Shell Shock's house and greeted the fellas. "Yo, man, what's happ'nin'?"

A chorus of greetings rang out from Cooder, Shane, and a few others who were lounging around in the den, smoking reefer. Shell Shock, who had been in a back room when I first came in, strutted out front with a cigar-sized joint dangling limply from the tip of his lips. He took a deep drag and handed it to me. "Hey, li'l ugly niggah, where you been all day?!"

I took the joint, sucked in, and exhaled slowly, letting the smoke ooze through my nostrils. "I been chillin', man. Got a lotta things on my mind."

Without responding, he walked over to the stereo, lifted the top to the turntable, and put on a record album by Marvin Gaye called *What's Going On.*

The music started and I settled back on the couch and listened, toking the joint whenever it was passed my way. Gaye's silky smooth voice, complemented by an alto sax, crooned through the large speakers, filling the room. I'd heard the album before but for some reason tuned in really close to the lyrics this time:

> *Mother, mother, there's too many of you crying.*
> *Brother, brother, brother, there's far too many of you dying.*
> *You know we've got to find a way*
> *To bring some lovin' here today . . .*

It was different from the romantic themes of most record albums. It dealt with a range of things that were going on in the country. Poverty. Racial unrest. The Vietnam War. The country was one big pressure cooker that seemed ready to blow.

Gaye sang:

> *Say, man, I just don't understand*
> *What's going on across this land . . .*

I sat there and thought about all the fucked-up things going on in the world, and in my life. I had no job, no money, no future. I felt lost, alone, out of place. My life was going down the drain, and I saw it happening and seemed unable to do a damn thing to stop it. I thought, *My moms is right. I'm goin' crazy. Losin' it.*

My mother had known for some time how troubled I was. She'd questioned me about the dark sunshades I sometimes wore at night.

She'd found a pistol in my coat pocket. She'd answered the telephone and had anonymous callers tell her they were going to fuck me up. After the fight with Bimbo, she called her minister to counsel me. She was worried and trying hard to figure out what to do with me.

I listened, and Gaye sang:

Nobody really understands . . .

I knew I was hurting Mama. There were times when I wanted to tell her that I knew she cared, but my macho pride got in the way and I could never bring myself to express my roiling feelings. Besides, I couldn't process my confusion sufficiently in my own head to explain it to somebody else. When they questioned me, my parents interpreted my stony silence as stubbornness. In truth, it was a reflection of futility. The gulf between what I instinctively knew was happening to me and what I could express was so broad that I gave up trying to explain.

Gaye sang:

We've got to find a way
To bring some understanding here today . . .

The futility ran so deep that it festered and churned inside me, quietly making gunpowder. I walked around feeling tense all the time. The only way I could balance the tension and the deep depression was to stay high—all the time. Like the rest of the fellas, I had started getting high earlier and earlier in the day. Some of them had begun drinking and doing drugs the first thing in the morning. I knew I couldn't let myself reach that point. That's one step from being a drunk, 24/7 on a park bench. But I was close enough that it worried me.

My dress and appearance were slipping. I'd started wearing the same clothes day after day, and didn't care whether the colors matched or not. I was starting the slow, steady process of wasting away. Cavalier Manor was filled with other guys going through the same drug-induced decline.

I rested my head on the back of the couch, stared up at the ceiling through glazed eyes, and thought about the changing times. Things in my world and outside of it were changing faster than I could handle. Even things between Liz and me weren't the same. Around that time, when we were talking once, I broke down crying and told Liz I felt like I'd never been loved and feared that I didn't have long to live. Later, Liz told my mother those things and I cussed her out for revealing my private feelings to somebody else. After that, it seemed like we started drifting apart.

When relations among the fellas and me started changing, I knew my life had spun completely out of control. The break with my man Bimbo was just another indication of that. I thought about what had happened, how far back Bimbo and I went and how tight we used to be. I didn't feel as tight with any of the fellas anymore. The deeper we got into the drug thing, the more paranoid and ruthless we became. Guys who'd been the best of hanging partners since way back when started turning on each other and ripping each other off.

I couldn't even trust Shell Shock, my tightest stickman. I learned this during one of the last stickups we pulled together. My old buddy Cooder came along and served as the getaway driver while Shell Shock and I went and took off some dudes leaving a Norfolk dance hall. We made good money off those cats, but on the way back to the car Shell Shock insisted we not tell Cooder what we'd gotten so that we wouldn't have to split it with him. Reluctantly, I went along, but later, when I thought about it, I concluded that if Shell Shock would rip off Cooder, he'd rip me off, too. After that, I didn't hang with Shell Shock so much anymore. The vibes started changing between him and me.

Marvin Gaye sang:

> *Mercy, mercy me,*
> *Things ain't what they used to be.*
> *Where did all the blue skies go . . . ?*

I toked on the joint and considered the future. It seemed so vague. Life seemed to be closing in. I felt trapped. I was unemployed, broke, and desperate as hell.

Marvin Gaye sang:

> *I can't find no work, can't find no job, my friend.*
> *Money is tighter than it's ever been . . .*

My favorite song on the album was "Inner City Blues." It captured the depth of the despair I felt setting in. It was the only thing that came close to explaining the frustration churning inside me. It was the first time I'd heard someone put it all together in words like that:

> *Aw, it make me wanna holler*
> *The way they do my life*

Make me wanna holler
The way they do my life
This ain't livin'
This ain't livin'
Naw, naw, baby
This ain't livin'
Naw, naw, naw, naw . . .

That's how I felt. I wanted to holler. Listening to that album and thinking about all my problems made me feel like crying.

Absorbed in my own thoughts and carried away by the reefer, I hadn't realized that everybody around me had stopped talking. The fellas were listening and thinking, too. I looked around the room and noticed the thick clouds of reefer smoke hanging heavily in the air. The lights were dim. It felt like all of time was suspended.

When the album ended, nobody said a word for a long, long time. Like the others, I couldn't speak. We just sat there, thinking.

Chapter 16 BUSTED

After graduating from high school, Liz got a job as a salesclerk at Robert Hall Village, a new department store that opened near Cavalier Manor. When she'd been working there awhile and gotten to know some of the other employees, we worked out a scam with several black cashiers in the store. After we got it down, I walked into the department store like a regular customer, got a shopping cart, and went on a spree: through the men's section to get things I wanted; into the ladies' department to pick up a few items for Liz; and then on to appliances. When I finished, my cart was filled to the brim. I pushed it to a counter, where a black cashier promptly rang up the price of one item, a three-dollar pair of socks, placed all my merchandise in large shopping bags, and stapled them closed with an attached receipt.

I paid the lady, then took my bags to the front of the store and walked past the jewelry section, where Liz stood behind the counter, watching nervously as I approached. Our eyes met briefly, then turned away, as if we were two total strangers. I walked toward the front door, past a security guard who glanced at my sealed bags and then turned his attention to something else. Once outside, I broke into a grin. We were over, like a fat rat.

I think Liz loved that rip-off because it was risky and exciting and made her feel like she was learning how to hustle. That hustle worked so well that we took Christmas orders from people in the neighborhood for jewelry, clothes, appliances—anything they wanted. We made a killing. In fact, Liz and I, along with some of the other employees who also were robbing the store blind, got over so well that the place eventually went out of business. By cleaning out the store and forcing it to close, we took away jobs that employed people in our community and we got rid of a business that brought revenue to the area. We didn't view it that way at the time, but we did ourselves in. Once the place closed, Liz had to find another gig and I looked around for another hustle to get into.

■ ■ ■

After all my other hustles fell through, I went back to what I knew best. There were several stickup teams operating from the neighborhood. I hooked up with Nutbrain and Charlie Gregg, two old-heads who I figured knew everything there was to know about working the streets. Nutbrain and Charlie Gregg, who were both three years older than me, were longtime swinging partners who had hooked up when they were both living in the projects downtown. They were as thick as thieves. They *were* thieves. I had supreme faith in their experience and skills as stickup men.

Nutbrain, who used to school us about sex when we were kids, was tall, slim, and jet-black. He was good with his hands and cool as ice. Nothing rattled him. Nutbrain, who lived about four blocks from me, didn't hang on the corner much. He'd walk past our block, doing his slow, old-man pimp, looking like he had somewhere important to go. He always kept a brown bag tucked under his arm. Occasionally, he'd stop on the block, chat with the fellas and me, pull a pint bottle from the bag, take a swig, and talk some more.

Although his nickname suggested otherwise, Nutbrain was smart in his own way. He didn't work often, but when he did, he specialized in on-the-job injuries. Every time I turned around, he was waiting on a check from some former employer who owed him compensation. He'd say, "Lemme hold somethin' till next week, man. I got some money coming in from a case I got when I hurt my back." I liked him a lot. He knew how to get over, and he was on the one.

Charlie Gregg was married, and had children. He worked a job, but needed money badly. I met him through Nutbrain. Charlie Gregg was brown-skinned, wiry like me, bowlegged, and cross-eyed as hell. He had bad feet that each looked like it wanted to take him in a different direction when he walked. Nutbrain jokingly called him Funky Winkerbean.

Nutbrain was the mastermind of the team. He could case a joint perfectly and figure a plan, just like that. I also liked his style. Unlike Shell Shock, he had ethics. If you worked with him, you never had to worry about getting your cut. And he focused solely on businesses, which Shell Shock and I had avoided. I knew there was no real money to be made unless I crossed the tracks.

I was right. We hit one spot and did good right away. Walked away with a grand apiece. It was a big step up from the chump change Shell Shock and I used to take from ghetto blacks. After that hit, I stayed up most of the night, counting the money over and over, marveling at what we'd done. It gave me a rush to know that I'd taken all that money from white folks and gotten away clean.

At the same time, there was this fear that had been nagging me for a while. It was a fear that the law of averages was closing in. This ripping-off couldn't go on forever. Cats all around me were getting popped for one thing or another, and being sent to the penitentiary, left and right. I figured that soon or later I'd take a fall, too.

Sometimes, when I thought about it, I didn't care. Sometimes I cared a whole lot more than I was willing to admit. Like the night Brain and I hit a supermarket on Military Highway. He'd scoped it beforehand and laid out the plan like a pro. We parked the car in a hotel parking lot nearby and walked across a large field to the store. Dressed in dark clothes, we entered the supermarket just before closing time. Brain told me, "Check the aisles and make sure all the customers are gone." I went up and down the aisles, stopping in one to pick up a Morton apple pie from the frozen-food section. I went to the checkout area, where Brain was waiting. He pulled the gun and calmly ordered a cashier to empty the registers. It took a minute for other store clerks to figure out they were being robbed. I was jittery. The place was so large, I feared somebody might appear from behind an aisle and open fire.

We got the cash, burst out the door, and began low-running, hard, across the lumpy field. All the while we're running, I'm thinking that this is going to be the one; this will be the time we get popped. I ran, thinking it, feeling it, remembering how Charles Lee got surprised in that house and wondering if it might end that way for me. I ran and listened, half expecting to hear a loud crack break the night silence, and to feel the hot sting of a bullet pierce my back. I listened, but all I heard was heavy panting coming from Nutbrain and me, the two of us breathlessly trying to outrun fate.

■ ■ ■

It's hard to move slow with fast money. Each time I went out on a job, I told myself it would be the last. And each time after that, I found a reason to go out one more time.

That was the case with the Sheraton hit. We went out mainly because of Charlie Gregg, who was pissed because he'd missed out on the supermarket job. So Nutbrain came up with the Sheraton Hotel at the Military Circle shopping mall. He'd scoped it out and figured it would be an easy, big-money hit. Fresh off the other job, I didn't really need money. When Nutbrain called, I decided I'd use the funds to do something nice for Liz. Buy her a gift: an expensive-looking dog. An Afghan hound.

I got dressed that night in a black skullcap and dark clothes. I went to the living room and paced back and forth, waiting impatiently for Nutbrain and Charlie Gregg to come and scoop me up. When my mother walked through the house and saw me standing there, peeping out the front curtain, she knew right away that something was up. She always got nervous when she saw me leaving the house. I was still on probation for shooting Plaz, and she wanted to make sure I didn't take another fall.

"Where you going?" she asked.

I igged her like I usually did. I acted like I didn't even hear.

"Don't go out there and get in no more trouble," she warned.

"I ain't gonna get in no trouble, Mama. I'm just goin' out for a while."

A car horn sounded. Charlie Gregg and Nutbrain had pulled up out front. I was glad. It would help me escape another awkward scene with Mama. I left her standing at the opened door, watching, straining to see whose car was out there and who was inside.

I climbed into the backseat of Charlie Gregg's Dodge Charger and greeted the brothers. "Yo, brotherman! What it iissss!?"

Nutbrain was his usual cool self. Charlie Gregg was pumped up. "Let's do it, baby! Let's make some money tonight!"

Riding down the interstate with music blaring from some eight-track tape, I sat quietly in the backseat and thought about what my mother had said. Normally, it wouldn't have bothered me. But that night it did. My intuition was burning again. It, too, was telling me I shouldn't go.

But I was committed. We were on our way, speeding on Interstate 264 toward the Norfolk tunnel. Nutbrain had figured that 10 P.M. was the best time to make the hit. We reached the Sheraton right on time, ready to make the quick walk into the door and take the few short steps to the registration desk, where, we were sure, thousands of ducats were waiting for us in the cash register.

But when we got inside, nothing was set up like we thought it would be. The hotel lobby, usually empty and unguarded, was crawling with white people dressed in tuxedos and gowns. There was some kind of special event going on. A policeman stood around watching, as if he half expected something to jump off.

Nutbrain scanned the crowded room and said what Charlie Gregg and I were already thinking. "Let's go, man. There's no happ'nin's here."

I took that as another sign that this was a bad night. But Charlie Gregg was set on making a hit. We went to a convenience store, bought some wine, and drove around drinking and looking for a quick pedestrian vic to roll. We drove onto Hampton Boulevard and a lightbulb came on in Nutbrain's head. "Yo, man, I know somewhere we can hit. Drive past that McDonald's down the street. Somebody comes in every night around eleven to pick up the money and take it to the bank. We can lay for him outside the door and take the shit from him when he comes out."

It sounded simple enough. Still, I was uneasy. It wasn't the original plan. We didn't have time for the usual dry run of the getaway route, and the white neighborhood where we parked the car looked like a foreign land. I felt we should call it a night, but I didn't say anything. I couldn't punk out.

When Charlie Gregg turned off the engine, Nutbrain turned around and handed me the gun. "Nate, it's your turn to carry the piece."

He'd carried the gun and done most of the work the last time we went out. Despite the wine I'd guzzled to numb my fear, I was nervous. It just didn't *feel* right.

As we entered the side door of the McDonald's, a beefy white man carrying a small, white, plastic pouch came out of the employee entrance. *Now!* My intuition told me he was the mark. But instead of drawing on him, I froze, then turned and ducked into the men's rest room nearby. Nutbrain and Charlie Gregg followed. Once inside, Brain said, "That was the man! He had the money in that pouch!"

The man had glanced warily at us, gone outside, and climbed into a parked van. I said, "Maybe we should get him while he's in the truck." Nutbrain poked his head out the door and saw that the man had started the engine. "Naw, he's about to pull away. We gonna have to do the store."

He said it like we had no other choice, like we couldn't just leave and try again some other time. Charlie Gregg nodded his approval, so I went along. After planning our move, we burst through a door that read EMPLOYEES ONLY. I flashed the silver-plated pistol and yelled, "Nobody move!"

The workers, stunned, turned and did what they were told. They left their cash registers, huddled in a corner, and stared, wide-eyed, at us.

As shocked customers ran out the side exits, Nutbrain and Charlie Gregg hurriedly emptied loot from the cash registers into food-carry-out bags with golden arches printed on the side. I stood guard near the door, pointing the gun and looking around. I didn't feel in control. There was too much light, too much space to cover, too many people in those ugly brown McDonald's uniforms looking right at our uncovered faces. Out of the corner of my eye, I noticed the store manager trying to ease his way into a side office. I pointed the .32 pistol at him and said, "Freeze!"

Minutes later, he tried it again. I aimed the piece at his face, tightened my grip on the trigger, and tried to decide in that split second what to do. I *swear* I didn't want to blow him away. All I wanted was to get the cash and dash. But I made up my mind that if he moved again, I *had* to smoke him. I hated him for putting that pressure on me. I didn't even know him, and I hated the hell out of him. Intuitively, I sensed he was an Uncle Tom, one of those head-scratching niggers, willing to put his devalued life on the line to protect the white man's property. I looked him in the eye and warned, "Move again, and I'm gonna bust your ass."

He remained still and kept his eyes fixed on me.

Once Nutbrain and Charlie Gregg had cleaned the cash registers, we turned and ran out the side door and sprinted to the parked car a block away. We sped off into the night. Two blocks down the dark street, we ran into a dead end. I knew then we were goners. Charlie Gregg wheeled around, sped out of the cul-de-sac, and turned onto Hampton Boulevard. A few minutes later, he looked in his rearview mirror and said, "The rollers are behind me."

Nutbrain told him, "Just be cool. Maintain the speed."

I sat in the backseat, tensed, bracing for the bust. A police cruiser pulled closer and flashed its emergency lights. Then others came from nowhere and surrounded us. In the seconds while Charlie Gregg steered over to the curb and stopped, adrenaline rushed to my head. Panicked thoughts came at me, rapid-fire:

Burst out and dash!

No! Shoot first, then run!

Finally, I heeded my strongest intuition: *Sit still. You're busted.*

After surrounding us, the policemen sprang from their cruisers with their guns drawn, pulled open our doors, and shouted, "Get out of the car! Get out of the car!" One cop grabbed me, pushed my chest flush against the side of the car, and clamped the cold steel handcuffs to my bony wrists. He shoved me into the backseat of a cruiser.

The emergency lights flashing overhead created a weird, dreamlike effect. Cars slowed, and motorists peered through their windows, trying to get a better look. Some cops waved them on and directed traffic, while others flashed lights inside and around the getaway car.

I stared blankly out the window and did something I had learned to do in years on the street when fear or reality became too much to face: I let my emotions go limp. That was my only protection against freaking out, my only guard against coming apart.

The police drove us back to the McDonald's, where the employees stood outside. They escorted the manager to the car I was in and asked him if I was one of the men who had robbed the store.

I glared into the manager's eyes, half hoping to intimidate him. He returned my glare, with a dash of contempt. "Yeah. He was the one with the gun." We drove off, beginning the long ride toward police headquarters.

■ ■ ■

A ride in a police car always feels like a long journey to me. I always have time enough during such a ride to review my whole life. I rode in the backseat, stared out the window, and let my mind wander aimlessly. I thought about crazy things. I thought about how much I hated being handcuffed, how much it pissed me off when cops locked the cuffs too tight around my wrists. I wondered why they had to cuff people's hands behind their backs like that. You can never sit straight up in the seat when you're handcuffed because your full weight comes down on you, squeezing your wrists painfully between your body and the backseat. Most guys I had ever seen riding in the back of police cars bobbled from side to side, like bottles in water, to keep from leaning back and crushing their hands. Over time, I'd learned to lean sideways and rest my head against the side window to keep my weight off my hands.

Riding down Hampton Boulevard, I watched the world pass and thought about the people I saw walking, carefree, along the sidewalks. *Where are they going? What are their lives like?* I wished I could change places with one of them. I wished I had listened to my mother. I wished I could rewind the last hour of my fucked-up life and reset its course. I wished I were somewhere else, anywhere but riding in a cop car.

My mind did a sweep of all the landmarks in my life, the kind of sweep described by people who have had scrapes with death. It certainly felt to me like my life was over. I was twenty, half burned out on drugs, depressed, and hopelessly lost. At some point in life—long before I ever held a gun—I had lost control. I tried to figure out what had gone wrong, and when. I wished I could vanish, go back to a point in time when life seemed, well, hopeful. Strangely, I thought about my third-grade spelling bee. I was an honor student then and felt so full of promise. I had made it to the competition finals but was eliminated after misspelling a word; I think it was "bicycle." *If I could go back to that night on that school stage,* I thought, *I would spell that word right and straighten out all the other things in life that had since gone wrong.*

My thoughts were distracted by the two white rollers sitting in front. They were laughing, joking about the stickup and predicting how much penitentiary time we would get. I wanted to lash out. I wanted to tell them, *Kiss my blaaack ass!* But I kept quiet.

We got to the police station, along with the cars carrying Nutbrain and Charlie Gregg. When we got out, Nutbrain made the mistake of saying something to his police escort. "Yo, man. These handcuffs are too tight." The cop smiled broadly, stepped behind him, and yanked them tighter. "Is that better?" Nutbrain grimaced.

They took us into separate rooms and started the process of interrogating us. Without talking with Nutbrain and Charlie Gregg, I knew what to do: *Don't confess shit, and don't give 'em any meaningful info until you talk with a lawyer.* That's what everybody yells when they get busted: "I want to talk to my lawyer!" It just seems like something you should say to let them know they can't push you around.

They took me into an office and sat me in a chair. Then they started the little cop head-games that had become familiar to me. A few of them stood over me with their shirtsleeves rolled up, like they were gonna do me in. A black detective did all the talking. When he asked me my name, I didn't answer at first. I considered giving them a hard time to show them I wasn't scared. But it was late, and I was too tired to play games.

"My name is Nathan McCall."

"Address?"

"Six Vaughn Court."

The black cop sat on the edge of the desk in front of me and said, "Tell us what happened tonight."

I said, "I didn't do nothin'. . . . I need to make a phone call!"

He looked at the others, indicating it was a waste of time trying to get me to talk. They laid off the crime questions and stuck to the basics.

When the interrogations, fingerprinting, and processing ended a few hours later, we were thrown into the bull pen, a huge holding cell, about forty feet square, filled with thirty or so drunks, junkies, and assorted other losers. The place smelled like piss and vomit. Guys were leaning against the grimy walls looking tired and pitiful. It was about two in the morning and the lights were dim. Everything was quiet. Nutbrain, Charlie Gregg, and I huddled near the bars and compared notes. Nutbrain was cool. Charlie Gregg, who seemed nervous, kept asking me questions. "How did it go?"

"It went all right."

"What did the rollers ask you?"

"The same old dumb shit they always ask."

Both of them had telephoned family members to say that they were locked up. I would have felt stupid calling my mother to say that I was in jail after doing exactly what she'd warned me not to do. *No*, I thought. *I'm gonna ride this one out on my own.*

But I called Liz at about 1:30 A.M. and told her the news. She freaked. "What happened?! What happened?!"

I calmed her down and gave her instructions on how to find out when and where I'd be taken for a preliminary hearing later that day. After we got that straight, we hung up. I thought about how glad I'd be to see her face.

Nutbrain, Charlie Gregg, and I talked some more, then decided to get some sleep. There was nowhere to lie down. The benches along the walls had been taken by the early arrivals. Some guys were trying to sleep standing up, like cows. They leaned on the walls, held their heads skyward, and closed their bloodshot eyes, like they were praying. Others were sprawled on the floor, sleeping hard. I staked out a spot on the floor and stretched out near the bars. The concrete was cold and smelly. I found a dingy half roll of toilet paper and slid it under my head to use as a pillow.

Lying on my back, I stared at the greasy ceiling and thought about the new mess I was in. Mama was right. I wouldn't be so lucky this time. I was penitentiary-bound.

In a weird way, that didn't seem so bad. I figured I might have been saved from something potentially worse. I had fully expected a more tragic fate: to be caught by surprise, like Charles Lee, the burglar; to go down in a shoot-out with police, like Prairie Dog. I knew that if I had come out of that car shooting, those trigger-happy cops would have blown me away.

Later that morning, Charlie Gregg, Nutbrain, and I were shackled to some other inmates and led downstairs for a preliminary hearing. We looked like shit. Our hair was nappy. We hadn't brushed our teeth or washed our faces. I know I smelled like the pissy odor that rose like a yellow mist from the bull-pen floor.

As we stood before the judge, I glanced around the courtroom, looking for Liz. I didn't see her. The judge asked us a few questions, then set bail for each of us at $25,000. I remember thinking, *Twenty-five thousand! I'll never get outta here!*

To get me out, my parents had to raise $2,500. Nutbrain's and Charlie Gregg's people had to do the same. Less than two weeks after the stickup, we all got out on bond, just in time for Christmas.

■ ■ ■

The bust made the papers, with a picture of the getaway car. My mother told me that a neighbor, seeing the photo in the paper, called the house to ask if the person identified in the photo caption was me.

My parents didn't have the funds for a great lawyer this time. The best they could afford was some white poot-butt dude. I could spot his kind a mile away. They get paid a thousand dollars or so to usher you up before the judge and try to make sure you don't get screwed too bad. They're great actors. They look and listen to your side of the story like they're really concerned, then, after they've let you blow off steam, they start coaching you on how to throw yourself on the mercy of the court.

Like Nutbrain and Charlie Gregg, I'd pleaded innocent during the preliminary hearing and asked for a jury trial. But my lawyer warned, "You don't want to take a judge through a jury trial. We've got no defense. It'll only piss him off, and we don't want to piss off the judge." We canceled the jury request, but I kept my innocent plea. Weeks later, I gave in and changed my plea to guilty. After reviewing the case, my lawyer said that given the strength of the evidence against me, I'd come out with a lighter sentence if we did it that way. "My guess," he said, "is that you'll get *some* time, but it won't be much."

Given my background and record, he predicted the judge would give me a five-year sentence—at most. That meant I'd be eligible for parole after fifteen months. I thought that maybe my lawyer had worked a deal, like the attorney I had when I shot Plaz. I figured I could do fifteen months standing on my head. I needed at least that much time to dry out and clear my mind.

■ ■ ■

On April 11, 1975, the court date, I was accompanied to court by Reverend Ellis from Norfolk State, my parents, and Liz. As I moved to join my lawyer at the defense table, Reverend Ellis gave me a biblical verse to recite to myself. It was taken from the Book of Romans, chapter 8, verse 28. I still remember it: *Everything works together for the good of those who love God, for those who are called according to His purpose.*

It turned out to be a very short hearing. Witnesses were there who could recount the robbery if called upon. The McDonald's manager and a couple of employees were also there.

The judge, an old white man, called out my name and launched into all that official jargon they use in court: "Nathan McCall is brought before this commonwealth of Virginia on a charge of armed robbery committed on December fourth, 1974. How shall you plead?"

At the prompting of my lawyer, I stood up, put my hands behind my back, and repeated my guilty plea. Without looking at me, the judge, sitting up high on his bench in his black robe, leafed through a file folder on his bench. Then he lifted his head and called me up front. "Do you have anything to say for yourself before I announce sentencing?"

Something about the tone and the nature of that question let me know this was going to be a bad day. I scrambled in my head to try to come up with something that might sway that man. I sensed that if I didn't come up with a helluva rap, he was going to lay some heavy time on me.

But it was impossible to say all that was weighing on my heart. I felt choked up inside, as if all the emotions and words had converged on my throat at once and gotten bottled up. Standing there, looking solemn, I mumbled some bullshit about being sorry for committing the crime, then hated myself for even giving it that feeble, embarrassing try.

After he was sure I'd finished, he said, "Anything else?"

I shook my head and glanced at my lawyer, hoping he'd come in and help me out. The lawyer came up, stood beside me, and ran off a rap that was even weaker than mine.

The judge nodded at the lawyer, then looked at me and said, "I sentence you to serve twelve years in prison."

The words echoed in my head. *Twelve years!* I felt faint, like the room was reeling about me. I heard screams in the back of the courtroom from my mother and Liz, but was too weak to look behind me with more than a fleeting glance. I looked at my lawyer, who stepped forward and pleaded with the judge. "Your Honor, please take into account the fact that this young man comes from a decent home and has never served prison time before."

The judge was unmoved. "I'm sorry, but he has to learn that he can't go around putting guns to people's heads." He brought down his gavel. "The sentence stands."

I stood there, stunned, the scene surreal. A bailiff walked up behind me and clamped handcuffs to my wrists. I glanced at my family in the rear of the courtroom. Their faces revealed their shock: A tearful Liz held her hands to her face in disbelief. My sobbing mother buried her face in my stepfather's chest. And Reverend Ellis stared blankly at the floor.

When the bailiffs led me from the courtroom, I dropped my head to conceal my misty eyes.

PART TWO

Chapter 17 DENIAL

Blackmen born in the U.S. and fortunate enough to live past the age of eighteen are conditioned to accept the inevitability of prison. For most of us, it simply is the next phase in a sequence of humiliations. Being born a slave in a captive society and never experiencing any objective basis for expectation had the effect of preparing me for the progressively traumatic misfortunes that lead so many blackmen to the prison gate. I was prepared for prison. It required only minor psychic adjustments.
—from *Soledad Brother*, by George Jackson

■ ■ ■

There were several guys crying in the holding cell where I was taken after being sentenced. All were black and all had gotten time. The dude with the lightest sentence, a tall, burly guy with greasy hair, was wailing loudest. He had a measly five years—the sentence I'd hoped for—and was boohooing like a baby. I wanted to strangle him.

We were issued thin mattresses and old, wrinkled jail clothes, and three of us were marched upstairs to a sixth-floor dormitory cell. When the guard closed and locked the doors behind us, I stood there and scanned my new home—I was in jail, the one place in America that black men rule. A gloomy mass of concrete and steel, it was one large open space that looked like an oversized lion's cage. The largest area was a dayroom with two steel picnic tables. At eye level in front of the tables, an old black-and-white TV sat on a wooden stand mounted to the bars. Across the room in the far corner were four fully exposed toilets. Another corner held an open area with two doorless shower stalls. Opposite that section was a sleeping area lined with bunk beds, like in an Army barracks.

The cellblock held about thirty-five inmates. All of them were black. It felt like I was in the Motherland with all those black faces around there. Some guys sat at tables in the dayroom and watched TV, played cards, and talked quietly. When we entered the cellblock, a few inmates glanced up at us, then went back to what they were doing. A few others watched closely in the way that jailhouse veterans study newcomers. I learned over time that the manner in which a person enters a jail cell provides some essential clues to those already there. Seasoned inmates can tell a lot about a guy just by how he acts and what he does when he first walks in. They can tell if it's his first time in jail or if he's a regular. They can sense whether he's scared to death or fearless. A new guy's demeanor determines who approaches him, when, and how.

An inmate walked over to the three of us and motioned for us to follow him to the sleeping area. He showed us vacant bunks, then watched while we got settled in. I picked a lower bunk near a corner, flopped down my mattress, and dived onto it. I stretched out on my back, put my hands behind my head, stared up at the ceiling, and thought about my predicament. I thought, *Twelve years. I'm never gonna make it.* I couldn't conceptualize it. Every time I tried to register the length of the sentence, my brain rejected it, spit it back out. I thought again about the trial. The judge had acted like he took it personal that I robbed that place. I understood what that was all about: I shot and nearly killed Plaz, a black man, and got a thirty-day sentence; I robbed a white business and didn't lay a finger on anybody, and got twelve years. I got the message. I'd gotten it all my life: Don't fuck with white folks.

I was startled by a voice nearby. It was the guy who had met us at the door. "Yo, man, what you in for?"

I answered without looking at him. "I got a robbery beef."

"What'd you rob?"

"A store."

"Oh yeah? How much time did you get?"

That was the wrong question. "Look, man, I don't feel like goin' into all that."

I turned over onto my side, with my back facing him. He rose and left to interview the other newcomers. I lay there and stared through the bars at the ugly mustard-colored wall across the corridor. There were several long, narrow windows along the length of the wall. From my bunk I could look through one window and see the night sky illuminated by thousands of speckled city lights. They were fluorescent streetlamps and moving headlights from cars going back and forth over the Elizabeth River tunnel-bridge to Portsmouth. I thought, *It will be twelve years before I go out there again. Twelve years!* I couldn't believe it. I went to sleep that night wishing I would wake up the next day and come out of this terrible dream.

■ ■ ■

Over the next few days, I noticed that something about this cellblock differed from others I'd been in. There was more order to this one. The inmate who'd greeted me the night before gathered the other newcomers, brought them over to my bunk, and explained the workings of the place. He said the cellblock was reserved for "motivated" inmates. Unlike in the Portsmouth jail, where guys could stay in bed all day and sleep their time away, inmates in this cellblock were required to "program" throughout the day. Inmates who went through the program could earn "good-time," days subtracted from their sentence for good behavior. It was something the jailers allowed to help control inmates, to provide an incentive for them to behave. "Guys from all over the jail try to get transferred here because we run the best shop in the house," the inmate boasted. "We program hard."

I saw inmates working together, filling buckets with water and gathering rags and cleaning detergents. They mopped floors and cleaned the bars and tables. The place smelled like ammonia.

A guy called Chicago ran the cellblock. He was a tall, muscular guy with a thick southern accent, and he was very articulate. The jailers addressed him by some alias, but the inmates had named him "Chicago" because that's where he was from. The word was, he was a street-gang leader who had gotten busted in Norfolk for robbing a bank. Unlike Nutbrain, Charlie Gregg, and me, he was supposedly a black revolutionary, who had done it for a *cause*. Like me, most of the guys in the jail had never spent time around a revolutionary before, much less talked to one. We all hated the white man, but few were committed to fighting him in an organized, disciplined way.

We had meetings in the cellblock, and when Chicago spoke, everybody sat quietly. He talked about what was going right and wrong in the cellblock. He talked with such authority that you assumed he *should* be in charge. When he talked, everybody paid attention, from the hardest-nosed thugs to the most bombed-out junkies. I learned over time that he knew his stuff. He was well versed on philosophy, politics, and law. He knew how to organize against the system. I'd never seen a black man who could handle white people so well. He spoke to white jailers like he was their equal, like they weren't keeping him locked up so much as he was *letting* them detain him for a while.

Chicago had real power in the jail. When he summoned guards to the cellblock, they came. He could have inmates shipped out of the cellblock at will. He had special arrangements with inmate workers in the cafeteria to get the best food. Anybody less dynamic than Chicago would have been roused by guards at night, taken to a solitary cell, and given a thorough ass-whipping to mull over. But if they'd done that to Chicago, it would have started a riot in the jail.

There were no whites in our cellblock. There were so few whites in the jail that the administrators were careful about where they placed them. I think the jailers knew it would have been unwise to put whites in our cellblock with Chicago around. When he preached about the legacy of slavery, he got inmates so fired up that they wanted to strike out, and whites in the cellblock would have been convenient targets.

Chicago also directed our daily "therapy" sessions. The sessions were designed to encourage self-improvement, but he used them for more. He talked about the double standard of justice in America, how blacks regularly got big time for petty crimes and how white boys routinely stole millions, and walked. Chicago also rapped about the need for us to challenge inhumane conditions in the jail. He tied the two topics together so eloquently that it made me feel like I was a political prisoner rather than a two-bit stickup man.

We also took time in those therapy sessions to talk about ourselves. Each prisoner took turns on the "hot seat," where he talked about his background and answered probing questions from other inmates. The object was to get us to look within, to talk honestly about the personality problems and distorted views that landed us in jail.

I learned through those sessions that most of the guys in the cellblock had grown up poor in and around the Church Street area, where Shell Shock and I had done most of our stickups. Many were so poor that they lacked money in their inmate accounts to order toothpaste and other essentials from the canteen. They gambled with cigarettes and bartered to get what they needed. A lot of them were in jail with small bonds that required only $100 or $200 to get out, but they remained confined for months because they couldn't scrape up the chump change from family and friends. Few had made it through high school, and a lot of them were functionally illiterate.

The majority of the guys had been arrested for drug-related crimes, but the criminal charges ran the gamut, from drug dealing to murder to flimflamming. Many of the guys were longtime hustlers who knew each other from the streets and had previously done prison time together.

The most popular old-head in there was a likable junkie in his early

fifties who had been in and out of prison all his life. His name was
Moses Battle. They called him Mo for short. He was the elder states-
man of the cellblock.

Mo Battle came to my bunk one evening after I'd been on the hot
seat. He introduced himself and said he was curious to know how
someone who had spent a year in college had wound up in jail. He
called me "Youngblood" because I was one of the youngest guys in
the cellblock. "Youngblood, you say you from Cavalier Manor?"

"Yeah."

"That's a nice neighborhood. . . . I know some people from Cavalier Manor."

We started talking, and I became as intrigued with Mo Battle as he
was with me. "Youngblood, you say you been to college?"

"Yeah."

He said, "I got my GED. In the penitentiary. I took some college
correspondence courses, too."

Well-spoken and shrewd, Mo Battle was a born teacher who read
a lot and loved to share his wisdom with younger guys like me. We
spent long hours in the evenings, sitting on our bunks, talking. His
favorite subject was philosophy. He saw philosophical meaning in
everything, including some of the petty shit that happened in the
cellblock. If two guys got into a rumble over food or cigarettes, Mo
had a theory about why they'd bumped heads. He theorized a lot
about jail guards, whom he hated. He said the difference in guards and
inmates was so slight that if you took away the guards' uniforms you
couldn't tell them apart. He said guards were "losers with little-dick
complexes" and a serious need to boss somebody—anybody—around.
One day, when one guard, a real knucklehead, came to the block to let
an inmate into the cellblock, Mo Battle said, "Look at him. I betcha
he comes in his pants every time he turns those keys."

Mo Battle taught me how to play chess. I'd never been exposed to
the game on the streets. Like him, the other guys in the cellblock who
knew how to play had learned on previous trips to prison. They
adapted the game to their street perceptions and described tactical
maneuvers in their own language. They called the queen, the most
powerful and versatile piece on the board, the "bitch." A guy describ-
ing how he was checkmated after losing his queen would say that his
opponent "took my bitch and fucked me up."

Mo Battle taught me chess by explaining its philosophical parallels
to life. "You can understand the game of chess if you understand the

game of life, and vice versa," he said. "In life, the person who plots his course and thinks ahead before he acts, wins. It's the same with chess."

One day, I made a move to capture a pawn of his and gave Mo Battle an opening to take a valuable piece. He smiled and said, "You can tell a lot about a person by the way he plays chess. People who think small in life tend to devote a lot of energy to capturing pawns, the least valuable pieces on the board. They think they're playin' to win, but they're not. But people who think big tend to go straight for the king or queen, which wins you the game." I never forgot that. Most guys I knew, myself included, spent their entire lives chasing pawns. The problem was, we thought we were going after kings.

Mo Battle also pointed out the racial symbolism in chess and how it reflected society. "The white pieces always move first, giving them an immediate advantage over the black pieces, just like in life," he said.

The most important thing that Mo Battle taught me was that chess was a game of consequences. He said that, just as in life, there are consequences for every move you make in chess. "Don't make a move without first weighing the potential consequences," he said, "because if you don't, you have no control over the outcome."

I'd never looked at life like that. I had seldom weighed the consequences of anything until *after* I'd done it. I'd do something crazy and then brace myself for the outcome, whatever it happened to be. I had no control over the outcome and no control over my life. When I thought about it, that was a helluva stupid way to live.

But on the chessboard, I eventually saw that I could predict—and, more important, control—outcomes if I considered the consequences of moves before making them. That gave me a whole new way of looking at things.

After Mo Battle shared his philosophy, I got hooked on the game. Over the months, I got a fair enough command of chess to beat most of the other guys and give Mo Battle a run for his money.

I was fascinated by Mo Battle's range of knowledge. He knew a little something about everything. It made me wonder why he wasn't doing more with his life than being a jailhouse sage. After I got to know him better, I asked him about the contradiction I saw in him. "Yo, Mo, if you got all this knowledge, why ain't you runnin' the country?"

As always, he came at me straight. " 'Cause, Youngblood, I'm one a' those dudes that got all the knowledge in the world while I'm locked up, but I can't execute when I get out."

"Why can't you execute?"

The sparkle in Mo Battle's eyes dimmed. "'Cause, man, I'm a junkie."

By his own admission, he was a slave to heroin, which he and other junkies in the cellblock pronounced "her-ron." He'd already written off his life as a failure. "I've already blown it, Youngblood. If I had gone down a different road, I think I could've been a college professor or a lawyer. But I got dealt a different hand. I'm a junkie. I got to have that her-ron."

He told me he had picked himself up and made many new starts after getting out of the penitentiary, but he'd fallen down as often. The frequency of those falls convinced him that the pull of heroin was stronger than his will to resist it. He said he had a loving wife and family who supported him during his trips to prison and through drug treatment programs, but he'd been more loyal to heroin than to them. Most of the criminal charges he caught through the years were either for possession of drugs or for ripping off people to get drug money. "It's like a woman in love with a man who she knows is no good for her, but who makes love to her so well that she can't let him go, even if he drags her into the gutter. That her-ron makes love to me, man, and I can't let it go."

He got his breaks from addiction when he went to prison. He seemed almost grateful. It gave him a chance to dry out, to read, think, flirt with all the possibilities of what he could have become. He and other junkies in the cellblock were taken to the dispensary every day to get their doses of methadone, which helped ease their withdrawal pains. He'd always say to me after he returned, "Don't be like me, Youngblood. You got a chance, man."

I seriously doubted he was right about that.

■ ■ ■

Ordinarily, after being sentenced, guys are shipped away to some prison, but the system was so overcrowded that we in the cellblock had to wait for openings at prison compounds. I spent six miserable months in the Norfolk jail, and after a while the days and nights merged into one continuous run, measured by the meals we ate and the routine we followed. For me, the toughest days were weekends, when I normally would be out partying. Most inmates were subdued on weekends because the weekends made them long more for the streets. I'd lie on my bunk and listen to tunes playing on a portable radio in the cellblock and wonder what was going on in the free world. The singer Minnie Riperton had a hit song out that depressed me. She'd sing, "Loving you is easy 'cause you're beautiful . . ." My heart sank and I thought about Liz every time I heard that song. It seemed that deejays played it fifty times a day, just to mess with me.

I marked time and kept up with what was going on outside by the letters I received from Liz: I learned that a popular guy in Portsmouth named Sweetwolf got forty years; two guys I grew up with got life sentences for robbery and murder; Shane got into a fight at Nick's pool hall downtown and went back and shot out the windows; Cooder caught a robbery charge. It seemed that guys I knew were going to the penitentiary and getting killed, like there was nothing to it.

Charlie Gregg and Nutbrain, who went to trial a month or so after me, each got eight years. They got less time because I was the gunman. They were sent to different floors in the Norfolk jail. We sent messages to each other through inmate hallboys approved to travel throughout the building. Sometimes, we paid inmate cafeteria workers cigarettes to deliver messages when we came through for chow.

Despite the many ways I learned to keep busy, time dragged by slowly. I spent much of that time in denial, believing that something would happen to get me out, that some high-level white people somewhere were going to review my case and realize that the punishment was too harsh for the crime. I had Liz and others write the judge, and even the governor of Virginia, asking them to reconsider my case. But time passed and nothing happened. When reality hit me, I settled in to do my time.

■ ■ ■

I was lying on my bunk on Wednesday, flipping through a magazine, when a guard appeared at the cell. "McCall, front and center! You've got a visitor!"

I jumped up, rushed to the sink for a glimpse in the mirror, and went through the opened gate. The guard escorted me to the tiny visiting room. When I stepped inside, I saw Liz and my parents on the other side of a thick glass partition that separated us. Bampoose, my grandmother, appeared from behind them and waved at me.

I smiled, waved back, and took a seat between several other inmates who were talking quietly through telephones to family members and other loved ones. I lifted the receiver and spoke to Liz. "Hey, baby. How ya doin'?"

"I'm all right. Monroe is O.K. Everybody's doing fine. How about you?"

"I'm fine." Actually, I was annoyed.

Liz picked up on it and said, "What's the matter?"

I asked, "Why did y'all bring Bampoose? I didn't want her to see me in here like this."

She shrugged her shoulders. "I know. But she wanted to come, so we couldn't say no."

"Yeah. I understand."

We talked a few minutes more, then my parents took turns at the telephone. Finally, my stepfather helped Bampoose to the seat. I'd only been locked up a few months, but it seemed Bampoose had aged a lot since I had last seen her. She looked frail and brittle. She put the phone to her face, smiled weakly, and said, "Hey, boy. How you doin'?"

"I'm fine, Bampoose. How 'bout you?"

"All right. They treatin' you good in here?"

"Yeah. The food ain't great, but I'm all right."

As I spoke, I felt myself choking inside. In all the other previous weekly visits from family and friends, I'd been able to put on a strong face, but the sight of Bampoose weakened me. I was ashamed for her to see me in jail. For all our lives, Bampoose had quietly set an example of hard work and sacrifice in our family. In her dignified way, she'd always been there to lend support to everybody and done what she could to help. Everybody wanted Bampoose to think well of them, and I was no exception. There was a song that reminded me of her. It was a tune by the Spinners entitled "Sadie." That was Bampoose's first name, and it seemed as if the song was written expressly about her. The song was about a woman who'd provided strength and support in her family. I thought about Bampoose whenever I heard that song.

> Sadie, don't you know we love you, sweet Sadie?
> Place no one above you, sweet Sadie. . . .

It also bothered me to think that with her rapidly advancing frailty, she might not live to see me get out.

When our ten minutes were up, I felt relieved. That was the one time I was glad to get out of the visiting room. At other times, I looked forward to those Wednesday visits like children look forward to Christmas.

■ ■ ■

On visiting days, the whole cellblock seemed to come alive. We played the radio louder and talked more. Guys waiting for visits paced near the cellblock entrance. Others climbed onto the horizontal supports to the bars to look through the windows, which overlooked the visitors' parking lot. I couldn't help noticing how much they looked like caged monkeys climbing the bars like that. Over time, though, I craved the sight of the outdoors so bad that I climbed, too. If you climbed high enough, you could see visitors drive up, get out of their cars, and walk into the building.

There was something else outdoors that caught my eye. In another parking lot, not far from the visitors' lot, lawyers and other people on official business left their cars while they came to the jail. There was an interesting contrast between the two lots. Most of the folks who parked in the visitors' lot, coming to see inmates, were black. Those parking in the business lot were white. I could distinguish the lawyers. They drove up in sleek Porsches, Mercedeses, and BMWs, and got out in their expensive suits carrying briefcases. I realized that white criminal lawyers had created a cottage industry supported almost exclusively by blacks. They built lavish lifestyles by profiting from our despair, and we cooperated fully, played right into their hands. I'd never thought about it until then.

■ ■ ■

I had known that with Chicago in charge, there was always a possibility of trouble, and sure enough, the kettle blew. Fed up with deteriorating conditions, Chicago called for a boycott of activities until some of the problems were addressed. Under his instructions, no one would go into or out of the cellblock for anything until we got some results. We drafted a list of demands that had to be met: Concrete steps had to be taken to ease overcrowding, improve the quality of our food, and give us prisoners more time to research our cases in the jail's law library. Chicago had requested a meeting with the jail administrator, but the administrator refused to meet with us.

Then, in a show of force, a battalion of guards in helmets and riot gear stood menacingly outside the cellblock entrance, brandishing clubs. The floor captain called out to the inmates bunched up near the entrance: "You all gonna cooperate, or do we have to come in and get you?"

Chicago, of course, spoke for us. "What you think we gonna do? You got to come in here and get us. And don't forget, you got to take some to get some."

When it became clear that the inmates were solidly united, the floor captain tried the old divide-and-conquer routine. "I realize that some of you fellas probably don't want to be in with the troublemakers. We're going to give you a chance to separate yourselves from this mess so you don't get hurt and damage your chances of getting out of here. All those who want to go to another cellblock can step forward now and we'll transfer you, no questions asked."

For a long moment there was silence. Then several inmates stepped forward and walked through the cage leading to the door. In my heart, I wanted to leave, too. I was afraid that if I took part in a riot, I'd lose my good-time or blow my chances of making first parole. But I couldn't bring myself to punk out. It just wasn't in me. So I stood there, ready to go down with everybody else.

When the inmates who had chosen to had left, the guards readied themselves to storm the cellblock. They prepared tear-gas guns to shoot into the place. Following Chicago's instructions, we all dampened towels and wrapped them around our faces to protect us from the gas. Just when it appeared the rumble was about to start, the administrator appeared. He pretended that he had just learned of the disturbance and asked what was going on.

Chicago spoke. "You know what's goin' on. We requested a meeting with you to talk about our grievances, and you sent your henchmen instead."

"That's fine," he told us. "But I can't have you taking over my jail. . . . Get some representatives together and come on down to my office and talk."

We picked Chicago, Mo Battle, and a few others. They left instructions that if they didn't return by the day's end, we should tear up the place. With that done, the standoff ended.

As a result of the meeting, some of the demands were addressed. Inmates were reshuffled to ease overcrowding. Jail officials claimed to have improved the food, but I saw no noticeable difference. The most significant change was our increased ability to use the jail's law library. At least once a week now, inmate representatives were allowed to go there for a few hours and do legal research for themselves and other inmates. Because I was considered "educated," I was among the representatives chosen to do research.

Of course, the jail administrator won the final battle. Under the guise of easing overcrowding, he changed the makeup of the cellblock until there was almost an entirely different group of people. I was sent to another cellblock down the hall. I don't know what happened to Chicago, Mo Battle, and the others after that. I never saw or heard from them again.

Chapter 18 NATIVE SON

One night, the familiar sound of jangling keys echoed outside my new cellblock. I looked up and saw two white men walking briskly down the hallway toward the entrance. One was a jail guard. The other, walking a step or two ahead, was a tall, influential-looking man who appeared to be in his fifties. Wearing an expensive suit and a white shirt unbuttoned at the collar, the man looked like he had just ended a long, tiring business day. When the two reached the entrance, the guard opened the door, let the man inside, then closed and locked the gate. The man stood there for a long moment, sighed wearily, and scanned the room.

By now, everybody in the cellblock had turned from what they were doing to study the newcomer. There were a few other whites in the cellblock, but he was different from anybody I'd seen come through those gates. Everything in this man's dress and manner suggested that he came from the upper reaches of a world I had only read and talked about. He had that saunaed, pampered look about him and seemed to be the kind of white man who was unaccustomed to being inconvenienced, let alone locked up.

Apparently unnerved by the prisoners' glares, the newcomer turned around, leaned his head against the cell bars, and stared out into the empty hallway. The guard returned minutes later and handed him a mattress and a set of crumpled jail clothes. A white inmate walked over and steered the new man to an empty bunk. They chatted quietly a moment, then the inmate walked away, leaving him there to get settled. I learned later from that inmate that my initial take on the newcomer was on the money: An executive at some high-powered business firm, the man had been busted for a white-collar rip-off.

He sat on his bunk and looked around, bewildered. I could tell by the tortured expression on his fleshy face that this was his worst nightmare. For him, the world had turned upside down and inside out: Black people were in the majority, and they ran things; white people were in the minority, and they were oppressed. Clearly, he had never dreamed he'd spend a minute even passing through our world.

He stayed anchored to his bunk the remainder of the night and part of the next day. He was still glued there that afternoon when we gathered in the dayroom to begin our group therapy session. Just as we were about to start, a guy called Titty Head (his head was shaped like a woman's breast) shouted to the newcomer: "Yo, Mr. Executive! I know you ain't used to bein' told what to do, but you gotta bring your pompous ass out here just like everybody else!"

The man's pasty white face turned beet red. With all eyes on him, he rose, walked slowly out of the sleeping area, and took a seat at one of the steel tables. We started the session, sending inmates to the hot seat. After several guys had spoken, Titty Head turned to the newcomer. "Okay, Mr. Executive, it's your turn to bare your soul."

I knew what Titty Head was doing. Everybody knew. He was taking a rare chance to strike back at somebody who represented the very system that made his life hell. This was his once-in-a-lifetime shot, a chance to get even, and he intended to milk it for all it was worth. We asked the man a lot of offensive, deeply personal questions, and he responded, trying to hide his resentment at having to answer to people he probably considered beneath himself. Titty Head in particular hit him with a lot of questions framed more in the form of accusations. "I bet you dog niggahs out on the job every chance you get, don't you?!"

Throughout the grilling, the few other whites in the cellblock kept quiet, taking care not to jeopardize their own fragile safety. I sat watching, enjoying the *hell* out of it, loving the sight of a powerful white man squirming in the clutches of powerless blacks. I suspected he felt indicted by his whiteness as never before, and I hoped he felt at that moment the same way I'd felt for much of my life: like an alien in a hostile world where he couldn't win; like the victim of recurring injustices against which there were no appeals.

We kept the newcomer on that hot seat and fucked with his head for hours. When the meeting ended, he retreated to his bunk, humiliated, and sulked the rest of the day. The following day, the brothers rode him some more, on the hot seat and off. They looked him up and down in the shower like he was a piece of shit and barked orders at him, reminding him constantly that his life was now subject to a whole new set of rules.

After a few days, the newcomer got out on bond. When the guard called his name and yelled, "Pack your bags!," he nearly *flew* to the gate and didn't even bother to gather most of his belongings. As he left, he looked through the bars one final time at the thirty or so black men eyeing him. His lips parted as though he were about to say something, but he kept quiet and walked on away.

Whites in general caught hell in jail, especially in my new cellblock, which was less disciplined and far rowdier than the other one I'd been in. White junkies, whose drug dealings had often taken them to inner-city spots, did well because they'd grown comfortable around blacks. But that was less the case with those sheltered, smug whites, such as that businessman we'd put through hell. They wore their racial fears and prejudices on their sleeves.

At night, when the lights went out, those whites who couldn't hold their own were harrassed, sexually and otherwise, by the wolves. One morning, I woke up and saw a young, long-haired white guy sitting on his bunk, staring dejectedly at the floor. His lips were swollen and his eyes were black and puffy from an apparent thumping he'd taken the night before. He was taken to the dispensary, then placed in protective custody. I heard through the rumor mill that he'd been raped and beaten by a few wolves while everyone else was asleep. Eventually, several brothers were fingered and charged with the rape.

Those and similar incidents involving whites reminded me that our little saying in Cavalier Manor rang true everywhere, especially in jail: "Payback is a motherfucka."

■ ■ ■

There were moments in that jail when the confinement and heat nearly drove me mad. At those times, I desperately needed to take my thoughts beyond the concrete and steel. When I felt restless tension rising, I'd try anything to calm it. I'd slap-box with other inmates until I got exhausted, or play chess until my mind shut down. When all else failed, I'd pace the cellblock perimeter like a caged lion. Sometimes, other inmates fighting the temptation to give in to madness joined me, and we'd pace together, round and round, and talk for hours about anything that got our minds off our misery.

I eventually found a better way to relieve the boredom. I noticed that some inmates broke the monotony by volunteering for certain jobs in the jail. Some mopped the halls, and others worked in the dispensary or the kitchen. When the inmate librarian was released from jail, I asked for and was given his job. I began distributing books on the sixth floor as part of a service provided by the Norfolk Public Library. A couple of times a week, I pushed a cart to each cellblock and let inmates choose books and place orders for literature not on the cart. I enjoyed the library work. It gave me a chance to get out into the halls and walk around, and to stick my face to the screens on the floor windows and inhale fresh air.

Beyond the short stories I'd read in high school, I hadn't done much reading. Naturally, while working for the library, I leafed through more books than I normally would have. One day, shortly after starting the job, I picked up a book featuring a black man's picture on the cover. It was titled *Native Son*, and the author was Richard Wright. I leafed through a few pages in the front of the book, and couldn't put it down. The story was about a confused, angry young black man named Bigger Thomas, whose racial fears lead him to accidentally suffocate a white woman. In doing so, he delivers himself into the hands of the very people he despises and fears.

I identified strongly with Bigger and the book's narrative. He was twenty, the same age as me. He felt the things I felt, and, like me, he wound up in prison. The book's portrait of Bigger captured all those conflicting feelings—restless anger, hopelessness, a tough facade among blacks and a deep-seated fear of whites—that I'd sensed in myself but was unable to express. Often, during my teenage years, I'd felt like Bigger—headed down a road toward a destruction I couldn't ward off, beaten by forces so large and amorphous that I had no idea how to fight back. I was surprised that somebody had written a book that so closely reflected my experiences and feelings.

I read that book every day, and continued reading by the dim light of the hall lamps at night, while everyone slept. On that early morning when I finished reading *Native Son*, which ends with Bigger waiting to go to the electric chair, I broke down and sobbed like a baby. There is one passage that so closely described how I felt that it stunned me. It is a passage where a lawyer is talking to Bigger, who has given up hope and is waiting to die:

> You're trying to believe in yourself. And every time you try to find a way to live, your own mind stands in the way. You know why that is? It's because others have said you were bad and they made you live in bad conditions. When a man hears that over and over and looks about him and sees that life is bad, he begins to doubt his own mind. His feelings drag him forward and his mind, full of what others say about him, tells him to go back. The job in getting people to fight and have faith is in making them believe in what life has made them feel, making them feel that their feelings are as good as others'.

After reading that, I sat up in my bunk, buried my face in my hands, and wept uncontrollably. I cried so much that I felt relieved. It was like I had been carrying those feelings and holding in my pain for years, keeping it pushed into the back of my mind somewhere.

I was unaccustomed to dealing with such deep feelings. Occasionally, I'd opened up to Liz, but not a lot. I was messed up inside, empty and afraid, just like Bigger. *Native Son* confirmed for me that my fears *weren't* imagined and that there were rational reasons why I'd been hurting inside.

I developed through my encounter with Richard Wright a fascination with the power of words. It blew my mind to think that somebody could take words that described exactly how I felt and put them together in a story like that. Most of the books I'd been given in school were about white folks' experiences and feelings. I spent all that time learning about damned white folks, like my reality didn't exist and wasn't valid to the rest of the world. In school, the only time we'd really focused on the lives of black people was during Black History Week, which they set aside for us to learn the same old tired stories about Booker T. Washington and a few other noteworthy, dead black folks I couldn't relate to. But in *Native Son* I found a book written about a plain, everyday brother like myself. That turned me on in a big way and inspired me to look for more books like that.

Before long, I was reading every chance I got, trying to more fully understand why my life and the lives of friends had been so contained and predictable, and why prison—literally—had become a rite of passage for so many of us. I found books that took me places I'd never dreamed I could travel to and exposed me to a range of realities that seemed as vast as the universe itself.

Once, after reading a book of poems by Gwendolyn Brooks, I wrote to her, not really expecting to receive a reply. She wrote me back and sent me an inspirational paperback of hers titled *Aloneness*. I was thrilled that a well-known black writer like her had taken the time to respond to me.

I was most attracted to black classics, such as Malcolm X's autobiography. Malcolm's tale helped me understand the devastating effects of self-hatred and introduced me to a universal principle: that if you change your self-perception, you can change your behavior. I concluded that if Malcolm X, who had also gone to prison, could pull his life out of the toilet, then maybe I could, too.

Up to that point, I'd often wanted to think of myself as a baad nigger, and as a result, I'd tried to act like one. After reading about Malcolm X, I worked to get rid of that notion and replace it with a positive image of what I wanted to become. I walked around silently repeating to myself, "You are an intelligent-thinking human being; you are an intelligent-thinking human being . . . ," hoping that it would sink in and help me begin to change the way I viewed myself.

Malcolm X made his conversion through Islam. I'd seen Muslims selling newspapers and bean pies on the streets, but I didn't know anything about their religion. I was drawn to Christianity, mostly because it was familiar. I hadn't spent much time in church. It seemed that all they did in churches I'd been to was learn how to justify suffering at the hands of white folks. But now there were Christian ministers active at the jail, and I became interested. They came around about once a week and talked to inmates through the bars, prayed with them and read Scripture. I started talking with them about God and about life in general.

It wasn't hard to accept the possibility that there was a higher force watching over me. When I looked back at my life, I concluded that there had been far too many close calls—times when I could have offed somebody or gotten killed myself—for me to believe I had survived solely on luck. I wondered, *Why didn't that bullet strike Plaz in the heart when I shot him? Why didn't I pull the trigger on that McDonald's manager when he tried to get away? And why wasn't I on the corner the night my stick partners were shot?* Unable to come up with rational answers to those questions, I reasoned that God must have been pulling for me.

My interest in spiritual things also came from a need to reach out at my most powerless point and tap into a higher power, something beyond me and, at the same time, within me. I longed for a sense of wholeness that I had never known but sensed I was entitled to. I set out to learn more about my spiritual self, and I began exploring the Bible with other inmates who held Bible studies some nights in the cellblock.

At some point, I also got a library copy of the book—*As a Man Thinketh*—that Reverend Ellis had given me in college. I immediately understood what he had been trying to get across: that thinking should be an *active* process that, when cultivated, can change a person's behavior, circumstances, and, ultimately, his fate.

When I first started reading, studying, and reflecting on the information I got from books, I had no idea where it all might lead. Really, it didn't matter. I was hungry for change and so excited by the sense of awakening I glimpsed on the horizon that the only thing that mattered was that I had made a start. I often recited the Scripture that Reverend Ellis had given me to read before I was sentenced: "Everything works together for the good of those that love God, for those who are called according to His purpose." *If that's true*, I thought, *maybe I can get something positive out of this time in prison.* It sure didn't seem like it. But it made me feel better just thinking it might be possible.

Chapter 19 HOMECOMING

Although I'd resisted the idea of marriage when I was on the street, near the end of my six-month stint in the Norfolk jail I was eager to take the vows with Liz. I came up with a lot of reasons to justify wanting to do it, but the bottom line was, on some level I wanted to make sure she'd stay around and help me do my time. Prisoners often cling to anybody they think can help ease the pain of doing time. It gives them a greater sense of security knowing that somebody has vowed to suffer through that hell with them. I saw dudes in prison claim to fall madly in love with old women friends they didn't look at twice on the streets. A woman could be cross-eyed, knock-kneed, and pigeon-toed and have the I.Q. of a brick, but to a dude who's been locked up a long time she's a thing of beauty and a treasure, sure enough.

When I raised the idea of marriage to Liz in a letter, she eagerly agreed. She'd wanted to get married before then. We'd gotten as far as the parking lot leading to the justice of the peace office once, then I made up some lame excuse to back out, leaving her in tears.

Liz and I got our blood tests and were moving forward with the planned jailhouse wedding ceremony when something unexpected happened. One fall morning in October, a week or so before the wedding date, a guard came to the cellblock entrance and shouted, "McCall, pack your bags!" It was my day to be shipped off to prison. I forgot all about getting married after that.

I was handcuffed and shackled to several other inmates and taken to a waiting van that had thick mesh wire covering the rear windows and contained two wooden benches on either side of the rear loading area, where we sat. We rode through the Norfolk tunnel and into Portsmouth, then headed onto Interstate 264. Midway along the highway, I caught glimpses of Cavalier Manor near Victory Boulevard. It felt creepy riding past my old stomping ground. It was a painful reminder that my life was now controlled totally by other people. As we rode along and Cavalier Manor faded from view, it dawned on me all over again that it would be years before I passed this way and saw that area again.

After two hours, the familiar city streets gave way to rural roads. I saw farmland, herds of livestock, and stately houses sitting on rolling hills. It looked like the kind of place where all the people hang big American flags from their front porches.

We got to Southampton Correctional Center, eighty or so miles from Portsmouth, and were taken to a reception and diagnostic center, a basement facility called the Receiving Unit. A large dormitory lined with about fifty bunk beds on each side of a room, it looked like a bomb shelter inside. The Receiving Unit was a way station for the prison system. Over the course of a month, inmates who came through there were given a battery of psychological tests and physical exams and were classified before being shipped to various prisons throughout Virginia. They were also assigned prison numbers while there.

My number was 10-63-83. That number became more important to me than my name. It was used to identify my mail; guards addressed me by it when calling me to the visiting room; it was stenciled onto my clothes and stamped into my brain. It became so much a part of my identity that years later, when I got out of prison, I used part of it as my secret computer code at work and have used variations of it for combination locks and bank-card codes.

Unlike prisoners in the general population at Southampton, who went in and out of their buildings every day, Receiving Unit inmates remained indoors round the clock, except at mealtimes. Each day we marched single file down the long sidewalks to the cafeteria to eat. Like clockwork, the established Southampton inmates lined up along the sidewalks at our evening mealtime to study us newcomers as we walked past. Some wolves whistled and taunted guys who looked sweet or scared to them. "Yo, hey, baby! Hey! Wha's your name?! You need some candy or cigarettes? You need somebody to take care a' you?" Others looked for friends or relatives they'd heard were coming through the Receiving Unit. Several times, I spotted homeboys. We acknowledged each other with waves and nods, but we weren't allowed to stop and talk.

Every other day or so, a handful of guys were shipped out of the Receiving Unit to other institutions or sent upstairs into the general population at Southampton. Administrators wouldn't tell us in advance where we'd be shipped to serve our time. I wanted to stay at

Southampton, where there were lots of homeboys from Portsmouth and Cavalier Manor. Eventually, I got my wish. One morning, my number was called and I was sent upstairs, along with several other inmates.

On the day I arrived on the yard, a group of the homeboys—Joe Ham, Bonaparte, Feetball, Marvin, Joe Burns, Pearly Blue, Tony Rome, and Chilly Bear—were standing around waiting, eager to hear the latest word from the streets. Some of those guys had been locked up for years and had no idea how much the block had changed since they'd left. Some wanted updates on Scobie-D and other well-known hoods ruling the streets. Others asked about girls they'd dated or wanted to date. "Yo, man, whatever happened to that big-leg gal who lived in Freedom Court?"

"She got knocked up and had a baby."

"What's that girl named Ramona doing these days?"

"She doing the same old same-old. I hadn't seen her much before I left the street."

We talked for hours and caught up on each other's lives. They offered to help me adjust in any way they could: choice food stolen from the kitchen, specially pressed clothes from the laundry, "Anything you need, homeboy, just let us know."

I went to my cell that evening riding a cloud. The comfort of familiar faces briefly made me forget the circumstances that had brought us together. For a minute there, it felt like homecoming in Cavalier Manor.

■ ■ ■

Except for the ever-present iron bars and the tall barbed-wire fence surrounding the place, Southampton vaguely resembled a college campus. It had five dormitory buildings, a large cafeteria, an administration building, a canteen, and a chapel, all of which ringed a huge courtyard.

My new living quarters were located in a long building painted an ugly lime green inside and lined from front to back with jail cells on two tiers. I was placed in a second-tier cell about the size of your standard bathroom. It contained a steel bunk with a paper-thin mattress, a small knobless sink, a metal storage cabinet, and a seatless commode placed near the cell door in full view of everybody who walked past. The cell was cramped, but it was mine. After living in dormitories for half a year, I felt like I was at the fucking Waldorf. I cherished my cell for what little privacy it afforded. I could retreat there evenings after chow, and chill, all alone, the rest of the night.

I noticed that some cats took an almost obsessive pride in their cell homes. They carefully decorated them with matching bathroom towels that they hung over sinks, used to adorn storage cabinets, and draped over cell windows as makeshift curtains. Some inmates got really grand and bought thick, expensive towels in coordinated, rich colors to make their cells look prison-plush. You couldn't tell *them* that their cribs weren't laid out. They acted like they lived in posh, high-rise condos instead of stinking jail cells. Watching them made me realize right away how you can lose perspective after being locked up a long time.

Inmates lived in two types of buildings. There were three C buildings, which had cells, and two R buildings, which had rooms. Southampton administrators had instituted a behavior-modification system where they moved inmates gradually from C-1 to more comfortable buildings and granted more privileges as inmates went for stretches of time without getting into trouble.

Inmates in C-1, where I started, were locked in their cells evenings and let out only to shower. Those who kept a clean record for, say, four months were "promoted" to the C-2 building, where they were allowed to play cards, mingle, and watch TV. Most inmates worked to get to the top of the two R buildings. They got their own room with a key, and were granted more freedom to come and go as they pleased. Advancing from a C to an R building was roughly the equivalent of moving from public housing to the sprawling suburbs.

C-1 was the wildest building at Southampton. More than half the guys there were old-timers who didn't give a shit about moving up. Some of those cats had so much time to serve that they had no hope of getting out and no incentive to follow rules. They couldn't care less if they got into a fight and made a short-timer miss parole. The hard-nosed among them walked around posturing like they were the baaddest niggers in the world, wearing vicious scowls and repeating Southampton's macho credo: "If you ain't no killer, don't fuck with me."

That bunch didn't worry me. I knew many of them were frontin', playing crazy-nigger roles to keep pressure off themselves. What concerned me most was the cats who were truly insane. Like the one inmate who walked around, eyes bulging, staring at the sky, and the many others who had that long-gone, faraway look. I wondered if one of them, in a fit of blind hysteria, might shank somebody out of the blue. I didn't want to be standing near one of the crazies when he went off.

In those first few months in C-1, I spent a lot of time taking the pulse of prison life, learning to identify the wolves, the hustlers, the thumpers, the loudmouth bluffs, the thieves, and the few progressive inmates in my building. From my second-floor perch, I saw all kinds of transactions among guys handing off contraband and paying off debts with cigarettes and cookies as they passed each other on the first floor.

By watching others' mistakes, I also learned some of the dos and don'ts of prison life: like, don't be seen getting too chummy with administrators—it makes the hustlers paranoid. And don't wear sling-shots. That's the prison name for men's briefs. It never occurred to me that there was anything wrong with them until I saw a white inmate, a newcomer like me, walk past my cell on his way to the showers wearing Fruit of the Looms. When everybody started whistling and making catcalls at him, I got the message: Men's briefs are tight-fitting, and anything tight-fitting is an invitation to trouble.

I also learned that some prison guards preyed on inmates as much as prisoners preyed on each other. One night, after the lights were turned out, I was reading by the light of the hall lamps. A white prison guard walked quietly to the nearby cell of a known black homosexual, glanced around nervously, then unlocked the door and let the inmate out. He escorted the inmate to the back of the building, toward the solitary-confinement cells. They remained there a good half hour before the guard returned the inmate to his cell. It didn't take a rocket scientist to figure out what they had done.

I spent most of my time reading, writing letters, and memorizing new words. After struggling through *Das Kapital*, by Karl Marx, I realized that my limited vocabulary made me miss the full meaning of much that I read. I decided that whenever I came across an unfamiliar word, I'd stop reading, look it up in the dictionary, memorize it, and use it in a sentence before I resumed reading. I then recorded the new words in a loose-leaf notebook and practiced using them in conversations. It took me months sometimes to get through a single book, but my speed and comprehension got better over time.

At some point in my reading, I ran across Rudyard Kipling's poem "If," which was so inspiring to me that I memorized it and recited it as my mantra every day. It's ironic that I got so deep into something written by a person who is widely considered a racist. But the poem has no racist overtones. In fact, it has a universal appeal. That poem challenged me to reexamine self-imposed limitations and encouraged me to fight nagging fears that I had ruined my life beyond repair. I recited it to myself sometimes after visits from Liz and my son, Monroe, who was then two years old. I recited it when I felt discouraged or blue. Later, when I got out of prison and went through other hard times working with white folks and trying to find my way, I recited it to help me keep perspective. One of my favorite sections in that poem said:

> *If you can dream*
> *and not make dreams your master.*
> *If you can think*
> *and not make thoughts your aim.*
> *If you can meet with Triumph and Disaster*
> *and treat those two impostors just the same . . .*

I was sitting outside on one of the building stoops, staring across the prison yard one day, when two of my homies, Joe Ham and Pearly Blue, came into view about fifty yards away. They bopped down the sidewalk toward the chapel and approached two white inmates standing there. They talked a moment, then Joe Ham hauled off and sucker-punched one of the whites in the face. Pearly Blue tackled the guy's partner, and the four of them got it on. Reflexively, I got up and started to run over to jump into it. Then I stopped and reconsidered. In that instant, a bunch of guards ran over and broke up the rumble. They slapped handcuffs on all four inmates and led them away to solitary confinement.

The word on the yard was that the fight stemmed from a gang-related beef over the sale of mash, homemade whiskey that some inmates sold. Joe Ham and Pearly Blue were tried by a prison panel and then each was placed in a dark isolation cell, where inmates were punished for breaking rules. Had I gone over to help them, I would have gotten locked up, too, and hurt my chances of making first parole.

The incident brought home the fact that there was a lot going on at Southampton that I needed to avoid—and made me realize that I needed to figure out where I fit in. Gang rivalries ran deep, and my homies from Cavalier Manor were in the thick of it. They led one of the two largest gangs at Southampton. Known as the Tidewater Gang, it was made up of inmates from Portsmouth, Norfolk, Newport News, and Virginia Beach. Its main rival was the Richmond Gang, made up of inmates from Richmond, Virginia's largest city. The Richmond Gang's members could be recognized by their dark, Ray Charles–like sunshades and the black silk stocking caps on their heads. The Tidewater and Richmond gangs each had its own football and basketball teams, a sizable interest in the mash marketed at Southampton, and a firm handle on drugs, street liquor, and other contraband smuggled into the place. They even competed for control of gay men—whom they called "boys"—who came to Southampton.

There were other, weaker gangs made up of black inmates from smaller locales, and gangs of whites, who banded together for protection. There were more whites at Southampton than in the Norfolk jail, but still, they were the minority. Inmates with no gang ties and those from other states had to fend for themselves. Those who couldn't hold their own standing by themselves got eaten alive, turned into somebody's boy, ripped off, or taken advantage of in some other way.

The gang scene posed a dilemma for me. Hanging with my homeboys offered guaranteed backup, which practically every inmate needs to live in peace. But it also made it harder for me to break with the past. Once it became clear what some of my homies were into, I spent less time with them and joined a group of guys who had formed a Christian fellowship. In weekly meetings held in the basement of one building, we read Scripture, sang, and talked about God. Some of my homies thought I was faking a religious conversion to try to make parole the first time up, but the spiritual change was very real to me. For the first time in my life, I was consciously involved in an ongoing search to understand the meaning of my existence, and the searching itself gave me a sense of purpose that I'd never known.

It didn't take long for my homies to notice that I'd distanced myself from them. One day, Pearly Blue came to me and said, "Yo, man, why ain't you hangin' with the fellas?"

I told him, "Hey, man, you know I'm trying to move in a different direction. I can't hang out and do that too. That would make me a hypocrite. . . . Nobody don't have a problem with that, do they?"

"Naw, man, we just noticed that you hang with them Christian dudes and always reading books and shit. That's no problem with us. But you know, other guys on the yard might start thinking maybe you turned to God 'cause you can't handle the time. They think you weak when you get into that Christian bag. . . . You know, this ain't exactly the best place to be turning no other cheek."

I saw clearly what Pearly Blue was getting at. He was trying to tell me that I couldn't afford to have my head tucked so high in the clouds that I couldn't watch my back. The environment was full of wolves looking for weaknesses to exploit, especially in newcomers.

Safety was one concern, but for me the real issue was allegiance, which I'd always felt strongly about. I was torn between old alliances and a new commitment to change. At times, especially on warm sunny days when all the gangs hung together on the prison yard, it felt awkward not being part of the hometown crowd. Torn between impulses to hang with my homies and break those ties, I played it by ear, hanging out with them sometimes and studying in the Christian fellowship most of the time. I wrestled with major questions: What if a rumble broke out involving my hometown gang? Would I help my homies or stand on the sidelines like I'd done with Pearly Blue and Joe Ham? If I wasn't committed to them, could I expect their help if I got into a beef with a member of another gang? I didn't know how I'd respond to certain situations, and it bothered me sometimes.

■ ■ ■

The prison was actually a large farm. Inmates produced all kinds of vegetables and raised livestock, which was used to feed prisoners at Southampton and at other institutions statewide. Inmates were paid thirty-five cents daily for their work. I often thought that if I ever got out of prison, I would jump at the chance to work for minimum wage.

Most of my homies had enough seniority to get plum jobs—in the laundry, the kitchen, the dental lab. As a new inmate, I was assigned to the "gun gang"; each morning, we were taken by truck to pick peas and other vegetables in the vast farm fields.

Down on all fours in rows of vegetables, plucking up food in the sweltering heat, I couldn't help wondering what it must have been like for my ancestors to toil like this with no hope of being freed. Always nearby was the symbolic "ol' massa," a white, shotgun-toting prison guard.

The entire compound seemed like one big plantation. The warden and his assistant were white, as were most of the top administrators. Some things let me know that a number of the whites who worked at Southampton had that southern, slaveholding mind-set, too. I saw it in the way they treated some inmates, especially one dude who worked with me on the gun gang. We called him Heavy. He was tall, fat, and jovial; the cat loved to laugh. He was uneducated, and the white supervisors made fun of him, to his face and behind his back. One day, my supervisor called over one of his white friends and said, "Watch this." Then he called Heavy over and said, "Tell us about niggers and flies, Heavy."

Heavy smiled broadly and recited:

Niggers and flies, I despise.
The more I see niggers, the more I like flies.

Then my supervisor and the other white man looked at each other—in the way that white people communicate with each other with their eyes when blacks are around—and slapped their thighs and laughed, like there was some deeper, private joke between them.

Although he was a likable guy, I hated Heavy for being that stupid. I pulled him aside a few times and said, "Man, don't you know they making fun of you?"

He answered, "Man, I ain't worried about them crackers. I just let them think I'm laughing with them. I'm smarter than them."

"So what are you getting out of it if you're outsmarting them?"

Heavy got serious. "I'm gettin' the pleasure of laughin' at them."

Sometimes, I wanted to take my shovel and bust him *and* our supervisor in the head.

I suppose the gun gangs had a meaningful purpose beyond providing us with food, but if there was some deeper value it was lost on me. To me, it was the kind of demeaning, backbreaking labor my stepfather had tried to prepare me for, the very kind I'd resisted most of my life. It threw me into a serious funk. One day, the farmwork got to me so much I rebelled outright. I was in a bad mood, feeling sorry for myself and wondering how much more I could take, when my supervisor barked at several inmates and me. "Load those feed bags onto that truck!"

I bent down and tested the weight of the bags, then protested, "These are hundred-pound bags! Can't we double up and throw them on the truck?"

When he ordered me again to do as he said, I exploded. "I ain't doin' it! Slavery is over! I'm sick a' this shit!"

Inmates stopped working and stared, the gun guard stiffened, and the supervisor moved closer and squinted his blue eyes threateningly at me. "I'm only gonna ask you one more time."

I glared back and stood my ground. "I ain't doin' it!"

The supervisor wrote up a complaint and sent me back to the hill, where I was thrown into lockup. When I thought about what I'd done, I realized that in my anger I'd forgotten to apply Mo Battle's principle of consequences. In that one act, I had lost the freedom I had, spoiling my prison record, and hurt my chances of making first parole. I got depressed, and then resignation set in, the same resignation that had taken over when I was arrested. It says, *Now you've done it. You've gone too far. You failed to consider consequences. Now it's time to pay.*

Within a few days, I was taken before a prison panel. I fully expected to be found guilty and placed in isolation. But I got lucky. The supervisor had charged that I "refused to work." The panel pointed out that I hadn't refused to work. I'd simply refused to lift those heavy bags alone. Because of the inaccurate wording in the supervisor's complaint, the panel dropped the charges.

I took that ordeal as a sign from God and a warning that I needed to work on my attitude. It made me think of a message I'd read in a book by Gwendolyn Brooks: *"When handed a lemon, make lemonade."* I decided to try.

After returning to the gun gang, I started working harder, doing more than my share and also doing things without having to be told. Nothing—not even shoveling shit from cow and pig pens—bothered me. I eagerly cleaned the pens and tossed hundred-pound feed bags and was the first to jump off the truck when we rode to the fields to herd cattle, repair broken fences, and feed the other livestock. After a while, I discovered that farmwork wasn't so bad after you got used to it. I realized that it's your attitude about the work you do that can determine how pleasant or unpleasant it is. For the first time, I understood what my stepfather meant when he said there was dignity in all work.

A few times, when my stepfather and my mother came to visit me at Southampton, I wanted to tell him what I'd realized. The words formed in my mind, and it seemed they got as far as my throat, but they wouldn't come out. So I held it all in and hoped he'd know someday.

■ ■ ■

Not long after the hearing, I was assigned to one of the most prestigious white-collar inmate jobs at Southampton: working in the prison library. I thought I'd died and gone to heaven. Getting that job meant I had access to all the newspapers, periodicals, and books in the library. It meant that I didn't have to work under slave conditions in the rain and cold with an armed white man standing over me. It meant I could finally go to work and return in clean clothes.

The library was a two-room building attached to Southampton's school, where inmates studied to get their GEDs. The larger of the two rooms was the area where inmates came in after work and on weekends.

There, they browsed through the books on the shelves, sat and read newspapers and magazines, or chatted quietly among themselves.

My job was to keep updated newspapers and periodicals on racks and shelves, to check books in and out, and to keep the place clean. I also led library-orientation seminars for new inmates. That helped me work on my speaking skills. Most days, after doing my chores, I browsed through books and magazines, reading anything that even remotely interested me. I loved being in a place where there were so many books. For once in my life it made me feel that I had total access to the world. I learned also that being able to find information is as valuable a tool as you'll ever pick up. I discovered how to use reference guides to research anything I wanted. I felt a sense of accomplishment whenever I tracked down some esoteric fact. And my getting the new job demonstrated something that hadn't been so clear before: that education commands respect, wherever you go. Compared to most inmates, I was educated, and that distinction benefited me—it helped me get that plum job.

The head librarian was a tall white dude named Mr. McCaffrey. A pipe-smoking, easygoing man, he preferred to stay in the back room ordering books and reading rather than hang out front.

Two other inmates worked in the library with me. One was a guy called Hop, a former member of the Black Panther party, who was doing ten years for armed robbery. Hop was very intellectual. We played chess and often debated whether Christianity was relevant to the black man's struggle for self-determination in America. Hop said Christianity was "the white man's tool, another way to keep niggers nonviolent so white folks can keep cracking them over the head." I argued that Christianity, specifically the black church, had always played a role in the black man's struggle, right on up through the civil rights movement.

My other library co-worker was a strange-acting white guy named Lee Hargrave. He was doing a life sentence in connection with the deaths of several elderly people who died on his shift at the Richmond hospital where he worked. It was one of the most highly publicized murder cases in the history of the state.

When Hargrave first got to Southampton, a short time after I got there, a rumor spread that he'd be assigned to work in the dispensary. Some inmates threatened to protest. Prison administrators calmed those fears by assigning him to the library.

For good reasons, Hargrave was paranoid. He knew he was being closely watched by everybody, inmates and guards alike. Wherever he went out on the yard, inmates stared at him and whispered. He responded by withdrawing as completely as possible from prison life. He never ate in the cafeteria with other inmates. He ate only snacks that he bought from the canteen and food that his parents brought him during Saturday visits. He spent most of his time after work in his cell, even when we moved up to other buildings.

Hargrave's face was a deathly white, and he wore large, box-shaped glasses. He always had dark rings around his eyes, like he had sleep problems. Although he was heavyset, he had a big waterhead that looked like it belonged on another, bigger body. He constantly bit his fingernails down to stubs. He wore cheap sneakers and always looked nervous, uptight, like he was about to break.

Hargrave's arrival at Southampton gave me my first sense of the strange pecking order that exists in prison. Under that order, guys serving time for murder and assault command the most respect because their crimes make them seem super-baad. Those locked up for robberies and dealing drugs can boast of being hustlers, and they are also admired. But people locked up for crimes such as rape, or crimes against the elderly or children, are considered weirdos and are sometimes threatened and attacked. Because of the nature of Hargrave's crime, Southampton administrators were concerned about his safety.

Hargrave came from an upper-middle-class family that lived in an exclusive Richmond suburb. It was evident that he'd spent little if any time around blacks. When he was assigned to work in the library, he took his time warming to Hop and me. I got to know him better after he joined the Christian fellowship group. Several of us in the group suspected that Hargrave might have joined more for protection from the wolves than out of some deep religious conviction. But we welcomed him anyway. Often, when inmates saw me talking with him, they'd pull me aside later and ask, "What's he like, man? Do you think he killed all those people?"

Initially, I always told them I thought he was too meek to do something like that. But over time, some things he did changed my mind. Once, after someone broke into his room and stole some of his food, Hargrave laced some of his other food with poison to lay a trap for the thief. I saw then that he was a sickie with a murderous heart.

It was the kind of incident that reminded me that I was in a sick place, a place that was to be my home for the next few years. Somehow, I was supposed to live in the midst of all that sickness and come out rehabilitated, healthy. Talk about solutions. It don't get any more messed up than that.

Chapter 20

TIME

I was standing in my cell doorway, checking out the scene on the floor below, when a white convict appeared in the doorway across from mine. He stood stark still and looked straight ahead. Without saying a word, he lifted a razor blade in one hand and began slashing the wrist of the other, squirting blood everywhere. He kept slashing, rapid-fire, until finally he dropped the razor and slumped to the floor, knocking his head against the bars as he went down.

Other inmates standing in their doorways spotted him and yelled, "Guard! Guard! Guard!" Guards came running, rushed the unconscious inmate to the dispensary, and ordered a hallboy to clean up the pool of blood oozing down the walkway. Later, when I asked the hallboy why the dude had tried to take himself out, he said, "That *time* came down on him and he couldn't take the pressure. You know them white boys can't handle time like us brothers. They weak."

It was a macho thing for a guy to be able to handle his time. Still, every once in a while, time got to everybody, no matter how tough they were. Hard time came in seasonal waves that wiped out whole groups of cats, like a monsoon. Winter was easiest on everybody. There was the sense that you really weren't missing anything on the streets because everyone was indoors. Spring and summer were hell. The Dear John letters started flowing in, sending heartbroken dudes to the fence for a clean, fast break over and into the countryside. Fall was a wash. The weather was nice enough to make you think of home, but winter was just ahead, giving you something to look forward to. Time.

I saw the lifers go through some serious changes about time. Some days, those cats carried theirs as good as anybody else, but other days, they didn't. You could look in their eyes sometimes and tell they had run across a calendar, one of those calendars that let you know what day of the week your birthday will fall on ten years from now. Or you could see in the wild way they started acting and talking that they were on the edge. Then it was time to get away from them, go to the other side of the prison yard, and watch the fireworks. They went *off*.

Especially the brothers. They were determined not to go down kicking and screaming and slashing their wrists like the white boys. The brothers considered themselves too hard for that. When the time got to be too much for them, they'd go fuck with somebody and get themselves in a situation where there was no win. It was their way of saying, "Go on, kill me. Gimme a glorious way to get outta this shit."

■ ■ ■

My time started coming down on me when I realized I'd reached the one-year mark and had at least two to go. I tried to cling tighter to Liz, but that didn't work. After I was transferred from the jail to Southampton, it seemed we both backed out on the marriage plans. She didn't bring it up, and neither did I. Liz's visits and letters slacked off, and I felt myself slipping out of touch with the outside world. When Liz did visit, she seemed distant and nervous, like there was something she wanted to tell me but couldn't get out. That drove me crazy, along with about a hundred thousand other irritations that constantly fucked with my head.

I thought a lot about the irony of the year 1976: It was the year Alex Haley published the slave epic *Roots* and the country was celebrating the two hundredth year of its freedom from tyranny. It seemed that every time I opened a magazine or walked past a TV set, there was talk about the yearlong bicentennial celebration. I'd heard white people brag about being free, white, and twenty-one. There I was, black, twenty-one, and in the penitentiary. It seemed I'd gotten it all wrong.

It's a weird feeling being on the edge and knowing that there's not much you can do about it but hang on. You can't get help for prison depression. You can't go to a counselor and say, "Look, I need a weekend pass. This punishment thing is taking more out of me than I think it was intended to take."

I didn't want to admit to myself that the time was getting to me that much, let alone admit it to somebody else. So I determined to do the macho thing: suffer quietly. Sometimes it got so bad I had to whisper to myself, "Hold on, Nate. Hold on."

Frustrated and depressed, I went to the prison and bought a green spiral-bound tablet and started a journal, partly out of a need to capture my fears and feelings, and partly to practice using the new words I learned. I adopted a journal theme—a quote I ran across by the writer Oliver Wendell Holmes—as encouragement to keep me pushing ahead and holding on:

I find the great thing in this world is not so much where we stand as in what direction we are moving. To reach the port of heaven, we must sail, sometimes with the wind and sometimes against it—but we must sail, and not drift, nor lie at anchor.

It made me feel better sometimes to get something down on paper just like I felt it. It brought a kind of relief to be able to describe my pain. It was like, if I could describe it, it lost some of its power over me. I jotted down innermost thoughts I couldn't verbalize to anyone else, recorded what I saw around me, and expressed feelings inspired by things I read. Often, the thoughts I wrote down reflected my struggle with time.

> *Each day I inspire myself with the hope that by some miracle of God or act of legislature I will soon regain my freedom. However, from occasional conversations, I find that many other inmates have entertained the same hope—for years.*
> May 21, 1976

Even the guys doing less than life had a hard time. Anything in the double digits—ten years to serve, twenty, forty, sixty—could be a backbreaker. I had a buddy, Cincinnati. Real outgoing cat. Every time you saw him, he was talking beaucoup trash. But Cincinnati was doing a hard forty, and it drove him up a wall at least twice a week. He fought it by trying to keep super-busy. With a white towel hung loosely over his shoulder and several cartons of cigarettes tucked under his arm, Cincinnati (we called him that because that's where he was from) would bop briskly across the yard, intent on his missions. He'd stop and jawbone with a group of guys hanging out near the canteen, then hand a carton of cigarettes to one of them and hurry off to the next meeting.

Cincinnati was one of several major dealers at Southampton who used the drug-peddling skills they'd learned on the streets to exploit the crude prison economy. In that economy, cigarettes replaced money as the medium of exchange. Favors and merchandise were negotiated in terms of their worth in packs of cigarettes. For twelve cartons of cigarettes, a guy could take out a contract to have somebody set up on a drug bust, or get them double-banked or shanked. Eight packs could get you a snappy pair of prison brogans from one of the brothers on the shoe-shop crew. For three packs each week, laundry workers would see to it your shirts and pants were crisply starched.

Cincinnati liked to get his gray prison shirts starched so that he could turn up the collar and look real cool.

The really swift dealers found ways to convert a portion of their goods to forbidden cash, which they used to bribe guards to get them reefer and liquor, or saved for their eventual return to the streets.

Cincinnati, who was about two years older than me and had logged a lot more street time, was penitentiary-rich. He decorated his cell with plush blue towels and stockpiled so much stuff that the rear wall of his cell looked like a convenience store. It was stacked from floor to ceiling with boxes of cookies, cigarettes, and other stuff he sold, "two for one," to inmates seeking credit until payday.

Watching cats like him, I often thought about Mo Battle and his theory about pawns. Cincinnati handled time and played chess like he lived: He failed to think far ahead and he chased pawns all over the board. In his free time off from the kitchen, where he worked, he busied himself zigzagging across the prison yard, collecting outstanding debts and treating his petty "bidness" matters like they were major business deals.

Cincinnati was playful and cheery most of the time. He was as dark as night and had a shiny gold tooth that gleamed like a coin when he smiled. Short and squat, he had a massive upper body and a low center of gravity, like Mike Tyson. In fact, his voice, high-pitched and squeaky, sounded a lot like Tyson's, too. It was the kind of voice that sounded like it belonged to a child. But nobody mistook Cincinnati for a child. He was a tank, and could turn from nice guy to cold killer in a split second.

He addressed everybody as "bro'." I'd see him on the yard and say, "Yo, Cincinnati, what's happ'nin'?" And if he was in a good mood, he'd say, "Bro' Nate, life ain't nothin' but a meatball."

But time came down on Cincinnati, like it did on everybody else. He had to do at least ten of his forty years before going up for parole. I could tell when he was thinking about it. I'd run into him on the yard and say, "What's happ'nin', Cincinnati?" He'd shake his head sadly and say, "Bro' Nate, I'm busted, disgusted, and *can't* be trusted."

Cincinnati was so far away from home that he never got visits. On visiting days, he usually went out to the main sidewalk on the yard and looked through the fence as people visiting other inmates pulled into the parking lot.

Other times, I could tell how depressed he was by the way he handled defeat on the chessboard. I beat him all the time and taunted him, but sometimes he didn't take it well. Just before I put him in checkmate, he'd get frustrated and knock one of his big arms against the board, sending the pieces crashing to the floor. Then he'd look up with a straight face and say, "Oh, I'm sorry, Bro' Nate. I didn't mean to do that."

We were playing chess one day when Cincinnati stared at the board a long time without making a move. I got impatient. "Go on and move, man! You gonna lose anyway!"

Ignoring me, Cincinnati kept his eyes glued to the board and didn't speak for a long time. After a while, he said, "Bro' Nate, I'm gonna make a break for the fence. I been thinking about it a long time. I got a lotta money saved up. I can get outta state. You wanna come?"

Any inmate who says he's never thought about escaping is either lying or telling the sad truth. The sad truth is, the only dudes who don't think about making a break are those who are either so institutionalized that their thoughts seldom go beyond the prison gates, or who were so poor in the streets that they had been rescued and are glad to be someplace where they are guaranteed three hots and a cot.

There were a few desperate, fleeting moments when I thought half-seriously about making a run. Southampton is ringed by a tall barbed-wire fence with electrical current running through it, but everybody knew the heat was turned off much of the time. Sometimes, I'd stare at that fence and think about how to scale it. I pictured myself tossing my thick winter coat on top of the barbed wire to test the heat and protect my hands, climbing quickly to the top, and leaping to the other side to make my dash before tower guards could get off a good shot. I'd mapped an escape route based on what I'd seen of the area while traveling with the gun gang. I'd thought it through like a chess match, move for move. That's why I didn't try. When I thought it through, I always saw a great chance of getting busted or leading such a miserable life on the run that it would be another form of imprisonment.

Looking at Cincinnati, I jokingly turned down his offer to run. "Naw, brotherman. I'm gonna squat here. I'm expecting a visit from my lady this weekend. I'd hate for her to come and find me gone. Besides, I can handle my bid. You do the crime, you gotta do the time, Jack!"

I forgot about our conversation until a week or two later, when the big whistle at the guard tower sounded, signaling all inmates to go to their cells to be counted. The whistle blew at certain times every day, but on this day, it sounded at an odd hour, meaning there was something wrong. After we went to our cells, the word spread that Cincinnati had made a break. He'd hidden in the attic of the school building, then scrambled over the fence after a posse left the compound to hunt for him.

Following the count, guys in my building (I was in C-3 by then) grew real quiet. Every time someone escaped, I got quiet and privately rooted for him to get away. I sat on my bunk thinking about Cincinnati, trying to picture him out in the pitch dark, his black face sweating, ducking through bushes, hotly pursued by white men with guns and barking dogs. I imagined him low-running across some broad field, dodging lights and listening for suspicious sounds. I imagined the white country folks, alerted to the escape, grabbing their shotguns and joining the hunt.

Some weeks after Cincinnati made his break, he got caught somewhere in the state. It saddened me. He was shipped to a maximum-security prison more confining than Southampton, and he got more time tacked on to the forty years that was already giving him hell.

Prison paranoia is a dangerous thing. It can affect a person to the extent that he becomes distrustful of anyone and everyone. Even though my woman has displayed no signs of infidelity, I find myself scrutinizing her behavior each week (in the visiting room), searching her eyes for the slightest faltering trait. I search in hope that I discover none, but hope even more that if there is, I will detect it before it discovers me and slithers back into some obscure hiding place.
June 4, 1976

I walked into the crowded visiting room and took a seat at the table with Liz. My intuition told me that something was up. She'd come alone, without my parents or my son, and her brown eyes, usually bright and cheery, were sad and evasive. In a letter she'd sent to me earlier in the week, she had said there was something she wanted to discuss. I sensed what it was, and I'd come prepared.

We exchanged small talk, then there was this awkward silence. Finally, I spoke, relieving her of a burden I sensed was killing her. "You're seeing someone else, aren't you?"

She nodded. "Yes."

There was a long pause as she waited for my reaction. I looked down at the floor and thought about what I'd just heard. My worst fear had come true. Liz couldn't hang. I'd have to do the time alone. I understood. She'd done the best she could. She'd been a helluva lot

more supportive and reliable than I would have been under the circumstances. The best I could do was be grateful for what she'd done.
Take it and grow, as she used to say. I tried to put on a brave face,
and I said, "I understand, really. . . . Well, nothing I can do about that
but wish you the best. I would like you to hang in there with me, but
really, I don't know when I'm gettin' outta here."

She listened quietly and nodded as I talked. When I finished, she
didn't say much. We sat there, bummed out, looking at each other.
Mr. and Miss Manor. Liz wished me well. Her eyes watered. Then
she said good-bye, and left.

I practically ran back to my cell that Saturday morning. I wanted
to get back there before the tear ducts burst. It was like trying to get
to the bathroom before the bladder gives out. I made it, went inside,
and flopped down on a stool. I turned on the stereo, slid in one of my
favorite gospel tapes, *Amazing Grace,* by Aretha Franklin, and closed
my eyes. The tape opened with a song called "Mary, Don't You
Weep." The deep strains of a full gospel choir, comforting the sister
of Lazarus after his death, sang in a rich harmony that sent shivers
through me:

> *Hush, Mary, don't you weep.*
> *Hush, Mary, don't you weep.*

When I heard those words, the floodgate burst and the tears started
streaming down my face. Streaming. The pain ran so deep it felt
physical, like somebody was pounding on my chest. I'd never been
hurt by a woman before. I had never cared enough to be hurt by one.
I sat there, leaning on the cell door, listening to Aretha and crying.
Inmates walked past and I didn't even lift my head. I didn't care who
saw me or what they thought. I was crushed. Wasted. I cried until
tears blurred my vision. Then I got up, picked up my washcloth,
rinsed it in the sink, held it to my face, and cried some more. Liz was
gone. I remembered that she had once told me, "I'll follow you into
a ditch if you lead me there." Well, I had led her there, but she'd
never promised to stay.

■　■　■

Sometimes I'd get grinding migraines that lasted for hours on end. I
figured it was caused by the pain of losing Liz, and the stress and
tension hounding me. When the frequency of the headaches increased, I came up with ways to relieve the stress. I'd leave the place.
I'd stretch out on my bunk, block out all light by putting a cloth over

my eyes, and go into deep meditation or prayer. Starting with my toes, I'd concentrate hard and command every one of my body parts to chill. Often, by the time I reached my head the tension was gone.

Then I'd take my imagination and soar away from the prison yard. I'd travel to Portsmouth or some faraway, fictional place. Or I'd venture beyond the earth and wander through the galaxy, pondering the vastness of what God has done. I developed a hell of an imagination by doing those mental workouts, and it put me in touch with my spirit in wondrous ways. When the concentration was really good, I'd lose all feeling in my body, and my spirit would come through, making me feel at one with the universe. It was like being high: It felt so good, but I couldn't figure out a way to make it last.

I just witnessed a brutal fight in the cafeteria. The atmosphere was certainly conducive to violence: hot, odorous air filled with noise and flies. The two combatants went at each other's throats as if their lives meant nothing to them. After being confined for an extended period of time, life does tend to lose its value. I pray that I can remember my self-worth and remain cool.
July 27, 1976

A group of us from Tidewater were sitting around, sharing funny tales from the streets and telling war stories about crazy things we'd done. When my turn came, I told a story about a near stickup on Church Street in Norfolk. "Yeah, man, we ran across a dude who had nothing but chump change on him. We got mad 'cause the dude was broke, so we took his change and started to take his pants. He had on some yellow, flimsy-looking pants, so we made him walk with us under a streetlamp so we could get a better look at them. When we got under the streetlamp, we could see the pants were cheap. And they were dirty. So we let the dude slide, and keep his pants . . ."

Everybody was laughing. Everybody but a guy from Norfolk named Tony. Squinting his eyes, he leaned over and interrupted, "Did you say the guy had on yellow pants?"

"Yeah."

"Goddammit, that was *me* y'all stuck up that night!" he said, pointing a finger at me.

Everything got quiet. The guys looked at me, then at Tony, then back at me. Somebody snickered, and everybody else joined in. I laughed, too, until I looked at Tony and realized he still wasn't laughing. He was hot. He looked embarrassed and mad as hell.

To lighten the mood, I extended my hand playfully and said, "Wow, man, I'm sorry 'bout that. You know I didn't know you then."

Tony looked at my hand like he wanted to spit on it. "Naw, man. That shit ain't funny." The way he said it, I knew he wasn't going to let the thing drop. I knew that stupid macho pride had him by the throat and was choking the shit out of him.

A week or two after the exchange, he came into the library, where I was working, sat in a corner, and started tearing pages out of magazines. The library was filled with inmates. I walked over to the table and said, "Yo, Tony, you can't tear the pages outta the magazines, man. Other people have to read 'em."

He looked up, smiled an evil smile, then ripped out another page and said, "What you gonna do 'bout it? You ain't no killer." The room grew quiet. I felt like all eyes were on me, waiting to see what I would do. I started thinking fast. Tony was stout and muscular and I figured he'd probably do the moonwalk on me if he got his hands on me. He was sitting down and I was standing. I glanced at an empty chair near him. I thought, *I could sneak him right off the bat, grab that chair, and wrap it around his head.* Then I thought about the potential consequences of fighting at work. I could lose my job, get kicked out of the library. I thought, *I gotta let it slide. I have to.* I looked at Tony, shrugged my shoulders, and said, "I ain't gonna do nothin', man. The magazines don't belong to *me.*"

Tony sat there, staring at me, and tore more pages out of magazines. I walked away.

Later that night, I thought about it some more. I thought about how he'd come off. I thought, *He disrespected me.* I was too scared to let that man get away with disrespecting me. I felt I had faith that God would take care of me, but whenever I got that scared about something, I relied on what I knew best—faith in self. So I prayed, then set God aside for the time being and put together a shank like I'd learned to make while in the Norfolk jail. I melded a razor blade into a toothbrush handle, leaving the sharp edges sticking out, like a miniature tomahawk. I told one of my buddies what I intended to do. "I gotta get that niggah, man. He disrespected me and tried to chump me down."

The next day, we went looking for Tony on the yard. We spotted him leaving the dispensary with a partner. While my friend kept a lookout for guards, I approached Tony. Without saying anything, I pulled the razor blade and swung it at his throat. He jumped back. I lunged at him again and he flung his arms in front of his face, blocking the blow. The razor slashed his coat. He held up his hands and said, "Hold it, hold it, hold it, man! Be cool. Everything's cool. We all right, man. I ain't got no beef with you."

I pointed the razor at him. "Niggah, don't you *never* take me to be no chump!"

"All right, bro', I was just playing with you yesterday."

I turned and walked away, relieved that he'd backed down and grateful that none of the guards standing on the yard had seen what went down.

My parents came to see me that afternoon. I went into the visiting room still hyper from the scene with Tony. As we talked, I looked at them and wondered what they'd say if they knew I had just risked everything I'd worked for to prove a manhood point. I wondered if Tony was going to try to get some get-back or pay somebody to try to shank me when my back was turned. I wondered if the time was coming down on me so badly that I was losing my grip.

At chow time that evening, my homie Pearly Blue came to the table and sat next to me. There was a slight smirk on his face. I sensed he was feeling a certain delight in knowing he'd warned me to hang tight with my homies to keep hassles away. "Yo, man, I heard you had a run-in with Tony."

"Yeah, a small beef."

"I told you these old rooty-poot niggahs will try you if they think you walk alone. . . . You know if you need to make another move on him, the homies can take care of it."

I kept looking straight ahead as I ate. "Naw, man. I got it under control."

I had no problems from Tony the remainder of the time I was at Southampton.

■ ■ ■

The one thing that seemed to soothe everybody in the joint was music. The loudest, most fucked-up brothers in the place chilled out when they had on a set of headphones. Some white inmates had musical instruments—guitars, saxophones, flutes—and they practiced in their cells at night. Most of the brothers didn't like hearing white music. The brothers would holler through the cell bars, "Cut that hillbilly shit out!"

But one white guy, from some rural Virginia town, was exempt from the hassles. He was a fairly good guitar player, and an even better singer. Every night, before the lights went out, he calmed the building with music. He sang the same song, and it reverberated throughout the place. He strummed his guitar and sang the John Denver tune "Take Me Home, Country Roads." He sang in a voice so clean it sounded like he was standing on a mountain crooning down into one of those luscious green valleys he was singing about:

> *Country rooaads,*
> *Take me hoomme,*
> *To the plaaace*
> *Where I beloooonng . . .*

When those lyrics floated into my cell, I'd sit quietly, lean my head against the concrete wall, and listen. That song reminded me of how lonely I was and made me think of home. It made me think of Liz. It made me think of my son, my family, my neighborhood, my life. Sometimes, when he sang that song, tears welled in my eyes and I'd wipe them away, get into bed, and think some more.

That song seemed to calm everybody in the building, even the baad-asses who were prone to yell through their cells. It had the soothing effect of a lullaby sung by a parent to a bunch of children.

Chapter 21 SEX

Each day, I find myself fighting an intense battle against sensuality. I have attempted to obliterate sexual thoughts, but obviously to no avail. I even tried drowning myself in books and comprehensive studies, but at the slightest reading interval those thoughts burst through my consciousness, filling me with frustrating tension. The battle has become so acute that excessive tension and headaches are becoming an integral part of my day. "Give your problems to Jesus," people say. But I wonder, does Jesus want to share my whorish lusts?

June 5, 1976

■ ■ ■

Just think. Before you got locked up, you were getting some every day, or at least every chance you got. You were throwing down hard, pushing up like it was going outta style. Then, a judge plays God and sends you to the dunce corner. Suddenly, you got *big* problems. You got a serious jones that won't let go, and you got energy coming out the yin-yang. That energy builds and builds until it fills your chest with heat—the heat of a thousand suns—and makes you so horny you get dizzy and aggressive and evil, all at once. It's the kind of feeling that makes you want to haul off and punch somebody for no reason at all, for no reason other than that you got *all* that energy and nothing to do with it. And you're in a place where everybody's got the same problem; everybody feels like Superman with a helluva hump on his back.

You ain't seen no tension until you seen *that* shit. You haven't felt any pressure until you've lived around dudes—hundreds of them—who act like they're in a desert with nothing but sand, and they start seeing mirages, luscious, eye-popping, thirst-quenching mirages. It brings new meaning to the warning "Watch your back."

■ ■ ■

When I was in the Norfolk jail, Mo Battle felt compelled to school me during some of our talks about the dangers I could expect to face when shipped to prison. He said, "The penitentiary is very different from jail, Youngblood. You got cats in prison that's been locked up a *long* time. Them cats are dangerous as wolves. They can play some serious head-games on you if you don't know what's goin' on."

Through the years in Cavalier Manor, I'd known enough cats who'd been to the joint to get some sense of what to expect. But Mo Battle ran down specific snags that he thought I should take care to avoid. He ran down a laundry list of traps that he said guys often slip into when doing their first prison bids. "Don't build up too much gambling debt, man, 'cause a guy can use that as an excuse to try to make you his bitch; don't trust nobody but your homies; don't let nobody—not even your homies—put their hands on you, man. I'm saying, don't even let 'em pat you on the back. That might sound crazy, but you'll understand when you get there and see how it is. Somebody is gonna wanna try you, man, and you gotta handle it."

Mo Battle made me nervous in some of those conversations. He made it seem like there was no way I could expect to go in, mind my own business, and do my time in peace. I was comforted by one thing, though: I knew I would kill if the need arose. If I had to, I'd shut down my mind and take a nigger out any way I could. That's a perverse thing to be comforted by, but facing the prospect of being threatened—sexually or otherwise—in prison, I felt good in knowing that I had the heart to do whatever was necessary to survive.

I didn't fear being raped or taken advantage of. I dreaded running into a situation that forced me to do something that might run up my prison time. In conversations in the cellblock, I heard nightmares about guys who went in with small, two- and three-year sentences, but got more time tacked on for coldcocking or shanking another inmate while under lock and key.

The thought of running up my time scared the hell out of me. I doubted I had the endurance to do the time I already had, not to mention more. I mustered hope by thinking in terms of making parole the first time up. In Virginia, an inmate is eligible for a parole hearing after serving a fourth of his time. I set my sights on doing three years and making parole the first time. That meant I had to stay out of trouble, stay squeaky-clean. So I made my resolve: *I ain't gonna bother nobody, but ain't nobody gonna take advantage of me.* Surviving was going to be a chess match that I *had* to win.

■ ■ ■

Evenings and weekends when the weather was nice, guards sometimes opened the fence to the ballpark and let inmates play basketball, football, and baseball or jog around the field. Remembering what Mo Battle had said about the need to avoid physical contact, I gave up basketball and football completely. Instead, I played Ping-Pong and went sometimes to the ballpark and sat on a long concrete wall, where dudes hung out and rapped.

Shortly after getting to Southampton, I was sitting on the wall with one of my homies—a guy we called Feetball—chatting about people we knew on the streets. A coffee-complexioned brother around the same age as me, Feetball was easygoing and loved to talk about the streets. Every time we got a chance to shoot the breeze, he'd steer the conversation to Cavalier Manor. "I was glad when I heard you shot Plaz, man. That niggah always thought he was baad. . . ."

He stopped in midsentence, looked curiously at another newcomer walking by, and said, "Look a' that guy. He looks just like Wanda Malone."

I looked at the inmate, blinked my eyes, and looked again. I thought, *Wanda Malone is a girl.* I looked at the guy a third time, focusing harder. Seeing no resemblance to Wanda, I turned to Feetball and said, "Man, get outta here! That guy don't look like Wanda!"

"Yes, he do. Look at his face. He got the same complexion and everything."

I gazed at the guy again, thinking, *Is this cat serious? Naw, he can't be. He must be joking, messin' with my head.* I fixed my eyes on Feetball, waiting for him to say he was just jiving, but he didn't crack a smile. In fact, he went on to talk about another subject, as if his comment about the inmate were no more unusual than a statement about the weather. "Man, I sure do hope they let us out to see that program on TV tonight. . . ."

I tuned him out. I was still thinking about his earlier observation, wondering if this bid had screwed up his head or if the accumulation of stints in the joint had finally caught up with him. Since he was around twelve, Feetball had spent more time in prison than out. He'd started going to reform school when I was at Waters Junior High, and he graduated right on up through the prison system like other people move through public school. By the time he reached age eighteen, it seemed he'd spent time at practically every prison in Virginia. It wasn't unusual for his older brother and him to be locked up at the same time. A lot of dudes at Southampton had brothers, sisters, and even mothers and fathers in other prisons at the same time.

Feetball had already been locked up at Southampton for several years when I got there, and the time didn't seem to get to him much. He never seemed disappointed when he didn't get weekend visits, and he never acted like the place bothered him. He was just doing time, like it was a natural part of life.

As Feetball went on talking, I stayed quiet and nodded every now and then, like I was paying attention. I didn't want to let him know he'd freaked me out. At the same time, I wanted to hear more, to see just how fucked up his head really was. I hoped he'd break off on his own and say, "O.K., man, I was just jiving you about that guy looking like Wanda." But Feetball kept on talking about other things.

At some point, the whistle sounded and we had to go to our buildings. Before we split, I hesitated briefly to give him one last chance to say he was kidding about Wanda. Instead, he said, "I'll catch you later, homes," and walked away.

I said, "Yeah, later," and started toward my building. As I walked, I shook my head, trying to figure out what it all meant. Inwardly, I knew: Feetball had seen so few women in recent years that some men looked like women to him. The frightening thing was, he wasn't even aware of it.

Later, when I thought about it some more, it scared me to death. It made me wonder if after being locked up a long time, I, too, would start seeing mirages.

■ ■ ■

At Southampton, there were chasers (otherwise known as "booty bandits") and chasees, cats who didn't have the will and heart to kill, even for the sake of keeping somebody, literally, off their ass. On the sidelines, there were cats who out of principle or revulsion chose to suck in the energy, suffer, and sit out the prison mating dance. They watched and watched out.

A homeboy in the Norfolk jail once told me that when he was last in the penitentiary, he took *two* shanks to the shower with him every night. "I draped a towel over my arm and hid the shanks under the towel," he said.

The cat probably never got clean, but he stayed pure.

Although I felt safe at Southampton with all my homies there, the level of paranoia was high enough to keep me alert. The first time I

dropped my soap in the shower, I looked around before bending down
to pick it up.

■ ■ ■

I was standing near the canteen, talking with some homeboys, when
a dude called Tooty walked by. One of the homeboys, a guy from
downtown, called out to him, "Hey, baaaby!"

Tooty turned sharply, squinted his eyes evilly, and said, "Go to
hell, punk!" Then he turned and stormed off. My homeboy glanced
at the others standing there, and they all smiled knowing smiles.

I was surprised that my homie would crack on Tooty like that, and
amazed that Tooty let him get away with it. After being locked up
awhile, I could tell by the way guys looked or carried themselves on
the yard whether or not they might have problems with the wolves.
Tooty wasn't someone I would have guessed would get hassled.
Before the exchange with my homeboy, I assumed he was as respected
on the yard as anybody else. We'd come to Southampton around the
same time and worked on the gun gang together. In that time, I got
the impression he was as hard as anybody on the crew and that he
could hold his own if the need arose. Dark-complexioned and bowlegged, he was about 5' 10" and solidly built. He was loud and cursed
a lot, like he was baad. But I questioned his heart when he failed to
put my homeboy in check. The law of *that* land dictated that he
should've gone to war.

After that exchange, my homies taunted Tooty regularly on the
yard—"Hey, baby, when you gonna gimme that brown-eye?"—testing him to see how he'd respond. It amazed me that guys weren't
ashamed to let somebody see them cracking on another man. In fact,
in a warped way, they were proud. It fed a macho notion widely
accepted in the joint: That a guy was even *more* of a man if he could
"flip" another man, turn him into a homosexual. They also called it
"breaking him down." If they thought they spotted a mental weakness
that they could exploit, they'd chip and chisel at it until they got
results. Sometimes it took months before they got a breakthrough;
sometimes it took years, which was no big deal for somebody doing
time.

Clearly, someone spotted something in Tooty—the way he looked
at somebody in the shower, or the way he carried himself—that made
them think he was ripe for being broken down. I wondered what they
saw, and I watched to see how that budding drama played itself out.

They jeered and teased him, and when he still didn't retaliate they turned up the heat, openly treating him like a woman, throwing him kisses and calling him "sweetheart" out on the yard. Then they turned up the pressure more, touching him, pinching his butt, and called him "girl." Finally, they made a major move.

I'd reached the R-1 building, where we had our own rooms with keys. There were guards in R-1, but they patrolled the halls less often than the guards in other buildings. One evening, I was heading to my room and heard a commotion coming from another room down the hall. It sounded like somebody tussling, bumping against the cabinets and bunk. I passed one of my homies in the hall and asked, "What's going on down there, man?"

"They running a train on Tooty."

At first, I didn't think I'd heard him right. Then, as I thought back to those wild days in Cavalier Manor, it sank in. *They're running a train. In the penitentiary. On a man! . . . Life is crazy, and it's getting worse.*

I went to my room and closed my door, afraid that if I stayed in that hallway too long, I might see something—or, rather, somebody—come out of that room that I didn't want to see.

The next day, word spread on the yard that Tooty was in the dispensary being "stitched up." Several months later, he was somebody's boy.

That whole ordeal taught me a lot about the power of the mind. It demonstrated that if you don't know who you are and if you don't believe fully in yourself, others sense it, no matter how much you try to front it off. My homeboys had psyched Tooty out by treating him like a woman until he doubted his own manhood. Then, when they had broken him down, they flipped him like a pancake.

■　■　■

I could always tell when the tension level was high. There'd be less joking going on, and allies hung closer together on the yard. The most telling sign this time was the posturing of dudes in the Tidewater and Richmond gangs. Members from each gang stuck tighter than usual on the yard, eyeing each other hard. I found out there were rumors of war.

Normally, it took a lot to bring those two gangs to blows. They talked trash to each other, especially when playing football or shooting hoops, but a mutual respect underlay it all. Yet it was understood that if a rumble jumped off, both sides were ready to throw down.

I went to Pearly Blue and asked him what was up. "You ain't heard, man? They competin' for this new bitch that just came outta the Receiving Unit. Her name is Pauline. They waitin' to see who she gonna choose."

" 'Who she gonna *choose*'?" I echoed, confused.

"Yeah, she just came on the yard and she ain't chose nobody yet, so the brothers are gettin' kinda uptight 'cause she looks gooood! She look just like a bitch."

The Richmond and Tidewater gangs each had their best rappers vying for Pauline's attention, and all kinds of candy, cigarettes, and other gifts were being sent to "her." That was another one of those penitentiary mating rites that had been around so long that old-heads acted like it was the most natural thing in the world.

All the chatter made me curious. There were a lot of closeted and openly gay guys at Southampton, but this was the first time I saw the excitement generated when a new, openly gay inmate came on the yard. I wanted to see for myself how the new guy looked. I only saw him once at a distance; then he disappeared. As soon as prison administrators found out about the tensions he created on the yard, they put him in protective custody to calm things down.

He stayed in lockup a long while, and tensions eased. I'd forgotten about it until one day when, as part of our Christian fellowship activities, I was visiting the lockup cells. (The administration let us go to the lockup area on weekends to "witness"—talk to inmates and try to get them interested in God and the Bible.) I'd finished talking with a guy at one cell and moved to the next, and there he was, standing at the bars, looking straight at me. I jumped back, surprised. Pauline looked *just* like a woman. He was about 5' 8" and very slender. Tan-complexioned and clean-shaven, he had long eyelashes and seemed to have plucked and arched his eyebrows like women do. His hair, long and straight, looked like it had been tinted a reddish blond. He even had his gray prison shirt rigged to look like a woman's blouse. Instead of buttoning it down the front and tucking it into his pants, like everybody else, he had left it unbuttoned and tied the tails together in a knot, revealing part of his flat chest and trim waist. His chin provided the only clue that he was a man. If you looked hard, you could see the outline of where he shaved.

I collected myself, then walked over to the cell and spoke to him. "Do you believe in God?"

"Yes, I believe in God. I was raised in the church," he said in a soft, high-pitched tone.

"Are you saved?"

"I accepted Jesus as my Savior a long time ago."

"Well, then, how did you get like . . . this?" I hadn't intended to be so blunt. It just spilled out that way.

He told me a long story about how he was molested as a child by a teenage uncle who was his baby-sitter. For a long time after that, he said, he'd been confused about his sexuality. He even got deeply involved in the church and asked God to help him resist temptation, but gave up fighting because the homosexual impulses were too strong. Although his real name was Paul, he said he preferred to be called Pauline. "I feel," he said, "like I was meant to be a woman."

On the streets, my homeboys and I had always called gays "sissies" and "freaks," and we'd hassle them. But listening to Pauline's story, I saw that he'd spent much of his life at odds with himself. I sympathized. Yet there was something about him—his feminine manner and the way he gazed into my eyes when he spoke—that made me uneasy. I enjoyed talking with him, but felt the need to get away. So I did. I bowed my head, recited a short prayer for him, then said good-bye and moved on to another cell.

Pauline was eventually released back into the prison population. Whenever I saw him on the yard, I spoke to him briefly and kept walking. He made me feel self-conscious and awkward, and I felt even more uneasy about the prospect of being seen—by guards or inmates—talking with someone who was gay.

Ultimately, Pauline chose as his man a smooth-talking, gold-toothed player who was the quarterback for the Richmond Gang's football team. They walked around the yard together, like a couple on the streets. The prison vets and wolves looked on jealously. Guys in the Richmond Gang gloated. "She" belonged to them.

■ ■ ■

Mrs. Pinkney was one of several teachers who helped inmates at the school work toward earning their GEDs. There was one other female teacher, but compared to Mrs. Pinkney she wasn't much to look at. A short, petite woman in her early thirties, Mrs. Pinkney was dark-skinned and thin-boned and had big brown eyes and full lips that glistened from the bright-colored lipstick she wore.

Other inmates stumbled over each other trying to open doors for her, carry her books, or do anything to command her attention for a few minutes. Every time Mrs. Pinkney went to the rest room, inmates rushed into the library to the men's bathroom. They'd punched a tiny hole in the wall, enabling them to peek down over the women's toilet next door.

Although I wanted to go, I didn't. I believed that if I saw what other inmates said they'd seen, it might drive me over the edge. Besides, I didn't want to give in so easily to Mrs. Pinkney. I was certain she was a tease. She had never said anything to suggest that, but after studying her dress and manner very carefully, I concluded she knowingly tortured us. She wore very high heels and fitted skirts that hugged the contours of her shapely body. And she walked slowly, swaying her hips gently, beckoning me, it seemed, to grab her around the waist and pull her to me. She wore strong perfumes that inflamed my nostrils whenever she was near. I said to myself, *She has to know she drives us crazy.*

I loved and hated her all at once. Like everybody else, I was drawn to her, but I resisted because I didn't want to join the list of guys whose hormones she controlled. In spite of myself, I gave in sometimes in other ways. Every time she came into the library, I grew dizzy and went to war with my emotions.

One day, she strolled over to the card catalog, where I was flipping through some titles. She asked me if we had any old issues of *Ebony* magazine. "I'm giving my class an assignment and I want them to research the material in those magazines."

"Yes, ma'am," I said. "I'll check for you." While she waited in the main section, I walked into the back room and began leafing through stacks of magazines piled on the floor. When I had gathered a stack, I took them to her and said, "Let me know if you need some more."

As she took the magazines, my hand brushed slightly against hers. The sensation lingered and I felt dizzy. I resumed working, trying hard not to stare at her. Still, when she sat at a table and casually began turning pages in the magazines, I watched from the corner of my eye. I drank in every detail about her, including the contrast of her bright red fingernail polish against the black-and-white pages she turned, and the way her black hair fell just so, revealing the base of her delicate neck. The neck I wanted to kiss. I fantasized about an exchange between us. In that fantasy, she confessed a secret desire for me that was stronger than my own lust for her. Every other inmate, I'm sure, imagined the same thing.

For a while, she and I were the only people in the library, and I couldn't resist taking advantage of that rare moment alone with her. I thought, *What if we talked and realized we had some common interests? Maybe she likes to read the same things I do.* I glanced at her, sitting in the corner, reading. I *had* to think of a way to get her to interact with me.

I returned to the storage room and tore through the stacks of magazines until I found more back issues of *Ebony*. I stood there with the magazines in my hand, trying to figure out what to say. I carried the magazines to Mrs. Pinkney, like a child trying to win favor with an adult. I took a deep breath. "Here," I said. "I found some more in case you need them." She looked up from her reading. "That's all right," she said. "These are enough." Then she gathered the magazines I'd given her, picked up her pocketbook, and headed for the door.

I was left standing there with an armload of magazines, hating her only slightly less than I hated myself for letting her make a fool of me.

■ ■ ■

Before prison, I'd been aware, but not really conscious, that there was a vast psychic difference between men and women. And I'd never really considered what women added to the world. Then I realized that if prison was any indication, a world without women would be crazy, stark raving mad. It became clearer than ever to me that women brought a lot to the table that the world couldn't do without. They brought balance, beauty of spirit, and sanity. Lots and lots of simple sanity. I'd seen some who were as messed up in the head as any man, but all things considered, women generally knew more about being human beings than most men I'd come across.

Women brought a dimension to life that I discovered only after being placed in a fenced-in universe from which they were absent. In the visiting room, I watched their mannerisms—the way they held their hands when they talked. I noticed how they dressed, and other little details, such as their earrings, hypnotized me. I could even pick up their perfume fragrances at tables near mine. Sometimes, while in the visiting room, talking with my parents, I'd hone in on the fragrance or mannerisms of a woman at a table nearby and my heart would float over there against my will. I'd fight off the urge to get up, walk over, and plead: "Please. Can I just sit here a minute and talk with you?"

Sometimes sexual tension got so heavy in my chest that I felt I might just explode, blow up in a puff of smoke. I knew I *had* to come up with some strategies to beat that energy down. For starters, I got rid of all those *Playboy* pinups in my room, and stopped cruising through freak magazines that would get me upset. When I realized that the sight of women on the screen also got to me, I damned near gave up watching TV altogether. I got so thoroughly out of the habit of watching TV that I seldom turn on my television set even today.

I also designed a regimen to help me keep myself in check. I'd rise at five, and write poetry or make journal entries until breakfast time. Then I'd go to work, eat dinner, jog, and stagger back to my room. Later, I'd go to the basement and lift weights to work that strangling tightness out of my chest. Exhausted, I'd shower, return to my room, and read until the lights went out. I'd put on my headphones, listen to music, and stare out that porthole of a window at the stars in the night sky, and think.

I thought more about women than I had in my entire life. I'd think about all the hatred and abuse the fellas and I had heaped on women, and I'd promise God that if I ever got out of prison alive, I'd never mistreat another woman as long as I lived.

Lying in the darkness, I'd caress myself and let my imagination soar beyond Southampton's long country roads to places where the world was turned upright. I'd pick up a date and we'd go out for the evening, to dinner or a movie; maybe we'd walk and talk. I imagined entire conversations I wanted to have with women. In my fantasy, the ending to my lovely evening was always the same. We'd go to my date's apartment, embrace, make love, and fall asleep, exhausted.

Then I'd wake up the next morning to the haunting, shrill sound of the prison whistle, signaling that it was time to start a new day.

Chapter 22 JIM

Two years into my prison stint, Liz had started writing me again, and we talked about the possibility of getting back together. I was also starting to have trouble with my Christian fellowship group. There were too many weirdos joining up to seek protection from the wolves, and it was becoming hard to talk with the Christians about all the things I was learning and thinking about. My mental and spiritual regimen had begun to make me feel whole for the first time in my life, and I wasn't about to give that up just to please some jackleg, wanna-be preachers.

Maybe that's why I started to listen to a guy named Jim, who was the most respected inmate at Southampton. A Richmond native in his mid-thirties, Jim was on the tail end of a life sentence for murder; he'd done close to fifteen years in the joint. He was admired partly because of the way he'd handled his time, but mostly because of his integrity and broad intellect. Unlike so many other dudes, who became mentally passive after years in prison, Jim had somehow remained a freethinker who'd stayed focused on the world beyond that fence. Using his prison time to educate himself, he'd evolved into a self-assured, articulate brother with an unyielding commitment to what he called "black folks' struggle." Administrators were so impressed with his intelligence that they allowed him to teach inmates at the institution's school.

I'd seen him around the yard a lot, but for a long time kept my distance. Jim hated the white man, and I was trying to internalize Christian love. By the summer of '77, I'd begun to fast once weekly, spending those days mostly in my room, praying, thinking, and reading everything from poetry to philosophy to books about nutrition. I read Pearl Buck's novels and Hermann Hesse and *The Prophet*, by Kahlil Gibran. I found myself drawn to the novels of Chaim Potok, including *My Name Is Asher Lev*, a book about a young artist that gave me insight into Jewish culture and whetted my curiosity about art, especially Picasso. I'd never known art could be used so powerfully to make social and political statements.

I experimented with a memory technique and learned how to recall up to one hundred numbers, words, and names in sequential order. There were times I got so deep into reading and fasting that I felt I'd transcended the constraints of prison. In those moments, it seemed not to matter whether I stayed behind bars another year or an eternity.

With all this going on inside me, I think that's why I became more curious about what Jim had to say. Some evenings, he held court on the yard, and guys gathered around and listened to him preach about the white man's evil ways. Eventually, I went with one of my home-boys, a guy called Mahdee, to check him out. Jim's message reminded me of what I had heard from Chicago, the black revolutionary I'd met in the Norfolk jail, and much of it was similar to the teachings of Malcolm X and the Muslims: "Don't you know white men are the most lying creatures on the face of the earth? They don't care nothing about the truth. They use falsehood to gain dominance over people and they use trickery to maintain that dominance. They run a game on black folks by trying to get them to think bad things about them-selves that aren't true and believe good things about white people that are outright lies. Think about it! White folks claim we're lazy and don't wanna work. Our people worked for crackers for two hundred years—for *free*, man!—because white folks were too lazy to work for themselves! Our women cooked, cleaned their houses, and raised their children because whites were too trifling to do their own work, yet they gonna call us lazy?! If you look around today, black folks still do most of the work that whitey don't wanna do!

"Check this out. White folks claim we constantly have illegitimate babies and abandon them. During slavery, they raped black women and fathered more illegitimate children than we can count! Why you think they're so many coffee-brown and light-skinned black folks like me and you? That's because we come from all those children that white men fathered and abandoned, man! And they try to pretend that it's *us* that's got a thing for white women. White men *live* for the day to get a piece a' black meat. Think about it, brother!

"I don't care what we produce or invent, white folks don't want to acknowledge its worth unless they can steal it and take credit for it themselves. Look at all the things black folks invented and had stolen from them! Look at how whites worship Elvis Presley. Black folks been singing soul music for years, and whites wouldn't give them their due, then along comes Elvis, imitating black soul, and they treat him like he's God."

Everything Jim said seemed to have the ring of truth. After he'd finished, I chatted with him and we hit it off real well. When he learned I was a Christian, he challenged me to rethink my commitment to "the white man's religion." He said white folks love for blacks to embrace Christianity because they use it to control us. He said whites encourage us to follow Martin Luther King, Jr., because he was a passive Christian, and they urge us to reject Malcolm X because he challenged us to stand up against white oppression.

"If Christianity is such an effective religion, then why hasn't it helped white people become more humane? Most of the white people in this country are Christians and still they're the most hateful, ruthless group of people on the face of the earth. Open your eyes, man! Black Christians are no better. They believe that they ain't righteous unless they suffer like Jesus suffered. Christianity got black people thinking we got to be crucified in this life in order to get peace in the next one. I want what's coming to me in *this* life, here and now, man!

"White Christians are also imperialists. Check anywhere in the world and you will find that where there are white people, there is Christianity and there are missionaries. They send the Christian missionaries in first to preach turn-the-other-cheek, then they come with their armies and conquer the people."

I began to see what he was talking about. Books I found in the library told me that whites in South Africa, Britain, France, Portugal, and Spain, not to mention America, had oppressed people of color whenever they encountered them. Practically every place I could identify where there were whites, people of color were suffering at their hands.

Jim was right about something else, too. The prison administration was very supportive of our Christian fellowship group. They knew Christian inmates were the most easily controlled. They made sure they provided space for our activities, often suspending rules to accommodate us. At the same time, the Muslims, who were considered more radical, complained that the administration was less supportive of them. The control issue sealed my split with Christianity. I wanted no part of anything used by white people to control blacks.

In his talks, Jim also focused a lot on history. He said it was important to understand the past because it shapes our present perceptions about ourselves and the rest of the world. He said white people think they're better than everybody else because they are taught a history of distorted facts that always present whites in a positive, superior light. "Think about it, man. They teach you that the white settlers who came over here were heroes, and we celebrate

Thanksgiving to commemorate their heroism. But check this out: When the settlers were starving, the Indians helped feed them. The Indians helped them survive through the winter. The settlers repaid them by killing them off and taking their land. Now you tell me, were the white settlers heroes or fucking barbarians?"

I thought about all the lies and the indoctrination I had absorbed all through school. Every year, teachers drilled into our heads myths about the heroic white pioneers who sailed from England and settled Jamestown, Virginia. Relics of that settlement have been preserved through the years to support the myths. I remembered that my fourth- and fifth-grade classes took field trips to the Jamestown settlement, which is about a forty-minute drive from Portsmouth, and visited replicas of the tiny ships the whites rode here. When I was young, I accepted my teachers' version of stories about Jamestown, and everything else I was taught, because there was no reason to question it. I figured that if it was contained in schoolbooks, then it must be true.

Throughout school, except during Black History Week, we were taught more about everybody else than about ourselves. I'll never forget that one of my junior high school history teachers made us memorize all the dynasties of the Chinese empire, from start to finish, in chronological order. Yet the story of Africans brought here as slaves was summed up in our history books in a few short paragraphs, almost as a footnote. On some level, that communicated the message that we were less important than everyone else. I wondered how my black teachers could permit such a thing. I understand now that they taught what was approved for the school system, and that while schools had been integrated for blacks and whites, administrators had still failed to integrate the information passed along to us.

In my reading, I also learned that we'd been grossly misled in school about the Indians. Our textbooks always portrayed Native Americans as primitive heathens who threatened to obstruct the settlers' noble mission. That version of history was promoted by TV westerns that showed "brave" cowboys battling "savage" Indians who attacked them for no apparent reason. When I was young, I thought those Indians were crazy, with their feathered headdresses and painted faces, riding horses and yelling like they had lost their minds. When I learned that those Indians were actually fighting to protect what was rightfully theirs—that *they* were the true heroes and that the settlers were the savages, like Jim said—it made me furious to know that whites so arrogantly distorted the truth.

I reflected on those and other myths that may have influenced my thinking as a child, and I realized that Malcolm X, Chicago, Jim, and so many other cats were right: Black people had been systematically brainwashed, and our parents had paid their tax dollars for the schools, biased textbooks, and curriculums that helped carry that out. Without realizing it, we'd been taught to hate ourselves and love white people, and it was causing us to self-destruct.

Jim and I started exchanging books and talking regularly about the effect of historical myths on blacks. We met on the yard most evenings after chow and talked with other guys who also did a lot of reading. In that group, I met some of the sharpest, most intelligent guys I've known, then or since. Most of them were dropouts who had long before lost interest in formal schooling. But once they got a whiff of some real knowledge—knowledge that was relevant to *them*—they educated themselves far better than any public school could have hoped to do.

We formed our own writers' guild, discussed world affairs and politics, and talked about what we intended to do when we got out. Those were the deepest discussions I'd ever had. We debated theories of the major philosophers: Spinoza, Kant, Hegel, Kierkegaard, and Sartre, among others. We dissected dualism, pantheism, and existentialism, and discussed questions such as: How can you appreciate good until you've known evil? Does essence precede existence, or does existence precede essence? Sometimes, during those conversations, I was struck by the strangeness of former robbers, drug dealers, and murderers standing in the middle of a prison yard, debating the heaviest philosophical questions of all time.

■　■　■

Jim, who also worked constantly to improve his vocabulary, taught me to play the word game Scrabble. He'd memorized many of the two-, three-, and four-letter words in the dictionary to help him score high points. We were often joined in fierce matches by Lee Hargrave, the serial murderer who worked with me in the library. One day, after Hargrave had won a game and left the room, Jim said, "Hey, man, we can't let this white boy beat us on the Scrabble board."

Initially, I didn't get it. "What's the problem?"

"Don't you know this cracker thinks he's smarter than us because he's white and we're black? Can't you tell that? He's always trying to bluff us with medical words he thinks we don't know."

I knew what Jim meant. I got that same feeling when I played whites at chess. I got the feeling that white boys automatically assumed they could beat me on the board because chess was a thinking person's game. I was black and they were white, and therefore they were better thinkers. They never came out and said it, but I could tell by their confident body language and their smug analyses of moves made during games that they assumed they were superior. That's why, whenever I played whites at chess, the fun went completely out of the game. It was war disguised as a game. Every nerve in my body stood on end and my mind focused sharply on every piece on the board; I was like a boxer, eyeing an opponent's every feint and move, ready to use sharply honed reflexes to make him pay dearly for the slightest mistake.

I suspected Hargrave thought he was smarter than everybody else at Southampton. He had an elitist air about him. Even after being at Southampton more than a year, he still rarely spoke to more than a few select people and still refused to eat in the cafeteria. While everybody else read *Ebony, Jet, Time, Newsweek,* and other mass-circulation periodicals in the library, Hargrave subscribed to his own—*Town and Country* magazine. Curious, I borrowed an issue from him once and leafed through it. It carried stories and pictures about rich white people who spent their time horseback riding, fox-hunting, and managing their stables and shit.

Whenever Hargrave's parents came to visit him, his father wore a business suit and tie and his mother wore a dress. Out of place in the visiting room with all those working-class black people, they looked stiff and formal, like Beaver Cleaver's parents on TV. Every time I went into the visiting room, his parents made it a point to come over to my table to say an artificial hello to my family and me. I sensed they were unaccustomed to interacting with black people, yet they were trying to encourage me to cultivate a relationship with their son. They were well aware that he was in constant danger because of his crimes against elderly people, and I suspected they viewed me as somebody who could help protect him if the need arose. But I wasn't about to let them use me. I knew that if those rich white people passed me on the streets, they would probably roll up their car windows and lock their doors.

After Jim pulled my coat to Hargrave, we came up with a way to cheat him "like white folks cheat us." Jim, who was a great defensive Scrabble player, made sure he sat in front of Hargrave to prevent him from getting openings to score high points. Whenever Hargrave took the lead, Jim and I secretly fed each other key letters to make sure one of us won the game.

Hargrave never won a game after that. I don't know if he caught on, but it didn't matter. No one else in our building played Scrabble. He loved the game, so he *had* to play with us, or not play at all.

■   ■   ■

In a way, Jim was also similar to Mo Battle, my mentor in the Norfolk jail. When he saw young guys with potential come out of the Receiving Unit, he'd take the time to school them about anything he could. He'd pull them aside and tell them the dos and don'ts of prison life so the wolves couldn't get to them. The wolves resented Jim because of that, but none made a move to do anything about it.

It amazed me to see how much the so-called tough cats respected Jim. Whenever he was around, they cursed less and toned down their macho posturing, as if he were an authority figure or a revered elder. Initially, that kind of deference, which bordered on fear, puzzled me, because Jim didn't carry himself like a knockout artist or anything. Brown-skinned and medium-built, he always dressed neat and spoke softly. He was clean-shaven, and he constantly carried books and newspapers tucked under his arms.

Eventually, I figured out that the characteristics that made him so widely respected had little to do with how he looked; instead, it was his manly demeanor. Ever since I could recall, I and everybody else I knew had associated manhood with physical dominance and conquest of someone else. Watching Jim, I realized we'd gone about it all wrong. Jim didn't have to make a rep for himself as a thumper. He could whip a man with his sharp mind and choice words far more thoroughly than with his fists. The wolves feared his kind of ass-whipping much more than a physical beating, so they kept their distance.

I decided that this was the kind of respect I wanted to command, and I noticed other guys who without being fully aware wanted to be like Jim, too. They strutted on the yard, looking super-macho, like killers, but acted differently in private. In those moments when they weren't profiling with their buddies, some of my tough-acting homies would stop by my perch on the yard or in my cell and ask, "What you reading'?" I sensed they wanted to improve themselves but didn't want their other homies to see them, because self-improvement wasn't a macho thing. Pearly Blue was one of them. He sometimes tried to draw me into deep private discussions about God and reality while sticking to the tough street vernacular that helped him maintain his macho facade.

As I learned more about our misguided ideas about manhood, I experimented with some of those macho dudes: Whenever I passed them, I looked into their eyes to see what was there. A few had that cold-blooded, killer look about them, but in the eyes of most of them I saw something I hadn't noticed before: fear.

Even in Big Earl. Big Earl was one of the brawniest, most outwardly fearless cats in the place. He was tall and jet-black, his muscles rippled though his T-shirt, and his thighs were so massive that all his pants fit too tight. Big Earl, who was thirtyish, was from a small, off-brand town in rural Virginia, but he didn't need homies to back him up. He walked around the yard, talking loud and intimidating other inmates like he owned the place.

One day, while walking down the long sidewalk on my way to the cafeteria, I spotted Big Earl pimping toward me. (He never said anything to me, Jim, or some of the others who were part of our progressive group.) As he approached, I fixed my eyes on his and kept them locked there. When we got closer, I kept my eyes fastened to his, not in a hostile gaze, but in an expression of serene self-assurance. Initially, he tried to meet my gaze. Then he turned his eyes away and looked toward the ground. I smiled to myself. I would have never been able to back down Big Earl in a rumble, but I had certainly backed him down with my mind.

Several times after that brief, silent encounter, I caught Big Earl watching me curiously. He never said anything. He just watched and turned away whenever he realized I'd caught him staring. I sensed he knew I'd figured that he wasn't as confident of his manhood as he pretended to be, and he felt naked, exposed.

I practiced the piercing eye contact with other guys like Earl and realized that few of the seriously baad cats could meet my gaze. That helped me see my homies and the other toughs at Southampton as they were (and as I had been): streetwise, pseudo baad-asses who were really frightened boys, bluffing, trying to mask their fear of the world behind muscular frames.

■   ■   ■

Jim made parole in 1977. The word spread fast across the yard that he would soon be leaving. This dude, who had been locked up since 1962—longer than anybody else there—was getting out, and it was regarded as a momentous occasion at Southampton.

The day Jim left, hordes of guys lined up along the sidewalk to watch him walk out. The guys in our group, including me, were saddened. It was always that way when good friends left. You were glad they were getting out, yet sorrowful because they had helped you do your time.

Before leaving, Jim chatted with us a few minutes, dropped a few more morsels of advice on us, then said, "Later, man. I'll keep in touch." That was the only time I ever saw a hint of apprehension on his face.

With his arms loaded down with a boxful of books and other possessions, he walked slowly to the administration building. He waved one last time, then turned, his head held high, and disappeared through the door.

Chapter 23 FREEDOM

In the late spring of 1977, I was approved for a two-day furlough. Under prison guidelines, I could go on furlough, if approved, once I neared my parole eligibility date. I'd knocked down more than two years in the joint and had less than one to go.

When my furlough date arrived that June, I went to the administration building to sign my release papers. Looking through a glass-and-steel cage, I could see my stepfather sitting on a bench in the hallway, waiting for me. When I walked through the cage, he stood, extended his hand, and smiled. We both stood there, vigorously shaking hands and grinning broadly.

"How you doing?"

"Fine." My lips quivered. "I can't believe this."

As we headed for the car, I thought of the many nights I'd lain on my bunk, trying to imagine how it would feel to walk through that door. It felt just like I thought it would—wonderful.

On the ride home, we talked about general things—how close I was to parole eligibility, how healthy I looked. My stepfather showed me his new CB radio. There were still uneasy silences between us, but the broad gulf that had separated us didn't seem as wide as it used to be. I'd realized during my time in prison that a lot of the lessons he'd tried to teach my brothers and me—especially lessons about the dignity of work—were on the money. Sitting there, I wanted to let him know that I was beginning to see life differently and to tell him I better understood where he was coming from. But I didn't say it. I still hadn't reached a point where I could express my deepest emotions to him. We rode, and I looked anxiously out the window at all the forgotten sights flying past and took in the warm feel of the bright summer day.

Two hours later, we pulled into Cavalier Manor. I nearly broke down and cried when I saw my old neighborhood. As we drove along, I scanned all the houses of people I knew and wondered what courses their lives had taken. We turned onto Darren Drive and wound around the curve leading toward our street. When we got there and drove up to the house, my mother was standing in the doorway, waiting. I went into the house, hugged her, then walked quickly through every room to refresh my memory. I went out back into the yard and checked out the once bald spots where my brothers and I had played sandlot basketball and baseball as young boys. I never knew home meant so much.

That afternoon, I walked to a friend's house, stopped by the 7-Eleven, and ran into some of the fellas—including Lep, Holt, the dude I did my first B&E with, and Shane—who had heard I was coming home. We talked a short while, then I left. I didn't want to spend much time with them. The entire time I was down, they hadn't written or visited me, and I was pissed. I remembered that when Holt had done his prison bid years before, I'd made it a point to keep in touch with him.

Later that day, Nutbrain came by. He and Charlie Gregg had recently been paroled. Seeing my man Nutbrain was like seeing an old war buddy. We posed for pictures in front of my stepfather's new Eldorado and caught up on each other's lives. Nutbrain said he was looking for work and trying to readjust. "I'm trying to get my act together. Things out here have changed a lot, man. It's strange."

Then Liz came by with Monroe, who was by then four years old. I was glad Monroe was still too young to understand that I was doing time. I played with him in the backyard, but still found it hard to connect with him being my son. What was different was that I felt a greater sense of responsibility for him than I had before.

I nearly came apart when I first saw Liz. She looked as beautiful as ever. We embraced, then stood back and looked at each other long and hard. Her eyes were sad and she seemed tentative, like she felt guilty about having left me and was unsure how she should act. She'd said in one of her last letters that she thought we should give our thing another try. I wanted to ask questions. What did that letter mean? Was she still dating? Did she have a man? But none of that mattered at the moment. All that mattered was that she was there and open to the possibility that we could try again. The three of us—Liz, Monroe, and I—spent most of the day at my folks' house, talking and eating.

The following night, my mother baby-sat, and Liz and I went to a hotel. She'd gotten reservations at one of the best hotels in the area, the Omni in downtown Norfolk, so that we could celebrate our reunion in style. I'd hoped that after a night of passionate lovemaking, we'd both conclude that we couldn't do without each other. I'd fantasized that we'd bring back the fire we once had and that everything would come together in a nice, tidy ending, like in the movies. But it didn't work out that way. It felt so strange being out of prison that I couldn't unwind. She was uptight, too. That night we talked, we argued, we cried, we mourned the passing of our relationship. We realized, even in bed, that our old chemistry wasn't there. We'd both changed and grown, it seemed, in different directions. The next morning, Liz drove me home and we said another tearful good-bye.

Sunday came around in no time. It felt weird riding back to prison voluntarily. On the way, my stepfather let me brood in peace. I think he knew how hard it was for me to return, and he realized that it was no use trying to lighten my mood with chitchat.

I got back to Southampton and my homies crowded around to get the latest scoop from the streets.

"How was it, man?!"

"Did you get over?!"

"Who did you see on the block?"

I finished talking with them, went to my cell, and went to bed early to brood some more. The furlough had come and gone so fast it felt like I'd dreamed it.

■ ■ ■

I grew seriously uptight when I got closer to parole eligibility. It was the kind of uptight where you can barely speak and your fuse is short, and everybody knows to keep their distance until you get through your hell. Dudes were getting turndowns left and right, and I was scared that my motivation—or sanity—would slip if I got denied.

I knew my case would be a tough call for the parole board. There were a few matters working against me: I was a repeat offender. I was on probation for another felony when I stuck up the hamburger joint, and both crimes involved the use of a gun. But there were also some things working in my favor. Except for a few minor infractions, I'd been a model prisoner, if there is such a thing. I'd stayed clean, obeyed the rules, and, most important, I had a supportive family to go home to, unlike many inmates, who had nowhere to go.

The trip home made me focus more on my future and try to figure out what I would do if paroled. I definitely wanted to return to college, but to study what? I'd considered studying to be a librarian when I got out. After reading about Margaret Mead's fieldwork with the Hopi Indians, I became so fascinated that I thought I might want to study anthropology. When I read Ernest Hemingway, I thought I might be a writer.

I also reminded myself of reality as I viewed it: White people pursue careers; black folks pursue jobs. I marveled that white people made livings in so many interesting ways beyond working at a shipyard or joining the Army.

Jim had urged me to learn a trade before leaving prison, and I knew that that, too, would help my parole chances. He said most of the guys in prison couldn't be rehabilitated "because they had never been habilitated in the first place." I looked up the word "habilitate" and concluded he was right. The definition said: "to make capable, qualify." Most inmates couldn't be *requalified* because they had never been *qualified* for anything before going to prison. The only skill most of those guys at Southampton could boast of was their knuck games, their ability to throw down.

Auto mechanics, dentistry, brick masonry, and several other vocational trades were offered at Southampton, but none of that interested me. Jim, who operated the printshop for the complex, taught me how to use the small printing press and, shortly before leaving, told me about a lucrative scam he'd run. He'd printed bogus copies of the canteen cards that were distributed to inmates as their monthly pay. He gave some fake cards to needy inmates and sold most of the rest to other prisoners at discount rates for cash. Whenever he got visits, he sent the cash home to be placed in a bank account so he'd have money saved up when he got out.

I decided to learn the printing trade. I wrote the warden and state prison officials, asking for a transfer to the minimum-security St. Brides Correctional Center, which had the only printing program in the state prison system. A month or so later, I noted in my journal when I got the good news:

> *Well, my transfer to St. Brides has been approved and now I am waiting to leave. I must get into the habit of stepping out into the unknown and making the necessary sacrifices for the things I want. My goals must be in focus at all times; I must eat, drink, sleep, and think college until I am there. . . . It's me against the world. . . .*
> *July 25, 1977*

Less than a month later, a guard came to my cell one morning and told me, "Pack your bags and go to the administration building." I was to be transferred to St. Brides.

■ ■ ■

The St. Brides compound is located in Chesapeake, less than twenty miles from Cavalier Manor. When I wrote my mother and told her where I was, she was thrilled. It was as if the closer proximity to home was a symbolic sign that I was also nearer to freedom.

Compared to Southampton, St. Brides was easy time. The atmosphere was more laid-back. Most inmates had little time to do and light convictions: burglary, drug abuse, parole violation. Others with serious felony convictions, such as mine, were close enough to parole eligibility to have their prison status upgraded to minimum-security. There were no wolves to speak of at St. Brides. It was understood that being in such a chilled-out place was a privilege, and guys seldom did anything crazy that might get them shipped to rougher compounds. The Richmond and Tidewater gangs also dominated at St. Brides, but the tension level was so low it didn't matter whether guys had homies or not.

The first day I got there, I ran into homeboys from Portsmouth and, of course, from Cavalier Manor: Red, Wink-Wink, Al Porter, Piggy Hume, and Reed. They were glad to see me and helped me get settled in, just like my homies had done before.

I got acclimated in no time. Most evenings after chow, I hung out on the yard, playing chess and shooting the breeze. At night, we watched TV or hung out at each other's bunks in the dormitory cells, like soldiers in a barracks, rapping about the streets and listening to music.

I found a lot of ways to keep busy. I entered and won the annual chess tournament at the complex. The win and the trophy (I still have it) were especially sweet because I beat an egotistical white inmate in the finals. I fasted for two days in preparation for that match and beat that white boy like he stole something. Jim and Mo Battle would have been proud of me.

Since I was close to home, more people were able to visit me. One visitor was my neighbor Greg, who had remained close to my family and who was living at home after being kicked out of the Army. I also got visits from Yvette Johnson, an old school friend I'd run into when I went home on furlough. I was so grateful for female companionship that I instantly fell for Yvette the first time she visited.

Overall, I treated St. Brides like an adventure. Going there and having to adjust to a new environment all over again helped kill time. That's what I needed in those last few months: to kill time, to keep myself preoccupied with so many challenges that time passed unnoticed.

■ ■ ■

While awaiting an opening for printshop classes, I worked in the kitchen. I rose early every morning, dressed in my white hat and Pillsbury Dough Boy uniform, and helped prepare inmates' meals. When mealtime came, I worked in the serving line, scooping food from the deep containers and loading it onto inmates' trays.

One day, a group of about ten people came through the kitchen as part of a citizens' tour. I was cleaning tables as they passed into the dining area and sat down. As I set glasses of tea on tables before them, I recognized one of the men in the group. It was Mr. Brown, my junior high school gym teacher. His hair had gone gray and he'd grown a mustache, but otherwise he looked the same. When our eyes met, he stared at me a long time, straining to remember. He pointed a finger and squinted his eyes. "Where do I know you from? You were in one of my classes, weren't you?"

"Yes," I said. "I took gym and health under you at W. E. Waters. I'm Nathan McCall."

"That's right. McCall." The Mr. Brown I remembered would have started jonin' on the spot, but nothing was funny now. I could tell he was disappointed and hurt to see me, one of his former students, doing time. He looked long and hard and remained silent, wondering, I assumed, what to say next. Then he asked, "What are you in for, McCall?"

I said, "Armed robbery."

He shook his head slightly. A wave of shame passed through me. I felt like I should try to explain, to let him know I expected to get out soon and assure him that I intended to straighten up. But what was there to explain? What good would it do?

Mr. Brown suddenly realized that the other visitors, all white, were staring. He stiffened and became self-conscious, lowering his voice when he spoke and occasionally cutting an eye at his white colleagues.

Eventually, the institutional guide urged the group to move on to the next phase of the tour. Before leaving, Mr. Brown leaned low toward me and said, "Hang in there."

"Sure. I'll see you around, Mr. Brown." I waved good-bye. I relived that fifteen-minute encounter over and over in my mind the rest of that day. I thought about how hard Mr. Brown used to jone and preach to guys in our class at Waters, and how many of his former students were either dead or in prison, like me. Seeing him made me remember how hard I'd studied for one of his midterm exams, and for some strange reason I still recalled snatches of the definition of one of the health terms I'd memorized but never quite grasped: basal metabolism.

I wished that I could've talked with him longer. Mr. Brown was one of many black people who had shown me and other students that he cared, and I wanted to let him know that I finally understood the value of such caring. I wanted to tell him that his efforts had not been in vain, even though, judging from my circumstances, that seemed to be the case. But Mr. Brown was gone, and there was nothing to do but grieve in my journal.

> *Today, I saw Mr. Brown, my former gym teacher from junior high school. I could see that he was hurt and disappointed to see me in prison. He had one of those "Where did I fail?" looks in his eyes. I wanted to tell him that he had been a good teacher to me. I wanted to convince him, to recite something that he had taught me in health class: Basal metabolism is the rate at which the heart makes up heat from the oxygen and food substances in the blood. . . . Maybe that's right. Maybe not.*
>
> *There are so many Mr. Browns out there who do their damnedest to teach the Nathan McCalls that there is a right way and a wrong way, a good way and a bad. And there are far too many Nathan McCalls who simply must learn the hard way.*
>
> *September 17, 1977*

No African American spends much time in prison without being exposed to the doctrines of black Muslims. Ever since the Nation of Islam was founded in the 1930s, it has drawn a lot of its converts from prison, where the Muslims have a captive audience of brothers to teach what they call "the plain truth."

The Muslims commanded as much respect as any group at Southampton. Always neatly dressed and well behaved, they walked around in their kufis, carrying copies of the Holy Qur'an and spreading their message of black salvation through self-reliance.

Brothers respected Muslims for being disciplined, religious people and, at the same time, warriors. The Muslims didn't believe in that stuff about turning the other cheek. Nobody messed with them, because many of them were hard-nosed cats who were eager to throw down for a righteous cause.

The Muslims at St. Brides were led by a guy named Rasool, who was respected there like Jim was revered at Southampton. When I got to St. Brides, Rasool watched me from a distance for a while, then sent two of his representatives to invite me to the weekly service that he led. I went to the service and later talked with him over a few games of chess. Initially I was skeptical, but after checking out the Muslims' beliefs, I was impressed. The group Rasool represented was the American Muslim Mission (not to be confused with the Nation of Islam, which is led by Louis Farrakhan). The Muslim Mission is led by Warith Muhammad, the son of onetime Nation of Islam leader Elijah Muhammad. When Elijah died in 1975, Warith and Farrakhan split because Warith wanted to lead the group to a more orthodox practice of the faith. They'd evolved a lot from the 1960s, when they railed about "Yacub, the big-headed scientist," who, according to them, created white people from a mixture of pig and dog.

Rasool explained all of that to me when we talked. He also turned me on to one of the hippest books I read in prison. It was a thin, simply written paperback titled *Natural Psychology and Human Transformation*. Written by Dr. Na'im Akbar, a black psychologist who is also a Muslim, the book suggests ways that people can develop their full potential. It grabbed my attention right off the bat because, after wasting so many years messing around in the streets, I was trying to do double time to regain direction and mental health.

In his book, Dr. Akbar uses the example of the butterfly, which goes through several incarnations—from a caterpillar to a flying insect—to reach full development. He says that human beings similarly have the potential to develop and transform in stages. He says we start off in a caterpillar stage as crawling babies, concerned solely with satisfying our most basic physical needs. Then we evolve into mental beings who are able to think and extend our desires beyond basic physical drives. Our highest and most beautiful stage of development, he says, is spiritual, a state that enables us to soar, symbolically, like a butterfly.

Dr. Akbar says that most people don't understand the developmental process and, as a result, don't even strive to reach their highest potential. In fact, he says, many people grow up and remain mentally locked in the wormlike first stage, the baby stage, where they focus solely on satisfying their base physical appetites.

When I reflected, I realized that my entire life before prison had been spent locked in that baby stage. Most of the dudes I knew had lived like that. In fact, when I *really* thought about it, it seemed that much of American culture was conditioned that way—self-absorbed, driven mainly by greed for material possessions, and uninterested in evolving to a higher stage or extending concern beyond self to other human beings.

Natural Psychology and Human Transformation helped me focus more intently on reaching my spiritual peak. Whenever I fasted and meditated, I could *feel* my spirit strengthening. I realized that there was an entire aspect of myself, probably the most important aspect, that I had completely ignored for most of my life. It was an enlightening discovery for me.

■ ■ ■

I got lots of what I had gone to St. Brides for. The printing program had a top-notch instructor and featured the latest equipment. I learned to operate offset presses, do studio photography, layout, and platemaking—the whole printing process, from start to finish. The instructor was a friendly, philosophical white man, who seemed to genuinely enjoy teaching. Some days, when class was over, he spent time chatting with us about the challenges we could expect to face when we returned to the real world.

He said—and I knew—that my chances of success would be increased greatly if I could find a decent printing job or get into college. More and more, I found that I enjoyed writing. I narrowed my career choices down to English literature and journalism. I tried to find out all I could about journalism; what it is that journalists do, how much they earn, etc. I recalled how two journalists at *The Washington Post* had used their reporting skills to kick a corrupt president square in the ass, and that seemed like the kind of thing I'd like to learn.

I wrote the head of Norfolk State University's journalism department, explained my situation, and told him I wanted badly to make a new start. The department head, Dr. Larry Kaggwa, wrote back to me. He also entered me in a competition that required me to write a paper explaining why I wanted to study journalism. I wrote the paper and won a one-year tuition scholarship. I was pleasantly stunned. It was the second time in months that I'd gone after something—something geared toward self-improvement—and gotten it.

Dr. Kaggwa's quick response also boosted my belief that black colleges and universities are committed to helping blacks beyond the classroom. I'll bet that if I'd written from prison to the department head at some white university, he probably would have notified the campus police or sought an order barring me from coming within fifty yards of his white campus. That help from Dr. Kaggwa would go a long way in helping me demonstrate to the parole board that I had solid plans to get rolling once I sprang.

About two weeks before my hearing, I got a last-minute plug from my printshop instructor. An inmate got his hand caught in one of the large presses. When he screamed, I ran over, turned off the machine, reversed the rollers, and pulled out his hand before it could be sucked into the feeders like a sheet of paper. His hand was cut up pretty badly, but he made out all right considering what could have happened. The instructor thanked me for reacting so quickly and wrote a letter of commendation for my prison file. I was good to go.

On the day I went before the parole board, I was so nervous I was nearly paralyzed. I was scared that I'd get in there, get asked a question, and choke. I was scared that when it was time for me to speak, all my suffering would come to the surface and all my emotions would bum-rush my throat, and nothing would come out. So I did deep-breathing exercises and prayed for the best.

I waited in a hallway with about six other dudes who were going before the board that day. All of us looked alike. We looked like choirboys sitting out there. We were spit-shined and scrubbed and lotioned down to the max. We all had our hair cut short. We had our shirts buttoned to the very top, and we were so quiet you could hear the roaches walking across the shiny floor.

But appearances didn't seem to sway the board. When dudes came out after meeting with the board, they were red-eyed and withdrawn. I asked one guy how he thought things had gone for him. He looked at me, shook his head slowly, and said, "It looks bad for the home team."

When my name was called, I went in and took a seat before the board members—several white men and a black woman—who sat behind a long table. It was a stern-faced, tight-butt bunch. No-nonsense all the way. They asked a few questions about my crime, my family, that sort of thing. Then, after several other minor questions, came the biggie: "So, Mr. McCall, what do you plan to do to better yourself if you get out, and what arrangements have you made to carry out those plans?"

If a cat hasn't given serious consideration to his future, really thought it out, that's the question that cold-cocks him. That's the one that renews his lease for another year. If he's wasted his time and neglected to improve himself, he can't answer that question convincingly. He's down for the count. TKO. With the parole board, you've got to come strong or not at all, because they've heard all the bullshit they care to hear, and they can smell it a mile away.

I knew all that going in. I knew I couldn't go in there half-stepping. I was prepared. My future? Shit, I had thought about it, prayed about it, and dreamed about it the entire time I was down. I had thought a helluva lot about my future—enough to know that I might not *have* a future if I didn't get sprung that first time up. When they hit me with that question, they hit the right person that time, because I was ready.

I rapped. I rapped *hard*. I rapped harder than I'd ever rapped in my life. I took all the skills I'd picked up rapping with those penitentiary philosophers out on the yard and threw the whole handful at the parole board. I told them all I'd done to improve myself in the nearly three years that I'd been locked up, and shared my plans to go home to my family and to enroll at Norfolk State. I told them that robbing that hamburger joint was the stupidest thing I could have done, and that I'd spent a lot of time thinking about that and other mistakes I'd made in my life. The bottom line was, I came straight from the heart. I came from so deep within the heart that I surprised myself. But I meant every word I said. I was changed. I knew it, and I wanted to make sure they knew it.

I'll bet those white folks on that parole board were glad when I finally finished talking. I'll bet they thought I'd never shut up. I'll bet that when I finished and left that room, they burst out laughing and said, "Damn! We need to hurry up and let this nigger out. This dude wants *badly* to get out of here."

But they didn't come off like that. They were very professional. When I finished talking, one of the parole board members said, "Thank you, Mr. McCall. The board will take into consideration all that you have said. You will be notified within the next month of our decision." They sent me on my way without a hint of the verdict.

■ ■ ■

Waiting for an answer was like waiting to be sentenced all over again. Those few weeks were as hard on me as the entire three years had been. I nagged my institutional counselor constantly to see if a response had come. He got mad at me for nagging him, and I got mad at him for getting mad at me. If he had been an inmate and not a counselor, we would have come to blows, because I was uptight as hell and I already had a full head of steam.

When my letter from the board finally arrived, I took it to my bunk and sat down alone. I looked at the letter in the sealed envelope a long time before even attempting to open it. I needed a drink, but since there were no bars open in the penitentiary, I had to face it straight. I gave myself a long talking-to before opening it: *Keep cool. You've done the best you could do. You've given it your best shot and programmed hard. Stay strong, no matter what happens.*

Then I opened the letter and I could hardly believe it. For a long while, I just sat there, staring at the words, reading the letter over and over, making sure I'd gotten it right. I thought, *I made parole. I made it. I'm getting out. They're gonna let me go. I can go home. Soon. I made it. I can't believe it. I made it. I made parole!*

Waiting for my February 3, 1978, release date was worse than waiting for the parole letter, especially in the final few weeks. There were times, crazy moments, when reason escaped me and I feared something weird might happen to make them revoke my parole. I'd heard horror stories of dudes who caught new charges while waiting to walk. Once, at Southampton, a dude got set up on a reefer bust only a few days before he was to leave. He went to court and got more time. I had no known enemies who would do that to me, but I knew that in the craziness of prison life, anything was possible. I wouldn't have been too surprised if my counselor had come to me and said, "The parole board notified me that they made a mistake. They sent the letter to the wrong person. You got turned down." That's the kind of stuff that happened sometimes. Any inmate with half a brain knows not to get too happy; he knows that it ain't over till it's over. He's not free until he walks out that front door. So I waited and struggled through the toughest few weeks of my entire bid:

> *Even though I have made parole, time is no easier to conquer than it was nearly three years ago. A day is still 24 grueling hours and a week is still an eternity. The fact that I will soon be freed has eased my present suffering very little, for in my heart I am serving a life sentence until the day I walk out that front gate.*
> *January 16, 1978*

In our final talk before I went home, the printshop instructor told me something I never forgot: "Make sure that whatever you do, you find a job in an atmosphere that is psychologically comfortable for you."

I appreciated the intent, but I needed that piece of advice like I needed a .25 automatic with extra clips. It was clear to me that, as a white man, my instructor came from a reality that gave him enough choices to be able to look for a *comfortable* work environment. But that was a foreign concept to me, a contradiction in terms. I knew that if I worked, I'd likely work for white folks. So how could that be comfortable? I figured that if I followed my instructor's advice and looked for a comfortable work environment, I'd be unemployed all my life, unless I worked for a black-owned business or started one myself.

I politely thanked my instructor for the advice and moved on, thinking, *He meant well. He didn't know no better.*

When I thought about it later, I concluded that his advice was better suited for those happy-faced white boys in my printing class. Using connections they had on the outside, most of them landed job guarantees at local commercial printshops before their prison release. It pissed me off that the white boys had the inside track, even in the penitentiary. They acted like they had it made, like they *knew* they were going to get back into the flow of things as soon as they were sprung. They were chilled, and I was nervous as hell, anxious and scared at the same time, wondering what would happen to me on the outside if things didn't work out.

> *I have observed that many whites here seem unfazed by their plight in prison. They regard confinement merely as a temporary restraint from their usual lives. And they face the future with optimism, confident that they have only to slip on a coat and tie, get a haircut, and shave for the establishment to forgive their transgressions. . . . But most blacks look ahead with apprehension, afraid that we may never be forgiven for our crimes—or the color of our skin.*
> *January 24, 1978*

I remember clearly that snowy February day in 1978 when I was released from the joint. My homies gathered on the sidewalk that morning and watched me leave. As I climbed into the car and my mother drove off, I cast a long, hard look at the prison, and tears began streaming uncontrollably down my face. I felt a strange mixture of pain and pride. I was mostly proud that I had survived, and I told myself, then and there, *I can do ANYTHING.*

Although it had been the most tragic event in my life, prison—with all its sickness and suffering—had also been my most instructional challenge. It forced me to go deep, real deep, within and tap a well I didn't even know I had. Through that painful trip, I'd found meaning. No longer was life a thing of bewilderment. No longer did I feel like a cosmic freak, a black intruder in a world not created for me and my people. No longer were my angry feelings about the vast white world simply vague, invalid impulses dangling on the edge of my mind. I knew the reasons for those feelings now. I understood them better, and, most important, I could express them precisely as they arose. I knew that there was purpose and design in creation and that my life was somehow part of that grand scheme. I had just as much right to be alive and happy as anybody else, and I wasn't going to let anybody, especially not white folks, make me feel otherwise.

PART THREE

PART THREE

Chapter 24 HOME

The house was completely quiet when we walked in. There was no one there but my mother and me. She'd left me to my thoughts during the emotional ride from St. Brides. When we entered the living room, she broke the silence and tried to lighten the heaviness of those fragile first moments home. "Well, boy, you finally made it outta that place."

"Yeah, Ma, I made it out." I kept walking to the back of the house. I could hardly talk. It was too risky. Talking would bring on another tearful breakdown. . . . I needed to be alone.

I dropped my belongings in my old bedroom, went into the bathroom, and ran hot water into the tub. It had been nearly three years since I'd been allowed to take a bath. In all that time, it had been showers, always showers, in a large tiled room with ten or more nozzles and as many loud, funky hardheads moving about. Now I could close the bathroom door and shut out the world. I could lock it and nobody would care. I climbed into the tub, sank down low, and let the water creep up to my chin. With eyes closed, I sat there, soaking, thinking, taking in the profound pleasure of it all. I tried my new reality on for size in a hundred different ways: *Home. I'm actually home. They let me out. I made parole. . . . If I want, I can get up now and walk out that front door and nobody will care. I can walk down the street and around the corner and won't get written up. I can go to the store. I can talk on the phone. I can ride a bus. . . . I'm home.*

It felt surreal, like an out-of-body experience, like maybe I was daydreaming it from a cell in the C-3 building at Southampton and might be awakened any minute by the sound of jangling keys or chattering inmates. But all I heard was the deep quiet of the house and the occasional soothing ripple of warm water splashing against my skin, flapping against the side of the tub.

In those first few weeks, I wore the consciousness of my new freedom like an overcoat. While riding a bus or walking through a crowded mall it would dawn on me: *I just got out of prison. I did three years. Now I'm out.* I never said it to people, but I felt it in every interaction and thought it at the oddest times, especially when learning new things and relearning old things. There were readjustments to make: being around elderly people, children, and dogs; walking through the aisles of grocery stores; seeing all those beautiful, wonderful women walking around, free and accessible.

Several times, I tested my freedom to verify it. I got out of bed late at night and walked through Cavalier Manor—just because I could. No guards came running. No whistles blew. No bells sounded. Nothing. It was real. I was home.

■ ■ ■

For a long time, everything felt alien, like one of those movies where a person is frozen in a block of ice, and when it thaws he discovers he's in the same place but in a different time. It seemed I was moving about at a different pace than the rest of the world; like for three years, the world had been speeding ahead while I'd stood still.

The first time I went through a checkout line at Earle's supermarket on Victory Boulevard, the clerk passed my items over a computerized scanner, which I had never seen. I was fascinated. It made me feel like I'd been locked away a hundred years. The first time I stepped out into traffic, it scared me to death. It had never occurred to me before then that you had to consciously *think*, to gauge and measure the speed of oncoming cars, before crossing a street.

Of course, the fashion changes were constant reminders of how long I'd been gone. The platform shoes and bell-bottom pants in my closet just wouldn't cut it. Mama gave me some money and I bought a pair of soft, thin-heeled shoes and blue flair-leg denims, and I wore them until they nearly fell off.

I knew I was seriously out of it when I ran across Slick. Walking down Cavalier Boulevard, I saw him across the ditch, pimping in the opposite direction, toward the 7-Eleven. Slick was a little lightweight chump when I left the streets. Now his frame had filled out and he was strutting hard, like an old-head. I yelled across the ditch to him and threw up my clenched fist in the Black Power salute. Slick raised his hand similarly, but flashed a different sign. Two of his three middle fingers were tucked under, like a partial fist, and the pinkie and index fingers stood upright, like antlers on a deer. After flashing that sign, Slick turned and bopped away.

Later, I demonstrated the sign to my brother Dwight and asked, "What does that mean?"

He said, "Oh, that's the P-Funk sign."

"P-Funk?"

"You know. Parliament/Funkadelic."

Parliament/Funkadelic was the hottest new black music group on the scene. I'd heard a few of their tunes on the radio at St. Brides, but still wasn't fully hip. Dwight showed me a picture of the group on an album cover. They looked wild and crazy, like a black rock group. I thought, *Damn. When I left the streets, people were doing the Black Power salute. Now they flashing the P-Funk sign. These niggahs gone crazy.*

There were also tense moments that taught me how much I'd really been affected emotionally by the whole prison ordeal. Shortly after I got my license renewed, I was driving my stepfather's Mercury Comet down Portsmouth Boulevard when the sound of sirens pierced the air. It was the shrill, urgent sound of trouble, coming from behind. I panicked. I wheeled the car off the main street onto a side road and pulled over to the curb. I sat there, horrified, waiting for them to come after me. My heart pounded like crazy. The sirens grew louder and louder, getting closer and closer. When it seemed they were right up on me, I looked in my rearview mirror in time to see a police car zoom past, its red lights flashing. Then they were gone. I took a deep breath, exhaled, and bowed my head.

Why had I been so shaken? I hadn't done anything wrong. I wasn't speeding. Then it struck me: The last time red lights flashed down on me, I wound up doing time. In my head, we were leaving the McDonald's all over again. I was driving this time and the cops were coming from everywhere, preparing to surround the car and close in for the bust.

I leaned my forehead on the steering wheel a few minutes, thinking about how scared I'd felt that night and at this moment. I sat there until I was sure everything was all right. When my heartbeat slowed, I started the car and drove off.

■   ■   ■

Not much had changed with the family since I'd left, except for Bampoose, who was frail and sickly. I went to visit her in the senior citizens' complex across town, where she'd moved after living in Norfolk for a while. Junnie was still away in the Army. Billy was married and still living in New York. My mother was concerned that Dwight, who had been drifting in and out of jobs around Portsmouth since he got out of the Army, was dabbling heavily in drugs. He and a strung-out lady friend were busted in the Jeffry Wilson public housing projects with some works in the car. He was placed on probation.

After all the problems Dwight and I had given my parents, they'd clamped down hard on my youngest brother, Bryan. Nine years younger than me, he was almost in high school and my parents barely let him leave the street without permission or go out after dark. Unlike Dwight and me, Bryan didn't know diddly-squat about the streets. My parents tightened the reins on him so much that my friends joked that if you took him to the other side of Cavalier Manor and left him, he wouldn't know how to find his way back home.

I called Liz to make arrangements to see Monroe. Part of me wanted to see her, too, to see if maybe we could rekindle our thing. I talked to Liz before leaving the house, but when I made the fifteen-minute walk to her family's place, it was her mother who answered the door. Liz was gone, she said. I got the message.

Monroe was sitting on the living-room floor, playing with toys. I went in and talked with him, trying to relate to him as best as I could. But it felt awkward trying to make conversation with a five-year-old. Besides, there was still no strong paternal connection. I'd been away from him for more than half his life. My affection for him felt forced. I could tell he didn't feel connected to me, either. He seemed to regard me no more differently than he did my brothers.

After that visit, I went past the 7-Eleven to check out the scene. Shane and a lot of the old-heads were there, hanging around outside the store, sharing a spot along the wall with some new faces I didn't recognize. Many were my peers' baby brothers. Young and brawny, they had that teenage cockiness about them that was once my style.

The guys at the store filled me in on everybody and gave me the latest scoop on Scobie-D. He was married with a few children and, they said, working at the shipyard. I couldn't imagine Scobe working for somebody, least of all the white man. Working for somebody meant you had to take orders. But he had to eat and feed his family, like everyone else. So he had to work and take orders, no matter how baad he was.

Even though he was mellowing, Scobe, with that flaming red hair and limp wrist, was still the baaddest cat in Cavalier Manor. Shane told me Scobe had recently "fucked up Frank Watford for pissing him off." Scobe had gotten into a beef with Frank at the basketball court behind Waters Junior High. Tall and dark, Frank was a basketball purist who cared less about rumbling than about popping the nets clean with a sweet outside jumper from the top of the key. He loved playing street ball, and he knew the game from way back when. Scobe got mad because Frank was checking him too tight. When Scobe started crying foul, Frank held his ground, trying to save face. Just like always, Scobe left to get his gun.

When he saw Scobe return with the piece in his hand, Frank made a break for the fence, which was more than seventy-five yards away. But he wasn't fast enough. Scobe cocked the trigger, took aim, and fired, striking Frank in the back in full view of everybody on the basketball court.

Frank was taken to the hospital. He lived and, to everybody's surprise, pressed charges against Scobe. Frank lost the case. Although there had been hundreds of dudes at the basketball court that day, nobody dared go to the trial to back up his story. So Scobe walked, and added another notch on his rep.

The whole thing blew Frank's mind. Shane said that the last time he'd seen Frank, "That niggah was ridin' a Huffy bike with balloon tires through Cavalier Manor, deliverin' newspapers. He had a nappy Afro and was mumbling to hisself. He's fucked up in the head now."

Shane gave me the lowdown on all the fellas from around our way, including himself. He'd been in and out of jail on lightweight bids. Nutbrain and Charlie Gregg were around, he said, but they'd been low-key since they got out of the joint. Most of the others, including Shell Shock, Lep, Frog Dickie, and Bimbo, were unemployed or working at the shipyard. Shane said the drug game was changing. "You can't even get a good four-finger O.Z. no more! A halfa ounce cost you thirty-five dollars."

After we'd talked awhile, Shane looked me up and down, as if noticing me for the first time. "So, my man, what's up with you?"

"Not much, man. I'm trying to find a job until I can start college."

"That's cool. . . . You wanna go to the Broadway Club with me Friday night?"

I paused before answering. That was the challenge I knew would come—to hang with the fellas, or not to hang. I wanted to stay away from the old spots. I knew the gang would want to hang out, get high, and do some crazy shit for old times' sake, but I didn't want to get into any of that. At the same time, I didn't want the fellas to say I'd changed. On the streets, they treat it like something bad if you hang with them, then change and start doing something different. They get a complex and start thinking that maybe you think you're better than them. If I didn't hang, I knew what they would say about me. I knew how Shane would run it down to some of the others: *Yeah, man, that niggah done changed. He talkin' proper, usin' big words and shit. That niggah done gone off to the penitentiary and got GRAND on us. Think he too good to hang with his boys.*

But I couldn't be too concerned about what anybody said. I had grown. I wanted to keep moving ahead in life and not even think about falling back into the old groove that had once had my head so messed up.

So I turned down Shane's offer. Then there was this strange silence. There was nothing else to talk about. When we both realized that, we split.

Actually, I didn't know where to go or what to do for fun, beyond the things I used to do. I kept a low profile. Yvette, the school friend who'd visited me in prison, became my haven. A dark-skinned, brown-eyed beauty with prominent cheekbones and an infectious smile, Yvette told me she'd had a crush on me in high school but stayed away after I hooked up with Liz because she thought I preferred red-bones. (I've since learned from a lot of dark-skinned sisters that they had complexes about their complexion when they were young.) Yvette and I spent a lot of time together talking in my parents' den. She sought refuge in me from her mother, who cussed her out whenever they disagreed. I sought refuge in her because I'd given up my old life and had nothing to replace it with.

I was grateful to her for being there, but besides her there was no one to talk to, no one as stimulating as some of the brothers I'd met in the joint. I was sure there were many intelligent, progressive people out there somewhere, but I had no idea where they were or how to find them. It was weird and I felt lonely.

■ ■ ■

My parole officer was a cockeyed young white guy with a big water-melon head and thin, stringy hair that he combed from one side of his head all the way across the top to cover his bald spot. Right away, I resented him. I resented the whole notion of being on parole. I felt I'd paid my debt to society—or whoever the hell felt they were owed— and that the slate should be squeaky clean.

During our first meeting, my P.O. lectured me about what I could and couldn't do. It was humiliating and made me feel like a child: I had to report to him once a month. I couldn't own a firearm. I couldn't vote. I couldn't travel outside the immediate area without his written permission. Finally, putting on his best stern-faced look, he added, "And you're not to associate with other ex-felons."

I wanted to slap my knee and laugh in that white man's face. I wanted to say, *Motherfucka, you may as well ship me to the desert to live, 'cause half the niggahs in Portsmouth are ex-felons.* But I didn't say it. I kept quiet and nodded my head, signaling that I understood.

Right away, my P.O. pressured me to find a job. He said I'd have to report to him weekly until I got employed. That was incentive enough to get hustling. The problem was, he also told me I was required by law to tell the truth on job applications. If they asked, I had to tell I was a convicted felon.

I hit the streets hard, starting with applications to area printshops. Armed with my Offset Printing and Lithography certificate, I went in feeling confident that I could talk knowledgeably about any phase of the printing process, and I did. At one point, a printshop in Norfolk was set to bring me on. They had openings. The interview went extremely well. The fleshy-faced shop supervisor was smiling at me big-time. "You'll like it here. You'll do just fine."

Then, as I sat there, he scanned my application. His big blue eyes stopped near the bottom—the section where they ask, *Have you ever been convicted of a felony?* I had put "Yes" in that section.

The supervisor looked at me, turned the application my way, pointed at that section, and said, "What's this about?"

"Well, uh, I was convicted of armed robbery and served three years. I'm out on parole." I heard the words as if they'd been spoken by someone else. The supervisor played it off, like it was no big deal. Then he went into that "We'll call you" mode and walked me to the door.

I knew it was over. I knew I'd never hear from him again, and I didn't.

Several times, I missed out on plum printing jobs like that one, jobs that I really wanted, all, it seemed, because I came clean about my record. It didn't make me feel good about telling the truth, especially to white folks. Most blacks understand that a brother with a rap sheet is commonplace, like being circumcised. But white folks take that shit to heart. They don't understand, and they don't forgive.

Job hunting is expensive. The little money I'd saved from working in prison was gone in no time. I had to rely on my parents for bus fare. My pride wouldn't let me ask them for much. I walked wherever I could, but most places I went were not within walking distance. The frustration of going from door to door to businesses in Norfolk and Portsmouth brought to mind a line about job hunting in a rendition of "Inner City Blues" by Gil Scott-Heron:

Walk a big hole in a brand-new pair of shoes
and you've had your first look
at the inner city blues. . . .

Every time I filled out an application and ran across that section
about felony convictions, it made me feel sick inside. I felt like getting
up and walking out on the spot. What was the use? I knew what they
were going to do. No white folks would hire me. It was bad enough
that I was black. A black man with a felony record didn't stand a
chance, no matter how many trade certificates or degrees he had.

The thing that irritated me most was that everywhere I went it
seemed white folks were always asking if they could "help" me. Every
time I walked into a store or into a building, white people rushed up
to me before I could get in the door good and asked, "May I help
you?" They'd look at me like I was a germ, like they thought I was
there to steal something or stick up the place. "May I help you?"
They always said it loud enough to make other people stop and stare.
I knew the deal. That was their way of alerting everybody else. That
was their way of announcing, "Beware! There's a *black* man in here!"

It still pisses me off now when white folks rush up to me and ask,
"May I help you?" Hell, they were doing everything in their power
to hold me *back*. When they asked if they could help me back then,
I wanted to cuss them out. I wanted to say, *Yeah, motherfucka, you can
help me! Help me get a JOB!*

Seeing how frustrated I was getting, my parents suggested that I
get away for a while, so I went to Washington, D.C., to job-hunt.
There, I lived with the family of one of my father's old Navy buddies.
I wandered around downtown D.C. applying for jobs at printshops
and other places. It felt refreshing being in a city where nobody knew
me. In D.C., I didn't have a street image to contend with. I had a clean
slate. But that comfort didn't last long. After a few weeks, I ran out
of money and had to return home and start the job search there again.

Over time, the frustration worsened. My P.O. kept bugging me,
and I stayed broke all the time. There was nothing to give Liz for child
support. Every now and then, she'd make some sarcastic remark about
me not doing anything for my son. For a while, I stopped going
around to see Monroe because I was so ashamed that I had no money.
I couldn't even afford to take Yvette to see a movie.

With no money, no car, no apartment, I began to feel like less of
a man, like I was a grown child depending on my parents. My

self-esteem started slipping. Every day I got more uptight and madder at the world.

One day, while driving my stepfather's car, I pulled into the drive-in window of the Burger King on Victory Boulevard. I ordered. "Gimme a fish sandwich, fries, and a shake."

The server, a white man who appeared to be in his mid-twenties, hurriedly took the order, handed me the food, and shut the window. I needed more change. I waited as the server spoke on the intercom, apparently taking orders from other customers driving in behind me. Noticing I was still there waiting, he frowned and opened the window to see what I wanted. I could tell he was annoyed.

I asked, "Could you give me change for a ten, please?"

Without saying a word, the clerk clucked his tongue in disgust, snatched the ten-dollar bill from my hand, and slammed the window shut. After changing the bill from the cash register, he opened the window and all but threw the money back at me. Quarters dropped from my hand and landed in my lap. The clerk rolled his eyes, slammed the window shut again, and waited for me to leave.

That old fire—the fire I used to feel all the time before I went to prison—resurfaced, and blood rushed *hot* to my head. Before I knew it, I'd sped the car away from the drive-in window and wheeled into a nearby parking space. I jumped out of the car, bolted through the front door of the Burger King, and leaped onto the front counter. All the nerves in my body had readied for battle. Just as I was about to swing my legs across the counter, a black store manager stepped forward and held his hand aloft, almost pleadingly. "Be cool, brother. Be cool."

Those few words, spoken in a soft, sincere tone that suggested that he understood, were enough to make me stop long enough to recon-sider my actions. I got off the counter and stood there, breathing heavily. Customers and other Burger King employees stopped and stared. The white server, his eyes wide, stood back behind the man-ager. I glared into his eyes and felt hatred seething in my soul. I wanted him bad. I wanted him bad enough to risk thirty days in jail. By then, I was feeling that if I could get across that counter and reach that white boy, I would try to knock his teeth through the back of his head. I'd punch him in his face and slam his head against the ice cream machine so hard he'd have nightmares about me the rest of his life.

Looking at the manager, I pointed at the white boy and said, "You better teach that *punk* how to treat people!" Then I turned and stormed out of the store.

■ ■ ■

I'd read somewhere that 85 percent of inmates return to prison within five years of being released. Just about all the guys I knew who'd gotten out were returning so fast it seemed they had been home on furlough rather than parole. Bonaparte stuck up a restaurant and was wounded during a shoot-out with the law. Another dude went back on an armed-robbery beef shortly after he got out. I'd heard Pearly Blue died in prison of hepatitis. Jim, who was living about ninety miles away in Richmond, was the only person who seemed to be doing all right for himself. He'd found a job, and had used the money he'd embezzled from Southampton to buy a small house and a brand-new sports car.

I knew I had to work hard to reach the five-year mark. And yet as the harshness of the outside world started taking a toll, fears began dancing around in my head. Doubts seeped in. All the spiritual and philosophical principles I had studied in prison seemed to go out the window when contending with the reality of that white man's world.

Oddly, there were times when I actually missed the solitude and security of prison. For three years, I hadn't hardly had to deal with racism. It hadn't mattered whether or not white people gave me a job. I was guaranteed work in prison, and I had a place to eat and sleep, three hots and a cot. I wondered if Bone and some of the others who'd gone back had subconsciously found ways to get busted because things got too heavy for them out in the world. I wondered if I might mess around and do the same. I'd read about the power of the subconscious, and I believed it was true. I figured that if I went back to the joint for anything, it would be for going off on some white person for insulting me. But there was always the possibility of getting busted on a humble, being in the wrong place at the wrong time. I was determined not to let anything like that happen, but every now and then I wondered about it and got uptight and started thinking that it just might happen if I didn't get a better grip.

One night, while driving my stepfather's car, I stopped at a convenience store. It was located on a small, deserted street. It was late and there was only one attendant in the store. While I browsed, he went to a back room to get something. When I went to the counter, I noted: *There's no one else here. No customers. No cameras.* When the clerk returned, I made my purchase and went back to the car. I climbed in and sat there a moment, thinking. I looked up and down the street, and there was no one in sight. I thought, *I can take this place by myself. I can stick my hand in my coat like I've got a gun, and take this place.*

I'd been doing that a lot lately. I'd enter stores, case them, and assess my chances of being able to pull off another job. *Just one job, no more. All I need is some funds to tide me over until I can find work. Just this one time.*

Every person who ever did time can tell you what he did wrong to get caught. Every one feels that all he has to do is rectify that one mental error and he's on his way. I knew what had gone wrong in the McDonald's stickup. We hadn't planned carefully. I *knew* I could do it right this time.

I sat there for a long while, struggling inside my head. It was a real rumble between right and wrong. It was a struggle that on the surface didn't make sense, an internal battle that should not have been taking place in light of all that I had suffered and learned from prison. And yet, there I was, thinking about making another hit.

Sitting there in the car, I thought my plan through like a chess match. I envisioned the job step by step and mapped out my getaway route. Then I thought about something else. I remembered that I had something that most cats coming out of the joint did not: I had supportive parents. I thought about my mother and stepfather, who had suffered through three years of hell with me, from start to finish. I thought about how hard they'd pulled for me since I'd gotten out. They gave me money. I had a place to lay my head. They let me use their car. They cared about me. *They cared about me.* I couldn't let them down.

I thought about something else, too. The lessons about perseverance I learned in the joint. I'd learned about the strength of the mind and seen that mental toughness, more than brawn, determines who survives and who buckles. When I left prison, I knew I was armed with a different kind of weapon than I had relied on before going in. I had knowledge.

I started the car and drove away.

One day I'm an inmate, looking out at life through a prison fence; the next day I'm a student, walking around on a college campus. Is this a crazy world, or what?

I took a few summer courses and started school full-time in the fall of 1978. It felt good being back in college. It was a concrete move to work at building a decent future. Norfolk State was a frenzied rush of faces: black, blue-black, dark brown, caramel, tan, beige, and damn-near-white. And everywhere, bright-colored shirts and beaucoup blue jeans. Blue jeans scuttling down sidewalks and across grassy fields. Blue jeans hurriedly entering and exiting buildings. Blue jeans standing in long, *really* long lines. Faded and rich-blue blue jeans, pimping, swaying, laughing, shouting, bunched in fraternity and sorority clusters, gearing up for high-walkin', shit-talkin' step shows.

Being in school and on scholarship at Norfolk State made me feel like I was *really* getting a second shot. Walking across campus near Corpew Avenue, I remembered that one night, five years earlier, Shell Shock and I had robbed several Norfolk State students just across the street. It was hard to believe this was the same campus where I nearly jumped from the balcony of the student union building while tripping on a hit of acid called orange sunshine. I was back, with direction and purpose this time. It would be head down and plow forward. No time for foolishness. No room for play.

When I started school, I was broke like a *big* dog. Dr. Kaggwa, the department head who'd helped me get the scholarship, knew I was low on funds. He got me a cafeteria meal ticket and arranged for me to get a $50-per-week job delivering the campus newspaper. For me, that $50 was like pig feet to a pork lover. After coming off a penitentiary gig making 35¢ a day, $50 a week was a *helluva* raise.

Every Thursday, I drove Yvette's Chevrolet Camaro to the printer in Suffolk to pick up bundles of the student newspaper. I got up around 4 A.M. on Fridays and dropped off the papers at various places on campus. Then I'd go back home, shower, and head to classes.

I worked extra-hard in school, especially on the student newspaper,

The Spartan Echo. Students on staff were friendly enough. Some
became friends, but I socialized with few of them. I couldn't relate.
They were into block shows, fraternity pledging, and school dances,
and none of that interested me. So I'd do my classwork, write my
news stories, chat awhile, and dash.

The school's journalism department was a tiny collection of rooms
tucked away on the third floor of the administration building. The J
school had a stingy budget and a staff of about five professors and
teachers. Norfolk State in general had its share of financial problems,
but students there got the kind of down-home, one-on-one nurturing
that blacks at big white universities miss out on. Years later, when I
crossed over into the white mainstream, I learned to deeply appreciate
Norfolk State. I saw that a lot of those blacks who had degrees from
prestigious white universities didn't know whether they were coming
or going; they didn't know who they were or what time it was.

The difference at black schools such as Norfolk State was that
professors didn't pull punches with us students about what we were
up against. They didn't try to pretend that everything was hunky-
dory in the mainstream world we were preparing for. We learned
about our specific fields of study, but a lot of the teaching revolved
around what it would take to deal on the white man's turf.

There were several teachers in our department who seriously
honed in on things like that. One was Harry Williams, a chain-
smoking student adviser on loan from *The Virginian Pilot–Ledger
Star,* the city's local newspaper. He was determined that no students
of his would pass into the white work world head-scratching and
half-stepping. He was harder on us than white folks could ever be. A
tall, dark, heavyset man with huge eyeballs that constantly rolled
around in his ten-gallon head, he hit us hard with brain-busting exams
and made us do long working hours in the student-newspaper office.
He came down hard on lazy folks and quitters. When a dude got mad
one day and threatened to leave school and search for newspaper work
with no degree, Harry Williams shouted at him like he was the boy's
daddy. "I'd like to see you quit! You'll go out there and get eaten alive!
This is a credential-oriented society! Without a degree you'll spend
the rest of your life fighting to be the king of nigger mountain!"

But there was one beef I had with Norfolk State and schools like
it. They prepared us to endure a system everyone acknowledged was
stacked against us. Professors in the J school and other departments
talked all the time about strategies students had to use to survive in
the racist media. It struck me as loony that we were actually being

taught ways to *endure* racism. I thought we should be learning how to *attack* that shit. It made me wonder whether I should even be considering going into the white man's system at all.

Some professors said that to make it in white mainstream America we had to assimilate, to study the white man and learn his rules. One teacher told me, "Do what you must to blend in. . . . Take up golf. Learn to schmooze. Do anything you need to do to get accepted into the club."

When recruiters came to Norfolk State to interview us, the assimilationist professors made sure we wore the "right" clothes—dark blues, grays, and black. One teacher lent me her copy of a book she said was a vital tool: *Dress for Success.* I gave the book back and asked her, "What's all this got to do with me being able to do my job?"

She looked at me like I was a child who didn't understand the complexities of the grown-up world. Then she said, "You might as well adjust yourself to the idea that these are the kinds of things you *have* to do to make it."

I thought, *I ain't gotta do SHIT but stay black and die.* Her kind of thinking undermined the idea that there were other options left open to blacks. Options such as starting and running newspapers on our own. It was as if some of our professors didn't even want to consider that. I debated with them sometimes about things like that, and talked with fellow students about doing for ourselves. Some listened and shared that dream. But others got that glazed-over look, like they'd gone off into another world. I understood. They were the descendants of slaves, still caught up in a serious dependency trip. All anybody they'd known had ever done was work for white folks their entire lives. College education or not, these students couldn't conceive of anything else.

■　■　■

Although Norfolk State is located outside my hometown, there were times when it brought reminders of my past. Like the encounter with Shirley, who grew up with me in Cavalier Manor. Leaving campus late one evening, I ran into Shirley, whom I hadn't seen in years. Growing up, Shirley had been set up on several trains by different groups of guys. The sight of her brought back images of a summer day when the fellas and I lured her to a friend's parents' house, then passed her around like cheap wine and sent her back out into the scorching heat.

When I saw Shirley on campus, she was practicing with the band near the football field. She was older than me; too old, I thought, to be in the band. But there she was, marching and twirling her clarinet like an eighteen-year-old. It was like she was trying to recapture some of the youthful innocence that had been stripped away.

Seeing her as an adult made me think about all the psychic damage we may have done to her. And here she was, trying to rebound and make a new life for herself, just like me. I wondered which of us faced the tougher task.

When our eyes met, hers dropped to the ground in a shameful look that said, *He knows my secret.* A wave of guilt passed through me, followed by an impulse to rush over and try to apologize. I walked over to her. "Hi, Shirley. How you doin'?"

"Fine." She smiled cautiously and looked away again. I wondered, *How can she ever trust men again? How can she move her life forward with such a painful past?*

I wanted to say more than an empty hello. I wanted to let her know that I was struggling to break from my past, too, and I wanted to encourage her to keep trying. But her expression suggested that I should say no more. It seemed that my presence brought out her shame. So I moved on.

There were other experiences that brought snatches of Cavalier Manor to me at Norfolk State. Like the day I was banging a typewriter in the student-newspaper office when a fellow student from Cavalier Manor told me the news. "Did you hear about Scobie-D, man?"

"No, what happened?"

"He's dead."

"Dead? Scobe?!"

The word on the wires was that Scobe had been depressed since learning he was terminally ill. He'd vowed to his wife that if he couldn't have her, nobody would. He took his small children to a neighbor's, shot his wife dead—some folks said it was an accident—then shot himself in the head.

I lost a lot more respect for Scobe after hearing about what he'd done. I'd already figured out that he didn't really understand what manhood was all about, but when he killed his wife like she was a piece of property, it confirmed that he wasn't half the man everybody thought he was. The warriors in the neighborhood were particularly stunned. We'd grown up believing that Scobe was so hard that he was devoid of the kind of emotions that could lead him to freak out like that. We'd thought he had defied life's problems and given the world the middle finger. Now he was dead at age twenty-eight.

Surprisingly, the local newspaper published a brief story about Scobe. In 1979, it was rare for a black person in Norfolk or Portsmouth to get that kind of press. It was an implicit acknowledgment that even white folks knew this guy's life had some larger meaning to some of us. Even so, the article revealed how little the reporter knew about the real story of Scobie-D and his impact on the dudes in our neighborhood.

The crowded funeral befitted someone of Scobe's street stature. I heard that practically every hood in Portsmouth went to see him "put away." I stayed home and paid private homage to Scobie-D. For a long time, he was our most perverted, enduring manhood symbol, our own black John Wayne. On the day of the funeral, I thought about the irony of how Scobe's life ended. Nobody could take him out, so he did it himself.

Chapter 26 ISLAM

In one of those bizarre coincidences that seem to follow me around in life, I found when I got to Norfolk State that Dr. Na'im Akbar, the Muslim psychologist whose ideas on human development I had studied at St. Brides, was teaching in the school's psychology department. So my first order of business was to go and meet this man, whose book *Natural Psychology and Human Transformation* had helped me view myself in a different light. We hit it off right from the start. Warm and sharp, he invited me to take a graduate course called African Psychology that he planned to teach that fall. After his conversion to Islam in the 1970s, Dr. Akbar had become a firebrand spokesman for the American Muslim Mission. He'd blended his training as a psychologist and the theology of Islam to draft some of his ideas about the process of human development. The cat was so heavy that some of his students from Morehouse College in Atlanta, where he'd taught before coming to Norfolk, had followed him to NSU.

In the African Psychology class, Na'im, as we called him, introduced us to a whole body of literature and black scholars unheard of in mainstream thought. We studied African cultures and religions and talked about our ancestors' traditional belief that God is present in all things. We talked about how that belief fostered our ancestors' sense of connectedness to all things in creation—animals, plant life, and other human beings. And we contrasted this perspective to that of white people in America, who Na'im said are guided by a worldview in which they see themselves as separate from, and superior to, the rest of creation. "That's what enables them to go into forests and desecrate whole sections of trees for money, or to kill animals en masse for stylish furs, or to conquer other people of the world everywhere they come into contact with them," he said. "As long as they see themselves as being separate and disconnected from other people, they'll feel no obligation to treat them as human beings."

Na'im didn't teach that white people were evil. But he interpreted their behavior in a way that helped us better understand the roots and nature of racism. He told us that whites, adhering to the value system of the West, place a premium on conquering people and developing objects. He said that while that way of thinking has led to the many technological advancements that have made the United States the most powerful nation in the world, it has virtually ignored advancements in human development and created a powerful country of dangerous, underdeveloped, primitive human beings.

As an example, he talked about the flaws of standardized tests that measure quantities of facts but can't measure such things as creativity and potential. By contrast, he said, "Look at African Americans, who generally don't score high on culturally biased standardized tests. We are the same people who, as slaves, took the leftover trash— intestines—that white folks gave us from the hog and turned it into a delicacy, chitterlings. We are the same people who took our hard time as slaves and created from it music—the blues and jazz—that the world loves. Those kinds of things are also a form of intelligence, but white people don't place much value on that kind of creative intellect."

That helped me understand why so many white folks walk around thinking they know every goddamn thing and why many blacks are so psyched out with deep-rooted complexes about what they *think* they don't know. I never did well on standardized tests in school. That stuff bored me stiff. I'd answer questions until I got tired, then lay my head on the desk. Since I never scored high on those tests, I never thought I had much on the ball.

Na'im's ideas about intelligence also made me think about the cats I came up with on the block, dudes who never finished school but, in their own way, were smart as hell. I thought about drug dealers like my old stickman Shell Shock. Given their business skills, I was sure they could run any corporation in America if given the chance. But they would never get an opportunity to do anything like that because they weren't considered smart by white folks' standards.

Na'im tossed out another idea that was foreign to Western thought. He said that sensitivity is a form of intelligence. This is a radical concept considering that most folks in our society, especially men, generally view sensitivity as a weakness, and it suggested to me that maybe women, who are clearly more compassionate and sensitive than men, are more highly developed human beings, and therefore more intelligent.

That class I took under Na'im was one of those rare experiences from which students come out forever changed. Years later, when I went into the system, the stuff Na'im laid on me helped me combat the psychological assaults by whites, who constantly questioned black folks' intelligence.

* * *

Largely because of Na'im's influence, I did in the free world what I hadn't done in prison: In 1979, I joined the American Muslim Mission. It was a change that had been coming for a long time. Islam seemed to address my nagging need to deal with my spiritual self and to worship in a faith that was not racially offensive to me. It got on my nerves every time I walked into a black Christian church and saw huge pictures of a long-haired, bearded Caucasian who was supposed to be Jesus. It let me know from jump-street that those preachers were messing up black folks' heads even more than they already were messed up. Without being aware, many black Christian preachers were promoting the notion of white supremacy, right along with white folks. The Muslims, on the other hand, were serious about prohibiting picture images of God or prophets in *any* race.

I was also drawn by the Islamic idea that you can see evidence of a Creator by studying the wonders of creation. When I learned Muslim lessons about the interconnectedness of nature and mankind, I could see it clearly: There is order to life, and man must find a way to get in harmony with that order.

But I also liked the Muslims for nonreligious reasons. They were survivors. Beyond some traditional civil rights groups, such as the N.A.A.C.P. and the Urban League, the Muslims were one of the few black organizations that had survived destruction by whites during the 1960s and 1970s. And they were realists. They recognized early on that all the civil rights begging and marching that black folks had done had produced very limited results for the masses of blacks. Unlike some of those mainstream, traditional black groups that kept plodding ahead, running into brick walls trying to gain acceptance into the system, the Muslims were willing to do something that black folks in general have had a hard time doing—change direction and try something different.

Also, I saw that the Muslims were committed to self-help and to establishing black institutions. They went out into communities and tried to do something to improve black people's plight. They sought ways to build their own schools so that their children wouldn't be brainwashed, and to build their own businesses to create employment and wealth that would benefit blacks. All that appealed to me.

It annoyed the hell out of me that even after the death in 1975 of Elijah Muhammad, the onetime leader of the Nation of Islam, when his son began steering the group away from hatred of whites and separatist beliefs, the media continued to depict the Muslims as militant separatists because of their emphasis on self-help and black empowerment. Every ethnic group in the United States has maintained some of its own religious, educational, and business institutions to preserve what it's about, and that's all the Muslims have sought to do.

The crazy thing was, no group of people in this country has been more separatist than white Americans. They did all they could to keep blacks out of their institutions, then turned around and accused the Muslims of being separatists simply because they stopped fighting to get in. It all struck me as deeply insane, and in joining the Muslims I wanted to get as far away from American insanity as I could.

■ ■ ■

I studied the Holy Qur'an, learned to speak some Arabic, and, in keeping with the faith, prayed five times a day. It was tough trying to get used to praying five times a day. It seemed sometimes that I prayed more than I did anything else. But there was value in it. During the course of any day, you can come unglued. By praying five times a day, you can bring it all back together—refocus on your purpose and goals.

My family, I'm sure, saw my devotion to Islam as part of some strange new Black Power trip. But nobody objected. Nobody said anything that indicated they didn't like what I was trying to be and do. My brothers were cool about it, and so were my parents. Mama was down for anything that kept me off the streets and out of the joint. She sort of watched me quietly and asked questions about Islam every now and then.

It was about the same with the fellas I'd once hung with. We were living such different lives that I seldom saw them. Shell Shock had stopped dealing drugs and gotten a job at the shipyard. Bimbo was working for the railroad. Shane was in and out of jail, and Frog, Lep, and the others were getting knocked around by life in various ways. Whenever I did happen to run into one of the boys from the old days, I could tell they were curious and puzzled, especially if I wore a Muslim kufi on my head. I'm sure they dismissed it as me being involved in "some black shit." That's what a lot of folks said when somebody they knew got involved in efforts to work for their people or raise their consciousness. "He done gone off into that *black* shit now. He wearing clothes like he think he an *African* or something."

Frankly, I didn't care what anybody thought. I knew what I knew, and I believed "that *black* shit" was helping me become a better person. So I kept pressing forward. For a while, my life, including work, revolved around the Islamic principles I studied. I got a part-time gig working with Rasool, the guy at St. Brides who had first explained Islam to me. He was now supervising a printshop in Norfolk. In my second year at Norfolk State, I went to school full-time days and worked nights, often studying on the job while the presses ran. It felt good working for a black man, even though white folks owned the place.

■ ■ ■

The Muslims emphasize the importance of marriage. Right away, when a guy joins the group, veteran brothers at the masjid, the local mosque, point out available sisters for the man to inspect. I understood the reason for the emphasis on marriage, but I thought they were a little too pushy about it. They talked about choosing a wife like it was as casual as picking fruit.

Yvette joined the Muslims shortly after I did. I suspected that she joined because of me, but she insisted that she was attracted to Islam for reasons of her own. Her joining didn't hurt our relationship, that's for sure. We grew closer and hung tighter after that.

After seeing Yvette and me leave the masjid together one day, a respected Muslim elder pulled me aside and said, "Brother, you know we don't believe in dating unchaperoned. Are you gonna marry that sister?"

I looked at him, cracked a defiant smile, and said, "I have no intentions of getting married. I don't know if we're compatible enough to spend the rest of our lives together."

The elder said, "That's the purpose of marriage. It gives you a lifetime to get acquainted." He said that if we both submitted to the will of Allah, "compatibility will come natural. You would be in harmony with each other because you will both be submitting to the will of God."

In short: The cat was telling me that Yvette and I couldn't keep hanging tight and sleeping together and remain active in the Muslim community. I shrugged off the elder's remarks and went on my way. But other guys made similar comments to me, and Yvette told me the Muslim women were laying the pressure on her, too.

I'd promised myself once that I would never get married unless I was madly in love. Although I cared for Yvette a lot, I wasn't in love with her. But after hearing all those remarks about marriage and seeing Muslim converts hooking up like there was nothing to it, I began to reconsider my position. I thought, *Maybe I can grow into this thing. Maybe I can learn to love Yvette.* In an act of faith and of affection for Yvette, I asked her to marry me.

Na'im performed the wedding ceremony in the summer of 1979. Standing there beside Yvette during the ceremony, I listened to Na'im preach about the virtues of marriage and wondered what the hell I was getting into. I thought about how a little over a year after getting out of the joint, my life had changed dramatically. I'd entered college, joined a religious group, and was now getting "hooked up," as we said on the block. It was scary and exciting at the same time. It was so much like me—living on the edge, trying to figure out what time it was.

■   ■   ■

But things fall apart. It's like that one tiny piece of thread that you pull at in a shirt, thinking it will snap. And it stays together, unraveling until you look up and the whole shirt is coming to pieces. That's how the next two years often seemed for me, even as my life was changing in ways I couldn't quite see. It happened with Islam, and it happened again in my personal life.

The first blow came when Na'im left. He accepted a teaching job at Florida State University in Tallahassee. While he was at Norfolk State, those of us in his class took our interaction beyond the classroom. We had monthly potluck dinners and Scrabble games, and held impassioned rap sessions about the impact of current events on blacks. It was just like the evening courtyard discussions at Southampton, but with women added to the mix. When Na'im left, the thread that held our intellectual potluck group together promptly fell apart. The members of our group didn't even think about getting together anymore after that.

Na'im was also missed in the masjid. The excitement generated by his presence and electrifying speeches, and the optimism I'd felt about the wonderful things we could accomplish with him there, leveled off.

After Na'im's departure, minor complaints I had about the Muslims seemed to magnify. In my view, some of their actions contradicted their aims. They talked a lot about building black institutions, but many of the men were slow to develop the educational skills and get the knowledge required to carry it out. I thought we needed to focus more on large-scale economic projects, but a lot of the Muslim men seemed unable to get beyond nickel-and-diming, selling jewelry, fruit, and bean pies on the streets.

When I questioned some of the Muslims about such contradictions, they played a lot of the same head-games that Christians play: If you question things, they try to make you feel that you lack faith. If you don't go completely along with the program, they say you're not a "true believer."

Over time, I began to look around and examine the individual lives of people in the masjid. Many were uneducated and poor, and it seemed they would stay that way. Few, it seemed, really understood the system they wanted to replace. That's when I began to wonder if the dream of nation building was just that—a lofty but unreachable dream.

There were also other things about the Muslims that bothered me—mainly, their almost fanatical obsession with avoiding pork. I'd stopped eating pork in the penitentiary before I even thought about becoming a Muslim, but I thought some of them took that pork thing much too far. Before they ate anything packaged, they carefully read the label to see if the contents had been cooked in pork or made from pork products. That was O.K., but it annoyed me that some of them were much more careful about what went into their bodies than what they allowed into their minds.

One day, a group of brothers came to my house. I offered them something to eat. While we were standing around in the kitchen, one dude glanced in my cabinet and saw something that he said might have been cooked in some pork product. "Say, brother, don't you know that this stuff has some hog in it?"

I said, "Naw, man, to tell you the truth, I hadn't noticed."

He said, "Yeah, it does. And this, too." By that time, he had his head sticking inside my cabinet, inspecting *all* my food. He even started reading the ingredients list on the side of a box of Rice Krispies!

That did it for me. I was seething, pissed off, not so much because he'd pointed those things out but because of a larger issue that had kept nagging me: How could they be so meticulous about something as trivial as what has or has not been cooked in pork and overlook more important matters, such as their need to get their overall education act together? That was a major blind spot I just couldn't abide.

I was also uncomfortable with the role of women in the Islamic faith. In the masjid, women were relegated to the role of mother, cook, all that traditional stuff, while the leadership positions were held by men. That ran against the grain of all the thinking and reading I'd done in prison to try to free myself from the sexism that had led me to be so abusive toward women before. I didn't want a subservient woman, yet I'd joined a faith where people had different ideas about equality.

While the men had less stringent dress codes, the Muslim women were required to wear long, flowing garb, even in the hottest weather, to ensure that no man besides their husband saw their legs, arms, and hair. The idea was that by covering themselves, they would not tempt men. I understood the logic, but it was a logic that relieved men of the burden of learning to control themselves.

Yvette quietly struggled with such issues, too. I asked her one day, "Aren't you tired of wearing that headpiece all the time?"

She said, "Yeah, it's beginning to ruin my hair."

I said, "The men don't have to cover their heads. From now on, you don't have to wear a headpiece. If anybody says anything to you about it, you've got my support."

That, I think, marked my first outward move toward a break with the Muslims. I'd become disillusioned and had begun to feel more confined with them than free. My attendance at the masjid dropped off gradually. Eventually, I stopped going altogether.

■ ■ ■

After we got married, Yvette and I moved into a low-income neighborhood in Norfolk. The small one-bedroom apartment was crawling with roaches. It was a dump, really, but it was all we could afford. For a short while, married life seemed like it might agree with us. We got along O.K., but the vibes were really bad between her mother and me. Yvette's mother made no secret of her wish that her daughter would have married a former boyfriend. Beyond that, I didn't know why she didn't like me. I resented that she could dislike me without getting to know me. That's how white folks treat blacks. I wasn't about to accept that. Whenever I went with Yvette to her mother's house, her mother would act aloof toward me. Yvette would always tell me things—silly, petty stuff—that her mother had said about me.

I guess Yvette wanted me to try to win her mother over, but I wasn't into brownnosing. I didn't back down from her mother's hostility. I told Yvette one day, "Your mama can go straight to hell." That didn't help our relationship at all.

But that wasn't the worst of it. One of the biggest problems we had in our marriage stemmed from Yvette's job. She worked with the

General Accounting Office, which audits government agencies. It turned out that there was a white man on her job who gave her hell, criticizing her Muslim faith and finding fault in everything she did. He made her feel that no matter how good she was she was not as qualified as him, even though they both held accounting degrees.

I tried to coach her, but Yvette couldn't muster the will and anger to fight him back. She was one of those peaceful souls who hate conflict. Generally, that was one of the attributes I found appealing in her, but when it came to dealing with white folks, it seemed like a liability. I told her, "White folks will eat you alive if you don't fight back. They love a black person who lets them get away with their crazy shit."

She still wouldn't fight back. That white man hounded her at work, and she brought her frustrations home to me. Sometimes, Yvette came home from work somber and beaten down; she slipped into monthlong depressions and would mope around the house not saying much of anything. She'd cry at night and tell me how she was sure she knew how to perform her job. It was pitiful. It made me so mad that I thought a couple of times about going up to her job to confront that cracker. But every time I thought about it, I didn't feel in control. I felt that if that white man said the wrong thing to me, I'd do something I'd regret.

Looking back, I think there was more to Yvette's unwillingness to fight than hating confrontation. I think that that white man tapped into some racial self-doubt that she hadn't overcome. It was as if, on some level, she believed she *was* inferior and assumed that the white man must have been right about her incompetence. She said things that let me know she was giving in: "Maybe I should quit my job and go back to school for a master's degree." She didn't need another degree. She needed to find an acceptable way to put foot up that white man's behind. But she didn't, and he beat her down.

I felt helpless standing on the sidelines watching my wife being psychically ripped apart. I agonized over the matter and tried repeatedly to help her overcome it, and even recommended that she get counseling. She wouldn't go. She couldn't get past what she thought was the stigma, the idea that counseling is for crazy people. Eventually, her prolonged depressions began to drag us both down. We began fighting over her unwillingness to fight back on other fronts.

We separated and, in 1981, got a quiet, uncontested divorce.

Chapter 27 **THE AUCTION BLOCK**

I just left a job interview with The Wall Street Journal. *A quarter of the way through the interview, I could see that that publication doesn't suit my interests and needs. It disturbs me to see how these recruiters come to black universities such as Norfolk State in search of one or two super-niggers to help them meet their EEOC requirements. It also bothers me to see us vying desperately to land that one token spot, hoping to be the "first" to integrate some newspaper office. After more than 300 years in this country, there should be no more black "firsts."*
    April 19, 1981

■ ■ ■

I graduated from Norfolk State with honors in May 1981—less than three years after getting sprung from the joint. I skipped the graduation ceremony. To this day, that remains one of my deepest regrets: I robbed my parents of the chance to see their son—the first in our family to earn a college degree—take the ceremonial march.

But I couldn't keep my mind on such matters as caps and gowns and ceremonies. I was too preoccupied with the thing that I dreaded most: taking my journalism degree and going into the white mainstream. Some things I saw while at Norfolk State convinced me that many white-owned newspapers had deep-rooted racial blind spots that would pose serious problems for me.

In early 1978, when I first got out of prison, a lot of newspapers had started a push to bring blacks onto their staffs. It was the tenth anniversary of the Kerner Commission Report, which had concluded that the lily-white media, which often ignored blacks in news coverage or portrayed them in a negative light, was partly to blame for the racial tensions that had led to the 1967 race riots in Newark, Detroit, and other places. But a ten-year follow-up study showed that few news organizations had increased their minority hires since 1968, and even fewer had promoted minorities to decent management jobs. About 60 percent of the nation's newspapers lacked a single nonwhite on their staffs.

The mad rush to bring on a few tokens seemed like an effort by some papers to avoid public embarrassment. They knew that a highly publicized discrimination case might show that the self-righteous newspapers that investigated racism in other institutions were just like the bigots they reported on. So recruiters rushed into the J school to "get a few."

When newspaper representatives came to the J school to interview students for summer internships, they ushered us in and out like we were products on an assembly line. Watching that process, I was bombarded with images of the auction block. It seemed that some of those recruiters were so anxious to find a token black that they over-looked any real talent we might have. If you could hold a fork and talk like white folks, you had already exceeded their wildest dreams. It was like they'd come in with their preconceived notions (we couldn't speak well, think, or write), but hoped anyway to find a few exceptional blacks who'd overcome those genetic flaws.

Some of us students felt insulted by the whole shameless search for a few "articulate" blacks, but others were starry-eyed and naive about the whole thing. They saw those recruiters as potential tickets to the American Dream, so they willingly bought into the minority numbers game. Their logic was, *Hey, we're using them to get what we want. Who cares if they think they're using us?*

I cared. I wanted a shot at an establishment gig, but it was hard to feel proud about accepting a job from someone who clearly thought so little of you. I had too much pride to let some tweedy, pencil-head white man piss on me and call it rain.

But it seemed there weren't many other ways to earn a living in my field. I'd looked into the possibility of working for a local black newspaper, but saw that they would pay me barely enough to live on. I felt I *had* to go into the white mainstream, if for no other reason than to see for myself what it was like working in the system. *Who knows?* I thought. *I may be pleasantly surprised.*

My hometown paper, *The Virginian Pilot–Ledger Star,* gave me my first summer internship after one of its columnists wrote about a homeless lady I'd featured in *The Spartan Echo.* The paper contacted me and offered the internship, which went O.K. Working among white journalists, I mostly kept to myself, but I still got a lot of good experience that taught me how to cover news. They invited me back the following year.

But after I graduated, they were reluctant to take a chance on hiring an ex-con full-time, so I interviewed at umpteen newspapers in several cities, including Kansas City, Raleigh, and Roanoke. I also made the first cut with a prominent newspaper that sent representatives to the J school to interview.

My second session with them was held over dinner in an exclusive Norfolk restaurant. It was an elegant, carpeted, high-ceilinged place with bright chandeliers and regal, high-backed leather chairs.

Of course, I was the only black there, besides waiters and the kitchen help. The room was filled with white people: flour-faced, blue-haired women and bald-headed, bloated men in expensive pinstripe suits. The whole place had a hostile feel. It was the kind of private club where they would've called the cops if I'd shown up alone.

Dressed in my one and only blue suit, I sat upright, fumbling every now and then, trying to find a resting place for my sweating hands. Sitting there across from my host, I reminded myself, *Remember the rules. Blend, as much as your pride will allow. Speak in crisp, clear Queen's English, hardening the d's, the t's, and the "ing"s. And don't forget: Sit straight, but not tall. That might be threatening to him.*

I don't remember the recruiter's name. He was an editor, a tall, thin man with a nervous twitch. He started with routine small talk, following that with the usual absurd questions they always ask: "What is your five-year career plan?"

My five-year plan? Sheeeiiit! A foot in the door, Jack, that's all I want. I cleared my throat and shot him a line. "I would like to get a few years' experience covering hard news, then I want to try my hand at feature writing, and maybe even move on into management someday." (I had no interest in management. It was a lie, calculated to show that guy he had an *ambitious* coon.)

The editor nodded, signaling his approval.

I crossed my legs, then uncrossed them, trying to relax. I would have sworn everybody in the room was staring at me, but they averted their eyes when I looked at them. I scanned the room and wondered, *Why am I putting myself through this?*

The waiter brought us menus. I saw nothing that even remotely resembled a meal I'd eaten before. No chicken or turkey, not even roast beef. I panicked. Then something familiar caught my eye. *Ah, salmon. Moms has made salmon before.* "I'll have the salmon."

Mr. Establishment proceeded to order some exotic shit I couldn't pronounce. The waiter brought bread. As we talked, my host picked up a knife, buttered some bread, and began chewing. He stopped several times to pluck crumbs dropped on the white tablecloth. He picked up the crumbs and began putting them into his mouth. I thought, *Here I am, uptight about my manners, and this motherfucka is eatin' off the table!*

Minutes later, the waiter brought something that looked like spruced-up seaweed—a salad, I guessed—set in the center of an elegant plate.

I noticed we each had several fancy forks and spoons. I couldn't recall which was used for what. I waited to see which one the editor would pick up first. He picked up the short fork, then continued with questions. "So, you like writing feature stories?"

I picked up my short fork, too. "Yes. I've written features throughout college and found that to be my strong suit. I like writing about people's lives and experiences."

The editor, who had a grayish complexion that made him look like he'd spent his whole life indoors, hung on my every word, trying, I suspected, to check out how well I spoke. "So, tell me more about yourself and your family. Did you grow up poor?"

Yeah, I was born down by the river in a little shack, just like every other darky you've read about! I cleared my throat. "Actually, I grew up in the next city, Portsmouth, and come from a working-class family. My stepfather is a security guard."

We talked for more than two hours, serving bullshit back and forth like hard volleys on a tennis court. As time wore on, I felt worse. From the pained smiles to the strained conversation, the exchanges were a sickening series of pathetic lies on both our parts. I hated him and he feared me. Then why were we both smiling so much?

When dinner ended, I was drained. I felt like I'd spent all evening pimping myself. I needed to go somewhere *really* black—like a bootlegger's house—and rinse the stuffy feel of that whiteness from my head. There was a crib, nicknamed the Pink Palace, in downtown Portsmouth, where you could go day or night and get some *real* food—collard greens, fried chicken with hot sauce, or a pig-ear sandwich—and nobody cared which fork you used. There'd be plenty of black folks there, drinking, talking loud, playing cards, and listening to Aretha or Otis Redding—deep-down, old-head soul.

It was tempting. But I went home, wrote in my journal, and considered the insanity of working so hard to get into the same establishment that devalued me.

■ ■ ■

The most promising interview took place in Muhammad Ali's birthplace, Louisville, Kentucky. One of my former classmates had gotten a job at *The Louisville Courier-Journal* and told me they were hiring. I went through the usual battery of interviews. When the day ended, I was drained but confident I'd landed a gig. They asked how soon I could start and told me to report to personnel the next day to complete my application.

The following day, when filling out the application, I ran across the question that always haunted me: "Have you ever been convicted of a felony? If the answer is yes, please explain." That queasy feeling returned to my stomach. I hadn't told them about my rap sheet, and I had another full year left on probation. *What should I do? If I don't tell, I've got this gig in the bag.* I left the question blank. When the personnel director picked up the application, I stopped her and whispered, "Excuse me. May I speak with you a moment?"

A middle-aged woman with an easy smile, the director said, "Sure, what do you need?"

"I need to explain something to you. I left this section blank for a reason," I said, pointing to the application. "I have a criminal record. I served time. For armed robbery."

She stiffened and looked at me. "Oh. . . . Well, I'll need to talk with someone else about this. . . . Wait right here. I'll be right back."

I squirmed in my hallway seat for more than an hour, trying to picture the high-level discussions that were probably going on. When the personnel director came back, she forced a smile. "O.K., we're all done. . . . We'll be in touch with you soon."

She didn't offer to tell me what was said by her higher-ups, and I didn't ask. But her tone and expression gave her away. I knew the lowdown. I knew I wouldn't get the job.

On the flight home, I cursed myself for letting them put me through that dog and pony show. I kept asking myself over and over, *Why do you take yourself through this shit?*

I didn't get the job, of course. I don't remember what, if any, reason they gave for not hiring me, but I'm sure it was because I came clean. I couldn't handle that. I'd served my time. I'd been punished for the crime and suffered, I thought, more than enough. I wondered, *Why do I have to keep paying for it, and what benefit is there in telling interviewers the truth?*

That's when I decided to take a more realistic approach when dealing with white folks, including my parole officer, who insisted I tell the truth about my record when seeking jobs. I decided that from then on, I'd get my foot in the door first and prove myself. Then maybe, *maybe,* I'd tell them about my past.

Chapter 28

CULTURE SHOCK

s I stood and walked across the newsroom, I felt them again: the eyes. Like radar, they locked onto me from the moment I rose from my seat, and remained fixed as I headed slowly to the file cabinets, where old newspaper clippings were kept. Returning to my desk, I looked straight ahead, pretending, as always, not to notice.

They weren't the evil, predatory gazes that I saw in prison. They were polite stares by curious white reporters, editors, and secretaries in the small office of the Portsmouth bureau, where I worked. After a month as a reporter for my hometown paper, *The Virginian Pilot– Ledger Star,* I began to get used to the stares. Well, I never *really* got used to them, but I resigned myself to the reality that someone always seemed to be watching, zeroing in on my every move. After all, I was a novelty—the only brother in the place.

I started with the newspaper in 1981. When all my other job prospects fell through, I went back and asked for a job. Because of my prison record, a bunch of bigwigs at the paper met and debated the matter. In what one editor later described as "a tough, close vote," they decided to hire me.

Finally, I had a foot in the white man's door. Here was a chance to check out life across the tracks. It blew my mind. In three short years, I'd gone from one extreme to the other: from prison to a white-collar establishment job—something I had dared not hope for.

I'd once resigned myself to the notion that if I ever did work for the white man, the best I could probably expect was a low-paying job as a deliveryman. Now I had done much better. I was getting paid to write, to do something I actually enjoyed. Getting that job boosted my belief in myself and marked another major confirmation that there *was* merit to the values I had adopted in prison. It made me wonder, *What else is possible?*

My parents were elated about the job. The phone lines burned from Portsmouth to New York to North Carolina as my mother spread the word among our relatives, and she boasted to local friends over the phone about her once wayward son: "You know, he works down at the newspaper now." For her and my stepfather, the newspaper job was a kind of joyful vindication for the hurt they'd suffered on my account all those years. They were also relieved. The job was an indication that I'd weathered the critical transition from prison to the real world. With a stable gig, it was far less likely that I'd start hanging on the block again or backslide into crime.

With my life stabilizing, my parents could focus on my brother Dwight, who was skidding fast on drug binges and long stretches of unemployment, which fed off each other magnificently to keep him down. By comparison, my other three brothers—Billy, Junnie, and Bryan—were doing well. They had jobs and stayed out of trouble, which was more than could be said for many we knew.

It always made the older folks in Cavalier Manor feel good to be able to point to young people who were doing well. Whenever I ran into my parents' friends around town, they'd beam and say, "I read one of your stories in the paper the other day. Keep it up!" Of course, they had only a vague notion about what I did at work. That didn't matter. The important thing was, I had a professional job in an office with white people.

Nobody was prouder than I was of what I'd done. For the first time in my life, I had a *real* gig. It was more than just a job. It was the start of a career. I worked in an office at a desk. I interviewed people and wrote for a living. The first time I wrote a story as a full-fledged reporter, I stared at my byline a long time. There it was, just below the headline: Nathan McCall. It felt good seeing my name in the newspaper associated with something other than crime. It gave me a rush seeing that name on a document that was read by thousands of people. Sometimes, if I had a front-page story in the paper, I'd stop by newsstands on the street just to stare at my byline. I'd wonder how many people in the region would see that name. I toyed with the idea of adding my middle initial—*J* for Jerome—but that seemed too grand, so I nixed the thought.

My new job paid enough for me to rent an apartment—my first one alone. Located less than a mile from the office, the one-bedroom unit had high ceilings and hardwood floors. It had a huge kitchen and a front porch with a swing and chairs. My mother eagerly donated pots, pans, linen, and dishes to help me get settled in. I'd bought a couch from Na'im Akbar for seventy-five dollars before he moved away. The place was sparsely furnished and crudely decorated, but it was mine. It was legit.

When I put on clean clothes to go to work, it felt just like I'd always imagined: dignified. In celebration of my new status, I went out and bought a few snazzy neckties and sport coats and made sure I went to work every day spit-shined and *clean*.

The most amazing thing was that for the first time in my life, I worked with white people who seemed civil. There was no oppressive supervisor. Reporters actually sat around, chatted, read the paper, and drank coffee before starting work. They took leisurely lunches, which they often wrote off on expense accounts. That was a major leap from punching a clock. As I wrote in my journal, it was all so wonderfully strange:

> *I have yet to grow accustomed to the free and easy nature of my job as a reporter. All my life, I've worked on jobs where white overseers stood close by and watched over my shoulders as I performed some menial, mindless task. They always were sure to make certain I never stole an extra minute or paused too long between strokes of the shovel. As a writer, I am now doing what I do best. It's difficult to believe.*
>
> *June 5, 1981*

All the benefits of the job made the white mainstream seem appealing in many respects, but they didn't come without a cost. Almost immediately after landing the job, I began to take on the subtle stresses brought on by the age-old burdens of race.

There were a few other blacks in the main news office in Norfolk, but I rarely saw them. As the only black in the downtown Portsmouth office, where we occupied the entire floor of a bank building, I could "feel" my blackness all the time. The differences between whites and me seemed magnified and discomforting. It was serious culture shock. I sensed that many white reporters felt the same when they found themselves in comparable situations—caught in the midst of blacks on the building elevator, for instance. When they saw blacks staring, their faces turned red. They'd get that embarrassed, uptight look and stare nervously at their feet or gaze at the lighted elevator numbers until they reached their floor. They looked like they couldn't wait to get away and back into the company of their own kind.

The eyes in my office gave me that same nervous feeling. Often, I looked up from my work to find one of my co-workers staring at me. Whenever my eyes caught theirs, they'd turn away. Their watching made me more self-conscious of the way I dressed, walked, and talked.

I modified my pimp, which was already toned down, and I was so self-conscious when walking across the room that I stumbled sometimes from trying to be so careful.

I wondered if they watched me so closely because I was black or because they knew about my prison record. Upper managers knew, but I wasn't sure whether gossip had filtered down to the rank and file. Paranoid about my past and afraid that other reporters might find out about it, I went to the newspaper's library files and searched for my name shortly after I started work. Certainly, there would be stories in there about a few of the run-ins I'd had with the law. I leafed through the files until I reached the *M*'s. Sure enough, there it was: McCall, Nathan. There were two clips inside the small manila envelope. One clip was a brief story, dated May 22, 1974, about me shooting Plaz at the carnival. The second clip, from early December 1974, was about the McDonald's robbery. It featured a photo of the getaway car and showed the gun on the floor. That life was so far from me now that it seemed I was reading about somebody else.

I took the file to my desk. *They won't be needing this anymore.* Later, I took it home. I felt scared and guilty about taking it, but I was more afraid of the prospect of white reporters passing crime stories about me around the newsroom.

In the office, I could also "hear" myself when talking with whites. I never heard myself when around my own people, but every time I went around whites, the subtly distinctive differences of tone and dialect in my speech and theirs stood out in my mind. They even used different words from those I used. They called people "jerks" and "schmucks," and their language in general sounded corny to me, compared to the stylized, lyrical way that black folks talk.

In a perfect world, such differences would be no big deal. But I remembered what Na'im Akbar once said: "Whites put a value on difference. To them, different is bad. Different is abnormal. Different is inferior. Being different is a professional liability."

Every now and then, in a feeble attempt to ease the racial strain, I caught myself altering my dialect to downplay the speech differences when talking with whites. "How ya doin'?" became "How are you today?" The words felt awkward and phony rolling off my tongue.

Whenever I chatted with the old black janitor who cleaned our offices most evenings, I automatically shifted back to my vernacular: "What it is?" I was always glad to see him and went out of my way to speak to him, as much to connect with another black person as to show him I hadn't forgotten who I was. He seemed to appreciate the gesture and always returned the greeting in kind. "Hey, young man. How you ta-day?"

The personal lives of my co-workers and me were very different, too. My lifestyle was as routine as the shipyard whistle that sounded every day. I went to work, went home, spent time with a lady friend, and went to bed. Occasionally, my childhood friend Greg and I hooked up for a game of chess, or I went to a movie. But that was it.

My white colleagues seemed to lead fuller, more active lives that included a broader range of fun and play. They had hobbies. They talked about camping, skiing, surfing, and hang gliding, stuff that I never would have thought to do. They went out to fancy restaurants all the time and talked in endless detail about the "ambience" and the food they ate. Their obsession with good food and restaurants puzzled me.

Compared to theirs, the existences of most black folks I knew seemed so contained. Most spent their working hours taking shit off the white man and devoted their free time to working off steam built up from taking shit off the white man. The old-heads drowned their stress in liquor. The young bloods did drugs. The old shouted in church. The young hit the nightclubs. For us, it was all about damage control.

It was obvious that many of my co-workers had had little exposure to blacks. They seemed overpolite and unsure how to relate to me. Likewise, I was guarded with them, remembering lessons learned from others' pain: *Keep them at arm's length and out of your personal business.*

There were always two conversations floating in my head when I interacted with whites. There was what I *thought* and what I *said.* Practically everything I said was calculated to counter some stereotype whites hold about blacks. If they brought up music, I responded in a way that said, *Yes, we listen to more than boogie-woogie and the blues.* Literature? *Yes, I've read Hemingway, Fitzgerald, and all the other white motherfuckas you think are so good.*

They seldom knew what I *really* thought and felt about things, and I made sure they got few chances to find out. Often, when a group of them were headed out to lunch, they'd ask, "You want to join us, Nathan?"

I'd lie, make up any excuse not to go. "No thanks. I've got some research to do."

It was the same if they asked me to join them for drinks after work. "No thanks. I'll have to pass. I've got too much to do."

I felt uneasy in social settings with whites. Barriers come down when scotch or bourbon takes center stage. People take liberties to pry and say things they might not ordinarily say in the sober setting of the workplace. No, they'd get no openings *here*.

Several whites at the paper tried to reach out and make friends. One reporter in the office invited me to go camping with him, and another occasionally suggested we play chess after work. Then there was Ron Speer, the portly, gregarious editor who was responsible for me getting the job in the first place. He'd contacted me at Norfolk State and campaigned hard for me to get that first crucial internship. A man in his forties who had covered the civil rights movement as a reporter, Ron was one of those rare bleeding hearts who had given a lot of thought to the damage his people had done to the lives and psyches of blacks. He was committed to doing his part to make things better.

Almost the stereotype of the hard-driving, heavy-drinking newspaperman who kept a burning cigarette dangling from the tip of his lips, Ron wore frumpy shirts with the sleeves rolled up and his tie loosened at his fat neck. Whenever we talked, he cracked jokes to try to get me to relax. He went out of his way to let me know that he was on my side. I guessed that somehow he really understood the challenges I faced. Shortly after I was hired at the paper, Ron told me, "If you have any problems or need help with *anything*, just come to me."

I sensed that Ron and the others were sincere, but still, I didn't open up to them. I couldn't. They were white, and I was convinced that the dumbest thing a black person could do was trust a white man. Ron and the others got surface rap from me, and nothing more. I saw them, and everybody else at the paper, as a hazard that came with the job.

I figured I could tolerate them for a while. I had no intention of staying in the white mainstream forever. I figured I would stay for a time, learn all I could from the best white newspapers around, then take my skills back to my people. Ultimately, I figured, I would work for a black publication or start one of my own.

■　■　■

While working for white folks, I couldn't avoid them altogether. Their rules wouldn't allow that. One rule was that attendance was expected at work-related social functions. So when I heard about a planned company party to be held in Norfolk, I panicked. At first, when one of my colleagues asked if I was going, I told him, "I don't think I'll be able to make it."

His eyes widened. "Oh, no. If I were you, I wouldn't miss this party. It could affect your career."

I felt cornered. In the weeks leading up to the affair, I agonized over the thought of being trapped in a social setting with a roomful of white folks for three or four hours straight. I'd have gladly traded that torture for a night in jail. Then I manufactured a bright side to persuade myself that it would be all right. *What the hell. I'll go. I haven't been to a party in a while. Maybe I can meet people and unwind a bit.*

It was nothing like any party I'd ever been to. Constipated-looking white folks dressed in sport coats and ties stood around chatting and smiling with drinks in their hands. They'd walk up to me, smile a phony smile, and say, "So, what interesting stories are you working on?" "What do you think of President Reagan's Star Wars proposal?"

I thought, *This ain't no fuckin' party! This is WORK!*

The social ceremony that ensued was easy to learn. It was like musical chairs: You clustered in tight circles of people, chatted about current events, and listened to corny jokes. Then you moved on to other circles and chatted about current events and listened to more corny jokes. You smiled a lot, drank a lot, and pretended to be having fun.

I felt more like an actor than a real person. Making my way through the maze of phoniness, I wondered, *What would the fellas think if they could see me now? What would Frog, Bimbo, and Shane say if they walked through that door?*

For much of the evening, I waited for the music to start. Later, looking around the room, I realized there would be no music and no dancing.

Black folks wouldn't even *think* of having a party without music. They would split in a heartbeat and talk about your ass on the way out. Standing there among those white folks made me realize that there were some aspects of hanging with the fellas that I really missed. In the old days, when we partied together, we had a ball, and some of those parties were incredible. Folks showed up so intent on partying that they brought their own tambourines and shakers to jam with the beat. There would be sweat flying, bodies gyrating, and loud noise, accentuated by occasional chorus shouts of "Party over *here*!" The music, a constant rhythmic thump, would be pumping and everybody would be grooving in a rhythm that seemed ancient, timeless.

It was at those times that it dawned on me that there was something special and thrilling about my people: our style, our manner and speech. Being among whites made me appreciate black folks that much more.

With no music at the company party, the rest of the evening was an endurance test. I stood near the wall, holding a drink I no longer wanted and cursing a clock that moved *far* too slow. When it seemed an appropriate time to slide—when some white folks started shuffling toward the door—I shot out of there as fast as I could. Driving home, I thought about the torment I'd just been through and wondered again if this mainstream thing was meant for me. That was the first time I'd ever gone to a party and left feeling more uptight than when I arrived.

Chapter 29 CLASHES

knew from the get-go that the crossover into the white mainstream would be very risky. I knew I'd be extremely uncomfortable entering a world that had never welcomed me. But never, not in my wildest nightmares, did I imagine that going inside the system would make me an outsider, uneasy with the folks I knew best.

■ ■ ■

At first, I worked as a general-assignment reporter, which meant that on any given day I could be assigned to cover anything, from politics at City Hall to soft feature stories in obscure neighborhoods. My job exposed me to sides of Portsmouth that were once foreign to me. When I was hanging on the block, I couldn't name anybody on the city council or school board. As a reporter, I met them, and learned all their names and most of their political agendas. Before, whenever I heard about decisions that affected the lives of blacks, I passively assumed they were irrevocable decisions made by faceless, powerful white folks who were out of reach. Now I got to see, firsthand, how the political process worked and how white citizens stormed City Hall when they wanted to get something done.

Blacks in Portsmouth seemed light-years away from understanding that process. They seldom organized and went to City Hall, mainly because they doubted it would make a difference. As a result, they were always reacting *after* the fact, always protesting after some historic black school had been closed or some right infringed upon—all because they hadn't been at City Hall when the deals went down.

Subconsciously, I think I'd bought into a notion that whites promoted among blacks: that the white politicians who ran the city (though there was always a token black on the city council) were born with the knowledge and expertise to do such things. Then, as I began to cover the city I'd grown up in, it became clear to me that a lot of those white folks were actually dumb as hell. Those were the same people who wanted to bring tourists downtown and whose infinite

wisdom led them to build a new jail overlooking the Elizabeth River—
on prime waterfront property.

■ ■ ■

In college, we were taught that the best journalists are "objective,"
that they cover events while keeping their feelings and views removed
from what they see. Most journalists, I believe, start out eager and
green and stupid enough to believe that line. Then they quickly learn
that the exact opposite is true: Journalists have feelings and opinions
about *everything*.

In my first year on the job, I ran into a lot of people and situations
in the city that offended me and tested my restraint. Like the good
white Christian man who called us out to write about his church's
donation of food, clothing, and shelter to help a family of Laotian
refugees get settled in America. When I interviewed him, he proudly
displayed a house that he and his fellow church members had worked
so hard to prepare for the foreigners. The house required so much
work, he said, because the previous tenants were a trifling family that
left the place a filthy mess. "And it wasn't black people living in it,
either," he said. Apparently realizing the color of the person he was
talking to, he blushed. "No harm meant by that."

Then there was the white, pistol-toting landlord whose family
owned a lot of low-income property in downtown Portsmouth, which
they rented to black women on welfare. Every month, around the time
when welfare checks were due, the landlord followed the mailman to
the women's houses and cashed their checks on the spot to make sure
they didn't spend the money before paying their rent. After cashing
each check, the landlord took out his month's rent, then moved on to
the next house. While he worked, an armed backup sat in a van nearby
to guard against would-be robbers. When I interviewed the landlord,
he said, "It's for the women's convenience. They don't have to go
anywhere else to cash the checks."

When I was growing up, the Christian dude and the landlord were
the kinds of white folks the fellas and I *prayed* to run across. Now that
I'd found some, I couldn't act on what I felt. They call it "professional
restraint." I had to swallow hard and hold my peace.

■ ■ ■

Any ex-con or former junkie will tell you that old homies get real
suspicious of a guy who makes an abrupt shift from prison gray to
suit-and-tie. Unless you've transformed into a cross-wearing, Bible-

thumping witness for God, they start thinking that maybe you got a break by snitching to the man on somebody. Street paranoia can be hazardous to your health, and if you're not in a big city where you can fade into the woodwork, it can get seriously claustrophobic.

It got that way for me after I started covering trials down at the Portsmouth Civic Center. When I was growing up, I was always going down there for one trial or another. I knew the Portsmouth Civic Center, and its courtrooms, front and back. But the instant I received that assignment, I knew it would create hassles for me.

My primary job was to write about the newsworthy courtroom cases. It turned out that the most interesting cases were criminal trials, and, of course, many featured cats I knew. Like Jason, a young lion who grew up a few blocks from me. Riding around in a new Coupe de Ville, profiling like they all do when they get a piece of change, he openly flaunted his success at "slinging dope." So it was no surprise when he was popped and promptly hit with a ten-year bid. Then there was Tony Rome, who'd served time with me at Southampton. He took an eighty-year hit on a similar beef.

I had to put the ink to both of them, and for the first time, I felt paranoid about my line of work.

■ ■ ■

Often, while walking through the Portsmouth court building, I'd run into old friends being led in shackles from one area to another. I'd try to avoid them for fear they'd blow my cover among court employees or colleagues who didn't know my story. Then, one day, my past nearly caught up with me. I was walking through the building on my way to lunch with a court employee and ran into a group of shackled inmates being led to trial. One, a guy called Dickie, spotted me and shouted, "Hey, Nate, how's it goin'? I heard you were out!"

I hadn't seen Dickie since I'd nearly O.D.'ed at his place several years before. I'd done several drugs at once, including acid and some herb soaked in embalming fluid. Suddenly, I felt myself leaving— soaring past the stage of being high—shooting right on out of the universe. Everybody abandoned me and left Dickie there to watch me die. Later, when I came to, I was stretched out on Dickie's ragged couch, and he was sitting there, praying that I wouldn't O.D. and bring heat down on him.

I hadn't seen or talked with Dickie since that night in 1974. I rushed over to him before he could blurt out more of my business, hoping my lunch companion hadn't heard what he'd said before. We chatted quietly a few moments, then he and the rest of the gang were led away.

I don't know whether or not the court employee heard Dickie's reference to me being "out"—he had been distracted by someone else passing through—but that brief encounter reminded me that my life was delicately balanced between two worlds and that, inevitably, my past and present would collide.

That almost happened in the case of Chilly Bear, another guy who had done time with me at Southampton. Bear was standing around, talking near a Dumpster in the Jeffry Wilson public housing projects one day, when two old-heads from Cavalier Manor drove up. Armed to the teeth, they parked the car, got out, and split up along different sides of the street, angling to get the drop on another dude they'd been tracking down. Seeing the ambush coming, the target drew his piece and ran for cover. A gunfight broke out, with both sides shooting at each other like cowboys in a western movie. When the shooting ended, Chilly Bear lay dead, caught in the cross fire.

The case was big news in Portsmouth because Chilly Bear had been a popular hood and one of the most heralded high school football linebackers to come out of the city. When the trial started, thugs from Cavalier Manor and downtown crowded inside the courtroom to check it out. As I stepped in there to cover the trial, I could feel the eyes instantly riveted on me. I knew many of those cats, and I tried to decide, *Should I go over and sit with them, or should I keep a professional distance?* I stayed away and sat quietly in the back of the courtroom, near the door.

During a recess, I went into the hallway to interview the prosecuting attorney. As we talked, fellas filed out and stood off along the walls, puffing cigarettes, talking and eyeing us.

I imagined how that scene must look to them—Nathan McCall standing in the court building, dressed in a suit and tie, talking to a white man and writing stuff down on a piece of paper. I knew what they were thinking. I knew because I would have thought the same thing about someone else if I'd still been hanging on the block.

I tried to ignore the strange looks, but thinking about it made me feel uneasy. I wanted to go over and say, "Hey, man, I ain't workin' for the lawman. I'm a reporter." But volunteering an explanation would have made the situation look more suspicious than it already did. Besides, I'm not sure they would've understood anyway. In their eyes, the newspapers and police were all the same—all part of that big,

amorphous, antagonizing white world called The Establishment—
and now they viewed me as a part of that.

Nobody said anything to me, but after Chilly Bear's trial, I heard
through the wires that some bloods questioned how I'd gotten out of
prison and gotten squared away so fast. I imagined what some of them
must have said: "How that niggah gonna take a fall, come back, and
get a better gig than most black folks who ain't never been locked up?"

It's hard to ignore talk like that. I considered going to one of my
bosses to ask to be taken off the beat, but that would have involved
revealing things about my personal life that were off limits to them.
So I lay low, waiting to see if there would be more serious fallout from
my appearance at Chilly Bear's trial.

There was. I returned home from work one day and found a sealed
note pasted to my front door: "Give up some money or I'm going to
the man on you."

I understood the warped logic that led to that stupid act. Somebody
assumed I'd hidden my past to get the job. I ignored the note and
pushed on.

■ ■ ■

Early in 1982, I ran into an old homie in Cavalier Manor while
heading to my mother's house. He looked me up and down. "That's
a nice-looking trench coat you got on, homes. It makes you look like
a lawman."

He said it half-jokingly, but I got the hint. I got hot around the
collar and went off on him. "Fuck you, niggah!"

He grinned cynically and pushed on up the street.

That exchange brought my frustrations to a head. Reluctantly, I
went to my editor and asked for another assignment. I didn't tell him
the real reason. I said something career-oriented like "I'm ready to
take on another challenge."

But I needed a change deeper than a simple switch in assignments. I
needed a complete change of scenery. I felt I needed to move to a city
where I didn't have to confront my past every day. It was time to leave
Portsmouth, and I decided that that was what I was going to do.

As a reminder of my new goal, I posted a sign in big, bold letters on
the wall, just above my bed: I'M LEAVING BY THE FALL, JOB OR NO JOB.

It was frightening to think of leaving home. Besides prison, I'd
never lived anywhere else as an adult but Portsmouth. But I told
myself I had to go. I *had* to go.

Chapter 30 FATHERS

One of the toughest challenges I faced in trying to get my overall act together was coming to grips with fatherhood. After my new job helped me get on my feet, I was able to do more for Monroe, but I still had trouble relating to him one-on-one. I suspected the difficulty stemmed from some buried, unresolved issues in my head about my blood father, whom we called J.L. I could also tell that in very different ways two of my brothers, Billy and Dwight, wrestled with these issues too.

Although I'd never acknowledged it, I think that on some level it bugged me that I was an adult and didn't know my old man from Adam. He and my mother divorced when I was less than two years old. As the oldest of my mother's three children by J.L., Billy was the only one with any memories of our father being in the same household as us. Around 1982, a few years before Billy moved his family to Portsmouth from New York, he started making it a point during visits home to track down J.L. and begin establishing the relationship they'd never had.

In fact, it was Billy who first took me to meet my father, whom I hadn't seen in more than twenty-five years. Talk about a *trip*. That one rated right up there with acid and wacky weed. When we went by his house, J.L. looked at me, smiled broadly, pushed open the screen door, and greeted us with the heartiness of long-long-lost friends. "Heeeeyyy, come on in! Come on in!"

I stepped inside first, followed by Billy. It felt weird being face-to-face with my old man for the first time in years. Standing in the middle of the modestly furnished living room, I wondered, *What now?* Was I supposed to hug this guy, shake his hand, or punch him in the face? I extended my hand and said, "How you doin', J.L.?"

"Fine, fine, I'm doin' just fine, Nathan! You lookin' good! Have a seat!"

We sat down, Billy and me on the couch and J.L. in an easy chair. Still smiling, J.L. said, "So, what's been goin' on?"

I said, "Not much."

There was an awkward silence. Billy, eyeing the uneasy exchanges like a referee in a boxing ring, broke the quiet with a lie. "We were planning to come over this way, so I thought I'd call and see if you were going to be around."

"Oh yeah? I just got home from work a little while ago. If you'd called fifteen minutes earlier, you'd 'a' missed me." J.L., a longshoreman, started running down the details of his workday, trying, I suspected, to avoid eerie silences. It wasn't easy. We were total strangers, brought together by bloodlines that seemed seriously thin. Yet he was my father, my old man. It seemed weird that we had so little to say. But what was there for strangers to talk about?

Sitting there, I studied every detail about J.L., looking for traces of myself. Medium-height and fat, he looked nothing like I'd imagined. He had dark brown skin and light brown eyes like mine, but beyond that he could have been any stranger on the street. When he spoke, a gold crown sparkled in his mouth, an indication, I guessed, that he was real hip when he was young.

J.L. was remarried and had a daughter and son, both a few years younger than me. They lived in a two-story frame house just off Tidewater Drive, a main street that runs through the center of Norfolk. Sitting there, I thought about how many times I'd driven past that street over the years with no idea my father was somewhere near. I also thought about a disappointing day, nineteen years earlier, when we were supposed to have reunited:

■ ■ ■

Shortly after we moved to Virginia in 1964, J.L. telephoned my mother and said he wanted to spend time with Billy, Dwight, and me. My mother let him speak with Billy, who was then thirteen. After he hung up, Billy came running to Dwight and me. He said our daddy had promised to pick us up soon and take us downtown to shop for school clothes. "He asked me what y'all wanted to buy."

Dwight, who was eleven then, said, "I want a leather coat."

I was nine. I took my cue from Dwight. "I want a leather coat, too."

In the two weeks before that visit, we wagged our tongues and bragged to our friends about our planned outing to see our "real daddy." To hear us tell it, J.L. was going to do everything, all the special things that daddies are supposed to do. We hadn't laid eyes on him since I was an infant, but he was going to make up for all those special moments missed—the first teeth pulled, the first report card, the first unsteady bicycle balancing act—and this shopping trip was just the beginning.

The days leading up to the visit were torture, like a thousand nights before Christmas. In that time, I wondered a lot of things about my daddy. I'd lie in bed at night and stare up at the ceiling, wondering how he looked, how he talked, and what his life was like.

When the day arrived, Mama drove us to downtown Portsmouth. J.L. lived less than ten miles away in Norfolk. We had to catch the tunnel bus to get there. Mama told us that J.L. would be waiting for us at the bus stop. And she added: "If he's not there, don't leave that corner until he comes."

We reached our stop and bolted off the bus and looked around for J.L. There was no one there. I had to go to the bathroom. There was a department store set back about twenty feet from the corner. Billy kept watch on the corner while I followed Dwight inside to ask a clerk if we could use the bathroom. She led us to a tiny room, smiled, and closed the door behind us.

I yanked down my zipper and frantically pulled at my drawers to get it out before the pressure broke. Pee squirted everywhere before I could aim it at the commode. Dwight grew impatient. "Hurry up, boy! J.L. might be out there waiting!" I quickly stuffed it back inside my pants and pulled up the zipper and felt warm drops of pee roll down my leg. We sprinted out the door and ran up to Billy. "Did he get here yet?"

Billy was getting antsy. "You don't see him, do you?"

A half hour passed and J.L. didn't show. As we waited, my mind raced ahead. There was so much to talk about. I wanted to tell him how smart I was in school. I wanted to tell him about our new house in Cavalier Manor. I wished I had some binoculars. I wanted to be the first one to spot J.L., the first one to step up to the car and greet him when he pulled to the curb. I knew what I was going to say. I was going to walk up to the car and say, "Hi, J.L. I'm Nathan."

An hour passed, and there was still no sign. We stood there, looking at the passing cars and believing with faith that could move mountains that, soon or later, our daddy would come. Whenever a car came in our direction, I'd lean over and look inside. Most of the folks driving by were white people. I spotted a black man driving a car that was coming our way. As he slowed the car, my heart pounded and my face brightened. I took a step forward and waved to make sure he saw us. The man turned the corner near us and drove on by.

When the wait grew longer, doubt began to set in. Nobody said it. The silence revealed it. As time passed, nobody said much of anything. We just stood there, watching, waiting, hoping.

After two hours had passed, it started raining. Without consulting Dwight and me, Billy walked slowly to a pay phone near the department store and dialed our home.

In the half hour it took for my mother to get there, I kept my fingers crossed, hoping J.L. would beat her to that corner. Every time a car pulled near us to the curb, my heart leaped, and every time one drove away without my brothers and me in it, my spirits sank. Finally, my mother came into view and we all dragged, reluctantly, to the car. We rode home in deathly silence. I stared out the window and wondered if we should have waited longer for my daddy. I wondered if maybe he might get there moments after we left and find us gone. I wondered if he had had a flat tire or something and couldn't get to us. I wondered a lot of things.

My mother and stepfather didn't explain to us then or later what had happened with J.L. One night, I overheard them talking about it in hushed tones, but that was it. My brothers and I didn't talk among ourselves about the letdown. In fact, the only person who said anything about it afterward was me. One day, out of the clear blue, I told my mother, "I ain't never going nowhere to wait for him again!"

But I never had to confront such a choice. I never saw or heard from J.L. again until I went with Billy to see him that day in 1982.

■ ■ ■

I'd often wondered how my brothers and I had been influenced by J.L.'s aloofness. Billy seemed most affected, in a desperate yet positive way. It was as if he used J.L. as a model for the type of father he *didn't* want to become. Billy was devoted to his three children, and he seemed determined to make sure they knew their wayward grandfather, too.

But it seemed just the opposite for Dwight, who'd been married briefly and had a son. Dwight seemed wholly unable to relate to the fatherhood trip. He'd go for months without seeing his son, who lived with his mother in Cavalier Manor, less than a mile from Dwight's apartment. He was almost as indifferent to his son as J.L. had been with us.

I think I was a frustrated combination of Billy and Dwight. There were so many unresolved issues haunting me. There were the two girls who had told me when we were teenagers that they were pregnant by me. Although I doubted that was so, I never resolved it with medical tests. After getting out of prison, I contacted the women to try to settle the matter, but gave up quickly. I suspect it was because I was scared to face what it might reveal and require of me. I was aware of the major contradiction: I believed that I courageously confronted life, yet I shrank from fatherhood, one of life's greatest challenges.

Then there was Monroe. He was certainly my child, yet I struggled to feel the bond that I thought fathers were supposed to feel with their children. At times, I looked at him and felt no more connected to him than to a stranger. I wondered: Had all those efforts on the streets to harden my heart taken their toll, or had J.L. passed along to me some fucked-up, coldhearted gene?

I fought to shed the warped values that had guided me before prison, probably the same ones my father had embraced when he was young: To us, children were double-edged swords, to be flaunted and dodged at the same time. They confirmed our manhood, yet they threatened to rob us of what precious little freedom we thought we had. Your options are narrowed greatly with crumb-snatchers in tow. You've got to play by the establishment's rules to keep children clothed and fed. You've got to work and, therefore, subject yourself to the white man. Children, like love, make you vulnerable to the world, and what black man wants to be more vulnerable than he already is?

My struggle to connect with Monroe brought to mind a time when I was in the Norfolk jail and had begun studying the Bible. One of the street ministers who visited the jail told a bunch of inmates that we would need to get the Holy Ghost and speak in tongues in order to confirm our salvation. For a time, I'd close my eyes tight and strain like hell, trying to force myself to speak in tongues so that I could be saved. Eventually, it dawned on me that salvation is less about what you *feel* than what you *know*. Then I relaxed, resting assured that I was saved.

At first, I strained hard with Monroe, hoping that the paternal bond would kick in. I went to his elementary school occasionally to check on him and picked him up from his grandmother's some weekends so that he could spend time with me. While I busied myself around the apartment, he'd leaf through my record albums and play songs he liked. That's when we discovered we had something in common. A love of music. We'd play records and talk about which recording artists we liked best.

Over time, he warmed to me. We established a rapport as I gradually learned how to relate to him. Then I relaxed, resting assured in what I knew—that I loved that little nine-year-old, and that if I tried hard enough I could make a critical difference in his life.

Then the growth of our bond was suddenly stunted. Liz got married, moved to California, and made plans to send for Monroe. He didn't want to go, and I didn't want him to leave. Yet I knew I had no right or authority to raise objections to Liz, who had been far more responsible than I'd been in caring for him. Whenever I tried to inject my views, she sharply reminded me, "You haven't been around for him." I backed off every time.

I didn't see Monroe the day he left. I felt too strange and fragile inside to see him off. My mother took pictures of him standing near his luggage before his flight to L.A. I looked at the photos later and saw the sadness on his face. It was a sullen, almost pleading look. I was saddened, too. Just when we were getting to know each other, he was gone and I was left to battle ghosts that seemed to be taunting me: distressing images of uncaring black fathers and the memory of my own detached old man, who fed such stereotypes.

■ ■ ■

A lot of those memories raced through my head while sitting there in J.L.'s living room. As Billy looked on quietly, J.L. asked me questions about my life: "Where do you work?" "Where do you live?" I answered in a monotone that made the exchanges seem more like a formal interview. I wanted to ask a few questions myself, such as, *Where the hell have you been?* But I didn't. If he didn't offer an explanation, why ask? Anyway, it seemed not to matter much anymore. I didn't need him now. I'd survived the period when I needed him most.

I suppose I'd felt hurt by his absence, but I figured I'd come to grips with that while in prison. I concluded that blood is *not* always thicker than water, and that fatherhood is not determined by bloodlines alone. Fatherhood is a state of mind. In that respect, Bonnie Alvin, the man who raised me, was my father.

J.L. and I talked on, straining to keep a conversation flowing; then I left with Billy, feeling somewhat better that another missing piece in my life had been supplied.

I visited J.L. on my own a few times after that. We got along well—better, in fact, than he and my other brothers did. He seemed suspicious of them because they had each borrowed money from him and failed to repay it. Unlike them, I never asked him for anything. For some reason—probably stubborn pride—I wanted always to be able to say I made it through life without *any* help from him.

During one visit, we sat on the porch and talked dreamily about things we wanted to do in life. I told him I would like to do some simple things that I'd missed out on while growing up in the streets. Maybe go camping or fishing. He sat up and looked at me. "You wanna go fishing? I go fishing all the time."

It amazed me that this guy assumed we could form an ongoing relationship after all these years, without him offering an explanation to bridge the gap. He seemed completely unaware that people need to know where they sprang from and who they're connected to. In all the years his three sons had lived in the next city, it never occurred to him that we *needed* to see him and our paternal grandparents in order to complete the picture of who we were. Because of him, my brothers and I had never laid eyes on J.L.'s mother and father, who lived a few hours' drive away in North Carolina. What's more, J.L. had never seen Monroe—my son—and it seemed not to bother him at all. *Pitiful*, I thought. *Just pitiful.*

When I left his house that day, he called out as I climbed into the car: "Call me when you ready to go fishing!"

I thought, *Call him? Call him? The few times in life I've ever seen this man is when I called or visited him. No, I won't call him. He needs to call ME.*

I decided then that I would never see J.L. again unless he initiated the visit. I'd wait and let him figure out that that was what he needed to do. Initiate.

That was in 1982. I haven't seen or spoken to him since that day.

Chapter 31 DATING

After the divorce from Yvette, I freelanced for a while on the romantic tip. But once again, my past complicated the present, making the dating experience more different than it had ever been. I could no longer hang with the streetish sisters I'd once run with. And besides Yvette, I had no experience dealing with women who were part of the new, professional world I'd gone into. I figured I needed to meet someone who was both streetwise and professional, and who could understand my attempt to deal in three conflicting worlds—among whites, working-class blacks, and bourgeois Negroes—and help me master that crazy high-wire act.

Finding such a person seemed hard, if not impossible. Most sisters I ran across were either streetwise and shallow or professional and sheltered. Like Rita. I met her at a party. She was fine as May wine, and mucho fun. She liked music and dancing and brought me much-needed relief from the stilted white world where I worked.

But Rita, a department-store salesclerk, was too superficial and contented for me. As long as she had a decent job, some nice clothes, and a relationship, she was good to go, but she had no sense of her potential to grow and expand. As far as I could tell, she'd reached her main goal in life when she graduated from high school. As for her future, the only thing Rita seemed sure about was her weekend plans. She was in touch with only her most basic feelings and guided by surface appetites. Na'im Akbar would say that she was still locked in the baby stage.

Rita and I hung out for a while, but I kept her far away from my professional life. I couldn't risk taking her to company functions. She talked about shopping sprees and hairstyles, manicures and clothing sales. She'd get eaten alive in social settings with my white colleagues, who loved to talk politics and current events.

I tried sharing books and ideas with Rita to ignite a mental spark, but often all I got in return was empty stares and this complaint: "You *think* too much."

The encounter with her and one or two other down-home girls

convinced me that I had to branch out, to check out some black professional women to see what was happening there. They were nice and far more stimulating than Rita, but they posed problems for me in other ways. Many were solidly middle-class women who'd led sheltered lives. It was hard for us to relate, especially on issues such as crime, politics, and the system. A date with one woman ended when she told me she firmly believed in capital punishment. Another said she routinely had background checks done on guys she dated to see if they had criminal records. I got a good laugh out of that one before laying her out.

Those professional women were perfect companions for company affairs, but they got on my nerves when we were all alone. I met one, Marie, while covering trials; she was doing an internship in preparation for a law degree. She was ambitious and smart, but she seemed to have no heartfelt convictions driving her. She talked about her career all the time, like that was all there was to life. People like her convinced me more of how thoroughly brainwashed some blacks were. And another thing: She liked to hang around white folks all the time, as if she thought that conferred some special status on her. She'd insist we dress up on weekends and go to fancy restaurants where she could order steak and sip cocktails among moneyed whites. After I peeped where she was coming from, it took me no time to pass on her.

My dealings with professional women weren't all bad. Some dates were fabulous nights right out of my prison dreams. And I learned through them that the dating scene among black professionals was far more complex than it used to be.

I realized that many black women are depressed. I'd known all along that we brothers were despondent, but I'd been unaware of black women's depression, maybe because it manifests itself more quietly. But I detected it in many ways, especially in the angst and utter frustration in their voices when they talked about black men. They're depressed partly because they see what's happening to us and they feel helpless, unable to stop it. They see us giving up, giving in, canceling one another out, and they know that it cancels them, too, because they're inextricably bound to us. They're depressed because there aren't nearly enough eligible and sane black men to go around, and that critical shortage is making them desperate and driving them crazy, as nutty as fruitcakes, just like us.

At the start of the eighties, I'd begun hearing a lot about the so-called shortage of "available" black men. I didn't believe it was true until I went into the white mainstream. Then I saw that there were a lot of single sisters in the professional ranks, and they seemed hard-pressed to find healthy, marriageable black dudes on their level to hook up with. The math was simple: After they subtracted those brothers who were locked away, gay, strung out, unemployed, or plain fucked up in the head from trying to cope in white America, black women often found the pickings slimmer than slim.

Whether real or perceived, the so-called black-man shortage started changing both men's and women's outlooks on things. One lady friend told me her father was so convinced that she and her younger sister would be unable in their lifetimes to find eligible black men that he'd begun preparing them early for the prospect of living alone.

Of course, a lot of brothers took their endangered-species status as an indication that they had it made. Some—those who didn't know any better—got the big-head when they found themselves in such great demand. One buddy used to say that being a single black professional man was "like being a child in a candy store."

But I saw definite drawbacks to the mismatched numbers. It screwed up the natural flow and dynamics of dating and fostered a sad, almost desperate, urgency among a lot of professional sisters. Sometimes, I found dates steering conversations to talk of commitment long before they knew whether I was worth being committed to. One woman told me shortly after we met, "I don't care what kind of problems you have—drugs, alcohol, whatever—I'm willing to work with you." Another woman, whose corporation job took her to a new, mostly white city, urged me to come along, and promised that her company would find me a newspaper job in her town or somewhere nearby.

Sometimes I got the impression during dates that I was being sized up, interviewed, and fitted for a bow tie and cummerbund. Often, I felt, such aggressiveness toward me had less to do with distinctive qualities I might have than with what I symbolized: They were searching for a buppie, a single black heterosexual male with a job. A white-collar job.

A lot of sisters claimed they weren't class-conscious in that way and insisted they'd take a working-class brother "if his head's on straight." But my experiences (especially later, when I moved to larger cities) led me to believe that in many cases that claim wasn't entirely true. I saw how they bum-rushed the white-collar cats in Armani suits.

It was so obvious that a lot of sisters were hung up on guys who fit the white-collar image that working-class brothers got hip and

figured out ways to pull the okeydoke. My barber, a dude named
Clarence, told me once that he regularly got business cards printed
with his name over some made-up executive title to impress "honeys"
who worked the happy-hour crowds. "Them gold-diggin' bitches go
for it every time. . . . And don't let me meet some broad that's lookin'
for work. I tell 'em I'm the director of personnel. I tell 'em, 'Baby, I
just hired a girl a few weeks ago, but I don't think she's gonna work
out. So if you gimme your phone number, I'll call you when I let her
go.' Man, you can't get rid a' them bitches then!"

That was fine if you were up to all that lying and frontin' and
carrying on. But if you weren't, the pressures brought on by the mad
rush for a "successful" mate made even casual dating seem like a
high-stakes, uptight affair. It made me a little paranoid, and it was the
same with a lot of other single black guys I knew. Often, when sisters
tried to speed up the pace of a relationship, we assumed they heard
biological clocks ticking inside their heads, while we heard time
bombs ready to go off.

■ ■ ■

One day, a Civic Center employee I knew introduced me to a friend
of hers, a woman named Debbie, who worked as a secretary at City
Hall. The three of us were eating at a restaurant when my friend
started talking about some fast-food chain where mice were found in
the food. "The woman took a bite into the chicken," she said, "and
realized she was eating a mouse. She sued the company."

As she spoke, I saw images of mice legs in my beef frank and gently
pushed my plate aside. Debbie looked at me and grinned. "You seem
to have lost your appetite."

We all laughed. That's when I really noticed Debbie for the first
time. Automatically, I reviewed the checklist in my head to see how
she rated on first impression. She seemed intelligent and had a sense
of humor. She was semi-professional, down-to-earth, and cute. Short
and copper-toned, she had high cheekbones like Yvette's, nice full
lips, and slightly slanted eyes that twinkled when she laughed. She
was twenty-nine, two years older than me.

After lunch, Debbie and my friend started up the sidewalk, headed
back to City Hall. Before moving on, I stood there, checking them out.
Debbie was slightly bowlegged, and her snug-fitting skirt revealed the
contours of a shapely frame.

A week or so later, I called her at City Hall and invited her to lunch.

"No thanks," she said.

"Then how about goin' out this Friday night?"

Pause. "Why do you want to go out with me?"

I must have said the right thing. We went out dancing that weekend. Afterward, I took her back to her parents' house in Norfolk. She said she lived with them because she'd come out of a live-in relationship with a trifling guy who'd ruined her credit. I parked in her parents' driveway, and we sat and talked. She told me she wanted to study veterinary medicine. I shared my plans to leave Portsmouth by the fall. When it grew late, I made a play for an overnight fling. "You wanna go to my place for breakfast?"

She said no. We talked some more; then, suddenly, she looked at me. "Let's go to your place."

That's how it started.

After that, Debbie often stopped by my apartment in her banged-up yellow Volkswagen Bug after she got off work. We'd sit on the front porch and joke and listen to music, or we'd go inside and cook, usually fresh fish. At the time, it seemed like a nice-enough casual relationship, something to tide me over until I moved away. But I was about to pick up a piece of wisdom that an older man had once shared: "There is no such thing as casual dating once a woman gives her body to you."

That summer, Debbie went into the hospital to have some fibroids removed. I visited her and took flowers. She lay in bed looking tired and worried. When I asked her how it had gone, she said, "The doctor told me that if I ever plan to have children, I had better have them now."

I thought nothing of it. I didn't even know what fibroids were.

■ ■ ■

I spent a lot of my free time after work at the Portsmouth library, trying to learn more about cities where I thought I might want to live. I narrowed my choices to Washington, D.C., Atlanta, and Oakland, places with reputable newspapers and a strong black culture. All other considerations were secondary. I saved money and decided to vacation in Atlanta, where I'd heard blacks were doing well. I took Debbie along and interviewed for a job at *The Atlanta Journal-Constitution*.

During my interview with the assistant managing editor, I didn't have to think twice about whether to tell them about my criminal past. Nor did I have to fill out an application and deal with the question I dreaded so much. As far as they were concerned, I was a choirboy, one of those trained, assimilated Negroes white folks love so much.

The timing was great. It just so happened that a lot of disgruntled reporters had quit or been fired after the paper's morning and evening staffs had been merged. I returned home, confident that I had a good chance to land a reporting job.

■ ■ ■

In any case, my mind was mostly on getting out of Portsmouth.

Eventually, the call came from Atlanta. They told me I could start the first of the year, in 1983. It was hard to believe I was about to leave the Portsmouth cocoon. My parents and the rest of my family were happy. The people at the *Ledger Star* were also glad for me. I felt sure I was on my way to something big: a big job in a big city where I could finally make the break from Portsmouth that I'd been dreaming of.

■ ■ ■

Debbie and I were at my place one day when she stepped close to me and said somberly, "We need to talk."

I sat down.

She looked squarely at me and said, "I'm pregnant."

I was stunned. "Pregnant? I thought you said you were taking birth-control pills."

She looked at me. "I must have missed one or two days."

The words hung in the air. I stared at the floor. *Pregnant.* How could I have fought so hard and come so far and have this happen? This wasn't *supposed* to happen. Not to *me.* According to the script I'd written for myself, I was supposed to move on to another city and live the rest of my life triumphant and problem free.

I looked at Debbie, who sat quietly watching me. "How do you feel about this?"

She said, "I want to have it. If I don't have this child, I may never be able to have children. You remember what the doctor told me when I got the operation?" She paused. "I'll abort if you insist, but I *really* want to have this child."

I looked into her eyes, searching for some telling sign, something— anything—that would give me a clue as to who and what I was dealing with. I wondered, Had this woman gotten pregnant intentionally? Had she planned this whole outcome? I'd heard about women who did such things. I'd heard stories about women who wanted babies so bad that they chose a man they wanted to father their child and manipulated things so that they could get their wish. But that was an ugly thing to consider. I didn't want to think about things like that. I didn't want to think about anything.

Over the next several days, I closed all the windows and doors to myself and denied I faced the dilemma confronting me. It was like something had happened that was so untimely, improbable, and wild that I was sure it couldn't be true. I just *knew* I was going to wake up any day now, any moment, and discover that it had just been a bad dream, a fucked-up nightmare. Then I'd get up from bed, go wash my face, shake it off, and get on with the real business of moving forward with my life.

I also thought—"hoped" is a better word—that maybe Debbie had gotten it wrong. Maybe her body was just messing with her head. Maybe her body was doing one of those weird things that women's bodies do every now and then where their period pulls a no-show for a couple of weeks and then arrives after nearly giving everybody a fucking heart attack. I just *knew* it was going to happen any day now and Debbie would come to me and say, "My cycle started. It must have been thrown off by some hormonal imbalance."

So, every day, I waited. But nothing happened, and time passed.

Months later, when I looked back, I concluded that the biggest mistake I made during that difficult period was that I didn't talk to somebody about it. I'm a big advocate of counseling now, mainly because of that experience. I needed badly to take that thing outside myself, to talk to somebody who had no emotional investment and get a clearheaded perspective on things. But I didn't. I couldn't. For weeks, I told no one, not even my mother. I couldn't tell anybody because I was too ashamed of myself for letting something like that happen. I felt stupid, and I didn't want to give anybody an opening to say, "You *are* stupid," not at a time when I was working so hard to build faith in myself and convince myself that I could live and function responsibly in this world and go for long stretches of time without doing something to jeopardize my freedom, happiness, and growth.

Finally, in the back of my mind, I knew I had a hole card: abortion. I knew that if all else failed, I could force myself to come to grips with that issue and persuade Debbie to do what needed to be done. I didn't have an intellectual position on abortion at the time. I was ambivalent about it. A white woman—of all people—helped me decide.

■   ■   ■

I'd transferred out of the Portsmouth office of the *Ledger Star* and was working in the Chesapeake bureau, which was run by Ron Speer. He came to me one day and said, "Nathan, there's a woman here who wants to talk to us about some protest taking place soon. Talk to her and see if there's a story in it, will you?"

I escorted the woman into the conference room, and we began talking. It turned out she was involved with a group planning an anti-abortion protest—really. After giving me the details of the planned demonstration, she looked me in the eye and said, "We've *got* to do this. . . . Do you know what the word 'fetus' means?"

Shaken and caught off guard, I tried to recover. "Sure. It refers to the embryonic stage of birth."

Her eyes bored through me. "No. 'Fetus' means 'little one.' That means that the life has already been formed. If the life has already been formed, it doesn't matter whether you kill it in the womb or outside the womb—it's still murder." She went on talking about the evils of abortion, convicting me with every word. It was as if she knew that I was considering pressing Debbie to do that very thing.

I sat there staring at her. She made me feel uneasy, like she knew my whole story all along and had come to chastise me. I felt like saying, "Go away, bitch, and let me think!" But she kept talking. I wondered, *Why did she come here at a time like this? Why is this happening? . . . Maybe this is the guidance I prayed for.*

I don't remember anything else about the conversation. When I left work that evening, I went straight to Debbie and told her that we would have the baby. I told her, "I really don't know you that well, but I don't want to hurt anybody. So I'm willing to try."

She was thrilled. She was delighted, and I was scared to death. All of a sudden, my whole life had changed. Suddenly, I was linked—for life—to a woman I'd known barely three months.

My future, which had seemed to be coming together so nicely, got real complicated. What about my new job and my plans to leave Portsmouth? I couldn't allow this crisis to block that. I decided to take care of my obligation from Atlanta and return home often to visit the child.

But as my moving date neared, the ghost of J.L. started hounding me: *If I go to Atlanta and leave Debbie behind, I will be separated from this child, just like I'm separated from Monroe. I can't allow that. I can't.* I felt I *had* to take Debbie. It would be risky stepping out in a brand-new city with someone I hardly knew. But I felt I *had* to try. Everything I'd learned in the previous five years suggested that if I did what I thought was right, if my heart was in the right place, things would work out. It was a principle of faith, the evidence of things not seen.

When I told my mother that Debbie was pregnant and that I planned to take her to Atlanta, there was this polite silence, a tacit acknowledgment that "Nathan has done it again." Neither she nor my stepfather said it, and I was grateful because I'd already beaten up on myself enough for everybody.

Debbie jumped at the chance to go to Atlanta with me. Her mother, father, and two sisters seemed warmer to the idea of her having a baby and going off to make a new life with a virtual stranger. Her mother and father congratulated us as if we were newlyweds. It would be years before I would fully understand that response. It would be a while before I'd learn what they all knew: that Debbie had been stood up at the altar—not once, but twice. She'd also been pregnant twice in one year, and the last time was just a few months before we met.

■ ■ ■

We pulled out of Portsmouth right after New Year's Day, 1983. I had a new car—a Nissan Sentra—a new job, and, having completed my time on probation the month before, a new freedom. All that, and yet I didn't feel free. Riding down Interstate 85 toward Atlanta with a pregnant woman beside me, I sensed I was heading into a bondage far deeper than any I'd ever known.

Chapter 32 THE BLACK MECCA

I fell in love with Atlanta from the jump. As picturesque and clean as any city I'd ever seen, it seemed to authenticate the glitzy images promoted in *Ebony* and *Black Enterprise* magazines. Long limos cruised along Peachtree Street downtown. Tall, gleaming buildings adorned the city's skyline, and couples strolled through lush green parks tucked into quaint courtyards here and there amid the skyscrapers. The southern-charmish feel and ultra-modern aura of the place combined to make Atlanta seem like the serious *joint*.

If you believed the tales floating among African Americans, Atlanta was "the Black Mecca," a place of boundless prosperity where jobs for blacks fell from the sky like manna from heaven. All you had to do was show up and some proud buppie would welcome you at the city's gates, whisk you away in a BMW, and drop you at the door to a well-paying, prestigious corporate gig.

In those initial months, it looked to me like *everybody* in Atlanta was livin' large. Walking down Marietta Street toward the Atlanta Journal-Constitution building, I saw well-heeled, bustling crowds of African Americans—scores of wonderful black faces—walking hurriedly, like they were going places. I'd never seen so many bloods dressed in business suits during working hours. In Portsmouth, most blacks downtown during the workday were clerical employees, city workers, or citizens plodding to City Hall to pay their water bills or going to court to face the man. Black men wore suits on Sundays or weekdays after 6 P.M., when they'd go home and shed blue-collar work clothes for nightclub duds.

In Atlanta, for the first time in my life, I saw my people seriously running things, controlling something other than the penitentiary or the rear-end lever of a garbage truck. For starters, blacks, who comprised a majority in the city proper, dominated the local political establishment. The mayor was black, as were most of the nineteen members of the Atlanta city council. Likewise, the Fulton County commissioner, the Atlanta fire chief, and the public-safety commissioner were all African Americans.

The black folks in Atlanta seemed more assertive and self-assured than the ones at home. Maynard Jackson, a feisty "Morehouse man" and Atlanta's first African American mayor, embodied that assertiveness. Among Atlanta blacks, he was a kind of folk hero, who did in the local political arena what Muhammad Ali had done in the boxing ring: He let white folks have it right between their blue eyes and talked beaucoup trash while doing it. When stubborn white business leaders tried to buck Jackson's efforts to ensure that minority firms get a fair share of tax dollars spent on construction, supplies, and services contracted out by the city, Jackson moved to block construction on the much-needed Hartsfield Atlanta International Airport until he got his way. When an old die-hard, racist police chief refused to resign at Jackson's request, Jackson created the black-led public-safety commissioner's office over the white chief to drive him out. Black folks in Atlanta loved seeing one of their own kicking ass.

There were more black-owned businesses in Atlanta than I'd ever seen, and a rich African American culture that featured goo-gobs of historic landmarks that kept me in wide-eyed awe. This was the cradle of the civil rights movement. This was the birthplace of Martin Luther King, Jr. His crypt was here, near the famed Ebenezer Baptist Church and down the street from the Southern Christian Leadership Conference headquarters. I went down Auburn Avenue to see it all.

I was surprised to find that so many of the civil rights giants I'd read about were still around. You're never too old for heroes. For the first time in my life, I could look around and take my pick: Andrew Young, Julian Bond, Hosea Williams, John Lewis, the Reverend Joseph Lowery, and Coretta Scott King, to name a few. Soon I would meet and write about them all and learn that they had problems and shortcomings, like everybody else.

I had friends in Atlanta, too. Several old schoolmates from Cavalier Manor had lived there a few years before I arrived. We often got together at each other's apartments on weekends and played Scrabble or cards and listened to music, ate, drank, and talked trash.

I was completely taken by Atlanta for a while, but after several months in town I realized it wasn't quite the middle-class paradise it was cracked up to be. Hidden on the black south side, in the shadows of the high-rises, were just as many—and probably more—poor, suffering blacks as I'd seen anywhere else. Atlanta was a white-collar town that thrived on hotels, conventions, and tourism. For the most part, unskilled laborers were out of luck.

And another thing: For all its glitz, Atlanta was still a big country town, with all the good and bad that comes with that. I learned quickly to distinguish between the transplants from other cities and those who were Atlanta-born and Atlanta-bred. Many of the home-growns, black and white, were as countrified as country gets. I could tell them by their scratchy drawl, that grating, Deep South twang that sounds like an untuned guitar, or their gaudy dress, the shiny James Brown shirts and cheap gray shoes. Chip, an old high school buddy who had lived in Atlanta for several years told me, "It ain't nothin' to see a niggah walkin' down the street wit' a pair a' spats on."

Shortly after arriving, I walked into a downtown barbershop to get a cut and was startled at what I saw. Men, lined up from wall to wall, sat in low chairs with their heads under dryers, while others got greasy touch-ups and fresh, oily Jheri-Kurls. It looked like a beauty salon. I turned and walked out. Farther up the street, I found another shop, where the scene was the same. It took several tries before I found a spot where a brother could get a regular cut.

It was country, all right. Bama Central. A cat with any kind of style could move in among the home-growns and become a star.

Bamas aside, Atlanta provided the escape from my old life that I'd yearned for. Here, I could start fresh with people who didn't know me from Adam, whose impression of me was shaped by the present day, not some wild thing I'd done a decade before.

For once, I felt that maybe, just maybe, I'd come upon a place where a black man stood close to a shot at competing with white folks on a level field. Maybe I could dream the same dreams that white folks dreamed, with a real possibility of making them come true. I was certain this was the closest blacks would get to the Promised Land. It *was* the Black Mecca.

■ ■ ■

Atlanta's potential as a Promised Land for blacks is tarnished by one fundamental flaw. It is nestled in the heart of a region where whites still cling religiously to their racist past. Atlanta is like a black island perched in the middle of a hostile white sea. Although the city is primarily black, the state is mostly white. Once outside the city, you can feel the seething resentment oozing from those crackers if they think you're from " 'Lan'a," that uppity nigger town.

I come from the South, too, but Georgia is different. It is the serious bastion of beer-drinkin'-flag-wavin'-pickup-truck-drivin'-card-carryin' nigger-haters. Dig this: As late as a few years ago, a Confederate flag hung prominently from the state capitol. The Ku

Klux Klan was still very active and often held rallies in Stone Mountain, just outside of Atlanta. Shortly after I got there, whites held a nationally publicized march in Forsythe County, not far from Atlanta, to protest the influx of blacks into that overwhelmingly white county. It was hard to believe this was the 1980s.

Some of my news assignments showed me that going ten miles in any direction outside the Atlanta city limits was like going back in time a hundred years.

On one of my first assignments, I was sent to a county fair to cover a watermelon-eating contest. That's right. A contest to see who can eat the most watermelon in a designated time. Of course, it set off alarms inside my head.

Ever since I'd first gone into the system, I'd remained seriously defensive about white folks' stereotypes of blacks, and I made sure that I did nothing that enabled them to typecast me. Knowing how much they enjoy seeing black folks dance, I refused to dance whenever I went to a party where there were whites around. If I went to lunch to interview a white person for a story, I'd never order chicken or other foods that they associate with blacks. Now here I was on hand for a damned watermelon-eating contest.

Standing in the middle of a crowd of mostly white farmers, I shook my head and wondered, *What the hell is going on?*

Minutes before the contest got under way, three young black boys, who appeared to be between ten and twelve, worked their way to the front of the crowd. I looked at them and got nervous, hoping like hell that they weren't there to compete. The boys stepped forward and signed up along with the fifteen or so whites there to try for the prize.

I scanned the crowd and saw the white farmers glancing at each other, grinning slyly as they looked at the black boys. I stood there, with pen and pad in hand, praying to God to not let one of the black boys win. But my worst fears were confirmed. The boys entered the contest and *turned it out*. One guy in particular went through watermelon slices like a buzz saw, knocking off big pieces like it was going out of style. He buried his face in the juicy stuff and never came up for air except to pick up a new slice. All the while I'm thinking, *Why me, Lord? Why do I have to see this shit?!*

When time expired, that boy had polished off twice as many slices as the second-place winner, who was also black. I felt nauseous.

White people were laughing at the boys, and the announcer also seemed to be in on the private joke. He grabbed the winner's hand and thrust it skyward, like a referee showboating a prizefighter. He shouted, "The winner!" The little black boy beamed proudly and accepted his prize, which I think was a new bicycle. All the white folks there clapped and grinned and looked at each other, winking to indicate they all understood the private joke: *Nobody loves watermelon like niggers.*

I did my job—taking notes and gathering quotes—but I was furious: mad as hell at the white folks secretly making fun of the boys; mad at those boys' parents for letting them come out there to make spectacles of themselves; and mad at the world for making me so racially sensitive that something so petty and innocent set me off.

Still, there were other assignments that tested my tolerance. We got word in the newsroom that a black man had been beaten by Klansmen in a place called Tallapoosa, about an hour's drive west of Atlanta. The night editor sent me and a white reporter to go and investigate.

When we got to the rural town late that night, it seemed desolate. It was a replica of the dusty, isolated towns I'd seen in cowboy pictures on TV. Had it not been for the cars on the streets, I would have sworn I'd gone back to the Wild West in the 1850s. Just like on television, the only establishment open at that time of night was a saloon. It was filled with rednecks, rough, leather-skinned cats in cowboy hats, boots, and wide belts. My partner, a guy named Gregg Jones, took one peek inside and his eyes got as big as two Kennedy silver dollars. He stopped me in my tracks and said, "I think you'd better stay in the car while I go in."

While sitting in the car, waiting for Gregg to return, I thought, *What if something happens? What an irony that would be: After all I've survived—the urban streets and prison—I come all this way, to the backwoods of Georgia, to get offed by the Klan. Life is wild.* The strangest feeling overcame me, one that has repeated itself occasionally since that night. I wondered, *What in the hell am I doing here anyway?* This reality seemed so remote from any I'd known or expected to know. I felt totally out of place—like a priest in a crap game or a white man in a rent party. At times like this, the breadth of my experience, from the streets to the mainstream, would dawn on me as if for the first time, and I would feel like I was dreaming.

It turned out the black man we'd been sent to investigate had been beaten for living with a white woman—I thought that sort of retaliation had gone out a long time ago. After we gathered facts and did our story, I was so glad to head back to Atlanta that I could've jumped out of the car and kissed the interstate when we reached the city limits.

Then there was the story that I did about a couple that had two seemingly healthy babies die mysteriously of sudden infant death syndrome in a small stretch of time. I went to the rural Georgia town and interviewed the husband and wife, who seemed more uptight over the idea of having a black man in their living room than over the death of their children. I went by the sheriff's office several times during the day to gather more information. As I prepared to leave town, the white sheriff pulled me aside and said, "I got somethin' ta tell ya." We sat down on a bench in the hallway of the small facility. "Some fellas called me on the phone taday and told me, 'You better tell that niggah to get outta town before dark or he may not make it.'" Then he smiled, searching my face for a reaction. It was a giddy, evil smile, like he was a co-conspirator in it all.

It pissed me off so much that I forgot to get scared. I gave him a message to take back to the boys: "You tell them that if they come at me, they better come right, 'cause I'm not a pacifist."

He was still smiling when I left, openly relishing the weird pleasure he got from trying to scare me. Driving home, I thought about Martin Luther King, Jr., and the other civil rights types who had willingly faced hostile people in towns like that one. I gained a new level of respect for those pioneers' courage. I wouldn't have had the heart to follow King. Nothing in me would allow me to submit myself nonviolently to the deadly abuse of southern crackers. My faith wasn't *that* strong.

In fact, my faith in the notion of divine justice was so weak that I considered getting a gun. If I was going to be going to southern towns like that one, putting my life on the line, I'd rather be armed. I figured that I'd rather be in a position to bust a cap into the first cracker that came my way. Then I dismissed the gun idea as a potential setup for disaster. If I got a gun, it wouldn't take much for me to use it, especially against some Deep South ofay with a hard-on for blacks. Then I'd end up right back in prison, where I started.

■ ■ ■

Like most newcomers at the *Journal-Constitution*, I was broken in on the evening shifts—3 P.M. to midnight or, sometimes, 6 P.M. to 2 A.M. It helped me learn the city. Most nights, I listened for action on the police scanner, often dashing from the office to get a company car and chase a fire or a shooting. One night not long after I'd started work, I found out from the police about a fight between two ambulance attendants at an emergency scene. Some guy had had a heart attack at a prominent Atlanta restaurant, and two ambulances from different companies had gotten there at the same time. As the man lay dying, the ambulance drivers fought over who would take him to the hospital to be treated.

Unlike in most jurisdictions, where ambulance services are city-run, Atlanta used privately owned firms, which charged emergency victims for transporting them to hospitals. Normally, when emergency calls came in, a county dispatcher rotated them, so as to spread the business evenly among the various ambulance services. But some greedy firms monitored police scanners for emergency calls, then tried to beat their competitors to the scene to collect the victims—and their money. This was known as "call jumping."

I wrote a story about the incident involving the heart-attack victim. Afterward, I looked into the problem of call jumping. It proved to be a reporter's dream. Police had reported several disturbing incidents, including one in which an ambulance driver, racing to jump a call, had run a red light and crashed into a car, killing the motorist, who happened to be a college honor-roll student.

I did a series of front-page stories that led county officials to investigate the problem and overhaul the entire system of dispatching calls to ambulance services.

After getting a lot of praise from editors, I made a pitch to cover a beat. It turned out that the only beat available was covering the Atlanta police. Eager to get on the day shift, I took it.

When I first went down to the police station, I wondered if I'd made a major mistake. I still didn't like cops. I hated their arrogant manner, the way they dressed, with keys dangling off their sides, and the way they walked with their arms hanging wide, like cowboys preparing to draw. They always seemed to have an attitude, like they were itching to walk up and spew their favorite macho line to provoke anger: "All right, move along, buddy."

At first, I confined myself to an office at headquarters, where the rollers left copies of police reports for journalists to sift through. Generally, I leafed through the reports and got story ideas from them, keeping my distance from the fuzz. Cops being cops, they were wary of me, too, and many were uncooperative when I called or went to their offices for interviews.

Then I met Detective Davies and that all changed. While I was walking through headquarters one day, he sidled up to me and said, "Yo, bleed, what it is?" Dressed in a leather jacket and slick, dark sunshades, he didn't look at all like a cop. He looked more like some brother I'd seen at a basketball court somewhere.

Taken aback, I asked him who he was. He told me he was an undercover cop who worked the streets. I hadn't known there were cops as cool as him. He was unconventional. Pure street. He talked more trash than a l'il bit and walked with a hard bop that would put pimpers to shame. Every time I saw him, he'd slap me a hard five and say, "Yo, bleed!" We hit it off from the start and hung out sometimes. He showed me the seedy parts of the city and turned me on to some good story tips. I often wondered when riding through the city with Davies what the fellas would think if they could see me cruising through town—in the front seat—with a lawman.

Davies introduced me to other cops, and I gradually loosened up around them. For the first time, I began to understand why a lot of cops have bad attitudes. Day in and day out, they deal with the worst on the human spectrum, and they are despised by a good number of the people they serve.

It both amused and amazed me that I was covering cops. I walked around headquarters carrying my own little secret. None of them suspected I was once their mortal enemy. I often wondered what they would do if they knew my background and that I had once detested them and their kind so much that I'd fantasized about taking potshots at them, guerrilla-style.

■ ■ ■

It was hard sometimes to separate myself from stories I wrote. Robberies, rapes, murders, drugs—I saw shades of my old life in all of that. And sometimes stories got to me. Like the time I beat the police to a crime scene only to find a dead cabdriver slouched in his car with a bullet hole in his head. I stood there for a long time staring at that hole, thinking about the time I shot Plaz and the times I'd been shot at. I felt blessed to be alive and living clean. Another time, I went to where a car had burst into flames on the interstate. When I walked up to the car, I saw a young boy sitting in the backseat, burned to a crisp. On the floor beneath him was a lone sneaker, about the size of one Monroe would have worn. The image of that boy has never left me.

Nowadays, when people ask how I am doing, I flash a pained smile and say, "Fine. I'm doing just fine." I don't think I'm a convincing liar, but I think people believe me because, by outer appearances, I

*should be doing fine: I have just started on a new job at one of the
nation's top-rated newspapers. I have just moved to what is commonly considered the best place for blacks to live in America. . . . I
should be feeling great. But I'm not.*

*Within me rages a turbulence that I can hardly contain. The
source of my anxiety is a life yet unborn, a soul that has not breathed
a single breath of this polluted air and, when it enters this world, will
probably know a time when it wishes it had never seen the light of
day.*

*That probably seems a terrible view for an expectant father to
hold. Perhaps if I had planned on having a child I would not be so
depressed. It was a decision made by the mother and executed with
my naive cooperation. Now I find myself faced with the unpleasant
decision of what to do, whether to remain in the household or move
into my own place. The decision has not so much to do with her. It
is the child that I'm concerned about, a child that didn't ask to come
into this chaotic, unhappy world. With one child already in California, thousands of miles away, how can I bring myself to separate
from another? I am afraid that if I do, I will end up supporting the
myth of the black stud who travels from household to household,
fathering children and then deserting them. And if I stay, that, too,
will be a compromise that I cannot live with. I cannot reconcile
myself to live in a household "for the sake of the children" or anyone
else.*

*It is a dilemma, indeed, one to which there are no easy answers.
I will have to resolve it, intelligently, rationally, and soon.*

Early 1983

Work was going well, but it was just the opposite at home with
Debbie. We seemed to get into a new argument every day. Before we
left Tidewater, she had assured me that her former job would cover
prenatal and birth expenses. Shortly after we got to Atlanta, she
checked again and learned that that wasn't true. Also, she'd promised
to find work until the baby was born. After we got to Atlanta, she
rarely left the apartment to look for a job. She had no money to help
with living expenses. She didn't even have a bank account (she said
her former fiancé had messed up her finances so badly that she
thought it best that she deal in cash). My savings dwindled, and more
and more, my attitude soured.

I generally know how I feel about most things, but I was more
ambivalent about that situation than about any in my life. Even as I

was moving forward with plans for the baby's arrival, I felt torn. There was a part of me that wanted to accept the situation and make the best of it. And there was another part of me that hated it because I felt I was being manipulated.

It just didn't *feel* right. Really, I didn't know how I was supposed to feel. All I knew was that it felt different than it had when Liz got pregnant. The difference was that I cared deeply about Liz and trusted her. Although I wasn't prepared for fatherhood when she got pregnant, there was at least an emotional connection with Liz that I could lock into. I liked Debbie, but beyond that there was nothing compelling about the relationship, and I felt guilty sometimes about feeling that way.

But Debbie acted like she was happy. She and her friends held a baby shower at the apartment. She constantly went shopping and came back with baby clothes, a crib, diapers, and other baby stuff. And she signed us up for Lamaze classes.

Reluctantly, I went. Sitting around in a circle with about eight white, happy-faced couples, I felt strange, out of place. They were married, and I was single. They seemed happy and excited, and I was scared and depressed. They looked like they were in love, and I was nowhere near it. During breaks, the women gathered in tight circles and chattered, comparing experiences and talking about shit like whether they were going to have a C-section and whether they planned to breast-feed. The men talked about health plans, hospitalization, and stuff.

I hated it when the instructor called on Debbie and me once to get inside the little hunky-dory circle and demonstrate a point she was trying to make about the partner's coaching role in helping ensure that the mother breathed properly. I felt like I was living a lie and that anybody who looked into my eyes could see it.

I went to the Lamaze class once or twice and then decided that it was too strenuous pretending to be half of a happy expectant couple. That wasn't the case, so why pretend? One day, when Debbie was getting dressed for another class, I told her, "I don't wanna do this."

She got pissed off and shouted her favorite complaint: "You're selfish! All you think about is what *you* want to do!"

I said, "What's wrong with me wanting what I want?"

We went back and forth, repeating the same gripes that we'd shared before. That's how the arguments usually went.

At times, Debbie seemed not to care a whole lot about whether I shared her enthusiasm about having a child. Her unbridled excitement sometimes bothered me. It was part of what made me suspicious of her. I thought she'd adjusted to the pregnancy much too quickly and eagerly for it to have been a mistake. I didn't want to think that about Debbie because she was such a nice person and seemed so genuine most of the time, but I couldn't help thinking sometimes that my pocket was being picked.

I rebelled against her because of all that. Sometimes, on my days off, I'd leave the house and, without telling Debbie where I was going, take long drives and think about my predicament. I'd ride around the perimeter of the city or go and hang out with one of my homeboys. I stayed in touch with an old girlfriend from Tidewater and rendez-voused with her a few times at a North Carolina hotel at the midway point. I'd return the next day and find Debbie red-eyed and dis-traught from crying all night. I didn't want to be mean to her, but I couldn't stand surrendering control over a life that I had only recently learned to command.

Debbie's family also played a big role in the discomfort I felt. They were real close. It was one of those families that if you got into an argument with one of them, all of them would jump in. On the one hand, I admired that closeness, but on the other, I thought it was dangerous. They had this blind mutual loyalty that led them to fiercely stand by each other, right or wrong.

I feared that Debbie wanted to use me to produce a carbon copy of the family she'd grown up in. Her mother was a housewife who adored family and children, and she was kind of domineering. She worked especially hard to see to it that family matters worked out like she thought they should.

Debbie's mother and two sisters were always on the phone with her, discussing preparations for the baby. I always got the feeling that they were the major players in this thing and that I was a secondary player.

I suspected that both Debbie and her mother wanted me to be like Debbie's father, who was the strong, silent type. A construction subcontractor, he worked hard, brought home the pay, and kept his mouth shut. He was a nice man, intelligent and gentle as could be. He didn't like conflict, didn't like to raise his voice. He was a go-along-to-get-along kind of guy.

Watching him during visits to our place in Atlanta, I understood where Debbie got her ideas about what a man should be. Seeing how she and her mother handled him, I understood why they came at me the way they did. Everybody has a price. I figured Debbie's father was the reason they got HBO. At their house in Norfolk, the mother and daughters would send him into the den, give him the remote control, and let him watch TV while they sat in the living room and made important decisions.

Her family was such a strong presence in my affairs that I felt like I was being double-banked all the time. They seemed intent on molding me to fit into their groove. No one came out and said it, but I got the impression that they thought my resistance was just temporary jitters, that eventually I'd break down and get with the program.

I got a good sense of what kind of family I was dealing with when Debbie's mother asked me on the phone one day, "What you all gonna name the baby, Nathan?"

Jokingly, I said, "If it's a boy we'll probably name him Hakim or Muhammad."

Before I could say "Just kidding," she exploded. "It don't make sense to name that child no African shit!"

I went off. "How you gonna get mad at me for what I want to name *my* child?!"

It was clear to me that she expected us to give the child some acceptable, European name. It has always amazed me how some black people are so brainwashed that they'd fight to preserve a life and culture detrimental to their own mental health. Over three centuries ago, white folks took away our names and assigned us theirs, and we've continued that confusing practice ever since.

That's why I applauded when young black girls started giving their babies crazy, made-up names like Tamika, LaWanda, Loquita. They may sound funny, but at least they're original. They're not slave identities.

When Debbie's mother and I clashed over the naming of the baby, I knew I was in for a bitter power struggle with her family that wouldn't easily go away.

■ ■ ■

I was at work on May 6, 1983, when Debbie went into labor. By the time I got to Grady Memorial Hospital, she'd already delivered a baby boy. Debbie had insisted on giving the baby a name she said she'd picked out long ago: Ian. I believe it's Scottish. When she named him, I thought, *Whoever seen a black Scot?* In a compromise, I gave him his middle name: Bakari, a Swahili name that means "of noble promise." Ian Bakari McCall.

I went to see Debbie briefly after the delivery, then went to the infant ward to see my son. Standing there, I felt the same sense of loneliness that I'd felt a decade earlier when Monroe was born. I stood there and looked at Ian for a long time. Bald-headed and shriveled, he looked old. He lay there, helpless and, no doubt, alarmed. Watching him, I thought about the implications of bringing another black male into the world to be dogged by white folks. I knew that there was no way Debbie could foresee what I saw in store for Ian. She saw only the joys of motherhood: baby food and nursery rhymes. I saw pain: job rejections and racial slights; self-doubt and maybe even self-hate. At one point, he squirmed and started crying. My heart sank. I wanted to cry, too, as much for myself as for him.

Chapter 33 BLENDING

In many ways, adapting to the white mainstream was a lot like learning to survive in prison: You had to go in and check out the lay of the land. You had to identify the vipers and the cutthroats and play the game by rules that are alien to nature and foreign to any civilized society. Prison primed me just right for that challenge.

Still, I was a little intimidated when I first arrived at *The Atlanta Journal-Constitution*. It was certainly a step up in size and prominence from *The Virginian Pilot–Ledger Star*. It had a higher circulation and a much larger staff, too. The newsroom was one massive open space filled with typewriters, computers, and rows of desks manned by eager reporters. Editors sat at broad desks in the center of the room, conferring with reporters and reading stories. It was the first time I had regularly been around *that* many whites before. Everybody looked like they knew what they were doing. I thought, *This is a big paper. These are experienced journalists. Maybe I'm not in their league.*

But learning the job was easy. The hard part was figuring out the newsroom culture and learning to interpret and respond to all those whites. Clearly, we were from different worlds. I found that the cues of one behavior that can be interpreted a certain way in one culture can have an entirely different meaning—or no meaning at all—in the other. Like something as simple as speaking when you pass each other in the halls. In black neighborhoods, we make a big deal out of it if you pass by somebody and don't say hello. It's offensive. Folks get mad and talk about your ass. In the newsroom, whites would speak to me one day, then I'd see them the next day and say hello and they'd look at me like I was from Planet Z. Or they'd speak to me in the office, and then when they saw me approaching in the street they'd look toward the walls or twist their heads halfway around their necks, like the girl in *The Exorcist*, to avoid eye contact.

That confused the hell out of me. I'd think, *What does that mean? Are they pissed off about something I did or said?* Over time, I learned that that's just the way many white folks are. It's no big deal to them whether or not you speak.

And then there was the black-male thing. I knew going into that newsroom that there was additional pressure on brothers, but I didn't know it was *that* intense, especially from white men. I always caught them looking at us, I mean studying us from head to toe, checking out our demeanor, the clothes we wore, our shoes, and how we coordinated our colors. Some of the brothers dressed nicely in outfits that were appropriate yet stylish. Occasionally, one of the white guys would make a snide comment about the way we dressed, as if to suggest that we somehow lacked substance because we paid attention to our appearance. They'd say things like "I'll bet you spend a lot of money on clothes, don't you?"

I knew what that was about. It was one of the many ways they revealed their jealousy. A lot of the white boys came to work looking frumpy. They ran polka dots and stripes in all directions, and their colors were so mismatched that it looked like they got dressed in the dark. They couldn't dress as sharp as the brothers and they felt insecure about it, so they tried to put us down. It was petty, but it was real.

It was also shocking to see how insanely insecure some of those white guys were in the men's room. Standing next to a white dude at the urinal one day, I noticed him looking down at my penis. The first time it happened, I thought it was my imagination. Then, after I began to pay closer attention, I noticed that it happened often with a lot of different white guys in the men's room. They just *had* to look to see if the myths about black men's penis size were true.

Sometimes, if I was in the mood, I'd fuck with their heads. I'd stand back from the urinal a few extra inches so they could get a *good* look.

■ ■ ■

There were all sorts of alliances and political intrigues that made up the zany culture of the newsroom. I arrived there just as the morning and evening papers had merged. New leaders were named and some heads rolled. There were the allies of the old regime, who were now on shaky ground. There were the allies of the new regime, whose careers were on the upswing. There were the white feminists vying for power. And there were the blacks, as usual, outsiders, trying to blend in and deal in the midst of all the aforementioned shit.

There were a lot more blacks at the Atlanta paper than there'd been in Norfolk. And these Atlanta blacks were different from most blacks I'd spent any real time around. Many had come from staunchly middle-class backgrounds and were second-generation college graduates. Some were stone-cold assimilationists, who had done everything the white man said you needed to do to blend in and get ahead: They'd gone to the nation's most prominent colleges and universities and learned all the things about white folks that you need to know to be considered intelligent by them. They were well trained but poorly educated. They could talk about Hemingway or tell you everything Shakespeare ever doodled on paper, but if you asked them about Gibran, J. A. Rogers, or Akbar, they'd shrug and ask, "Who are they?" They were the most pitiful ones, the ones who surrendered so completely to white domination that they were alien to themselves. Racism was so painful for them that they denied its existence. They would be the first to tell you, "There's no real racism anymore. We have to stop making excuses for our own shortcomings." If they overheard you talking about white folks, they would be the first ones to come to whites' defense: "You sound angry." The suggestion was that, somehow, if you had allowed racism to make you mad, then you were defeated. I felt the opposite. I felt that any black person who had *no* anger was defeated.

Many of the blacks had gone beyond undergraduate school and gotten master's degrees. They talked white and thought white and even dressed goofy like the man: blue sport coats, high-water khakis, and penny loafers. Away from the office it was crewneck sweaters, high-water khakis, and deck shoes. They boasted of vacations in Europe, where white people go. One dude, a brother who worked in the sports department, even went out and bought a pickup truck so that he'd belong. I knew he wasn't hauling anything. I think he wanted to feel a part of the good-ol'-boy culture, those white dudes in the sports department who drove pickups, too. It was sickening seeing how much white folks had scrambled their brains.

I often thought about how out of place some of those white-acting black cats would look walking through Cavalier Manor. They'd get eaten alive. If the serious joners honed in on them, they'd get ripped apart, from their paddy-boy shoes and tight-butt walks to their bald faces, which they kept shaved to avoid looking intimidating.

Blacks weren't immune to the neurosis that characterized the newsroom, either. They seemed uptight, nervous just like everybody else. Cordial but cautious, some of them seemed reluctant to speak to me when I first got there. They seemed hesitant to openly acknowledge the presence of another black. It was as if they didn't want whites to know that it made a difference to them that another black had come

to work there. The truth of the matter was that it made a *big* difference. In journalism, where there are so few African Americans in
newsrooms, we're always delighted to see other black faces. It's the
same thing that happens to white people when they find themselves
amid a sea of black people at a subway station or somewhere: When
the subway takes them someplace where there are more whites,
they're thrilled.

Although the *AJ-C* had its share of handkerchief-heads, many of
the blacks were cool and down to earth. We got together sometimes
for dinner and drinks and even an occasional party. It felt good being
in a work environment where there were at least some people on my
job I could relate to. Even for those of us who didn't relate well
personally, we were drawn together by a common bond: We were in
white folks' territory, and like it or not, we needed each other to
survive.

■ ■ ■

I knew from the get-go what white folks thought of us. I knew they
were afraid of us and that if I expected to do O.K. I had to be
decidedly unaggressive and unthreatening. Yet I kept hearing my
managers say, "We want people to be *aggressive*." That's the kind of
double message that makes brothers crazy. If we're aggressive on the
job, white folks get intimidated; if we're unaggressive, they knock us
for being passive and we don't advance.

I got my first lesson about restraint in the newsroom from a
brother. I'd completed a story and turned it in; then a white editor
made a lot of changes without discussing them with me. I got hot and
went back and changed the story to its original form.

When the black editor found out about it, he pulled me aside and
talked to me. "Hey, my man. Be cool. You can't lose your cool like
that."

But white reporters lost their cool all the time. Some white reporters, especially those considered stars and golden boys, went off on
editors in front of everybody and it was routinely dismissed as mere
temperament. But I couldn't get away with being temperamental. I'm
a brother.

The double standard reminded me of the days when my brothers
and I were very young and my mother warned us not to "act like
niggers" when we went to public places. The white kids acted like
niggers all they wanted, but when we got rowdy, somehow it was a
crime.

Such double standards on the job worked a serious head-trip on me, making me second-guess the sort of instinctive judgment that had guided me all my life. There were times after the story-changing incident with the editor when I should have been aggressive and I wasn't. Once, while I was working the night shift, an editor in his early fifties called me to his desk. As I walked forward, he said, "Will you hurry your ass up?"

I was nearly floored. Walking toward him, I asked myself, *Did he really say what I thought he did? Maybe I didn't hear that right. I couldn't have heard it right. No. No way. . . . If he did say that, then what does it mean? What should I do? Should I straighten his monkey ass here and now, or report it to some higher-up tomorrow? . . . Maybe I'm being super-sensitive.*

I second-guessed myself so much that I ended up doing the worst thing possible: nothing. Deep down, I knew I'd heard him right. Every time I saw that editor after that, I thought about how he'd disrespected me and I regretted not putting him in check. If he'd said something like that to me on the streets, I'd have put my foot so far up his ass he'd have tasted shoe polish. But we were on his turf. He knew it, and he knew I knew it. I had to be cool and let it slide.

If I had straightened him out, all he would have needed to do was casually suggest to some management person that I had a "chip on my shoulder," and it would be Good-bye, Nathan McCall. They might not have fired me outright, but they would have started nitpicking and fucking with me, working on getting me out of there. That's the code phrase they use when they want to get rid of black men: They say we have a "chip on our shoulder." They know they can get a response then, because no white person wants to run across a black man with a chip on his shoulder. They get images of Nat Turner, slave rebellions, and throat-slashing and shit. White men can throw tantrums in the workplace all day and all night, and they're excused as "eccentric." But the second a brother shows some aggression, he's got a chip on his shoulder. He's *got* to go.

I had a hard time interpreting white folks' behavior in a lot of situations. Sometimes I'd try to make sense out of behavior for which there was no rational explanation. Like the actions of Brenda Mooney, the city editor, who ran the day-to-day affairs of news reporting. She was an insecure white woman trying to rise in the ranks by proving to white men she could be just as oppressive as them. She even wore the women's version of blue and gray wool power suits, which looked like they'd been stretched on her big torso. She acted strange sometimes and would have you scratching your head, wondering if you really saw and heard what you thought you saw and heard. Whenever I talked to her about news stories, I felt her eyes raking my body, not in a sexual way, but in a deeply curious way. Invariably, she'd focus on my tie, half listening, then say "O.K." and walk off abruptly, leaving me standing there, puzzled.

Brenda had phobias that seemed to increase by the day. Like her fear of elevators. She'd often come into the sixth-floor newsroom huffing and puffing like she'd been running track: She'd walked up six flights of stairs because she was scared of the machine.

She seemed to try to compensate for her insecurities with a fanatical devotion to work. Although the city editor's job required people skills, she had a terrible way with people and was universally despised in the newsroom. Yet she'd been promoted from reporter to city editor in a few short years. At first, watching Brenda Mooney's career rise confounded me. I thought, *This woman is crazy. . . . But if she's crazy, then why has she been promoted to work over me and so many other people?* I looked around and saw other people as nutty, obsessive, and insecure as her, and they were moving up and being promoted, too. The people who were self-assured and humane in their dealings with others went nowhere, but the crazies went straight to the top. It made me scratch my head and question my own perceptions. *Maybe they're not crazy. Maybe that's normal and I'm the one who's confused. Maybe these people know something I don't know.*

I realized that the people, black or white, who survived in the system were those who learned to adjust to, rather than challenge, the system's insanities and to conform to its rules. I knew I could never adjust fully to the establishment, but decided that maybe I would adapt easier if I conformed a little more. I thought, *Maybe I take things too personal. Maybe I read too much into things. Maybe a lot of the things that I think are racial are really my imagination. These are fairly nice and intelligent people. None of them has called me "nigger" or "boy." . . . Maybe I should just play along with the establishment game and not be so . . . different.*

I tried for a minute. I walked around there, quiet and unassuming, and tried to be aggressive as a reporter while being unaggressive when relating to co-workers. I even went out and bought a pair of Bass Weejuns, those thick-soled penny loafers all the white men wore in the newsroom. I decided that maybe the shoes I wore were too black-looking and stylish. "Flamboyant" is the word white folks like to use to describe us. I thought that maybe if I wore some paddy-boy shoes and toned down my dress, white folks would stop staring at me so much and they'd see that I'm not so different. A friend who went with me to buy the shoes thought I'd lost my mind. He looked at them and said, "Why are you buying *these* things?"

I got mad and blew my cool. "You don't understand the pressure I feel!" I knew there was no way I could explain it, either.

Anyway, I wore those penny loafers several times and then gave up. It just didn't work. I knew from the days at Waters Junior High that brothers have to have their pants fall over their shoes a certain way for them to look right. The pants can't be high-waters and the tongue of the shoe can't ride too high. Otherwise, your shoes will push the bottom of your pant legs up and you'll look goofy. White boys might not mind, but no *real* brother wants to look goofy. When I wore those Weejuns to work, not only did I look goofy, I felt goofy. They didn't feel right when I walked. They didn't let my pant legs fall right. I looked down at my feet and all I could do was shake my head. I was conscious of those shoes every second they were on my feet.

After wearing them awhile, I put the Weejuns in my closet and left them there. They're still there now—right beside my prison brogans—with about a half inch of dust on them. I kept the brogans as a memento of what I'd been through in prison. I kept the Weejuns as a testament to the time I almost lost my way in the white mainstream.

■ ■ ■

When I reached the corner down on Auburn Avenue, a group of reporters was already gathered there, covering the press conference. With notepads and microphones in their hands, they listened intently to the preachments of civil rights warrior Hosea Williams. I'd been sent to cover the press conference. I don't remember what it was about. All I know is that I was excited about the prospect of meeting Williams, who had been one of Martin Luther King, Jr.'s, lieutenants in the movement.

Once the press conference formally ended, Williams hung around to take additional questions. Since I had arrived late, I tried to get fresh quotes. Speaking in his gravelly voice, Williams looked at me and said, "Which news organization are you with?"

I said, "I'm with *The Atlanta Journal-Constitution.*"

His eyes widened. "*The Atlanta Journal-Constitution*!? That's one of the most racist newspapers in the country, and you down there Uncle Tommin' for them!? Don't you know I demonstrated against that paper so that black folks like you could get jobs there!? And y'all ain't done no better than the white folks at that paper. A bunch a' Uncle Toms . . . !"

I was baffled. *How could this be? He's calling ME an Uncle Tom? ME? This is crazy.* I thought that Hosea Williams, of all people, should understand the nature of my struggle in the system. Hadn't he and others like him demonstrated during the civil rights movement so that my generation could get into the system and try to change it? So now what was he saying? Was he saying that I should *not* be in the system? Was he saying that I had to be unemployed and down-and-out to be considered a *real brother*? It was unclear to me where he was coming from and apparent that he had no intention of explaining.

As he spoke, the other reporters—all blacks who worked for black-owned newspapers and radio stations—stood back and watched quietly. They seemed embarrassed for me. I was more than embarrassed. I felt humiliated.

Williams went on ranting for what seemed like forever. I stood there, listening, but getting impatient. I didn't know which of the many impulses shooting through my mind to obey. I wanted to fight, drop my pen and pad, and throw down. I wanted to curse. I wanted to forget about being a journalist and defend my honor. Calling me an Uncle Tom was a sin, like talking about my mama. Before he could finish talking, I let go. "How can you say that about me?! You don't know me!"

That only fired him up more. "You a puppet for the white man . . . !"

I had to back off. It was clear that it was useless to argue. I couldn't explain. What was there to explain? I couldn't shout him down. Nobody shouts down loudmouthed Hosea Williams. I had to absorb the punishment and chalk it up as one of the risks of the job: being rebuked by my own people.

When it was over, I dragged myself back to the newsroom, reeling from a lashing I thought I didn't deserve. It was weird. It was one of several times since I'd become a journalist that I had had the frustrating experience of being cited by other blacks as one of the enemy, as a part of an establishment that worked methodically and consistently to cripple their lives.

As much as that incident angered me, I could relate to Hosea Williams's rage and understood the kind of frustration that ran so deep it turned black people against each other the way he'd turned on me.

I'd heard complaints about the paper from other blacks here and there and knew what they meant when they said the *AJ-C* was racist in its coverage of black communities. These blacks were bothered by subtle things that whites at the paper seemed unable to grasp: the way blacks were consistently depicted through the eyes of white writers and photographers, who promoted a narrow, distorted view of black life. The only stories the paper thoroughly covered about blacks related to protests, sports, discrimination, poverty, and crime. White writers and photographers seemed unable to conceive of black life being broader than that.

When I was covering cops, my editor—unconsciously, I think—differentiated the importance of stories based on whether the events had occurred on the black or the white side of town. If someone was murdered on the south side, where most Atlanta blacks live, the editor would say, "Gimme a brief," meaning, type up a few paragraphs and forget about it. If, however, someone was murdered on the affluent white north side, he would say, "Let's check into it. Let's see who it is." The connotation was that if the murder victim was white, he was obviously "somebody," but if he was black, it was just another worthless life.

Those kinds of slights kept me on edge, and I found myself in the curious position of being an insider carrying around the same rage as outsiders like Hosea Williams.

■ ■ ■

The year 1983 was pivotal for me. I started a new job in a new place. A son was born, and it was the tenth anniversary of my high school graduation. High school reunions have a way of putting you in touch with what Kahlil Gibran called "the procession of life." You see how people have changed through the years. You learn about their weddings, their children's births, and even their deaths. I went back to my reunion feeling proud of how far I'd come since high school. My former classmates didn't make a big deal of how I'd turned my life around, but they acknowledged their pride in another way: They asked me to give the keynote address.

I talked from my heart and held back tears as I looked around the room and saw all those people, folks who'd grown up with me way back when. I realized I loved them on a level I couldn't explain. That love surfaced for all of us when we did a special ceremony for former classmates who had died. LaFrancis had been killed in a car crash—we used to play stickball in her mother's backyard. Brenda had died suddenly of some illness, leaving behind a child for her mother to care for. And Steve, who first turned me on to tunes by Oblivion Express, had recently killed himself.

I left there determined to remain mindful of the brevity of life and to make sure that I appreciated other people. There were no guarantees they would always be around.

By then, my grandmother Bampoose was troubled by kidney problems that had her in and out of the hospital. I went to see her during one of my visits home. Standing over her bed, I wondered if she had always been that short and thin. It seemed impossible that this was the woman who had once carried our entire family. She looked so weak and frail. I sat and talked with her awhile, the entire time eyeing my watch, wondering if I could get away to visit one more person before leaving town. I left and returned to Atlanta, promising to spend more time with her the next time around.

Not long after I got to Atlanta, my mother called to say that Bampoose's condition had worsened. I waited for more information, trying to decide if I should hop on a plane to see her again. But I'd already seen her for the last time.

I was in the kitchen when the next call came, a few days later. It was my mother. "Bampoose just died."

"Oh yeah?"

"Yeah, she died this morning."

"When's the funeral?"

"I don't know yet. We're trying to make funeral arrangements now."

"O.K., just let me know, and I'll be there."

"O.K." She hung up.

As I put down the phone, it struck me that our conversation had been oddly distant and impersonal. I don't think the finality of the news had registered with either of us. It didn't hit me fully until I went into the living room and sat down. *Bampoose is gone. My grandmother Sadie Benton is dead.* The quiet little pillar who taught me to play checkers and sent me to the 7-Eleven on Saturday mornings to buy biscuits and molasses. *She's gone.* How could that be? There had never been a time when Bampoose wasn't around. She'd always been a fixture, as steady in my life as my mother.

Then the tears came, first the moisture that clouds the eyes, then the sobbing bursts. I just sat there, thinking about my grandmother and all the things between us that had been left unsaid. Whenever I'd gotten into trouble with the law and Mama had had to scrape up bail money or money for lawyers, Bampoose had always pitched in. Once, when my stepfather refused to pay out more money for lawyers' fees on my behalf, Bampoose dug deep into her big pocketbook and gave what she had. No hesitation.

I felt I'd never paid her back. I'd never given her the fulfillment of knowing that her faith in me was not wasted. And I regretted rushing off and leaving her during that last hospital visit.

Before Bampoose passed, I had been philosophical about death. Death, I thought, was not an ending to mourn but a promotion to another, perhaps better, state, a recycling in an eternal journey that ultimately leads somewhere peaceful and sublime. But when Bampoose died, I understood the sadness part, too. You simply miss the person, and the thought that he or she will never be around again is painful. I understand now more than ever.

After Bampoose died, I thought about the song that had always reminded me of her: "Sadie," by the Spinners. Every time I hear that song now, I think about Bampoose, and my eyes water. I choked, and my eyes watered again, while writing these words.

I held up O.K. at the funeral until we got to the grave site. Then I broke down again. Watching them lower Bampoose's casket into the ground, it occurred to me that she'd never asked for much in life: a game of checkers, a wrestling match on TV, some corn bread and buttermilk every now and then, and she was fine. I suppose she never asked for the ceaseless toil, either—working as a domestic for white folks so that she could take care of her children and her children's children. She lived for sixty-eight years. Yet it seems she never really lived at all.

Chapter 34 A MEASURE OF PEACE

I see now why old-heads tell young folks to take their time. I understand why they say, "Get to know people and their families before you plunge into affairs." Had I followed those conventions, I probably wouldn't have gotten hooked up so quickly with somebody so wrong for me. But I did get hooked up, and it cost me so much pain and so much time on the emotional roller coaster that to this day I haven't completely recovered.

■ ■ ■

On the day Ian was born, I left the hospital reeling. I was disoriented. I needed somebody to talk to about the confusion I felt. I needed escape—a fifth of bourbon or a cigar-sized joint. If I had those, I thought, I'd get high as a kite and let the drug deaden the pain.

Instead, I gassed up the car and rode around, cruising through Atlanta's black south side, glancing at people walking along the streets. It dawned on me while watching them that appearances reveal very little about people. I had no sense of their travails, and they knew nothing of what I was going through. We all looked cool, in control, on top of things.

Yet I was an emotional wreck. My self-pity at that moment was enormous. My life was more complicated than ever. Now I had two sons—two young, endangered black men—to steer through this crazy, racist world while trying to figure out how to get through it myself. I had two sons by two different women, neither of whom I was in love with or married to. And I had *serious* fatherhood fears haunting me. I kept wondering, *How am I going to handle the responsibility of another child when I'm already having so much trouble learning to be a good father to the first?* It looked bad for the home team.

The complexity of the shit I was dealing with was mind-boggling. Although I didn't understand it at the time, matters of race were once again a key factor, lingering in the shadows like they always do: I'd hooked up with a woman apparently desperate to nail down a brother to realize her family dreams amid widespread fears that there weren't many decent black men left. And she had cut into me at a time when I was hypersensitive about how I was perceived as a black man. Race played a key role in how I viewed my domestic situation, how I responded to Debbie's actions, and, ultimately, how I got myself into deeper doo-doo while trying to clean up my act.

I was dogged by racial stereotypes about irresponsible black baby-makers. I didn't want others, black or white, to see me that way. And yet, on the surface, it was beginning to look like I was a Mack Daddy in a suit and tie. Paranoid, I kept my private life as secret as possible from my colleagues. Except for a very few select black folks at the paper, I didn't socialize on weekends with any of them. If my colleagues were to come to my apartment, they'd see that I had a live-in partner and a young child, and I felt uncomfortable with that. It wasn't the establishment way of doing things. The establishment considered such arrangements "illegitimate."

Also, it was extremely important to prove to myself that I didn't fit the stereotypes. I knew I'd changed, but that new birth suggested otherwise. It cast doubts in my own head. All that stuff haunted me and clung like a pit bull.

Sometimes when I thought about it, it seemed that the best solution to that mess would be to legitimize things, to remain with Debbie and become a family man, to do the Ward Cleaver thing. Then my shit wouldn't appear to be so ragged.

But it wasn't so easy. After I'd lived with Debbie for several months, it became clear to me that we were two very different people whose outlooks on life, values, and goals were nothing alike. I thought she was so hung up on her family dreams that she ignored what was going on in the rest of the world. She said I was so consumed with black consciousness that I was unable to relax and enjoy the simple things in life, such as the family vibe. We had serious arguments, loud knock-down-drag-outs that always went in circles and usually ended with her calling me selfish and wondering aloud why I couldn't want what she wanted in life. She'd say, "What's wrong with what I want?"

And I'd say, "Nothing. There's nothing wrong with what you want in life except that you can't force me to want what you want. It doesn't work that way."

She always got to me, though, when she put it another way. Sometimes, she'd say, "What's so wrong with wanting to have a family? That's the most natural thing in the world."

When she said that, she struck a sore spot. After hearing the Muslims preach so much about the virtues of family, I'd accepted it as a good thing. Mostly, though, when she raised that issue, it tapped into a well of doubt that I had about myself. I knew that my value system had been so screwed up when I hung on the streets that some of my natural inclinations might be out of whack. And I feared sometimes that my reluctance to form a family with Debbie was an example of my imbalance. I wondered if perhaps I should be more family-oriented and, since I had a ready-made family with me, get with the program.

Sometimes I tried. Sometimes I told myself, *Just cooperate. Maybe you'll eventually learn to like it.* I'd go with Debbie to see her friends, and she and I packed up the baby and drove to North Carolina sometimes to visit her relatives. Always, I felt like an actor, playing the role of the warm husband and proud father to keep up a front. Lord knows I tried, but my heart wasn't in it.

The heart is a stubborn thing. It don't give a shit what you tell it to do. It does what it wants, and it can't be trained to do otherwise. Although there were times when I really felt I liked Debbie, I couldn't will myself to accept as permanent the situation that I was in with her. I couldn't get my heart to cross over into love to save my life. The magic just wasn't there.

■ ■ ■

Although we were an eleven-hour drive away from Norfolk, Debbie's family visited so often that it seemed sometimes like they lived right around the corner. Her mother was so excited about the newborn baby that she couldn't stay away. She was happy that Debbie finally had the baby that she'd wanted, and I could see that in subtle and not so subtle ways she was trying to move the union into the next phase: marriage. One day, when Debbie's mother was visiting, she walked over to me and said, "Nathan, now that you all have a baby, you should be thinking about getting married."

I was standing in the kitchen. I said, "No, I ain't thinking about getting married."

She said, "Well, if you were man enough to lay down and do what married people do, then you should be man enough to take the responsibility for it."

I went off. "I'm not getting married, and nobody's gonna make me!" Hearing my raised voice, Debbie, who had gone to the back of the apartment, rushed into the kitchen to see what was going on. When I told her, she grew quiet.

That wasn't the end of the family troubles. That summer, Debbie decided to send the baby to her mother for a while. I protested. "He's too young. I thought you were supposed to keep the baby with the parents so that he can bond with them in his first months."

But it was a done deal. Debbie's mother wanted to keep the baby, and she got him. I got overruled.

Then Debbie's sister came to live with us in our two-bedroom apartment. The youngest of the three girls, she had just finished college. She was self-conscious and somewhat shy. Nice, but not warm. She had personality quirks, like anybody else. Tensions rose between us, however, when it came to resolving those little differences that can make life hard in a crowded household. Like her unwillingness to wash our clothes along with hers when she went to do the laundry. And her insistence on taking Ian out of his crib at night when we were trying to get him used to sleeping alone.

I appealed to Debbie to talk with her sister about those things, but I ended up having to do it myself. I'd forgotten: *They don't take sides against each other.*

The arguments between Debbie and me worsened over time. Then I saw a side of her that I hadn't seen before. One day, we were arguing in the bedroom and she pushed a stereo speaker on me and hurt my hand. Another time, she got mad and hit me—hard—with a lamp. I learned through those and other experiences with Debbie that some women are as abusive in relationships as some men. It's rare to find women who'll do it, but some figure they can kick your ass up and down the street and you're not going to do anything because men aren't supposed to hit women. Some know that they have the law on their side, and they take full advantage of it. Debbie was one of those women.

Minutes after the lamp incident, I went to Debbie's sister, who'd seen and heard it all, and I appealed to her to talk to her sister. She gave me this blank stare, which I took to mean, *We're family. We don't take sides against each other.*

Debbie's tendency to get physical scared me. I knew I had a temper, and that if I hit her back or merely tried to protect myself she'd call the cops. I'd get locked away, my prison record would be brought into it, and the thing could mushroom into a big old mess.

I felt vulnerable, like I was in a potentially explosive situation that I couldn't control. That's when I decided to do something fast. I moved out.

I found a trendy-looking apartment on Edgewood Avenue, just blocks from downtown. It was a cozy second-story apartment with hardwood floors and a wood-and-plate-glass front door that looked out over a spacious deck and provided a splendid view of the city. For the first time, I got to experience Atlanta as I had originally planned to—alone. One of my fantasies was to live a stable, responsible life as a bachelor, to get all my affairs in order, and to get on top of life without some external obstacle hampering me.

For a while, I tried to pretend to myself that Debbie didn't still live in Atlanta. I got back into the market and began hanging out, hitting the happy hours to check out Atlanta's singles scene. But Debbie wasn't going for that. One day I looked out my front door and saw her standing across the street, watching me. She was just standing there, holding Ian on her hip. Another time she showed up at my place, unannounced, late at night. I had company over, a lady friend I'd met. Debbie rang my apartment, but I didn't answer the intercom. She kept ringing so much that one of my neighbors must have grown impatient and buzzed her in. Once upstairs, Debbie banged on the door, loud and hard, prompting a neighbor to come into the hallway and threaten to call the law. My guest got so scared that she went and hid in the bathroom until Debbie left.

That kind of blind irrationality frightened me, but it didn't stop me from dating other women. I desperately wanted to find that special someone with the right blend of intellect and worldliness, and I felt Atlanta had a lot of such women to choose from. That's when I got a better sense of the stress among black professionals in the dating scene. Black professionals in Atlanta had all the problems that I'd seen in Tidewater, but on a larger scale.

One night, while mingling at a game party thrown by a colleague, I met Alicia. She was fine, a dark-skinned beauty with a short natural, full lips, and big, pretty eyes. She had that ethnic style about her— dangling earrings, copper bracelets, loose-fitting African garb—that I love. She was intense but not solemn. She had a good sense of humor, was spiritual and cerebral, and her black identity was well intact. A schoolteacher, she was about to start her own business to get out of the system.

We had big fun together. We'd go to movies, go dancing, or sit up at my place and listen to music and talk about everything. But a couple of months or so after we started dating, she raised the commitment issue. "Nathan, I think it's time for us to talk about where we're going."

I responded in the dumb, evasive way men often do. "How will we know where we're going until we get there?"

"Then I need to know what it is we have."

"You know what we have. We have a fine relationship."

"I need something more."

"I'm not sure I can give more. Anything more and we'll be engaged."

The truth was, I wanted to give more. But I couldn't. I felt obligated to Debbie and Ian in a way I couldn't explain—to Alicia or to myself. I felt that obligation so strongly that I felt like I was sneaking around, even though Debbie and I had formally split.

Unable to get a commitment from me, Alicia called off the relationship.

Over time, that developed into a disturbing pattern with me: I met nice, intelligent sisters I liked a lot. We dated, but when they wanted to take the relationship to another level, I got scared and moved on. That nomadic life got frustrating, especially when I went out with the wrong women. Eventually, I realized I may have missed out on something special with Alicia. And watching those people I knew who seemed to enjoy family stability made me think seriously about settling down. I even started feeling guilty about enjoying so much freedom, and wondered, *Maybe I gave up too soon on Debbie and my son.*

I'd often wondered if I'd moved too fast and given up too soon on Yvette. The divorce from her was one of those experiences that taught me something about myself that I didn't much like: I'd invested a lot of energy in learning to believe in myself but never quite learned how to believe in others. Having left Debbie, I felt as if I'd continued an ugly pattern that I needed to break.

But Debbie, I thought, couldn't offer me a healthy relationship. This was the same woman who'd thrown lamps and overturned furniture during arguments. Yet I found myself willing to submerge the memory of all that when hounded by guilt. And I started rationalizing, trying to convince myself that our relationship hadn't been all that bad and that it could get better if given a chance.

Despite all the problems we had, I still thought Debbie was a nice person, and she was still attractive to me. I started spending more time with her again, testing the waters to see if the relationship deserved another shot. Sometimes I'd spend the night with her, then lay low at my own place a few days and assess things. Then one day in December 1984, about a month after I started seeing Debbie again, she told me she was pregnant.

Life has a way of making a liar out of you. When I'd gotten out of prison, I'd told myself there was nothing I couldn't handle. Now I was forced to admit that this was too much for me.

■ ■ ■

I now know how it feels to go for stretches of time that are unaccounted for. It's entirely possible that I went into shock. All I know is that I ranted on endlessly, refusing to accept the truth of what she said. "Why," I asked her, "did you offer to use the Pill as our method of birth control, then neglect to take it regularly? No way. No way. There is no way this is happening again!" How could it be true? I could halfway accept the possibility of an accidental pregnancy once, but twice? I told Debbie, "There is no excuse for a thirty-two-year-old woman to accidentally get pregnant twice in the 1980s. This means you are either terribly stupid or terribly manipulative, and I don't want to be associated with a woman who is either of those!"

I exploded so powerfully that it frightened me. I cursed her and called her everything but a child of God. I wanted her to abort, but she said right off, "I have no intentions of aborting."

For weeks, life stood still. I tried everything. I told her that she would either abort or have no support from me. I even tried to get her to sit down with a few couples we knew and discuss this thing rationally, get some objective feedback. She wouldn't budge. She wanted another child.

Depressed, I took some time off from work and went to Texas to visit a woman friend and think. For a full ten days, I stayed at my friend's apartment while she was away at work. I jogged, read, pondered my life and the cycle of insanity I seemed unable to shake. I wondered if I was addicted to turmoil and thought again of a deep-rooted fear, the fear that I was programmed to fail, that no matter how close I came to forging a successful life, I'd eventually find a way to blow it.

When I returned to Atlanta, I called Jim, my old mentor from prison, to get advice. Jim told me that he was dealing with the exact same thing—a woman he was dating had gotten pregnant. Jim was furious. He said the same thing that I had—that the woman had assured him she was on the Pill and that he suspected her negligence was intentional.

Despite all his anger and all his suspicions, Jim went on and got married for the sake of the child.

On August 19, 1985, I went to the delivery room, put on a hospital gown, mask, and sterile gloves, and waited for the C-section to begin.

The doctor began cutting, hacking at Debbie's stomach as if sawing her in half. Blood gushed and squirted everywhere. A light-headed sensation came over me and my legs felt weak. It was the first time in my life that I nearly fainted. It was also the first time I witnessed the wonder of a baby being born.

Doctors inserted an instrument into Debbie's abdomen to widen the passageway. The obstetrician reached in and wrenched out this tiny, rubbery-looking body that resembled a bloodied, mangled Cabbage Patch doll. He slapped its behind and it gasped and gulped desperately for air, wriggling, thrashing wildly. Then it let out a deep, agonizing, convulsing wail. The doctor glanced at it, looked at me, and announced, "It's a girl." He wiped her off and handed her to me.

Two emotions shot through my head when I took that girl into my arms. First there was fear. *A girl? Oh, shit! The fellas and I ran trains on girls! How will I help her get through that?* I was scared because I knew that a daughter would be subject to the insanity of men. White men would try to exploit her. Brothers would abuse her. Most sisters caught hell coming and going. As Zora Neale Hurston once said, black women are the mules of the world.

Gushing love was the second emotion that swept through me. I held my newborn daughter, looked into her eyes, and melted like butter. I've heard much about the chemistry between fathers and daughters. None of it prepared me for what I felt. All of a sudden, none of my troubles had meaning. None of her impending challenges mattered. All the stress and hassles of the past nine months seemed worth the experience of that baby girl, and I was suddenly grateful to her mother for protecting her life.

Since Debbie had named Ian, my son, I insisted on naming the girl, and I made sure she wasn't named after anybody white. I named her Maya, after the writer Maya Angelou. I gave her a Swahili middle name, Nailah, which means "One who succeeds."

Every time I think I've seen it all and experienced all that this life has to offer, I get hit with a new experience that thrusts me into a totally new reality. Today, I became the father of a baby girl. She is beautiful!

Now I face the challenge of raising her—a black female—in this sexist, racist world. What a charge! Meeting the challenge is going to require some serious reorganizing of values, time, money, and energy.

August 19, 1985

After Maya's birth, pressure to marry Debbie mounted. We now had two children out of wedlock, an extremely embarrassing and uncomfortable situation for me. Debbie's mother added to my anxieties, suggesting that I ask for her daughter's hand and prodding for an explanation of why I'd not already made that move. I told her, "Because I don't want to." Beyond that, there was an even greater reason for me to resist: Besides the pregnancies, there were several things about Debbie that I found deeply disturbing and dangerous.

Then Debbie's mother turned to my parents for sympathetic ears. She told Mama that Debbie's father was so upset over his unmarried daughter having two children that it was affecting his health. From time to time she'd ask my mother, "Why won't Nathan marry Debbie? Does he think he's too good for her?"

It worked to some degree. My mother also began broaching the topic whenever we talked. One day, while talking with me on the phone, she said, out of the blue, "Maybe you should go on and get married."

There weren't many people who could make me change my mind about such things. But my mother meddled in my affairs so rarely that I listened whenever she ventured to say something about my personal life. I paid attention and thought about what she said while trying to figure out what to do.

One of the other people who helped me figure things out I'm sure has no idea how his words affected me. His name was Charlie, and he was a Georgia good ol' boy from way back. He'd spent much of his journalism career at the *Journal-Constitution* and was preparing to retire.

For some reason, Charlie took to me. Maybe it was because we sat so close. My desk was set directly across from his, so close that if either of us raised his head from his work he looked right into the other's eyes. Or maybe it was because he considered me one of the more tame blacks that he could tolerate.

Like a lot of Deep South whites, Charlie always felt he was under siege. The world was closing in on the South, and everybody, complaining blacks and liberal whites, was threatening his precious way of life. I think he hated liberal whites more than he hated anybody. When one of those liberal whites walked across the newsroom, Charlie would look at him contemptuously, lean over toward me, and whisper, with his mouth twisted sideways, "Nathan, I'll betcha that guy's a fuckin' queer."

Clearly, he was homophobic, but beyond that he was extremely nice. Whenever he made one of his frequent trips to the cafeteria for coffee, he'd rise, pull his belt up as high as it would go around his round gut, and say, "Nathan, I'm going downstairs. Can I get you a cup of coffee or a soda?" If I said yes, he'd insist on paying.

I didn't know how to deal with this guy. I didn't know whether to ignore his offensive slurs or challenge his narrow views. Sometimes, when he made remarks to me, I just pretended not to hear. But he never seemed to catch the hint.

Around the time I was considering the whole issue of marriage to Debbie, our newspaper ran a front-page story revealing that 75 percent of the black children then being born in the nation were born out of wedlock. It was another one of the many stories suggesting that blacks in America were coming apart. I slipped into a blue funk that day at work because I was included in that statistic. I dreaded the thought that Charlie or anyone else in that office, white or black, would find out that I'd brought three out-of-wedlock children into the world.

Charlie came in that morning, sat down across from me, squinted his eyes, and said, "Nathan, me and my wife were discussing that story about the number of blacks born out of wedlock, and we couldn't believe it. I always thought blacks were very religious people."

I was livid. I was mad enough to leap across the desk and punch him in his face. Instead, I held my peace, got up, and stormed off. *Why do white folks always stand in judgment of us? Why do they always take such a one-dimensional view of things?*

Every time I saw him after that story ran, I felt convicted and conflicted and determined to get that monkey off my back. Charlie's words stung me sufficiently to make me consider doing my part in proving white folks wrong. *Maybe I should get married, like everybody says.*

For the second time in several years, the views of some unsuspecting white person figured in one of the most important decisions of my life. Charlie's words had nearly the same impact as those of the woman who had come to my office in Virginia and scared the hell out of me with her abortion speech.

It was Debbie who finally forced me to make up my mind. She told me one day that she planned to move back home to Norfolk. "Things aren't working out for me here," she said.

It took all of one second for the meaning of that to sink in: It meant I'd be separated from my children again. I'd likely be a stranger to them, just like my father, J.L., was a stranger to me, just like I was a near stranger to Monroe (although I flew Monroe to Atlanta each summer, it still seemed inadequate). That settled it, I told myself. I couldn't let that happen with Ian and Maya, too. I'd *have* to get married. Marriage would resolve a lot of problems nagging me.

Asking Debbie to marry me called for the same desperate resolve that I had used on the streets to summon the will to bash somebody's head, enter a dark house, or hold up a store. I would go through with it and prevent myself from thinking about it or changing my mind. I proposed to her in a bland, matter-of-fact way that must have given me away. She sought reassurance that I was serious. "Does that mean you love me?"

I paused. "Yes, I love you." It was a lie, and I suspected she knew it. It's like the woman who asks the morning after you have taken her to bed on the first date, "Do you care about me?" You say anything you think she wants to hear, and she accepts it, not because she believes it but because she *wants* to believe it. Debbie wanted to get married. She wanted to believe.

I called friends and told them the news. They congratulated me, but none expressed joy. A few even tried to warn me that Debbie might not be the right person. Some urged me to reconsider, which annoyed me because I knew they were right. But I figured peace of mind was worth more than any hardships I might face. The only way to get peace of mind was to at least try to do what was right.

After the proposal, Debbie and I got into an argument that I never thought I'd have. When I suggested that she either keep her maiden name or use a hyphenated combination of both hers and mine, she got mad. She insisted on dropping her maiden name and taking on mine. I don't remember the explanation she gave, but I remember during the argument scratching my head and saying, "Wait a minute. I thought I was doing something *good* by suggesting that you maintain part of your family identity. I thought a lot of women nowadays considered that the progressive thing to do."

But she made it clear who she wanted to be. It would be "Mrs. McCall."

In the time leading up to the wedding, I called all the ladies I had been involved with and told them my plans. I had lunch with Alicia, who looked at me sadly and shook her head. "It's strange," she said. "I try not to be manipulative because it's the wrong thing to do, but it seems that the women who manipulate win all the time."

■　■　■

I was so scared I might change my mind that I set the wedding date smack in the middle of the congressional primary race between John Lewis and Julian Bond, which I was covering for the *Journal-Constitution*. White folks at work couldn't understand why I would take time off in the middle of such an important campaign, but I didn't care. I was on a mission that was critical for me.

In the few months before the wedding, I moved out of my apartment and back in with Debbie and the children, and returned to life in a fog.

■ ■ ■

Debbie and her mother did all the planning. It was to be a Christian ceremony, conducted by Debbie's mother's pastor. The wedding would be held in Norfolk's Botanical Gardens. I went along with whatever they said, just like Debbie's father would have done. *Just tell me where to stand and what to say.*

It all felt so strange on that June wedding day in 1986. Among the guests, especially those in my party, was a subtle air of cynicism. I felt people searching my eyes, looking, I guessed, for signs of fear and doubt. If they looked closely, it was more likely they saw relief. At the same time, standing there at the altar, I couldn't help thinking that Debbie and her mother had defeated me and that I was possibly on my way to becoming a carbon copy of Debbie's old man. But I refused to let such thinking get in my way. I was on a mission, driven by a purpose that was larger than them. I kept looking at Ian and Maya and thinking, *This is good for them. This legitimizes things.*

I stood where I was told and repeated the vows as the minister prompted. When it was over, Debbie and I kissed and were legally joined. I felt nothing that remotely resembled joy. But that didn't matter. Debbie looked happy. Her mother looked happy. I'd paid my dues to two of the children I had brought into the world. *Maybe,* I thought, *I will find a measure of peace.*

Chapter 35 BABYLON

In 1984, my bosses assigned me to help cover City Hall. At the time, I knew nothing about politics, except what little I'd picked up working at my first newspaper. But I couldn't turn down a chance to take on a plum beat such as City Hall. Besides, for me there were compelling reasons to be interested in politics: Andrew Young was the mayor of Atlanta and was plugged into the national political arena. He and other prominent black Atlantans would figure into that year's presidential campaign, which included Jesse Jackson.

I actually got excited and felt optimistic. With campaigns and elections involving more blacks came the hope that maybe we could gain a measure of control over our destinies and get the system to work for us for a change. I was curious to see, close-up, just how much we benefited from having blacks involved in politics.

I saw in Atlanta that we benefited in the sense that black political leaders could use the city government as a vehicle to hire other minorities and to ensure that black businesses got a fair share of the city contract dollars. But beyond that, there was only so much they could do to help the masses of black folks. There were only so many jobs the city government could provide. To employ more people, the city needed help from private industry, which was composed primarily of white businesspeople. That's where the major breakdowns occurred.

Covering City Hall, I saw how white-run businesses, such as banks, actually undermined development in black communities. One year, a reporter at our newspaper won a Pulitzer Prize for a series of stories he did on redlining in the Atlanta area. His research showed that white banks turned down home-improvement and mortgage loans for blacks at a much higher rate than they turned down loan applications for whites with less income. Here was the real kicker: The research showed that the loan-default rate among whites was much higher than the default rate for blacks, yet whites were able to get bank loans much easier than blacks. The bottom line was, white bankers relied on their racist assumptions about black people to guide their judgment. As a result, blacks often were denied loans that would have helped them improve their neighborhoods, raise property values, and improve their quality of life.

Learning that kind of stuff pissed me off. It countered the notion—often repeated among handkerchief-head, assimilationist blacks—that racism is just a harmless attitude that should be ignored. It's an attitude, true, but one that translates into policies that make life unnecessarily hard for blacks.

I was also curious on the City Hall beat to see how African Americans handled power. During the civil rights movement, before blacks began gaining political offices in substantial numbers, we often stood on the outside of the political arena and proclaimed that we could be more righteous leaders than the whites then inside the system. I wondered if that was true. I discovered over time that although it is good to have blacks in office, in some respects black politicians are no different than whites. For politicians, black or white, politics is a game. It's all the better if the public benefits, but most of the time it's about winning—winning reelection or winning a debate or getting one up on an opponent in some political maneuver.

One day, after watching a particularly petty squabble among black Atlanta city council members, I complained to one councilman I had gotten to know pretty well. "What's wrong with these folks, man? I thought they had a stronger sense of purpose than that." The councilman, Bill Campbell, smiled and said something I'll never forget: "Nathan, there are two things you never want to see being made: laws and sausage." I'd never seen sausage made, but the process of lawmaking was sometimes nauseating.

It was especially interesting during my four years covering City Hall to watch Mayor Andrew Young. He is a fascinating man with a brilliant sense of world politics. Talking with him about his civil rights experiences was like taking a stroll through history. Andy, as we called him, was very approachable and down-to-earth. He'd take time to chat, even when his schedule was tight, and he was generous to a fault. He even took time out once to take pictures with my brother Billy and his family when they came to Atlanta to visit me.

It was nothing for Andy to appear at a press conference with Coretta Scott King as a favor to her and the King family. When she summoned the press, we reporters either didn't show up or we left early because everyone knew that you rarely got useful information from Coretta Scott King. I covered a couple of press conferences where she didn't even allow reporters to ask questions. But when

Young lent his presence, gobs of reporters showed up and stayed until the press conference was over.

Although I liked Andy personally, I cared less for his political style. He served the same role in politics that he had in the civil rights movement: He was a peacemaker, a conciliator (unlike Hosea Williams, who would loud-talk and browbeat you). When Andy first ran for office to succeed Maynard Jackson, white business leaders put up a white candidate against him. He was elected largely on the black vote, but in office he bent over backward to work with the very whites who'd opposed him. He cooperated royally with the chamber of commerce to help attract business investments and persuade corporations to relocate to Atlanta. There was no greater salesman of Atlanta than Andrew Young. He traveled the world pitching Atlanta as a haven of racial harmony, tossing around slogans that the chamber of commerce created to promote the city. Sometimes they called it "the International City" or "the City Too Busy to Hate."

The problem with promoting such grand untruths is that by failing to acknowledge racial problems one makes no headway in overcoming them. Atlanta was no more international than Tuscaloosa, Alabama. Everything was seen in terms of black and white. And it certainly wasn't a city too busy to hate. Whites didn't want to share contract dollars with blacks. They didn't want blacks living near them on the north side. And they resented the loss of political clout and at times did everything they could to undermine black leadership.

During his two terms, from 1982 to 1990, Andy's popularity declined a lot with local blacks, who felt he wasn't assertive enough in pressing black communities' agendas. They wanted him to do like Maynard Jackson had done: tell racist white folks where they could get off.

But there was a method to Andy Young's approach. I think he labored under the assumption that if you proclaimed often enough that there was racial harmony, white people would catch on and begin working to help create some harmony. It was an extension of the civil rights strategy to appeal to the conscience of white America. What it showed me was that Andy hadn't yet accepted a harsh reality about white America: When it comes to blacks, whites have no conscience. Whites don't bend unless forced to bend. They don't give one inch if they don't have to.

The only time I saw Andy really get fighting mad was during the 1984 presidential campaign. He was supporting Walter Mondale, but Mondale's campaign was falling apart. At the Atlanta convention of the National Association of Black Journalists, Andy said Mondale's campaign was being ruined by "smart-assed white boys" who didn't really know what they were doing. I understood his frustration. Here he was, politically seasoned and world-renowned, and young white boys who didn't know diddly were running the presidential campaign, screwing it up and ignoring advice and input from Andy and others. Practically every working black person in America could relate to that. It was a classic example of white male arrogance.

■ ■ ■

In the 1980s, something ugly filtered down from the national leadership that made me hone in even more on politics: Open hostility toward blacks came back in vogue. Bigots now had the president of the United States, Ronald Reagan, on their side. Six-gun Ron's single phrase—"welfare queens"—had become white America's rallying cry, the catchall explanation for every problem the country faced. To hear some white folks tell it, shiftless, unpatriotic black people and their reliance on government assistance were breaking the U.S. Treasury. Unqualified blacks were taking money and jobs that should go to honest, hardworking whites. In short, black people were single-handedly bringing down the country.

Yet, with Reagan's blessing, big-time white corporations plundered the country, acquiring other companies in hostile takeovers and firing employees, wholesale, without a thought. Multinational corporations exported jobs to foreign countries for cheap labor. Corporate presidents got fat benefit packages while their employees were laid off or given salary cuts. *These* were the real anti-patriots, and nobody got hostile toward them. But some white Americans would get so angry they couldn't see straight whenever they heard about some black welfare mother who might have gotten more food stamps one month than she was entitled to.

That kind of absurdity kept me hot under the collar. I was mad at Reagan for using black people as scapegoats for the insanity he helped inspire, and mad at white Americans, who demonstrated every day how naive, gullible, and selfish they are. I walked around furious all the time, so mad sometimes I had to actually calm myself. I kept hoping the rest of black America would see what I saw and get mad like me. Mad enough to do something about it, to take to the streets, cast out on our own, do anything other than pray and tolerate the shit being slung at us.

Jesse Jackson's campaign brought some relief. I think his run for president brought a mild ray of hope to millions of African Americans fed up with the status quo. His chances of winning were slim to none, but it felt good having somebody who represented a real alternative to the white bread that was running things.

I watched the campaigns closely and held ongoing telephone debates with Jim, my Southampton mentor. I felt that the campaigns held great promise for blacks, and he felt that focusing on politics was a waste of time. "We can't look to politics for our salvation, brotherman, because white folks control the rules of the game," he said.

I argued, "They can't stop somebody who learns to play the game as well as them. Jesse has his shortcomings, but he can play the game."

We both watched as the campaigns unfolded and telephoned each other when there were developments that bolstered our opposing positions. Over time, I saw what Jim meant. The Democratic party treated Jesse more like an agitator, an outsider, than a qualified candidate. I saw that some of the questions raised in the media about Jesse didn't seem to apply to other candidates: *Is he qualified? Would his ego get in the way?* The popular question that bothered me most was, *What does Jesse want?* The implication was that he couldn't possibly want to be president of the United States. He was a *black* man.

Watching the political developments, I couldn't help but think of my high school graduation, when I'd told a yearbook staffer that I wanted to be the first black U.S. president. I knew then that that bullshit about equal opportunity wasn't true. Here we were, eleven years later, and my assessment was still right.

When I told Jim that he'd won the argument, he said, "See what I mean? It doesn't really matter much that Jesse has learned to play the game. When confronted with a black person who plays the game as well as them, white folks simply change the rules."

■ ■ ■

Andy and other black political leaders in the city tried to keep up with what was going on at the *Journal-Constitution,* particularly as it related to blacks. During a time when black reporters were having meetings with management to discuss our complaints, he called me into his office. "So, what's going on with black folks at the paper? Is it something that we can help with?"

It warmed me inside to hear that kind of concern. Black leaders in my hometown would never have been that plugged in. Part of me wanted to spill it all, tell him how blacks were simply tolerated at the paper and left out of important news decisions being made by smart-assed white boys who knew nothing about the people they covered in this largely black city. I knew he had the power to mobilize Atlanta's black communities in a big way. The idealist in me wanted to reach out, to say, "Let's join forces, Andy, and take them on. We'll start our own black paper and do our own thing if we have to."

But there were other concerns. For good reasons, journalists are trained not to trust or get too chummy with politicians, black or white. They'll buddy up to you to the point where, eventually, you can't write about them objectively when the time calls for it. I didn't think Andy was that devious, but I wasn't sure. I hated being torn like that. My first allegiance was to black folks, but politicians' allegiance is to politics. Andy was compassionate, but he was also an astute politician.

In the end, I followed my instincts, which told me to watch what I say. I gave Andy a brief review of what was going on but never spilled my heart the way I really wanted to.

■ ■ ■

As a lot of the white folks at the paper saw it, the real competition in the newsroom was between white women and white men. Both sides seemed quietly annoyed that blacks wanted in. They weren't openly vicious about it. They just didn't think black journalists were qualified to compete on their level.

In subtle ways, management promoted the notion that every black who came through the newsroom door was an affirmative-action hire given a job that he wasn't really qualified for. A white reporter told me once that when she asked for a raise, a manager told her she couldn't have one because they had to give raises to the black reporters on staff: "You know. Affirmative action." The manager failed to explain to her that blacks weren't being paid on a par with white reporters.

But it seemed none of the whites, male or female, wanted us competing on an even keel with them. Especially not us black men. On many levels, they were scared of us. I guess they saw black men's aggression on basketball courts and on street corners and they knew what would happen if we ever got hip to the establishment game and transferred that aggression into their arena. They feared they wouldn't stand a chance if they had to compete head-to-head on an even keel with us. So they had to give themselves an edge—they put shit in the game. With the help of management, they floated whispering campaigns. *You know those black reporters can't write so well. . . . They're O.K., but they're not aggressive enough as reporters. . . . They can't handle complicated stories.*

That was their unspoken justification for not giving blacks good assignments, and it was the same approach taken during slavery. An act of cruelty was made to appear to be a gesture of compassion. Why free slaves if they're too dumb to fend for themselves? Why give black reporters plum beats and complex assignments if they can't handle them?

Every black journalist feels those patronizing airs from whites and hears those myths whispered, almost sympathetically, a million times in his career. So every black reporter who comes into the newsroom comes in on guard, carrying the burden of proving himself against such painful indictments, constantly aware that the slightest error in grammar, sentence structure, or story construction will be cited as undeniable proof of what white folks have always suspected. It's a heavy burden.

Success in journalism is tied directly to a writer's psychological state. You need to be relaxed to write well. But blacks at the *Journal-Constitution* never had that comfort. They were too busy battling the myths. It worked a number on everybody, if in no other way than to require a huge expenditure of energy fighting the stereotypes. Even if we won, we lost.

Because of the myths, I could never seem to settle down and relax and write with flair the way I knew I could under normal circumstances. Every time I sat down to a computer to type a story, all the stereotypes shot through my head and I had to battle to push them out. *They say we can't write well. They say we can't write fast. They say . . .* Sometimes, I'd have to take deep breaths and give myself pep talks to chase the myths away so that I could do my work. But it's hard to set them completely aside. You can't forget. You know you can't slip, or your white bosses will say, "See, we gave him a chance but he was incompetent."

And if you slip, it can break you. I saw it happen to a reporter named Cassandra, who started at the paper about a year after I got there. She started on the night shift. General assignment. One day, she made a mistake in a story that required the paper to print a correction. Then Brenda Mooney, who ran the city desk, and the editor who supervised Cassandra made a big fuss about it, and after that, Cassandra's editor stopped giving her good assignments. She was given only lightweight stories, like weather reports. Sitting just a few seats away, I could see Cassandra begin to doubt herself. Every time she sat down at her computer to write, I saw her hands trembling on the keyboard and her eyes focused so intently on the screen that it looked like she was about to crack.

Then Cassandra made another mistake in a story. I understood why. I understood that you can get so nervous about making a mistake, so tense about it, that it becomes a self-fulfilling prophecy. Cassandra's editor decided to get rid of her. I never heard the editor say it, but I saw it in the way she treated Cassandra. She put the freeze on her, giving her fewer and fewer story assignments. Some evenings, Cassandra would sit at her desk all day and not get a single assignment. I saw editors walk past her and get reporters who were busy on one story to work on another one when Cassandra could have done it.

Eventually, Cassandra's self-confidence fell so far she couldn't recover. She was a nervous wreck, fighting the myths and verifying them at the same time. Eventually she gave up. She left the paper and took a job at some lesser publication in a larger city. I don't think she ever recovered from that experience.

When I thought about what they did to Cassandra, I realized that it was a variation of the same thing that happened to Tooty, the guy my homeboys ran a train on in prison. Even though Tooty was a man, they treated him like a woman until they psyched him into believing he just might be more of a woman than he realized. Even though Cassandra was equal to that editor and every other white person in the newsroom, she was treated like an inferior so consistently that she accepted it and gave in, the same way Tooty eventually gave in to being treated like a woman.

What made it so bad was that Cassandra was a small-time schmoozer. Unlike me, she went out drinking with white folks in the office, including the two women who eventually cut her throat. She went biking with them. She trusted them, and they cut her down without batting an eye. Whenever somebody asked what happened to Cassandra, they ran for cover, and spoke in the coded way that some whites speak when talking about blacks: "Well, you know, she had some problems."

I felt sorry for Cassandra. I pitied a lot of the blacks I saw. For good reasons, they came into the system believing the promise that if you make sure you're qualified, and if you assimilate and work twice as hard as white people, you can be anything you want to be. But the promise wasn't kept, even though some blacks did everything—even change their appearance and contort their personalities—to try to blend.

The most difficult loss for me was Michael, a guy in his midtwenties who wrote for the paper's business section. His editor said he wasn't happy with Michael's work. I could tell Michael's confidence was crushed, in much the same way Cassandra's confidence had been destroyed. He was ready to give up. I told him, "Naw, man, you can't do that."

By then, I'd heard that story many times, especially from the business section, where the editor, who was white, seemed insecure about the fact that several black reporters working under him held master's degrees from the nation's top schools. Michael had earned an undergraduate degree in journalism from the University of Pennsylvania and an MBA from Wharton. On top of that, he was one of the brightest young brothers I'd ever seen. He was a Paul Robeson type, a cat whose intellectual interests were so broad that it blew my mind. If he had been a white boy with that kind of promise, they'd have put him on a management track from day one. Instead, Michael's editor had been hounding him to quit. During an evaluation, he cited a couple of mistakes Michael had made in stories over a few years.

Michael, another black reporter named Susan Howard, and I stayed in the newsroom late one night and made computer printouts of all the corrections printed as a result of mistakes made by white business reporters. What we found was no surprise. Some reporters had required numerous corrections in a single year—more than Michael had in his entire stay at the paper.

Armed with that information, we had Michael prepare a formal, written response to the business editor, refuting the allegations. The editor backed off, but he didn't let up completely. He found other ways to hound Michael until my man grew weary of fighting. Michael got special approval to take an extended leave—which the editor eagerly granted—and went off to Africa for a summer. He never came back to the paper.

After we lost Michael, I grew even more discouraged about the prospect of trying to survive in the white mainstream. Our problem at the *Journal-Constitution* was the same problem blacks faced everywhere: No matter how we tried to fit in and help improve the system, we couldn't win for losing.

■ ■ ■

In a strange way, it was a comfort knowing that I wasn't the only brother catching flak on my job. Friends—other folks I knew around the city—were also catching serious hell. One of them was my buddy Harun, whom I'd met at Norfolk State.

Harun worked for United Way, where employees were encouraged to wear conservative business clothes. Tall, slender, and brown-skinned, Harun had a mustache and a thick goatee. He wore the required business suits, but added an African flair to his dress. He'd drape a strip of Kinte cloth over his shoulder, or slap a colorful kufi onto his head.

Harun's supervisor, a nervous black guy, constantly rode his back about his style of dress and worried that it might frighten or offend some of their best white clients. "My supervisor said I make white folks feel uncomfortable," Harun told me. "I asked him, 'How am I gonna change my appearance to please white folks? That's impossible. White folks are scared of black men, period. They don't wanna have to look at our asses. White folks get uncomfortable if brothers are too tall, too short, too light, too dark, too quiet, too loud, too anything. You just can't please them motherfuckas no way you try.'"

I sensed that Harun's problems ran deeper than white folks' fears—that most of all his garb bothered his supervisor. Many evenings, we'd get together at his place or mine, play chess, and talk about the establishment and how crazy it was. To lighten the mood, we'd jone each other about what we were going through. I called the white man on his job "Mr. Charlie," and he called white folks where I worked "Mr. Gilmore," which he pronounced "Mr. Gilmo." He'd say, "Mr. Gilmo ain't gonna let you write what you wanna write," or "You better be thankful to Mr. Gilmo for bein' good to you." And we'd laugh until our sides ached, even though we were both hurting inside.

Whenever we got together, he always had a tale about his handkerchief-head supervisor, who thought Harun was an embarrassment to other blacks on the job. "Man, this cat is whiter than white folks," he'd say. "You should see him checking me out every day when I come into the office. I went to work the other day wearing a bow tie. White cats wear bow ties to work all the time, and it's no big deal. But when I walk in there, I get all these smart-assed comments from him about me lookin' like a militant Muslim."

Sometimes, Harun got deeply depressed and talked longingly about getting out of the system. He talked about that like I used to talk about being freed from prison. But he couldn't take off and leave or lash out at his boss like he wanted. He had responsibilities. He was married and had two children. He always had the sense that he could never get to who he really was because he was always under pressure to be somebody else. Harun had the soul of an artist. He had never taken formal art lessons, yet he could paint like a master. He had never taken music lessons, yet he learned African drumming. I'd always had that same feeling of being restricted by forces beyond my reach and never knowing what I could *really* be and do. I feared that the longer I stayed in the system, the further I would get away from who I really was.

Harun turned me on to a whole new subculture in Atlanta that I hadn't really been exposed to much before. He lived in the West End, a trendy area on the black side of town. There were a lot of Muslims, reefer-smoking Rastas, and old-head revolutionaries there. They all shared a distaste for the system and a desire to create alternative lifestyles more suitable to them. We'd go to one of their cribs and they'd be sitting around, smoking cigar-sized spliffs, listening to music, and rapping about the evils of "Babylon," the white man's depraved civilization. They called white folks "baldheads" and "culture vultures" because, they said, whites devalued blacks to our faces while at the same time trying to steal and capitalize off our creativity in everything—dance, music, art, style, inventions, etc.

I liked that bunch of folks more than any other I'd cut into. They were streetwise yet well-read, rough-hewn but politically astute. Many of those cats made yearly pilgrimages to Africa and talked of their yearning to make it their home.

I laughed to myself about the fact that while most other black people were busting their butts to get into the system, these folks were scrambling to get out. A lot of them had figured out ways to survive outside the system and keep from working for the white man. Some worked as street vendors, selling incense on corners downtown. Others sold fruit and T-shirts and hustled in various ways. Some even sold reefer to keep afloat. They bartered and worked at the neighborhood co-op to keep food costs down and ran their own schools to teach their children.

One of the guys I met in the West End was called JuJu. A jeweler, he was known all along the East Coast as one of the finest in his profession. I don't know what had happened in life to make JuJu so bitter, but he refused to even talk to white people. He let his wife do any negotiations that required interaction with whites. There were many whites trying to do business with JuJu. A prominent white-owned store chain offered him a lucrative contract to make jewelry exclusively for its stores nationwide, but he turned it down because it would require too much involvement with baldheads. He could have made a lot of money if he'd been willing to venture into the white world, but he said money was less important to him than his sanity.

I once knocked guys like that who wouldn't deal in the system. I thought they were copping out because they were scared to compete toe-to-toe with the white man. But after working in Atlanta, I began to understand why brothers opted for alternative hustles rather than work a nine-to-five. They knew Babylon meant them no good. They understood that they couldn't win in the system without giving up a lot of themselves.

Harun also turned me on to reggae music. I'd heard it in passing before but not listened closely to it until one night when we were playing chess at his place. I fell in love with reggae. Its spiritual lyrics and political messages were in tune with how I felt about being a black man in this country. Some days, when work was really getting to me, I'd leave the office on my lunch hour, go home, and put on some serious Bob Marley. I'd crank up the volume loud and try to blast all that whiteness out of my head. Then I'd return to work, pumped up and able to make it through the rest of the day.

Things eventually got better or worse for Harun, depending on how you look at it. He grew dreadlocks, and, as might have been expected, his supervisor tried to drive him off the job. Finally, when he and his wife separated, he packed up and left for Oakland, California, to try to develop his skills as an artist. Before he left, I bought one of his paintings, which reflected his wish to be liberated from Babylon. I still have it today. It's a huge painting of a black man with long, flowing, colorful dreadlocks, jogging along a deserted, sun-swept beach—free. In the background, there are birds flying in the shadow of a bright red setting sun, inscribed with the faint outline of the continent of Africa.

I stayed mad so much about one thing or another that I felt at times like I'd explode. I began to wonder how long I'd last in the white mainstream. The racism at work never ended. I could feel it in exchanges with whites all the time. It was always there, just below the surface, and it took a toll on me.

There is a liquor store at the intersection of Pryor Street and Memorial Drive downtown, just five minutes from where I worked. Every evening when I drove past the store after work I'd see twenty to thirty down-and-out brothers hanging around on the side of the building, bumming coins to buy some brew. It reminded me of the days when I hung on the side of the 7-Eleven in Cavalier Manor, stealing, gambling, and bumming money from patrons to get some of that sweet Wild Irish Rose.

Some evenings, when I was really feeling low and wondered how long I would last in the system, I'd ride real slow past the liquor store and reminisce about the old days at home, the camaraderie I enjoyed and the warmth I felt, even when we were standing in the cold. I'd look into that Atlanta crowd and see myself and the fellas: Shane, Bimbo, Frog Dickie, Lep, Turkey Buzzard, Shell Shock, and Cooder.

I'd look at the guys outside the liquor store and long for the days when life seemed so simple, when I was far away from white folks, as far as the end of the universe. I fantasized about pulling the car into the parking lot. In my fantasy, I'd get out, take a spot beside the dudes along the wall, chip in my few coins, and take the wine bottle when it was passed my way. I'd guzzle down the wine and wait for it to travel to my brain and deaden all the pain and frustration I felt inside. I'd get pissy-drunk and harmonize on tunes by the Temptations, join in on the lively debates about boxing, politics, and women. I'd chill, just like the brothers on the side of that store.

But there was no way I could do that now. I'd crossed the tracks and become a card-carrying member of the white mainstream. If I pulled into that driveway and got out, the fellas at the side of the store would instantly peg me by my uniform: the necktie and monkey suit.

They would identify me, as Hosea Williams once did, as an Uncle Tom, an Oreo, the white man's puppet.

So I always kept going. I always drove past the store and went on home and prepared to face another day on the plantation.

After nearly a year and a half at the Journal-Constitution, *I realize that the time has come for me to prepare to leave. . . . This is unhealthy, and my health is more important to me than any job.*
   March 23, 1984

Less than three years after that journal entry, I was on a flight headed to New York for a job interview and wondering why it had taken so long to do what I should've done all along. I'd concluded it was time to leave the white mainstream and go to work for blacks. Considering my training, the most logical place to look was the black press.

I landed a job interview with *Black Enterprise* magazine. I had done freelance stories for the magazine since 1983, when I first got to Atlanta. A former college mate was an editor there and fed me story assignments all the time. Finally he contacted me and said, "Nathan, I just thought I'd let you know that we're hiring. We need some good journalists, and I recommended you. We're planning to revamp the whole publication and move the magazine in a different direction."

I had mixed feelings about the job. Whenever I published stories in *Black Enterprise,* I felt a sense of pride, like I was giving something back to my community. But as time passed, I began to suspect that the publisher was more concerned with using *Black Enterprise* as his personal organ. Whenever I wrote personality profiles that alluded in the slightest way to controversy involving prominent blacks, those passages were cut. I grew tired of writing one-sided fluff pieces suggesting that all was well in black America when I knew that that was untrue.

And then there was the issue of money. Everybody knows the black press pays a lot less than the white-owned media. I'd have gladly taken a pay cut to get some purpose to my work and some peace of mind, but with a wife and children there were limits to how low I could afford to go. Before leaving for the interview, I devised a proposal: I'd take a pay cut if they allowed me to work from Atlanta, where the cost of living was lower.

I got to New York and went to the magazine's offices. There was the usual battery of interviews. Then came time to talk to the managing editor, a smart, easygoing woman whom I had worked with on stories before. After we got the small talk out of the way, she went to the point. Yes, she said, they were planning to make some editorial changes to revamp the magazine. No, she couldn't give me any assurances about the direction of the magazine. And then, on the issue of pay: "The most we can pay you is twenty-five thousand dollars per year, and you would have to move to New York."

I was shocked. That was much less than I was making in Atlanta. With a family, that would be like committing financial suicide. Disappointed, I turned them down.

I returned to Atlanta determined and desperate to find a way out of the system. I looked into every option that crossed my mind. I contacted the publisher of the local black weekly, *The Atlanta Daily World*, to talk with him about working there. I talked with some of my old college colleagues about us starting our own newspaper.

Like Harun, my old buddy who grew dreadlocks and moved to California, I desperately wanted out of Babylon. I even looked into the possibility of moving to Africa to start a new life. Years before, when I was about three, our family went to live in Morocco, where my stepfather was stationed in the Navy. I was too young to appreciate the experience of living in North Africa, but I remember that my brothers and I loved it there. My parents did, too. They said it was the first place they'd ever lived where they didn't have to enter through back doors and heed WHITES ONLY signs everywhere they went. They liked it so much that they tried, unsuccessfully, to get an extension of my stepfather's tour of duty. We left after two years and returned to Norfolk in 1959.

I always wondered if I could go back there or somewhere else in Africa and feel what it's like to live in a place where I was welcome. Two African students I'd befriended in Atlanta while doing a story talked with me about their home in The Gambia and the prospects of me making the transition to their way of life. I wanted to try it but I needed an income source, some job possibilities. I concluded I couldn't move my family there on a wing and a prayer. Finally, that idea was nixed, along with the others.

But I *had* to get away from the white mainstream. I thought, *What if I simply walked away from it all?* I knew my friends and family would think I'd lost my mind. I could hear them talking: "He put *all* that effort into gettin' in, now he talkin' 'bout gettin' out? The boy gone crazy, chile. Had a *good* job workin' for white folks and he walked away. He oughta be shot, hard as jobs are to come by these days."

I couldn't help it if they wouldn't understand. They didn't see all the energy invested and the draining battles fought at work around issues of race. When I first went into the system, I assumed, like many blacks, that whites could be won over if I proved myself. Once they worked with me and realized I was just as smart and skilled as them, they would drop the racist assumptions they used to justify holding me and other blacks back. But I saw now that racism ran deeper than a few misconceptions. I realized I could spend a lifetime trying to prove myself and nothing would change.

That period of searching for an alternative was rough for me. I had the feeling of driving a car, running on empty, searching frantically for a filling station, fearing that I would run out of gas and wind up stranded on some deserted road. For the first time in a while, I was very uncertain about my future, and insecure. I felt like they said in an old song I used to hear: "Nowhere to run, nowhere to hide."

■ ■ ■

Stanley showed up in Atlanta all of a sudden one day, tired from the eleven-hour drive from Portsmouth. He hadn't even called anybody to say he was on his way. It turned out that he'd shot someone in Portsmouth over a drug debt and needed to lay low until things cooled down. Chip, one of my homeboys who lived near me, brought Stanley by the house. "I need a place to chill until I can find my own spot," Stanley explained. "Can you put me up for a while?"

I'd bought a house by then, and it had become sort of a way station for struggling relatives and guys from home who came through needing a hand. "Sure, man," I said. "No problem. No problem at all."

Stanley, who had gone through high school with me, had become a big-time drug dealer in Portsmouth. We hadn't hung out together, but I usually saw him or heard about him whenever I went home to visit. Whenever he cruised past the hangout spots in Cavalier Manor—the swimming pool or the 7-Eleven—the dope fiends got real excited and tried to flag him down. They'd run across the field toward his Jeep, yelling his name, arms flailing in the air. If he didn't feel like being bothered, he'd toot the horn and keep on pressing.

During the couple of weeks he stayed with me, I let Stanley sleep on my living-room couch. Although she didn't complain much, I got the feeling that Debbie didn't like the idea of having strange guys come through and stay with us. She'd be cordial, but more low-key than usual. I always made sure that visitors didn't stay long.

In the evenings, when I got home from work, Stanley and I would sit around and talk about how much our lives had changed. He ran off a list of people who were strung out. He was married and had a son, and he said his wife was pressuring him to give up the drug game and go legit. "I'm gonna give it up and go for a shot on the straight side, man," he said. "I don't wanna be tryin' to raise my son from the penitentiary."

He'd been a welder at the shipyard before giving it up to deal drugs. He said he intended to find a job in his field in Atlanta and send for his family after he got established. He eventually found work welding for some private company, but things didn't go as planned. He'd come home evenings, shower, change clothes, and sit around moping about the hassles on his job. Every day, he'd come home a little more depressed. I could tell he was trying to make a straight go at it, but it just wasn't working.

One night I was sitting in the living room, listening to music, when he came home. Debbie and the children were asleep in bed. He had a brown bag in his hand. He opened the bag and held up a bottle of peach schnapps. "Want some?"

Just like my old man used to do, I'd started drinking more lately to forget about work and problems at home. "Yeah, man, bring me a glass."

He brought two glasses into the living room, sat down, and poured two drinks. I gulped mine down and poured another. Stanley pulled out some papers and rolled a spliff. We toked and listened to music, each of us off into our own thoughts. Finally, Stanley broke the silence. "Ya know, I don't think I can hang, man."

"What you mean?"

"When I was workin' the street, money was flowin' in faster than I could count it. Now I'm gettin' paid twice a month, and these white folks act like they doin' me a favor by payin' me for the work I do. I can't do this, homes. This just ain't my thang no more."

I understood. Once he'd had a taste of being his own boss, it was hard for him to go back to work for somebody else, especially somebody who was giving him a hard time. "So what you gonna do, man?" I asked him.

"I'm gonna do some dealing here in Atlanta for a while, then maybe go back home and take it from there."

I remained quiet. It's strange how the logic shifts when the mind is desperate. The logic still functions, but it switches completely to another track. I thought, *Maybe Stanley's on to something.* When he was self-employed, he was independent. Free. He had been disciplined. He'd bought a couple of houses and had some money stashed.

All he had to do was stay one step ahead of the man. In a way, it seemed that cats like him were smarter than the rest of us. They saw the handwriting on the wall. The choice was clear: the system or the streets. They knew there was no need for trying to blend into the system. All of us were aware that working in the system carried a price: humiliation on some level. We shared the lingering fear that the racially integrated work world, with its relentless psychological assaults, was in some ways more perilous than life in the rough-and-tumble streets. At least in the streets, the playing field is level and the rules don't change.

I wondered, *What if I could make enough money to get out of the system for a while and clear my head?*

I looked at Stanley through a thin haze of smoke. "You think I can make some money doing this?"

I could tell he was surprised. Here I was, supposedly with a good job and doing well. All the fellas at home on the streets talked about how well I was doing in the white folks' world. Now I was talking about backtracking into the life. At first, Stanley seemed puzzled, but I think he understood. The system is the system, no matter how good it seems. "Yeah, man," he said. "There's *big* money to be made."

Not long after our talk, Stanley started making the rounds in Atlanta and got his own spot. Within several weeks, he knew more people than I had met there in a couple of years. A few times, Stanley paid me to let him leave his stash at my place and sent a few people there to make pickups. He told me he would let me come along when he made his next big coke buy so I could see how it's done. Although I had sold reefer and acid once, I knew nothing about handling cocaine.

One day, he came by, picked me up, and took me with him to a house in southwest Atlanta. It was a rambling ranch-style brick house in a neighborhood where you wouldn't believe anything illicit was going on. A guy called Benny answered the door. We went inside. The lights were down low. It was like déjà vu. Besides Benny, there were two guys and a woman. I knew what that was all about. They were the parasites. They were the ones who had no money to buy it themselves. They hoped to benefit when the sampling started.

We sat around, talking and listening to music, in a large open area that included the den and the kitchen. The druggies had that impatient look on their faces, that anticipation that sooner or later, somebody's gonna light up and they'll be right on hand when the pipe is passed.

Benny pulled out the cocaine for Stanley to test. Stanley examined it warily. Working with the precision of a chemist, he poured the powdery stuff into a test tube, added a pinch of baking soda to harden it, then added some water, which he measured carefully. As he worked, everybody in the room watched silently, hungrily eyeing that test tube. Stanley pulled a cigarette lighter from his pocket, flicked it, held the flame under the test tube, and let it cook. He added a few drops of cold water and shook the gluey substance in the tube until it hardened into a rock that, when shaken, clanged the sides of the tube. He then took the rock out and placed it in a pipe.

Stanley took a long, hard drag from the pipe, then passed it to me. "Inhale slowly, man, then hold it in." I inhaled, but it didn't work. "No, man, inhale it slowly, then hold it and work the hole in the pipe."

I glanced around the room at the others. They looked anxious, irritable. No worse sight to a junkie than seeing good drugs wasted.

Clumsily, I tried one more time, then passed the pipe along to the next man. They passed it around the room, each one careful not to hog it too long. When it was all gone, everybody sat back in their seats, glassy-eyed, soaring.

At some point, the woman got up from her seat and crept over to the counter where Stanley had cooked the stuff. She studied the countertop carefully, looking for particles of cocaine that might have dropped. Dazed, she seemed to have forgotten that anybody else was in the room. She ran her hand slowly, carefully, across the top of the counter, then leaned down until she was eye-level with the counter-top. Then she swept her hand across the counter again, gathering particles on a piece of paper. She found only a few white particles, but she walked away from that counter smiling triumphantly, like she'd struck gold, and sat back down.

The whole scene reminded me of the madness I'd known years before. It made me think hard about what I was about to get into. I learned something important about myself in that moment. I learned that I couldn't return to the life, even if I wanted to. The brutal harshness of that world conflicted sharply with what I had become. How could I return to that, given all I'd learned about life and God over the years? How could I deny that knowledge and live with myself? No. No matter how rough times were in Babylon, I had to give in to what I knew was right.

Thinking about all that, there was only one thing left to be done. I looked at Stanley. "I'm ready to ride, man."

He glanced at me, then flashed a knowing grin. "O.K., boss." He completed his transaction and grabbed his jacket.

Benny walked us to the door. When he was sure he was out of earshot of the others, he said, "We gonna freak this skank when her head gets bad. You sure you don't wanna get a piece a' that?"

I'd never been more certain about anything in all my life. I said, "Naw, man. I gotta go."

I walked out of that world and never looked back.

Chapter 37 DANNY

Sitting at my desk, working, I noticed a tall, lanky white dude walk into the newsroom and head toward my row. He was casually dressed: a silly-looking stingy-brimmed straw hat on his curly head, a lightweight mustard-colored zip-up jacket, paddy-boy slacks, and a pair of those shoes construction workers wear. No sport coat or tie. He was dressed so casual I assumed he'd come in for a story interview. Then he walked straight over to the aisle where I sat, plopped a notepad down on the empty desk behind me, and took a seat. I thought, *Just what I need. Another cracker near me.*

I stood up to go to the supply cabinet. Before I could leave, the new guy sprang from his seat, extended his hand, and said, "Hi. I'm Danny. Danny Baum." He was three inches from my face, smiling like there was something funny. I shook his hand. "I'm Nathan." And I walked away.

Later, I saw Danny walking across the newsroom. He had a goofy demeanor—long strides, arms swinging wild—like a northern Gomer Pyle or Mr. Green Jeans on *Captain Kangaroo*. A white woman reporter who sat near me leaned over to another white reporter, pointed at Danny, and whispered, "That's the new guy. Do you know what he did? He moved into a *black* neighborhood. Everybody's talking about it. *Somebody's* got to talk to him." Apparently unaware that I overheard, they burst out laughing, as if this new guy—this crazy northerner—had done the stupidest thing in the world. I looked at them a minute and thought to myself, *Uh-huh. These are the same pseudo-liberal crackers who will get up in your face and swear they're not racist and they don't see color. Yet they thought it was hilarious that a white guy was so color-blind that he'd moved into a black neighborhood.* I decided that the next time a white person told me he didn't see color, I was gonna call him a liar to his face. Let him know that he can't insult my intelligence and get away with it.

After I finished going off on white people in my head, I turned my thoughts back to this Danny guy. What kind of a person *was* he to move into a black neighborhood? Was it a mistake on his part or did he do that intentionally?

Newsroom gossip held that he had come to *The Atlanta Journal-Constitution* from *The Wall Street Journal*. Normally, that's considered a step down professionally. *The Wall Street Journal* is, after all, one of the top newspapers in the country. When asked why he left the *Journal* to come to Atlanta, Danny had told someone, "The people at *The Wall Street Journal* were too stuffy and pretentious. I decided I'd get a real job with real people who would let me chase fire engines and write about it."

In the following weeks, I watched him closely to see what he was about. It didn't take long to see that there was something different about this cat. Other people in the newsroom, blacks and whites, recognized it, too. I found him to be different in a pleasant way. Whenever he said something to me, there was a straightforwardness, a childlike honesty, that I didn't get from most other white people. With him, I didn't feel the hesitancy I felt from other whites or the racial baggage getting in the way. And he'd ask me the damnedest things out of the blue. One day, he slid his swivel chair back near mine and asked, "Why aren't black reporters more aggressive around here, Nate?"

It was the kind of thing I knew a lot of whites around there wondered about but were afraid to ask for fear of sounding racist or for fear of revealing that they were, in fact, racist. But Danny didn't seem to care. I concluded it must have been because he was secure in his mind that he wasn't racist, and he had nothing to hide. He was simply curious. He didn't know, so he did what any intelligent person should have done: He asked rather than assume. I respected that about him and found that, in spite of myself, there was something about this dude I really liked.

Since we sat so close to each other, we began rapping a lot at our desks. I learned Danny had done his own examination of the white mainstream and reached some of the same conclusions as me: that it was totally fucked up, that they needed to scratch all the rules governing the macho corporate game and go back to drawing stickmen on cave walls because that's about how far they'd come in human development. By the time he came to *The Atlanta Journal-Constitution*, Danny had decided that he was no longer going to play the game by their silly rules. He didn't brownnose the bosses or try to join the white folks' privileged insiders' club in the newsroom. He didn't try to get in with all the *right* people to gain an edge. In fact, he held management in contempt and talked about them as much as I did.

When Hosea Williams led a march in Forsythe County to protest the racism and open hostility to blacks who moved there, Danny took part in the march, even though our bosses had ordered reporters to stay out of it for the sake of objectivity. When he did that, I concluded that this dude was *truly* wild.

■ ■ ■

One day, Danny slid his seat near mine and said, "Nate, how about coming over to my place for dinner this weekend?"

"Lemme see what I've got planned," I said, "and I'll get back to you on that." I didn't have anything planned. I said that to buy time to think about it. Thinking about it, even *considering* spending my free weekend time at a white person's house, was a major leap for me. Had it been anyone else I wouldn't have had to think about it at all. I'd have declined without blinking an eye. But I considered it with Danny and decided, *What the hell. I'll give it a try.* Besides, I wanted to see just where he lived and ask him why he had moved into a black neighborhood.

I went to Danny's place that weekend. He definitely lived in the 'hood. He'd rented a detached house in a working-class neighborhood in Hosea Williams's council district. Danny was dating another reporter at the paper, Meg Knox, who lived in Savannah and worked for the paper's bureau there, several hours from Atlanta. She seemed just as laid-back and cool as Danny. We ate, then went into his living room, sat down, talked, and drank beer. It was the most comfortable I'd ever felt around white people. I didn't feel like Danny and Meg were judging me by their standards all the time. They didn't try to pretend there were no differences between us, like everybody else I knew. They celebrated our differences, and we joked about contrasts in the way blacks and whites talked, cooked, dressed, danced, and did everything else.

At some point, Danny told me he'd moved into this black neighborhood because he could get the best deal for his money there. "I like this house. It has a porch and a yard. The neighbors are friendly. . . . Actually, I'm thinking about buying it."

We talked about our tastes in white music and black music. I told them how I'd learned about white music—about the time I stole those tapes out of some white person's car. Danny played a tape for me and explained why a particular white artist I'd asked about was currently so popular. The singer was Bruce Springsteen, and the tape was *Born in the U.S.A.*

We talked a lot about race. I guess it helped that Danny was Jewish. Danny told me that he'd had his share of brushes with racism, and it didn't sit well with him. He asked me about Louis Farrakhan, whom he said frightened Jews with his statement that Hitler was a great man. "Nate," he asked, "why does Farrakhan hate Jews?"

I said, "I don't agree with everything Farrakhan says, but I don't think he hates Jews. I think he's widely misunderstood and his comments are often taken out of context. He's simply pro-black. A lot of white people assume that if you're pro-black then you must be anti-white. . . . You have to listen closely to what Farrakhan says to understand where he's coming from."

He asked to borrow a tape of Farrakhan so that he could hear it for himself.

We talked about a lot of other things. I was surprised to learn that he had actually read books written by black people: James Baldwin, Richard Wright, Ralph Ellison. It amazed me that a white person would do that when it wasn't required of him. He seemed equally as surprised to learn that one of my favorite authors was the Jewish writer Chaim Potok.

I left Danny's place late that night surprised that time had passed so quickly and shocked that I had actually spent a weekend evening— voluntarily—with whites and had a grand time. In return, I invited Meg and Danny over to my place for dinner. They met Debbie and our small children. It was one of those evenings when the differences between Debbie and me seemed to vanish, a night when there were no arguments about in-laws and money problems. After we put the children to bed, the four of us sat on the front porch and laughed and talked for hours. It was the first time I'd had any white people over to my house.

■ ■ ■

After a while, I found that I looked forward to talking with Danny. We grew closer and, in jest, gave each other silly nicknames. I started calling him "Danny Boy," and he called me "Nate McMann." He'd walk into the newsroom, look at me, and say, "Nate McMann, how ya doin', bro." I'd say, "Fine, Danny Boy, just fine."

At some point during the two years he lived in Atlanta, somebody broke into Danny's house. I felt strange about that. On its face, it supported the stereotype of crime-ridden black neighborhoods. I

wondered if it would conjure up racial stereotypes and send him
running for cover, as it would many pretentious liberal whites I'd
seen. But Danny treated it like any break-in. It didn't seem to matter
to him whether the burglar was black or white. He stayed right in the
neighborhood until he left Atlanta. More than anything else, that told
me that this cat was for real.

■ ■ ■

When Danny found out that I had a bike, he suggested we get together
and go riding one Saturday morning. I agreed, and we were on. He
pulled up to my place the following Saturday driving an old green
station wagon he'd bought from a colleague. We threw the bikes in
and he drove deep into the country. We picked a turnoff spot, parked
the car alongside the road, and unloaded the bikes. We rode for hours
and talked about everything. I asked him tough questions about
whites. He asked me tough questions about blacks. He'd offer his
theory on a matter, then wait for my response. I respected his sincer-
ity—so much so that I even confided in him that I'd been to prison.
I hadn't told anyone else at the paper about my prison past, not even
other blacks.

The country road was deserted, except for an occasional passing
pickup truck. After a long period of silence, Danny came at me with
another question. "You're pretty angry inside, aren't you, Nate
McMann?"

"Naw, Danny Boy, I'm not angry. I'm fuckin' furious."

Danny frowned. "God, Nate, you think about race all the time.
Give it a rest, man. It ain't healthy."

I told Danny I didn't have a choice in the matter. "You can sit
around and intellectualize about race when you want to, and when you
get tired of it you can set it aside and go surfing or hang gliding and
forget about it. But I can't. Race affects every facet of my life, man.
I can't get past race because white folks won't let me get past it. They
remind me of it everywhere I go. Every time I step in an elevator and
a white woman bunches up in the corner like she thinks I wanna rape
her, I'm forced to think about it. Every time I walk into stores, the
suspicious looks in white shopkeepers' eyes make me think about it.
Every time I walk past whites sitting in their cars, I hear the door locks
clicking and I think about it. I can't get away from it, man. I stay so
mad all the time because I'm forced to spend so much time and energy
reacting to race. I hate it. It wearies me. But there's no escape, man.
No escape."

When I finished talking, I felt like I had preached a sermon. I didn't realize I had so much frustration bottled up until I let it out on Danny. At first, I wondered why I had told him so much of what was going on inside my head. Then I realized that despite all I'd said in the past about not caring what white folks thought, I cared a lot. In fact, I had spent my whole life reacting to what they thought. The notion that one of them cared, really cared, about what I thought moved me. Danny was the first white person I met whom I actually saw trying hard to understand. It meant a lot to me that he tried because he wanted to and not because he had to. By the same token, he helped me see the world through white eyes and helped me better understand the fear and ignorance behind prejudice.

I learned something else from Danny that hadn't been clear to me before. I learned how little even the most highly educated white folks really know about blacks. He was very well educated and yet he struggled to understand some of the most basic things about black life in America. He struggled because in school he hadn't been taught diddly about blacks. Even though he saw us every day and interacted with us, we were puzzles to him. That showed me that the education system in this country has failed white people more than it's failed anybody else. It has crippled them and limited their humanity. They're the ones who need to know the most about everybody because they're the ones running the country. They've been taught so little about anybody other than white people that they can't understand, even when they try.

During one of our bike rides, we stopped and sat down on the side of a grassy mound to take a break from the scorching sun. About a hundred yards behind us, there was a huge white house sitting on a large tract of land. We were sitting there, talking and tossing pebbles onto the street, when a white man crept up behind us. "Hi," he said.

We both said hello. I expected the man to tell us to get the hell off his grass. Instead, he said something that startled me. "You guys look hot. I've got a full-sized swimming pool in my backyard if you want to take a swim."

Initially, his words didn't register with me. In my mind, there was something wrong with that picture. After all, this *was* Deep South Georgia and we *were* in some country town. I'd come out there half expecting to encounter hillbillies with gun racks in the windows of their pickup trucks. Now this cat was inviting us—a black and a white—to take a dip in his swimming pool?

Danny looked at me and I said, "No thanks. We're about to leave."

The man was almost insistent. "Really, I don't mind. Help your-selves and cool off if you want."

"No, we've got to leave."

The man smiled warmly and said, "O.K. If you change your mind, feel free to come on over."

"Thanks."

We got up and rode off. Later, I reflected on what that might have been about. I think the white man was moved by the picture of a white guy and a black dude sitting on the side of the road, rapping. I could be wrong, but I think the sight of us warmed his heart and he wanted to take part in our interracial communion for reasons of his own. Danny and I never discussed it, but I never forgot it, because gestures like that were so rare in my experience.

■ ■ ■

Danny told me sometime in 1987 that he and Meg planned to go to Africa to travel and work as freelance writers for a while. Initially, I felt envious that he, a white guy, would get the chance to go to my homeland, which I'd never been to as an adult. I told him how I felt: "See, you white motherfuckas get to do everything in the world you wanna do."

He insisted, "Nate, there's nothing stopping you from doing what you want to do in life. You can go to Africa, too."

That started a running debate. "No, I can't, Danny. You don't understand. You white boys can take off from work anytime and hitchhike across the country or spend a coupla years hoboing in Europe. Then, when you get ready to resume your career, the white establishment will welcome you back with open arms. But if I tried to do some shit like that, Mr. Charlie's gonna wanna know where I been and why there's a gap on my résumé. He's gonna want me to give an account of any time that was not spent slaving for him."

I had no frame of reference for Danny's opinion. All I knew was that every black person I had ever met had lived life aware of the limitations imposed by race, and that those who had tried to do what they truly wanted were met with intense opposition. I felt it was easy for Danny to think there were no ceilings because he hadn't known any.

Danny didn't win me over on that issue before leaving Atlanta, but he dropped a piece of advice on me that changed my thinking about something else. He said, "Look, Nate McMann, you may not believe this, but there are several white people in the newsroom who are *really* good people. You should give them a chance before writing them off as racists. Get to know some of them. You might be pleasantly surprised."

Later, I thought about what he had said. I thought about those whites who had tried to be friendly and the semi-meaningful talks I'd had with some of them in the newsroom: Among them was a political reporter who seemed sincere and two editors I had grown to like. *Maybe*, I thought, *I should open up more and be receptive to the fact that there are some good whites in the world.*

Somehow, just thinking that thought made me feel better. I realized that I needed to know that there might be other white people like Danny and Meg, and that there was some reason for hope in this deeply disturbed nation of ours.

Danny and Meg just left for Africa. Of all the white people I know, they are among the very few I can call friends. It's sad, this gulf between blacks and whites. We're so afraid of each other. . . .
January 10, 1987

Chapter 38 YANKEES

In the South the past is not dead. The past is not even past.
—William Faulkner

■ ■ ■

Old Danny Boy was right about one thing. Once I became more receptive to some of the friendly whites at *The Atlanta Journal-Constitution*, they proved to be O.K. (Before leaving for Africa, he pulled my coat to the cool ones and the closet racists.) Some of them were as sincere as any bloods I knew. One, an editor, engaged me in long talks that were as deep and funny as those between Danny and me.

My interaction with whites eased some of the tension I felt in the newsroom. It wasn't so traumatic being at work around them, and I even loosened up enough to begin going to lunch and to drinks after work with some. After I got to know some of the whites pretty well, I told one of my homeboys one day, "You know, there *are* some good white folks out there."

He shook his head and looked away, like he was pondering it. "Yeah, there are some good ones, but the ones that are bad are *really* bad."

We laughed ourselves silly.

A lot of the pressure I felt to leave the system was eased by some major personnel changes at the paper. In an effort to convert the *Journal-Constitution* into "a world-class newspaper," the owners went out and recruited some of the top journalists in the country to run it. They started with a guy named Bill Kovach, who had served as the Washington bureau chief of *The New York Times* and who had a reputation as a journalist of impeccable skills and integrity. After pulling together his own team of people from the *Times,* Kovach came in right away and reworked the entire paper, changing its appearance and writing style.

Kovach's arrival virtually split the newsroom into two camps.

There were those who were happy to see somebody come in, break up the entrenched good-ol'-boy system, and raise our journalistic standards. And there were the Deep South compatriots, who didn't like change and could stomach it even less at the hands of a "Yankee."

I heard that term a lot in Atlanta. Whites in and around that area still mourned the loss of the Civil War, as if it had ended only a few months earlier. And they strongly resented outsiders, especially the Yankees they deemed responsible for shattering their splendid plantation culture. They glorified the days of white-run cotton plantations and black handkerchief-head nincompoops depicted in *Gone With the Wind*.

It occurred to me that if these white people hadn't yet gotten over a war fought more than a hundred years ago, they hadn't even *begun* to deal in their heads with modern racism and equality.

Watching some of those good ol' boys huddling conspiratorially in their clusters, grumbling all the time about "them damned Yankees coming in and taking over," you would have thought they were planning to fight the fucking Civil War all over again. Some got mad and quit. Kovach fired others. It was interesting seeing white people warring against each other like that. I enjoyed watching the carnage.

Kovach's arrival revealed something to me about whites in the Deep South that I hadn't fully understood before: They have a deeply rooted inferiority complex that really *does* stem partly from that stupid war. I figured those northern whites must've worked a *mojo* number on their minds and humiliated them so badly that they passed that humiliation down through generations in the same way black folks had passed along the humiliation of slavery. What really got to the good ol' boys was that Kovach's actions indicated that the old bunch running the paper was incompetent, which, I guessed, supported the myth of the dumb hick southerner. I concluded that southern whites' inferiority complex may be the reason they cling so desperately to racism. They need to feel they are superior to *somebody* in the world.

Kovach didn't just upset the people working under him. He managed to piss off his bosses just as much. I think his bosses assumed he'd come in and be the typical executive newspaper hypocrite—talk about impartiality and aggressiveness in journalism and overlook the newsworthy sins of powerful people who bought advertising. But Kovach refused to get cozy with the powerful. When an executive from Coca-Cola, one of the most influential corporations in Atlanta, invited Kovach to dinner, Kovach turned him down. That upset top management terribly. When that happened, I became convinced that he was one of the few white managers on that level who actually believed in the journalistic ideals he preached. Others talked a good game but used the rhetoric of journalism like Reagan and Bush used the rhetoric of patriotism—to manipulate and deceive.

Kovach's arrival was poetic justice for blacks in the newsroom. For a while, we walked around gloating, with looks on our faces that said, "Well, whaddaya know. These crackers were so persistent in trying to prove *us* incompetent, now come to find out *they* were faking the funk. . . . They don't take it so well when the tables are turned."

Compared to the tough times we had had under the old regime, blacks (and women) were in hog heaven after Kovach got there. We got opportunities to do things that had been closed options before. I didn't know whether or not he was less racist or sexist than anyone else, but he seemed to offer equal opportunities, and that's all any of us could ask. Clearly, Kovach was smart enough to know that black journalists were valued assets in a largely black city. As soon as he took over, he promoted some blacks to the city desk and made sure others were included on major stories done by the paper. He promoted me to City Hall bureau chief.

When he began utilizing blacks, some whites in the newsroom started mumbling that affirmative-action shit again. But I knew what that was about. I knew the real deal: Some white people are so accustomed to operating at a competitive advantage that when the playing field is level, they feel handicapped.

■ ■ ■

In the short span of time that Kovach was at the *Journal-Constitution*, I got to travel out of town on more assignments than I had in my entire time in journalism. I went to Miami to cover a mayors' conference, and to New Orleans for the Republican National Convention. I even went on a trip to Europe with Andy Young and a group of other politicians and businessmen in a trade delegation seeking to attract business to Atlanta. I hadn't been out of the country since I was four, when the family lived in Morocco.

First we went to Switzerland, where delegation members met and dined Swiss dignitaries and made pitches promoting investment opportunities in Atlanta. Then we caught a train over the Swiss Alps to Milan. There were more tours, luncheons, and dinners. I wrote stories about the trip and sent them in from a laptop computer. I trailed Andy Young everywhere as he dazzled Italian dignitaries with his knowledge of the intimate details of world politics.

At various times during the trip, the irony of my being abroad dawned on me. The experience was so far from anything I'd ever imagined I would do that I wondered how I'd gotten there. Sometimes, I'd stop in the middle of an activity and ask myself, "What are you doing here? Only a few years ago, you were in prison. Now here you are in Milan, Italy, with Andrew Young. . . . Life is incredible." That dawning was like a quickening of the spirit. When that happened, it seemed my consciousness was suspended and I could feel all the power and wonder of the universe flowing through me.

At the end of the trip, the delegation leaders threw a final dinner to celebrate the success of the trade mission. After we ate, the host asked various people to say a few words. Andy spoke, and was followed by other delegation members. Then, surprisingly, the host turned to me and said, "Now we would like to hear from our journalist friend."

I was speechless. I wondered, *Should I make some comment as a journalist, or speak from the heart?* I wanted to speak from the heart, to tell them what this experience *really* meant to me. I wanted to tell them that I had never imagined in my wildest prison dreams that I would get an experience as enriching as this. I wanted to say all that and more, but I couldn't. The words wouldn't come.

When I realized that everybody around the huge table was watching and waiting for me to say something, I choked up even more. They looked at me like they feared something was wrong, like they thought I might be about to have a heart attack and were wondering if someone should call a paramedic. I glanced at Andy. He, too, appeared concerned. Desperate, I forced some words out of my mouth. It probably didn't make sense, but I had to say *something*.

When I finished, there was an eerie silence in the room. Then someone spoke up and rescued the moment, and the celebration continued. I could tell some of the people were embarrassed for me. I was embarrassed for myself. I felt so bad I wanted to get up and bolt from the room.

After dinner, I retreated to my room and sulked. How had I allowed that to happen? Why had I not been able to steel my nerves and do what I was called upon to do? I felt frustrated, yet I understood why I'd choked. I had been called on at precisely one of those moments when I was in the middle of a dawning. Mentally, I had been far away, basking in the splendor of that moment and savoring my connectedness to the universe.

This has been the most rewarding of my six years as a journalist. I have traveled to Milan, Italy, and Zurich, Switzerland, with Mayor Andrew Young. I went to Miami, Florida, for a conference of black mayors and a National Association of Black Journalists convention. I have interviewed for jobs in New York at Black Enterprise *magazine. I also have traveled to Richmond, Virginia, and Tennessee. Furthermore, I bolstered my career at* The Atlanta Journal-Constitution *with strong stories about City Hall and I am bureau chief over two other reporters.*

These experiences solidify my belief that I can do anything I set my mind to do. The possibilities are boundless.

What is also clear to me is that my achievement efforts will be hampered or helped by my mate. I need someone who is goal-oriented, who really knows that dreams are attainable. Although I am married, I look past my wife because she has no sense of direction and she is not motivated enough to even draw upon my resources and drive. For these reasons and more, I must terminate the union. If I don't, I'll face a life of unfulfilled dreams.

. . . The sad thing is that we have two beautiful children who undoubtedly will suffer some personal deprivations. That pains me, but not more than the prospect of spending the remainder of my days with a woman I neither love nor respect.

October 3, 1987

Debbie telephoned me in the newsroom just as I was putting on my coat to head out for an interview. "Nathan, this is Debbie. I'm at Georgia Baptist Hospital."

"What's the matter?"

"It's Maya. She got real sick this morning. I took her to the doctor and he said he's afraid she may have meningitis. He told me to rush her to the emergency room."

As she told me that the doctors were then examining our two-year-old daughter, her voice broke and she started crying.

I rushed out of the newsroom and headed toward the downtown Atlanta hospital. While speeding through traffic, my mind ran the gamut of possibilities. Of course, the thought that haunted me most, the one I refused to think about too hard, was the possibility that Maya would die. I uttered a prayer and struggled to steel my nerves. "God, *please* don't test me this way. I can handle anything but this."

I felt that if Maya didn't pull through, *I* wouldn't make it, either. I'd be a walking, breathing, living dead man.

I reached the hospital within fifteen minutes and found Debbie pacing in a waiting area. We talked with the doctors about Maya's condition, and they told us they would have to conduct tests to determine if she really did have meningitis. They performed the tests and admitted her to the hospital. When we went to her room, she was lying inside a crib with needles in her arms and an oxygen tent surrounding her. The doctor said, "It may be several days before we can get her condition under control."

Debbie and I decided that we should be with Maya around the clock. She pulled days, and I went there every night after work. Maya was subdued. She sprang to life, however, whenever I left the room to go to the bathroom or to get a soda. She'd wail hysterically until I returned. Some nights, after she had fallen to sleep, I sat there in a chair near the crib and stared at that young soul and wondered, *How do you get them through life? How do you protect them and minimize their hurts?*

After nearly a week, Maya's condition improved and doctors said she would pull through. It turned out that she didn't exactly suffer from meningitis but had some related condition that could lead to it. We took our daughter home and celebrated her impending health.

Debbie and I worked well together when faced with emergencies like that. We got through a brief scare with cancer that she suffered, as well as the many frightening bumps and bruises the children got. It was the calm times we had trouble managing: the times when all was quiet, everyone was healthy, and we were forced to look at each other and acknowledge that there was something vital missing from our marriage. We still argued a lot, about everything: how we should celebrate Christmas with the children, her mother's frequent visits and long stays, money problems, me staying out too late at night with Chip and Claxton, my two homeboys.

I was constantly reminded of how different we were, even in the way we interacted with other people. Debbie, who worked as a secretary at Emory University, had a few friends she had met on the job, but she did most of her socializing with her family and the family of her ex-fiancé, who also lived in Atlanta. I met lots of smart and stimulating people through my work and formed new and healthy social networks that I hadn't had in Portsmouth. I cut into a group of people who worked at City Hall, and we often got together on week-ends for food, drink, Scrabble, and conversation with our families. Within the group were several women who were intelligent and pro-gressive, the kind of women I enjoyed being around. We'd get into

involved debates about politics, current events, books, and other
things. Debbie was cordial toward them but maintained her distance,
and she was so quiet when around them that it began to make them—
and me—uncomfortable. Initially, I thought that maybe she suspected
I was trying to hit on one of the women in the group, so I encouraged
her to get to know them better in hopes that she'd see that the
relationships were strictly platonic and legit.

Then one night, something happened that showed me that Debbie's hang-up ran deeper than female jealousy. I took her to a big party
being thrown by some black Atlanta politician. All kinds of other
politicians and folks from the city's black gentry were there, including
one of Andy Young's top assistants. Spotting me, the assistant walked
over, and I introduced Debbie as my wife. The assistant said, "My
pleasure meeting you," and asked her a question to get the conversation going.

Debbie just looked at him and smiled sheepishly, like he wasn't
talking to her. The guy repeated the question, and the reaction was the
same. She froze, just like she often had when my City Hall friends
were around. I cut in and changed the conversation to try to rescue
my wife. I was embarrassed, the assistant was embarrassed, and, I'm
sure, Debbie was embarrassed, too. The incident brought home something that I'd suspected but was unsure of: Debbie was intimidated by
intelligent and influential black folks, so much so that she withdrew
when around them.

That discovery made me reluctant to take her places that required
a lot of social mingling. After that, I started going out alone as often
as I could, and that heightened tensions even more at home.

For me, life at home was a compromise. There were the joys—
being there with my children and nurturing them—and the strains of
trying to work a marriage doomed from the start. There were moments when family life made me feel serene and in harmony with the
natural order of things. But there were too many times when hassles
kept me out of sorts.

No matter how bad things got, I was determined to hang in there
for a while for my children's sake. I had to see to it that they got off
to a better and healthier start in life than I had. My parents had done
a good job—the best they could. But they came from the old school,
a generation that seldom talked to children or got into their heads. I
wanted to try a different, more hands-on approach to child rearing.

With Monroe, I'd blown that chance to make an early impression.
Before going off to prison, I'd always felt like an outsider, neither up

to the responsibilities nor entitled to the full rights of a father. But with Ian and Maya, I had a direct, in-house impact on how they were being raised. There was a chance to do it right. To instill in Maya a strong sense of herself so that she wouldn't grow up feeling dependent on men. To provide Ian a healthy blueprint of manhood devoid of all that macho bullshit. To show him it's all right to hug and kiss his father and to say "I love you."

I was determined they would also be taught to love themselves and their blackness. There were no white dolls or Santas in our house, no pictures of white people on our walls. There were black faces in their children's books, and lots of warm, nurturing interaction with their parents.

It was just the opposite with their mother and me. We drifted further apart, battling against differences too vast to overcome and heading toward an end that we both knew was near.

Chapter 39 THE PAST

Often, during those years after prison, it seemed that I was spending the second half of my life trying to straighten out all the mistakes made in the first. Every time I thought I'd overcome my past and gotten over the hump, something would come creeping up from nowhere and put shit in the game.

Sometime in 1987, a call came in from a woman at *The Washington Post*. They had an opening in one of their Maryland bureau offices and wondered if I would be interested in applying.

That was a hell of an honor. *The Washington Post* is the major leagues. Practically every journalist, black or white, wants to work his way up to the *Post* or *The New York Times* or *The Wall Street Journal*. I took the offer as an indication that in covering City Hall I'd gained some valuable experience that just might serve me well. Since I'd begun covering local politics I'd received similar calls from other newspapers, and I'd actually interviewed at a few.

I sent the materials the *Post* wanted—my résumé, my best news clips—and they scheduled a date for me to fly to D.C. I knew that the *Post* had recently promoted a black to be assistant managing editor in charge of their Metro section. That made me feel more comfortable about interviewing there. Still, there was something about the prospect of interviewing at the *Post* that concerned me, the same thing that popped up anytime I considered a job anywhere. It was the three-year gap on my résumé. People usually wanted to know what I'd done from 1975 until 1978. I wasn't inclined to tell them I'd spent those years studying at Penitentiary State University. Nor did I feel comfortable making up bogus jobs to fill in the gap.

Weeks before the interview, I agonized over whether to tell the paper about my prison past. I knew the *Post* did more thorough background checks than most other newspapers. They'd begun doing that after 1981, when it was discovered that a reporter who had written a Pulitzer Prize–winning series about a young heroin addict had made up the story. The reporter, Janet Cooke, was black. The *Post*'s management learned later that in addition to lying about the story, Cooke had also lied about the college she'd attended. I was certain the *Post* would do background checks to avoid future embarrassments.

My intuition told me, *Tell the truth and be at peace.* But, recalling the painful experience in Louisville, where I thought I'd landed a job until I 'fessed up about my prison past, I wrestled with the issue and then decided to seek outside advice. I talked with an editor friend, who suggested I tell the truth. Then I talked with an older cousin, who reiterated something I'd been taught all my life: Never be truthful to whites. "Don't tell 'em *shit*," he said. That settled it. I'd withhold any details about prison and see what happened.

The interview was far more involved than any other I'd experienced. I talked with several people over the course of about two days. I met the legendary Ben Bradlee, the raspy-voiced editor, and other bigwigs I'd heard and read so much about. A few of the people asked about the three-year gap. I told them, "I dropped out of college and spent that time trying to find myself." I thought, *Yeah, white people can relate to tryin' to find yourself. No one else on earth spends more time tryin' to find themselves than white people.* They all nodded, indicating they understood.

But the reaction of Milton Coleman, the black assistant managing editor, was different. When I told him I'd spent the three years trying to find myself, he asked, "What did you do with that time?" His eyes bored right through me. I shifted uncomfortably in my seat. "I worked in a library and spent the time reading and thinking about what to do with my life." It was the truth, but not the whole truth.

We got through that conversation, but I sensed Milton wasn't fully satisfied. He didn't say it, but something in his manner suggested he wanted to know more.

Following that interview, I was happy to learn that I wouldn't be asked to fill out a job application. That surely would have contained the standard question, *Have you ever been convicted of a felony?* I hadn't decided how to respond and was glad I wasn't forced to make an on-the-spot judgment call.

I returned to my hotel room exhausted but confident that the interview had gone well. Before leaving, I got subtle indications from a few people with whom I talked that they felt I was a strong candidate for the job. I went back to Atlanta and waited. Several weeks later, I was sitting at my desk, working late, when my telephone rang. I lifted the receiver. "Nathan, it's Milton Coleman."

The minute I heard his voice, I knew I was busted. It was the same

intuitive knowing I felt that night at the McDonald's. The alarms
went off in my head. I braced for the blow. We exchanged greetings
and small talk, then he launched into his purpose for calling. "Nathan,
there's something I need to talk with you about. Someone at your
former paper in Norfolk told us that you've been to prison. Can you
tell me why you didn't tell us about that?"

I wanted to ignore the question and run away. Just drop the
receiver and haul ass. A whole host of regrets flooded my mind. I
regretted ignoring my intuition. I regretted staying at work late. I
regretted having gone on the interview in the first damned place. *Why
did I let these people complicate my life? I had a secure job and a buried
past before they called. I had to go and get ambitious. Now I gotta cop
another guilty plea.* In another life, I would have copped out completely, even after learning they had the goods on me. I would have
gotten mad and given the world the middle finger. *"Fuck it, man, I
don't wanna talk about it and you can't make me!"* But this new life held
me to different standards. So I took a deep breath and prepared to face
the firing squad.

I explained to Milton why I hadn't told them about my past. I told
him what happened several years earlier at the job interview in Louisville. "You may not believe this, but I agonized over it a lot before
coming to Washington."

I half expected him to cut me short and end the conversation, but
he listened. He listened to the full explanation, then said, "I understand." He said he would explain it to the other people involved in the
decision-making process. "I have to tell you that some of them are
against you because they feel you lied to them. I'll get back to you and
let you know the outcome."

I sat there at my desk for a long time thinking of the implications
of what had just gone down. I felt I'd let myself down in the worst way
and let down all the black people who would ever interview at the *Post*.
Janet Cooke lied. Nathan McCall lied. They would check the teeth
and fingerprints of every black who came through that door. *Damn.*
In running from the past, I ran right into it.

I was choked up inside. When I felt myself about to break, I got
up, walked calmly to the men's room, went into a stall, and wept
like a baby. After several minutes, I collected myself, wiped my
eyes, and gave myself a good talking-to. *You've been through too
much to have to go through this again. Don't take yourself through it,
man. Put an end to it.*

I returned to my desk and called Milton Coleman. When he came to the phone I said, "Milton, I've thought about our conversation and I'd like you to remove my name from consideration for the job. . . . I don't want to go through this."

After a brief silence, Milton said, "I understand." (I figured that he, at least, understood hardship. He had been in the news a lot during the 1984 presidential campaign because he had contributed information to a colleague's story revealing that in private conversations Jesse Jackson had referred to Jews as "Hymies" and to New York as "Hymietown." Louis Farrakhan, who supported Jackson's campaign, added to the controversy by implying in a speech that Milton should be killed for betraying black people. Those had been tough times for Milton.) Later in our conversation, Milton revealed that he understood my feelings on a deeper level. "I have a brother who got into trouble with the law once, and I know what he's been through."

I said, "Then you *do* understand."

"Yeah. . . . I'll have them take your name out of the hat."

There was a pause. Then Milton said, "Look, man, I don't want you to be discouraged by this experience. It's got to be rough for you, I know, but sometimes we grow from experiences such as this. I promise you that I'll keep an eye on your work and we'll keep you in mind. Who knows? Maybe in a few years, when all this blows over, we may want to reconsider you."

It meant the world to me to talk with somebody on his professional level who understood. It struck me that few black people in this country come from families where no one has been to prison. To some degree, we all understand.

Before hanging up, Milton offered a piece of advice that I have never forgotten. He said, "At some point, you're going to have to realize that although you have been to prison, you have since built a track record in the work world. You don't have to spend the rest of your life hiding past mistakes. You can now trust your track record, tell the truth, and put the past behind you."

I said, "Thanks, man. I'll think about that."

After we hung up, I went back to the rest room and cried some more.

■ ■ ■

One day, during an argument, I told Debbie that I was so displeased with the lack of stimulation in our relationship that if I didn't see some improvement soon, I planned to file for divorce. I also told her that I planned to go to Miami to visit my homeboy Cooder—without her.

Against her wishes, I left for Miami, and she packed up the kids and met her relatives in Wilmington. When I returned a few days later, Debbie met me at the door and handed me a thick wad of papers. She had filed for divorce, alleging mental cruelty and all that other standard bullshit they include in such papers.

That action started a long and painful process that led us to court in early 1988. As my marriage broke down, it was different at the newspaper. Under Kovach, I found myself wanting to explore new opportunities opening up. I made it known to my bosses that I was interested in becoming an editor. That would be another plus on my résumé and would broaden my options down the road if I wanted to dash to another newspaper. Besides, I wanted to see if I could do it. I wanted to enter the world of white management and see if it was as esoteric as they tried to make it seem.

I applied to go to a popular fellowship program called the Multicultural Management Program, which was run by a black journalist, Ben Johnson. Held at the the journalism school of the University of Missouri, the monthlong program was designed for reporters and management types on all levels to sensitize some to issues relating to minorities and to prepare others to deal with racism in the workplace.

I left for the program in the fall of 1988, at a time when I needed a diversion from my domestic troubles. When I arrived on campus, I met the group, which was a motley crowd of about twenty people: blacks, Hispanics, Asians, whites, and even some Native Americans. We were escorted to rooms in a wing of the graduate-student dormitory. Some fellows complained about the cramped rooms, but I felt right at home. My dorm room reminded me of a prison cell.

We started the program with a seminar, the first of many we would have every day until we left. The group leader, a tall, slender white man with a genuine smile, led off by asking us to talk about ourselves. People were guarded. We held back those parts of ourselves reserved for only those we trust. It remained that way through the first week.

Then, one Friday evening, after the grueling schedule had begun to take its toll, we all limped back to the dorms. Someone suggested, "Hey, let's get some beer." I had a boom box and some cassette tapes. We went to a room, milled about, talked, and listened to music. One by one, others drifted in. Then we started dancing—black, white, Asian, everybody started throwing down—and before long the affair grew into a full-blown party. We laughed, sang, got drunk, and took pictures as the racial barriers came down. It was as if all at once we realized that it really didn't matter what color we were. We were all human beings, brought together by a common experience. Aside from the time I spent with Danny, I'd never experienced anything like it.

I think that party and the closeness that evolved among us was a new experience for the others, too. During that month, we learned about each other's cultures and shared feelings about the rest of the world. The two Native Americans talked a lot about the impact of racism on their people. They told about the despair—the high alcoholism and suicide rates—diminishing their once thriving tribes. One of the Native Americans, a woman, broke down in tears while telling the group about their struggle. "You have no idea how frustrating it is as journalists trying to educate whites in the newsroom who are ignorant and arrogant at the same time," she said. An Asian American's eyes also watered as he recounted his troubles trying to make it in the white work world.

Listening to them, I realized how self-centered I'd been as a black man. I had come to think of the word "minority" as being synonymous with "black." Even when campaigning for the hiring of more minorities in the newsroom, I had been concerned solely with blacks. But through those sessions, I learned that Asian Americans and other minorities were as essential as anyone to changing the media.

Often, during those weeks, outside speakers came in to take part in seminars and panel discussions. In one of the seminars, managers from several of the nation's newspapers were brought in to talk about the difficulties they faced in trying to hire minorities.

One of the speakers, a guy from *The Washington Post* named Tom Lippman, led into his presentation by saying, "I want to tell you two stories that I think will give you some indication of how difficult it is to achieve what it is we're talking about here. The first one is a story of a young man who we were interested in hiring about a year ago. By all accounts he was very good at his job. He works for a serious newspaper, does very well, has satisfied every demand placed upon him by his editors. He was quite likable. He happens to be black, and we were getting ready to offer him a job. I can tell you, though, that because of our own experiences with a certain minority journalist whom I don't need to name, my newspaper is much more careful than it ever was in the past about checking references on people and finding out exactly what their backgrounds are."

Before he went on, I braced myself. I knew he was talking about me. I felt it inside. I knew it was my past haunting me again. Lippman continued. "In this case, we discovered on a reference check that this young man had served time on a felony conviction . . ."

Blood rushed to my head so quickly that it made me dizzy. I sat there, wondering what to do. My first impulse was to interrupt him and let him and everybody in the room know that he was talking about me. But I knew that if I stood and tried to speak, I'd lose control and go off on that white man.

I shifted in my seat, trying to decide how to handle it. Then, when the question-and-answer session started, I couldn't resist. Looking at Lippman, I said, "I didn't get the point in the example you used about the guy with the felony conviction. How does that reflect upon the problem you have finding minorities in the newsroom?"

While he babbled some response that didn't directly answer the question, I decided to keep quiet and see how my colleagues responded to him. As soon as he finished talking, hands shot up in the air. One woman said, "You expect us to believe that *The Washington Post* cannot find qualified minorities because all of them have prison records?"

Another person asked, "What did his prison record have to do with his qualifications for the job in the first place?"

One by one, the fellows attacked Lippman's logic, and one person even told him, "Such racist thinking is exactly the reason programs such as the one we're attending are needed in the first place."

The group's reaction to Lippman warmed my heart. They made it clear that their concerns were not about the *Post* rejecting an applicant for being less than forthcoming, which it had every right to do, but that Lippman was wrong in implying that prison records are common among minority applicants. I felt good that they had come to my rescue without knowing it was me they were defending.

When the session ended, I walked over to Lippman, who was standing near a wall, looking red-faced, and pulled him off to the side. I said, "You know that guy you mentioned with the prison record?"

He looked at me curiously. "Yes?"

"That was me."

His eyes grew as big as two fifty-cent pieces. "That was you?!" He apologized so loudly and dramatically that he caused a scene. "I, I, I'm sorry. Gee, I didn't know. I'm sorry. I really am sorry."

I told him that there was no need to apologize and that I wanted him to know that the example he cited for being unable to find minorities was inappropriate. He apologized some more and we parted.

Later that day, I went to dinner with a group of program fellows and told them I was the job applicant with the prison record who had interviewed at the *Post*. They were surprised. Then they got mad all over again and launched into a debate about whether the group should complain to the *Post*. Some wanted to write to the *Post* to complain about Lippman. Others argued that it wouldn't do any good.

I told them to let it drop. I didn't want to appear to be crying over spilled milk. But I could tell they all shared my hurt and anger over what had happened.

Experiences such as that drew us closer together. That and the time we spent together. We ate breakfast together, spent entire days in the seminars together, then went to dinner together and often rapped or hung out together until bedtime. After a while, we were like one big rainbow family.

When the program ended, I knew I'd taken part in a rare and special human experience that I would cherish for the rest of my life. I sensed that the others felt the same.

We had a farewell program on the final day. Each of us got up and went to the front of the room and talked about how deeply the program had affected us. The talk I remember most was given by a white guy from San Antonio; I remember it not so much for what he said as for what he did. Despite strong efforts to hold back, he broke down in tears. I knew why he was crying. Everyone in the room knew. We had learned that the racial differences that we had considered so profound were not so broad after all, and we felt better equipped to go out and preach the gospel of multiculturalism. The Missouri experience strengthened our wavering hope, and that realization brought us tears of joy.

■   ■   ■

Bill Kovach left *The Atlanta Journal-Constitution* sometime in 1988. He got into a disagreement with one of the bigwigs and quit. You would have thought they would have tried to keep him. Under him, the paper won a number of Pulitzer Prizes after years of going without winning many. But they readily accepted his resignation. A lot of other people left the paper after that. Kovach's leaving was a clear indication to them that the management of the *Journal-Constitution* had decided that the strain of being a world-class newspaper was too much for them. The management was much more comfortable with mediocrity. While a lot of people in the newsroom mourned the loss of Kovach, the good ol' boys who had survived his purges rejoiced. To them, Kovach's departure was a victory of grand proportions: A Yankee had been run out of town. The South had finally won.

■ ■ ■

Before he left, I had an encounter with Bill Kovach I'll always remember. I walked back to the foyer leading to his office and told his secretary I needed to see him. She told me, "Have a seat." Sitting there, I thought about what I was about to do. I'd been thinking about it ever since the experience with Tom Lippman at the Multicultural Management Program. I'd also thought about what Milton Coleman had told me after my interview at the *Post*, and I'd concluded that Milton was right: I *had* built a track record, and it should be strong enough to help me overcome my past. Being up-front about my prison record was the only way I could guard against its haunting me. I decided to tell Kovach.

After several minutes, his secretary said, "Go right in."

A white-haired man in his fifties, Kovach was a square-jawed cat who had dark shadows circling his eyes. It gave him a raccoonish look. Sitting at his desk, working, he looked up and stopped what he was doing. "What can I do for you, Nathan?"

"There's something I need to talk with you about."

"O.K." He sat erect. "What is it?"

I got right to the point. "I have served time in prison."

"Oh? What for?" His tone and expression didn't change.

"Armed robbery." I waited for a visible reaction. There was none. Then he gave me a strange look, as if he were wondering why I had bothered wasting his time with such trivia. After a few minutes, he said, "Is that all?"

I thought, *Is that all? Is that all?!* It was enough to make some white folks run screaming from the room with their arms flailing. I cleared my throat and answered, "Yes."

"Is anybody giving you shit about it?"

"No."

"If anybody gives you shit about it, let me know."

That was it. I sat there a minute, waiting to see if he had anything else to say. He said nothing. I looked into his eyes and he looked into mine. Then I rose and walked out of his office, stunned, wondering if that scene had really occurred.

Chapter 40 THE BROTHERS

Greg, our longtime family friend, visited me in Atlanta from time to time. When we were young, Greg and my brother Dwight hung tough together, but as we got older, Greg and I grew pretty close. He would come to Atlanta on a Friday morning, party two or three days, then head on back to Portsmouth and return to the daily grind. I thought it was strange when he showed up suddenly one fall afternoon and said he was there to stay. Like almost everybody else at home, Greg had worked at the shipyard for several years. Then he quit his gig to sell insurance full-time. He was trying to build his clientele when he decided to relocate. When I asked him why he came to Atlanta, Greg said, "Man, I just needed to clear my head and get a change of scenery. Portsmouth was dragging me down."

I suspected he was running from something, but that was O.K. We were all running, trying to overcome the feeling of rootlessness in the system and make a way for ourselves. Greg stayed with us for a while, then found a job and an apartment not far from where we lived. He seemed to be getting on his feet, then something happened. He changed. He started borrowing money. Increasingly, when I saw him, he had a different look. Greg had always had a sense of pride about the way he dressed and carried himself. But whenever he came around, he looked ashen and desperate. One day, Greg would come by and his hair would be uncombed. The next day he'd be wearing the same threads he'd had on the day before. I knew he was dabbling in cocaine, but had no idea what else he was doing or how much. Then one day, Chip, one of my homies, told me, "Greg is fucked up on that shit. He hittin' that pipe almost every day."

"Naw, man, not Greg."

My homie was insistent. "Man, don't underestimate the stuff they got out there now. It's more powerful than the stuff that was on the streets when we was out there. They got some shit out there now called crack. They say that shit will knock your socks off in a minute and put a *go-rilla* on your back."

Despite what I'd seen at that drug house I went to, I refused to believe the drug scene was any worse than it had ever been. Drugs are like fashions. One year, one drug is in style, then the next year they come out with something new. I argued to my homie, "When we were doing all that acid, people said that was the worst thing in the world. Now they saying this new stuff is worse than anything that's come down the pike. This stuff will blow over, just like everything else. People will try it, and when the novelty wears off they'll move on to something else."

When it got really bad for Greg, he stopped coming around to my place. I think he was embarrassed for Debbie and the kids to see him falling apart. But I kept up with what was going on with him by checking with my homies from time to time. I ran into Chip one day and he said, "Yo, man, the repo man got Greg's car yesterday. And I heard he lost his job."

The next thing I knew, Greg had gone back to Portsmouth. His mother sent him money to catch a Greyhound bus back home. When I talked with my mother a short time afterward, she told me Greg had checked into a drug rehab center called the Serenity Lodge.

I hated seeing Greg go through that hell. Outside my family, I'd known him longer than anyone else in my life. We could talk about anything, and he loved to play chess as much as I did. When I was in prison, Greg had visited me more times than my own brothers. I *had* to go home and lend him some moral support.

When I got to the Serenity Lodge in Portsmouth, I was ushered into what looked like a lawyer's conference room. Greg came through the door. Unlike the last time I'd seen him, he looked scrubbed and rested. We greeted each other, then sat down and rapped. I said, "Wow, man, I must be slippin'. I didn't even know you were *that* bad off until I heard they took your ride. You should've come and told me you were having problems."

Greg said, "I couldn't tell you I was havin' problems because I hadn't admitted it to myself, man. You know I always been able to handle drugs. I was doin' that shit for a long time and handlin' thangs. I was doin' good. Then that stuff started gettin' the best of me and I couldn't figure out how to get away from it, man.

"It got so bad one time, Nate, that I got in front of a mirror and stuck a gun to my head and said to myself, 'Man, with all these problems you got, all you gotta do is pull this trigger and you won't have to worry 'bout gettin high no fuckin' more.' I wanted out so bad, but I didn't know how to get out.

"I even tried to turn to Islam for help. I went and bought a Qur'an and read it every day. Some days, I'd be at home with the Qur'an in one hand and the pipe in the other.

"Sometimes I would think I had it beat. I was upstairs one day prayin' for God to take this shit from me. I told Him I didn't never wanna do drugs no more, and I promised God I wouldn't. Then the dope man came to the door and I *flew* downstairs. He gave me enough snow to use and then gave me some to sell so I could get myself straight. I packaged it up to sell, then ended up puttin' it in a pipe and smokin' it all up. After that, I had to pay the dope man every week when I got paid.

"Man, I sold everything I had but this gold necklace around my neck. My moms gave me this necklace as a gift. When I thought about sellin' that to get some money, I knew I was bad off. I refused to sell it, though."

Then I asked, "So, man, how you feeling? You think this rehab is gonna work for you?"

"Yeah, man, I love it. I think I'm gonna make it. I don't never wanna do no drugs no more."

We talked some more, then Greg said, "Hey, man, there's some other people here from Cavalier Manor gettin' treatment. When I told 'em you were comin', they said they wanted to see you. They'll be comin' through here in a few minutes."

A few minutes later, Charlie Gregg, my old stickup partner, came through the door. "Yo, Nate, what it iiis, baby!?" I had lost track completely of Charlie Gregg after we got out of prison. I heard through Nutbrain every now and then how he was doing, but had no idea that he, too, was strung out. Then, a few minutes later, a woman I had grown up with came through the door and hugged me. Before I left, several other people I hadn't seen in years came into the conference room to say hello. It was just like a reunion in Cavalier Manor.

When I left there that evening, I had to bear witness that Chip, my homie in Atlanta, was right—the drug game had progressed to another level.

■   ■   ■

Going home to Portsmouth always helped me keep abreast of the happenings in the streets. Every time I went home, I'd see something or run into somebody who gave me something heavy to think about. I could always find out who were the current knockout artists and get a line on the latest pseudo-big-time drug dealers in Cavalier Manor.

All I had to do was cruise up to the 7-Eleven or go anyplace where cats hung out and I'd get the scoop. I'd usually ask somebody, "Who's the man now?" and they'd say, "Lo is the man" or "Poochie is the man" or "JoJo is the man." That meant that the person they named controlled most of the drugs coming into the area. I'd usually see the man cruising through the 'hood in a Coupe de Ville or slick sports car, profiling and stopping at all the drop-off points.

None of them lasted. No matter how sharp any of them were, they eventually got busted, robbed, or shot. They usually lasted just long enough to flash the cars, the clothes, and the fat wads of cash that convinced the up-and-coming young bloods on the block that the drug game was worth a try.

Going home also helped me keep up with how the fellas around my way were doing. During one trip home, I saw Ba-Ba, the guy I'd stayed with years before when I'd run away from home. I was washing my car in front of my mother's house when I looked up the street and saw this tall, broad-shouldered dude coming toward me with a little boy in tow. When he got closer, I realized it was Ba-Ba. I hadn't seen or heard from him in years. The last time I saw him, he was selling blood to the blood bank in Norfolk to get drug money.

When he reached my mother's house, we hugged, slapped five, then stood back and looked each other over. Whenever I ran into dudes I knew from the old days on the block, I went out of my way to show them that I hadn't changed. Of course I had changed a *lot*, but I talked more slang than usual to let them know that I hadn't gotten grand on them or started acting white. I said, "Ba-Ba, where you been, man, shackin' with some babe?!"

The smile left Ba-Ba's face. "Man, I took a fall. I been locked up the last five years. I just got out on parole a few days ago. I was walking through the 'hood and I thought I'd come by here to ask your moms where you were."

"Wow. What a coincidence. I'm livin' in Atlanta, man, but I'm in town for the weekend."

"Yeah?"

"Yeah. What you do time for?"

"It was a drug tip. Got busted on a humble. Judge gave me twenty years. Made parole the first time up. . . . It was a bad fall, man. I took the rap for two other dudes. It shouldna went down like that, but it did. You know how that is."

"Yeah, man, I know how it is. Where'd they send you?"

"They sent me to Camp Twenty-two. It wasn't bad. We did lightweight roadwork. Where did you do your bid?"

"I did my first two years at Southampton. I did my last stretch at St. Brides. Everybody was at Southampton: Bonaparte, Joe Ham, Feetball, the whole crew. Who was at Camp Twenty-two with you?"

"Man, they had a lotta young boys from the Manor that you wouldn't even know. Younger brothers of dudes we grew up with. They playin' the crazy-nigger roles like we used to do. . . . Every now and then, some old-heads would come through from the Richmond pen."

I could see Ba-Ba was feeling the strangeness of having just gotten out. The free world and the people looked peculiar to him. I remembered how weird and out of sync I'd felt when I first got out. It took two years before I felt fully readjusted. I knew the adjustment would be hard for him at his age. It made me feel grateful that I'd done my time when I was younger and gotten it over with.

Ba-Ba spoke, almost as if he knew what I was thinking. "This adjustment is gonna be hard for me. I'm too old to be goin' through this shit. I got this kid. He's five years old. His moms was pregnant when I got popped. I hadn't even seen him before I got out. Now I gotta figure out how to raise him."

The little boy fiddled around impatiently, occasionally tugging on Ba-Ba's leg.

We talked some more and reminisced about the time I ran away from home and went to stay with Ba-Ba and his grandmother in Norfolk. Then Ba-Ba said he had to leave to take his son back to his mother's house. We exchanged phone numbers and promised to keep in touch.

Seeing Ba-Ba and some of the others reminded me how much life was taking a toll on brothers everywhere. There weren't many in my bunch you could point to and say, "He's doing fine." After I finished washing my car, I climbed in and cruised up and down streets in Cavalier Manor, just to do a mental tabulation of the casualties. I'd look at the houses and think about the people I knew and review their stories. It seemed I could associate every other house I passed with some tragedy. There were Steve and his brother, who both committed suicide, and Charlene, whose husband murdered her. Charlene had taught me how to hand-dance. And there was Jack, who blew his old man away with a shotgun blast. Ronald Bailey and Gibbs had gotten killed. The list of those dead was far too long for guys our age. Worse still was the list of those brothers who were drug zombies. They were breathing, but were more dead than alive. Teeth missing from their mouths. Skin pallid and ashen. Eyes vacant, and hearts cold as ice in winter. It was depressing, and reminded me why I couldn't bear to go home too often or stay too long.

It seemed that everywhere I looked, brothers were down-and-out. Every city I went to, I'd see hordes of grown black men in their twenties, thirties, and even their forties, hanging out, hustling for chump change, and wasting away. They'd be wearing the latest sneakers and have their shirttails out and hats on backward, like they were still teenagers, frozen in adolescence. Haki Madhubuti, the black writer, lamented in one of his record albums how so many brothers seem to be standing still while the rest of the world passes them by. He said, "While the white boys are walkin' on the moon, brothers are runnin' down to the Moon Lounge on Hot Pants Night." I kept saying, to myself and to other people when we talked about all the lost potential in black men, "Brothers gonna work it out. Brothers gonna get it together." But there was little visible evidence to support that claim.

Sometimes, I'd get mad at the brothers, especially those hanging idly on street corners, thinking they were baad. At the same time, I understood why they were having such a hard time getting it together. I knew why so many young brothers, and black people in general, were losing their minds. They look up and see that they're catching hell from the cradle to the grave, and that the whole fucking country is pointing fingers at them and saying it's black people's own fault that they're catching hell. They're beating the pavement, trying to find work, and nobody will hire them, and white folks cite them as examples of people who are trifling and don't want to work. And those blacks who have jobs are catching hell, trying to move up the ladder, like everybody else, and the same white folks who hold them back accuse them of being lazy and unambitious. Times for brothers were getting rougher when it seemed things couldn't get any worse. When I think of all that brothers have to go through in this country, I am reminded of something I once heard someone say: "If we ain't *in* hell, we sure can see it from here."

Every time I watched brothers playing pro basketball on TV it pissed me off. I'd look on the floor and see that most of the players were black. Then I'd look in the stands and see that most of the people there were white. I'd see those white folks cheering for brothers like they love them to death, even though they despise them in any other

arena they try to go into. The basketball court was the one place
brothers seemed self-assured. They did things that required amazing
coordination of timing and thought. They moved with the speed and
grace of gazelles. And they welcomed pressure and made last-minute
clutch plays that were outta sight. I concluded that brothers shone so
well shooting hoops because the basketball court was the one place
white Americans let them know they believed in them.

■　■　■

Often, when I went home, the word spread on the streets around my
way that I was there. Whenever the fellas saw a car with Georgia plates
parked in front of my mother's house, they'd stop by to see if I was
in town. One day, while I was standing in my parents' driveway, a
sleek, luxury-model green Mercedes-Benz pulled up. A tall, heavyset
guy climbed slowly out and walked toward me. He walked with a
pronounced limp and leaned heavily on a cane. It was Bimbo. I'd
heard the news over the wires about a recent accident that had
changed Bimbo's life. Depending on who you talked to, it was a tragic
mishap or a godsend. Bimbo was working for a railroad company in
Newport News when he slipped and fell on the tracks. Before he could
pull his leg away, the boxcar moved, severing his foot. The railroad
company settled in a deal that gave Bimbo millions of dollars to be
paid in installments for the rest of his life. Bimbo, once the least likely
among us to succeed, was now a millionaire.

After exchanging greetings, we climbed into his ride to go and get
something to eat. As we drove through Cavalier Manor past the
baseball field, some of the fellas hanging out there spotted Bimbo's car
and began racing full-trot toward us, arms flailing. "Bimbo! Bimbo!
Bimbo!" Bimbo glanced at them, snickered, and kept driving like he
didn't see them. "That's Marvin and them. Now they know I got all
this money, they always tryin' to catch up with me to get a loan."

We went to dinner and talked, and I learned more about what life
had been like for him since our hanging days. Like me, Bimbo had
been through a lot. He'd been married a few times and was trying to
find something meaningful to do with his life. Since his accident, he'd
been miserable and lonely. He said he had been hounded by guys from
the neighborhood ever since they learned of his new fortunes. "The
pressure got so intense that I moved to Williamsburg and got a big
fence to keep people out. That still didn't keep them niggahs away.
Kenny Banks paid Frog Dickie to show him where I live. He came
over and asked me for money to help finance some business deal."

We talked about everything—who had recently gotten killed or been sent to the penitentiary, who had gotten married or divorced, who was hitting the pipe or the bottle, and who was just plain struggling. We came up with a whole list of guys who had completely lost their minds: Pokey, Skip, Melvin, Ronald, Derrick. Bimbo said Derrick got jumped by some downtown boys. "They beat him with pipes. He ain't been right in the head since. . . . Whiskey Bottle is out of it, too. My moms told me that Whiskey came to the house one night asking for help. He said he was seeing snakes and that they were crawling all over him. Whiskey is now a vegetable, man. His sister got legal custody of him."

Bimbo added, "It's wild how so many guys are coming apart."

I told him that I could remember when I felt like I was coming apart, especially during that time before I got sent away to prison. I asked Bimbo, "Remember when I went berserk and cracked that cane over your head?"

He grinned and said, "Yeah, I *definitely* thought you had gone crazy."

"It was nothing personal, man. I was just mad at the world and you were somebody I could focus my anger on. It's easy to lose your mind when you're lost like that."

Bimbo said, "Hey, man, when's the last time you saw Shell Shock? You and Shell Shock used to be seriously tight."

I told Bimbo I'd only seen him once, on Cavalier Boulevard. "After we caught up on each other's lives, there wasn't much to say. We were like strangers. It was hard to believe we were once best friends. In spite of all the years we hung together, stole together, ran trains together, and fought together, our thing just fizzled after I went to prison."

Bimbo said, "I think Shell Shock has become bitter. He always had big Superfly dreams, bigger dreams than anybody I knew. Remember, we'd be sitting down in his mom's house, smoking reefer, and Shell Shock would say, 'I'm gonna make some *big* money. Buy me a limo and get a private plane and shit.' Now Shell Shock is workin' at the shipyard and reality has kicked him square in the ass. Ain't gonna be no limo or private jet. He gotta punch a clock and scramble to pay bills, like everybody else. I don't think he takin' it very well."

Then Bimbo got around to asking me what I knew everybody wanted to know: "I heard you workin' for the newspaper in Atlanta. What's it like goin' to work in a suit and tie?"

"It's strange, man. I been in the system about eight years now and

I'm *still* not used to it. It's like being on the front lines in Vietnam. You never know when white folks are gonna come at you, but you know they're gonna come and you gotta be ready to do battle.

"Being in the system, man, you gotta know how to handle stress. Remember when we used to go round looking for white boys, and when we'd find one we'd beat him until we got tired?"

"Yeah. We kicked some serious ass then."

"Man, that used to take the stress outta me. Sometimes I wanna do that now, even though I'm a grown-assed man. Sometimes I wanna take one of those white boys where I work and bang his head against a wall or stomp him in the ground until all the stress leaves my body. Nothing I know of, not even Olympic sex, relieves tension as completely as when we used to fuck up white boys."

Bimbo said, "So you don't like the system, huh?"

"I like it sometimes, but often I think about getting out. There are some good people, but the system is ruthless, man, more ruthless than the streets will ever be. They may not shoot and cut each other the way brothers do on the streets, but they're more brutal. They cut and shoot you in ways that don't draw blood, but the pain runs deeper and lasts longer.

"And there are some of the strangest black people you've ever seen. If you put some of them behind a wall and heard them talk, you wouldn't know they were black. It's not just the way they sound, but the way they *think*. It's like they've been trained by white folks to think like them. They ain't no use to nobody."

Bimbo looked at his dinner plate and said, "I wouldn't wish white people on my worst enemy. . . . Sometimes, man, I just wish black people would take to the streets and tear this motherfucka up, like we used to talk about doin' when we was comin' up."

"Hey, man, they too busy noddin' out. They too doped up and cooled out to tear up anything. Drugs have taken all the fight outta them."

Then I changed the subject. "So, Bimbo, how you feel about having all that money?"

"It's O.K., but it ain't everything. I'm thinkin' about openin' up a business. What would you do if you had this money?"

"I'd tell the white man to *kiss my ass*. I'd travel, read all the books I wanna read, and write what I wanna write. Money is freedom, man."

Bimbo and I stayed at the restaurant talking until the place closed. I glanced up, and workers were cleaning the tables and looking at us like they were anxious for us to leave. Bimbo dropped me back at my mother's house and we split. Of course, we exchanged phone numbers, but I've spoken with him only once since that night. I called a second time and he'd had his number changed. I assumed he did that to duck the brothers.

■ ■ ■

Often, when I went home, I'd spend most of the time at my parents' house. That made me feel good. They were proud that I seemed to have turned my life around. I knew my parents and my brothers still didn't quite understand how I'd done it, and I sensed at times they wanted to ask. But *how* I'd done it was less important than *that* I'd done it. My stepfather made it a point from time to time to tell me, "I want you to know that we're real proud of you."

I'd get a lump in my throat. I'd look him in the eye, then I'd have to turn away. I hadn't understood him when I was young, but now, after getting a taste of the real world, the white world, I understood perfectly why he had been the way he was.

My mother seemed to be preoccupied with trying to save my brother Dwight. Junnie was winding down a career in the Army. Billy was working two jobs to support his family. And Bryan, the youngest, was working at Blockbuster Video and living at home. Dwight was off parole, but he was always in and out of labor jobs, living from paycheck to paycheck. Every time he got his own apartment, he'd get evicted and have to regroup all over again. Every time it seemed he was about to hit rock bottom, my mother would take him in or give him money. Sometimes he came by the house to eat a good meal. Other times, when the tension between him and my stepfather was thick, he'd stop by for a plate and keep pushing. Whenever she sensed Dwight was really bad off, my mother would have Bryan take him a plate wrapped in aluminum foil or she'd persuade my stepfather to let him back in the house, even after she vowed not to do it anymore.

I kept telling Mama to let Dwight go. His weakness was taking a toll on her. Almost every time I visited or called the house, she had a story to tell about Dwight: "Guess what Dwight did? We cosigned for him to get a car and he stopped making payments on it and messed up our credit."

She would always say, "I ain't lending Dwight no more money because he don't never pay it back." Then I'd talk to her again and she would say, "I ain't got much money. I had to lend some to your brother so he wouldn't get put out in the streets. I'd hate to see the boy livin' in the streets."

I hated seeing my mother go through that and got mad at Dwight sometimes. I kept telling her, "You have to let him fall before he can begin to lift himself up. As long as he knows you're going to bail him out, he'll continue getting into jams."

She'd listen, but go right on helping Dwight. So the revolving door continued turning.

I didn't want to give up on my brother, either, but I didn't want to see him hurting my mother so. She worried about him all the time. I understand now that that's just the nature of a mother's love. A boy's blood daddy will get fed up and throw him into the streets on his head, but a mother is connected to her children in ways men don't understand.

Besides, my mother had reason to have faith. She had had plenty of reason to give up on me one time, but she held on until I pulled through. So it wasn't too hard to understand why she held on for Dwight. She felt she had a reason to believe.

■ ■ ■

Driving down Martin Luther King, Jr., Boulevard, back in Atlanta, I pulled behind a brother driving a beat-up Cutlass Supreme. He was gangster-leaning, cruising real slow in the passing lane, like he had nowhere to go and couldn't care less if other drivers did. I rode behind him for about a block, then switched to the right lane and shot by him to try to beat the yellow light. Too late. It turned red. A few seconds later, brotherman pulled up beside me at the light and tooted his horn. I looked over. He put on a killer scowl and said scornfully, "Yo, slim, you in a hurry?"

It pissed me off. I thought, *He gonna hold up traffic, then get* grand *on me for passing him.* I said, "Yeah, I'm in a hurry."

"Well, I ain't." He was staring hard now, like he intended to chump me down.

I thought, *I ain't no chump. I'm a man, just like him.* I said sarcastically, "I can see *you* ain't in a hurry."

He felt challenged when I didn't back down. "You don't like it?"

My turn: "Naw, I don't like it."

"Pull over when the light changes. We can settle it right here and now."

"O.K., I'll be there." A grown man with a wife, children, and a professional job, I was ready to toss all that aside and get downright *street* with some dude at a stoplight. It was all so silly, so juvenile, and counter to what I was trying to be about, yet I couldn't resist the temptation to demand respect. It was all so small, but on the block, the sheer pettiness of a thing is often what gets folks killed. Brothers die in such confrontations every day.

Show time. That was my constant struggle and perpetual fear: that I'd cross some cat who hates his own skin and takes it out on me because I look like him; that I'd inadvertently bump into some dude willing to put his devalued life on the line to prove a foolish manhood point.

So there I was, at a stoplight, preparing, for all I knew, to meet my Maker. I didn't know if he was armed, and he didn't know what I had. But we were both ready to take it to the hoop and see where it led.

The senselessness of the situation dawned on me in the seconds before the light changed. In a fraction of a second I calculated the possibilities and weighed the potential for loss and gain: *He must be armed. Fistfighting went out with Afro picks and platform shoes. Even if by chance homeboy is an old-school rumbling man, I'll win no trophies or awards for throwing down with him.* I told myself, *Nathan, let it ride. Walk away from this one while you can.*

When the light changed, my man put on his blinkers and pulled over to the side of the road, like he had promised. I pulled up beside him, tooted my horn, then drove away.

Chapter 41 HELL

I had forgotten how painful life can be. Now, with my divorce pending, it reminds me that life can be very painful, so painful that it becomes a physical ache, a strained feeling in the heart area that can only be relieved by time. I've weathered some tough storms in my 33 years. This one ranks right up there with the toughest of them.
March 11, 1988

■ ■ ■

Compared to my divorce, doing time in prison was like a day at the beach. Divorce is *hell,* pure and simple, a classic example of how screwed-up and backward-thinking the court system is. More than in any other ordeal in my crazy life, my frustrations with the courts during and after my divorce showed me that the folks running the system don't have a clue.

Nothing in that process works as it should. Nobody has figured out a way to make divorce fair to all concerned. Some women get shafted beyond belief, while others abuse the system and use the courts to slam-dunk their men. Some men abandon their parental duties and skip out, certain that the system can't or won't track them down. Those men who *do* try to be responsible for their kids often get pushed aside and financially beaten down, it seems, in retaliation for those who don't. And children get caught in the middle of all that mess.

Divorce. Somebody gets fucked up *real bad,* no matter which way it goes.

■ ■ ■

Debbie and I had to go through an endless series of hearings and postponements that stretched out for more than a year before the final court appearance. That provided ample time for hostilities between us to simmer and grow. We shared a tension-filled house and nothing more. We slept in the same bed, but barely spoke to each other except to take care of household matters. All the while, Ian and Maya swarmed happily around us, too young to fully understand the depth of the conflict between their parents.

Debbie and I knew we couldn't live together anymore, yet neither of us wanted to leave the house. I wanted to stay because it was *my* house, bought with *my* money. Debbie said she wanted to stay because she had the kids. Actually, her reason was nobler than mine, but I couldn't see past my anger enough to realize that.

Being in the house together created an atmosphere that was volatile and scary at times. One night, when Debbie and I got into an argument, she came charging at me, swinging wildly and banging me with her fists. Ian heard the ruckus and came running from his bedroom into ours. Maya came behind him. Ian started crying, and Maya cried, too.

Ignoring the children, Debbie kept swinging. I grabbed her wrists to keep her from hitting me, and we both fell onto the bed. She got madder then. As the children screamed, she ran to a phone and called the police. By the time the cops showed up, she'd calmed down enough to let me convince her to send them away.

The incident showed me that Debbie knew her greatest weapon against me was the law. After that run-in, I was sure that if anything funky went down, I'd be back in jail.

■ ■ ■

Whenever I step into a courtroom—for anything—I get flashbacks of the past and see terrifying images of white ghosts sentencing me. I always get ready to bend over because I know I've got it coming. I always think about something we used to say on the block: "Be sure to take a jar of Vaseline with you to court 'cause you gonna get fucked."

On the day of the final hearing, I sat in the courtroom with my palms sweating and my head throbbing, furious that I had to go before an old white man to get permission to dissolve a relationship that was already dead.

I was mad at everybody, including my lawyer. When I'd fallen behind on my legal bills, he stopped working on the case. I went to the bank and got a five-thousand-dollar loan to cover the fee, and he got back on the case again. He made it *real* clear that, first and foremost, he was about money.

Of course, Debbie's family all came to town and sat in on some of the trial. I looked across the room at my wife and her mother and thought about the irony that the same two people pressing for me to get married were now clamoring for my head. *They gonna use the system to punish me 'cause I wouldn't get with the program.*

During one of her trips to the witness stand, Debbie unleashed a bomb that left me nearly floored. She told the judge, "Your Honor, I'm afraid of Nathan. He has been to *prison* for violence."

I was stunned. I considered that the ultimate betrayal. It was clear that she understood racial dynamics well enough to use my prison past to her benefit. I thought, *Go on. Tip off the judge. Let him know there's a dangerous black man here who needs to be controlled.*

I sat there and listened as her lawyer used legalese to call me every kind of no-good motherfucka in the book. "He did willfully" do this and "he maliciously" did that. The thing that bothered me most was that they tried to make it appear that I didn't want to support my children. I kept wondering, *How can they even suggest that? I got married for the sake of the children.*

The case was simple to me. Debbie wanted the house and a thousand dollars a month in child support. I couldn't afford to pay that much, live, and send money for Monroe, too. But it didn't seem to matter what I couldn't do. In the end, I got hit with support obligations that I couldn't possibly meet—five hundred dollars a month in child support. She got to stay in the house and I was ordered to pay the mortgage, nearly seven hundred dollars each month. The total came out to about twelve hundred dollars a month, half of my take-home pay.

When the judge brought down the gavel, I felt like I'd been sentenced to do time all over again. I was crushed. Humiliated. I felt like I was being punished because the marriage didn't work. All I could do was shake my head. *One of the few times in my life when I really tried to do what I thought was right and I get kicked square in the behind.*

On the way out, I asked my lawyer, "What am I supposed to do, go live in a homeless shelter? What about the costs associated with getting a new place after kicking out all those legal fees?"

He said, "You've *got* to pay it or they'll throw you in jail." Then he reminded me that I had to pay him, too.

I said, "But I'm not saying I refuse to pay child support. I'm saying I *can't* pay that full amount and survive. Isn't there somebody I can talk to to explain?!"

"No." Then he looked at me and did what lawyers often do. He shrugged his shoulders and said, "That's just the way it is."

That's just the way it is. People in the system say that all the time.

Like there's no way in heaven that a thing can be changed, because they're locked into an established way of doing that thing. Like they can't bring common sense into the system to correct a proven flaw. *That's just the way it is.*

When I left the courtroom and walked through the shiny halls, I saw Debbie's family down at the elevator, skinnin' and grinnin' and congratulating her.

■ ■ ■

Claxton and Chip went with me to help remove my possessions from the house. Chip and I were in the basement gathering things when Claxton appeared at the top of the stairs and called down to me: "Yo, Nate, there's somebody here to see you."

I went upstairs and saw two policemen standing in the living room. One of the officers said, "Your ex-wife called and said you're taking things from the house that don't belong to you."

Debbie appeared from a back room. The lawman asked her what possessions I was taking that weren't mine. She pointed to a piece of artwork that I'd taken down from the wall. The artwork had been a gift, given to me by Chip and his girlfriend before I got married. I dug into my pocket and whipped out a court-approved list of my possessions and showed the lawman that the artwork in question was included on the list. Seeing that, the cop got mad as hell. He turned to Debbie and got on her case hard for needlessly calling the police on me. "Why would you do something like this?! Don't *ever* do anything like this again!"

Debbie looked sheepishly back at him and kept quiet.

The scene was pitiful. It was so pathetic that I didn't even get mad. When I looked at Debbie standing there, I saw clearly the extremes she'd go to in order to get at me. I felt ashamed that others saw it, too, and that they knew that I'd married someone who would stoop so low.

The cops left, and for a moment the living room was silent. I stood there, looking disgustedly at the woman who was once my wife. She glared defiantly back at me. And Claxton and Chip looked on, shaking their heads in disbelief.

■ ■ ■

They called it "joint custody." What it really meant was that Debbie got the children and I got to "visit" them every other weekend. I had no say in decisions about where they went to school or in anything else involving their lives. As it turned out, Debbie's parents had more access to Ian and Maya than I did. It was frustrating, and my lawyer kept telling me that there was nothing I could do. *That's just the way it is.*

Even the visitation itself was rife with strains. I never knew what to expect when I went over there, so I'd take Chip along to serve as a witness in case something ugly jumped off. Once, when we got to the house, there was no one home. No note, nothing. I knew Debbie was expecting me because I'd just talked to her by phone.

After that happened more than once, I filed a contempt action to have the judge force her to comply with the visitation order. We got into court, and when the judge learned that I'd fallen behind on child-support payments, he refused to hear my complaint about visitation. I told him I was doing all I could to raise the money needed to catch up. He looked at me coolly and said, "I suggest you file for bankruptcy."

The message from the judge was clear to me: The courts view the father mainly as the money source. *That's just the way it is.*

■ ■ ■

In no time, I got caught in that recurring cycle that body-slams lots of men after divorce: Every time I fell behind on support payments, Debbie filed an action to take me to court. Every time I went to court, it forced me to spend money on legal fees. (The judge would order me to pay her lawyer, too.) That was money that could have been used to help catch up on support payments.

It went round and round like that until I'd exhausted all my savings on legal fees and support payments, and gone deep into debt. I applied to banks and credit unions, and couldn't get another loan. After getting an apartment, I had no money to live on and had to hit up my parents and friends for money. All the while, I kept wondering about life in the fucking system, which just didn't seem to be working for me.

I knew it was just a matter of time before I fell so far behind that they'd lock me up for failure to pay child support. Desperate and depressed, I began to think illogically. At one point, I thought about dropping everything, just quitting my job and going underground to get white folks off my back.

None of my domestic problems related directly to my race— divorce is a universal hell—but when compounded with all my racial stresses, the divorce and its aftermath took a greater toll. My head was messed up so bad that I'd go for days sometimes without any sleep.

Even now—five years later—I still have occasional problems getting to sleep at night.

Sometimes, when I thought about what I was going through, I felt sorry for myself and wondered why I seemed to spend most of my life catching hell. I'd think, *Maybe this is God's way of paying me back for all the hurt and pain I've dished out to other folks. Maybe I need to accept it as divine justice and quietly take my lumps.*

At other times, I looked at it another way: that the anguish was the price I had to pay to be able to live with myself and face the world; that two of my children could say that their parents had been married, no matter how brief or ugly that union had been.

■ ■ ■

Every now and then, I ran across other dudes who'd been through the same hell as me. We'd spend hours comparing notes and sharing horror tales. Every one of them had a piece of divorce-related advice to give. Sometimes they said things I needed to hear. Like the one friend who told me, "No matter what goes down, take the high road. It's important that you be able to look back on this and feel good about the way you handled yourself."

Sometimes cats told me things I didn't need to hear. Like the tale about one guy who took matters into his own hands when his wife wouldn't let him see his children and the courts refused to do anything to enforce his rights. "He knocked that bitch's front teeth out," a friend told me. "He got thirty days in jail for it, but you know what? Every time he goes round there to get his children now, she hands them over and don't give him no problems."

Those rap sessions carried a lot of weight with me and sometimes affected what I thought and did. I decided that I wanted to do what was right—take the high road—but the notion of knocking out Debbie's teeth also carried some appeal for me.

One day, I went to the house to try to talk with her about calling a truce so that we could stop making lawyers rich. As I sat on the couch, she stood over me, ranting. She went off. Blah, blah, blah, blah . . . I sat there, quietly listening. Suddenly, I couldn't make out what she was saying anymore. Her lips moved and her arms flailed, but I couldn't hear. Without being aware, I'd slipped into a zone. I've been in that zone before. I went into it just moments before I shot Plaz. It's a semi-conscious state where nothing gets absorbed and all logic and reason shut down for the night.

I looked at Debbie and thought about all the anxiety she'd put me through. I thought about the incompetent court system and how it seemed that nobody cared what was happening to me. I thought about taking the high road, then about the cat who'd "knocked that bitch's front teeth out." Something inside me said, *Yeah, knock her front teeth out. You can do thirty days in jail standing on your head.*

That familiar tightness formed in my chest, that fight-or-flight feeling that used to come over me in the old days on the streets. I felt it rising, like vomit just before it convulses you and forces its way out of your mouth. I felt myself about to leap up and punch her in the face. I felt it coming over me, and I got scared. I knew that if I got up from that couch and took one swing—*one swing*—it would get *good* to me and I wouldn't stop. I wouldn't stop until I was completely exhausted or until my ex-wife was stone cold dead. As I sat there, mute, the voices of divorce veterans kept whispering, competing for control: *Knock that bitch's front teeth out. No, take the high road.*

I'd recently read an article about the benefits of counseling. Written by a psychologist, the article said that people don't realize they have to take care of their mental health in the same way they tend to their physical health. The writer said people routinely go to doctors for physical checkups, even when they know there's nothing wrong with them. People should go to counselors, he said, for mental checkups.

That made all the sense in the world to me. I thought about that article as I sat there contemplating whether or not to attack my ex-wife. I decided, then and there, that I needed counseling. I got up from the couch and walked out the door without saying anything, leaving Debbie still in the living room, raising hell.

The next day, I contacted a counselor and went in for therapy. The counselor was a white woman. She seemed to understand right away what I was going through. Seeing how hyped and uptight I was, she prescribed some medication to chill me out. She also gave me her beeper number and said, "Now listen. I want you to put this number in your wallet and keep it with you at all times. I don't care where you are—if that feeling ever comes over you again, call this number and talk to me."

It was comforting to know I had someone to call if I needed advice. That, more than anything, helped me eliminate thoughts about turning violent again. I came close to the edge once or twice after that, but each time, the assurance that I had someone to turn to was enough to calm me. That counselor doesn't know it, but she probably saved Debbie's life.

■ ■ ■

I've come to believe that there's a higher force looking out for me, and it moves on my behalf, right on time. Early in 1989, I got another call from *The Washington Post*. As Milton Coleman promised, they'd kept an eye on me. They called to invite me back for another job interview. They had an opening on their City Hall staff and wanted to know if I was interested.

After more than six years in Atlanta, I knew it was time to move on. I also knew I had to escape a domestic situation that was bringing me down.

I went to the *Post* interview feeling confident that I'd reached the point that, two years earlier, Milton Coleman had told me about: I'd done enough in my career to overshadow my prison past. I had built a track record.

I interviewed with the usual battery of people and found it easy to talk about the embarrassment that had occurred in 1987. For the final interview, I was ushered into a large office in the back of the news-room, where Ben Bradlee, the paper's famous executive editor, sat behind a desk, talking to Leonard Downie, the managing editor. We talked about a lot of things and finally got around to discussing the flap of two years earlier, when they'd found out about my prison record. Speaking in his raspy voice, Bradlee asked, "Why didn't you tell us?"

I told him about my experience in Louisville, where I thought I'd lost the job because I came clean. "I vowed after that that before I told anyone else about my past I'd first get a foot in the door to prove myself."

Bradlee said, "Did Bill Kovach know about your prison record?"

I said, "Yes, I told him."

"What did he say?"

"Kovach said he didn't care about that. He told me that if anybody gave me a hard time about my prison record to let him know."

Bradlee smiled, looked at Downie, nodded, and said, "Good for Bill."

I knew then that I had the job.

Chapter 42 **THE BIG TIME**

On a hot summer day in 1989, reporters crowded into the conference room at City Hall and jostled with photographers and television cameramen competing for choice spots. The reporters, acting like one big inquisitive family, gossiped while they waited for the mayor to appear. He was already late. No big deal. He was always late.

But this was Washington, D.C., not Atlanta, and I was feeling a little nervous as I sat near an aisle toward the front of the room. Everybody else there seemed to know their way around City Hall. They knew what buttons to push for news tips and where to find information they needed. I would have to watch and learn.

Suddenly, there was a rumbling near the door. Reporters rushed to their places and readied their cameras and pens. The mayor was coming. In walked Marion Barry, tall, dark, confident, and dressed to a T. He sported a dark, tapered, pinstripe suit coordinated perfectly with a heavily starched shirt, a matching tie with a gold tie pin, and dark Florsheims, the kind the hustlers wear on the black side of town. Surrounded by an entourage of security men and assistants, Barry stepped coolly through the doorway, paused for a second to straighten his tie, then scanned the gathering and stepped to a podium before a hundred microphones. Like soldiers, reporters snapped to attention and immediately began hurling questions and sparring with one of the most controversial, charismatic local politicians in the country.

By the summer of 1989, the media had already begun doing stories about Barry's rumored drug use and womanizing. That made him the hottest news topic in the nation's capital. I found it inconceivable that such rumors could be true. How could the mayor of one of the most highly visible cities in the whole wide world be so stupid? How could the person who was a folk hero to local blacks, who went around to city schools urging young children to "Just say no" to drugs, be so boldly hypocritical? *No way,* I thought.

During the press conference, reporters almost lunged at the mayor with questions about his behavior. Barry looked directly into the television cameras and told the world that he had never used drugs a

day in his life. In fact, he said, he abhorred drug use and was committed to fighting the scourge of drugs tearing apart black communities
in Washington and across the nation. As arrogant and cagey as any
politician, Barry answered those questions he wanted to address and
refused to answer those he didn't like. He weathered the scrutiny like
a pro and seemed to relish sparring with reporters he knew by name.
I sat there quietly, fascinated by this intelligent man who was haunted
by self-destructive tendencies and irresistibly drawn to the streets.

After several minutes of addressing more mundane questions about
the city budget, Barry abruptly ended the circus, leaving reporters
hanging with many unanswered questions.

Before leaving, the mayor walked down the aisle through the
throng of reporters, speaking to some and joking with others while
straightening his tie and primping in his tailored suit. When he
reached the spot where I sat, he stopped, looked me up and down, and
said, "What's your name?"

I took the inquiry to mean that if he didn't notice every reporter
in the City Hall press pool, he certainly noticed every *black* face in the
bunch. "I'm Nathan McCall."

"Who you with?"

"I'm with *The Washington Post.* I'm going to be covering the city
council."

Barry said, "Where you from?"

"I came here from *The Atlanta Journal-Constitution.*"

He nodded. "Atlanta, huh?"

"Yeah."

Pause. He gave me a hearty slap on the shoulder, grinned broadly,
and said, "Welcome to the big time." Then he strutted off.

■   ■   ■

Indeed, I had finally reached the big time. Washington, D.C. The
capital of the so-called Free World. The president of the U.S.A. lived
in and operated from this city; the White House was just a few blocks
up from City Hall. Less than a mile away, the U.S. Capitol sat
majestically at the end of the Mall.

Washington was one of the most beautiful cities I'd ever seen:
electric, pulsating, with its bustling traffic and historic government
buildings, its sidewalk cafés and basement bars, its brownstone row
houses and trendy high-rises. Riding through the streets, I remembered how I used to go to Washington with my classmates on field
trips in junior high school. We'd save our money for months, then

take the four-hour ride on chartered buses and tour the museums and historic monuments. I'd never thought I'd be living there.

I rented a seventh-floor apartment in the southwest section of town, near the waterfront. The apartment had a splendid view of the Capitol. It was within walking distance of the Mall, all the famous monuments, and the Smithsonian museums. It was not far from work, and it was close to theaters and good seafood restaurants.

It felt good being farther north. I knew I had left the Deep South when I stopped seeing leather-faced white men in Red Man caps and flannel shirts driving pickup trucks with rifle racks. I hoped that something I'd heard all my life would prove true: that the racial dynamics were better farther north. Certainly, I didn't feel the open hostility in D.C. that had kept me on edge in the Deep South. At a glance, it seemed to me that whites in D.C. were a more sophisticated, better-educated bunch. I figured the racial tolerance would be higher there because D.C. attracted people of diverse cultures and nationalities from all over the world.

Still, there were early indications that my hope to escape the burdens of race was asking for too much: when I saw black elementary school–age kids standing on corners with Windex and washcloths, begging motorists to let them clean their windshields for coins; when I saw white people at stoplights roll up their car windows at the sight of homeless black beggars, then hand dollar bills to homeless whites.

I got my personal initiation into D.C.'s own brand of racism when white workers in stores and restaurants went all out to please white patrons but dragged ass on me; when taxi drivers routinely passed me by, then stopped to pick up whites standing a few feet away. Finally, I was forced to acknowledge the thing that I'd often heard other blacks say: that it doesn't matter whether it's North or South, racism afflicts the whole U.S. of A.

■   ■   ■

D.C. has a larger, more entrenched black middle class than Atlanta. On the positive side, these blacks seem more assertive and politically astute. On the other hand, they are illustrations of a widely held view of middle-class blacks everywhere: In spite of all their money, skills, and potential, they're one of the most confused, alienated groups in the land. Middle-class blacks in D.C. are some of the most bourgeois, pretentious, snooty black folks I've seen anywhere. Some act like they are fourth- and fifth-generation aristocrats.

I got my fill of that pretentiousness one night when in an effort to meet more people I went to a meeting of a black ski club. Everybody there was boasting about their world travels. "Oh, honey, I just got back from Barbados. I had a *wonderful* time!"

"Oh? I need a vacation, chile. I'm thinking about doing Aruba next month. I'm *sooo* tired! I went to South America on business for a few weeks, and I just got back. I need a break."

They fronted hard, but I guessed that half of them were probably one paycheck away from being exposed. I felt like standing up and saying, "Look, we're all descendants of slaves, so let's cut this pompous shit!"

After listening to them tell lies and put on airs for half an hour, I left and never went back.

Anytime I want to get in touch with *real* black people in a city and take the pulse of street life there, I scope out a funky barbershop in a serious working-class neighborhood. I found the perfect spot in northwest Washington. Half the barbers, I was sure, had taken up their trade during prison stints. They had cocky penitentiary mannerisms that I recognized from Southampton, as well as that rock-hard musculature from pumping iron. They wore their hats while cutting hair, and talked as loud and crazy as their customers.

There was a constant stream of brothers and sisters in and out of this place, and a lot of them didn't come in for haircuts. Some of the cats who came through there were small-time hustlers and druggies who stopped in and offered "good deals" on shoes, shirts, jackets— whatever they'd stolen that day. Others went straight to the back of the shop, where the owner took a cut on card and crap games held in a smoky room.

My barber was an old-head in his early fifties, known around the neighborhood for being quick-tempered and hip. He kept a pistol in his drawer and a fifth of scotch, which he nursed constantly in a paper cup. I learned to get in his chair before Friday evening, when he was juiced up and his clippers were unsteady. I'd go in there some Fridays and he'd already be dressed to go out on the town after the last head was cut. He'd have on a wide-brimmed hat and a bright red shirt with a butterfly collar opened wide so you could see his rope-sized gold chain. He'd also be wearing a pair of pants that matched his double-knit jacket, which looked like the upper half of a walking suit. If you told him he wasn't clean, he'd probably shoot you with that piece he kept stashed away.

I liked that shop because I could always get a good bet on the latest boxing match, pick up on the latest street slang, or get a line on the working-class view of politics in D.C. Going there was a bit like hanging out at the 7-Eleven at home without being exposed to the risks. Sometimes I'd repeatedly forgo my turn in the chair while trying not to be so obvious about the fact that I just wanted to extend my stay.

■ ■ ■

Going from *The Atlanta Journal-Constitution* to *The Washington Post* was like going from college football to the pros. It seemed that practically everybody in the *Post* newsroom was a pro at what he did.

I spent my first few weeks at the *Post* in disbelief. I knew I'd gotten there by my own doing, yet there was a kind of shock that I had actually pulled it off. The first day I walked into the newsroom and went to my assigned desk, there was a nameplate already there. It read simply: Nathan McCall. I stared at the name as though detached from it, then let these words roll softly off my tongue: *Nathan McCall at The Washington Post.*

Almost every morning I'd enter the Post building on Fifteenth Street and wonder at the fact that I was entering a historic institution, a place where reporters were so good they'd actually brought down a president of the United States. And here I was, an ex-con, a former armed robber, working among them. That irony made me dizzy. It seemed like another installment in a big, continuous dream.

I spent a lot of time gawking, like a young stargazer, at all the legends I'd read about. Ben Bradlee bopped through the newsroom, sporting his starched two-tone shirts and matching ties. Katharine Graham, the owner of the paper, drifted through from time to time. Once I went to an in-house workshop on investigative reporting led by Bob Woodward, one of the two reporters who had broken the Watergate story.

Although I was awestruck, I constantly reminded myself that I was there because I, too, had something on the ball. I thought, *I deserve to be here as much as anyone in this room.*

Still, the *Post* felt like a strange and alien world to me. Many of the people there, I learned, were silver-spoonish, trust-fund babies raised and educated in the insulated Ivy League. They were smart, but in a narrow, elitist way. They could expound at length about all kinds of esoterica, and they knew all there was to know about the intricacies of politics and people around the world. Yet they seemed to know nothing about blacks in the city where they lived and worked, or about those African Americans sitting in the newsroom next to them.

I hadn't been at the paper more than a week when I spotted Tom Lippman, the guy who had implied a few years earlier at the Missouri seminar that the *Post* had a hard time finding minorities because so many of them had criminal records. As soon as I saw him I wanted to rush over and say, "See! Even guys with criminal records can do O.K. if given a chance."

When he saw me he averted his eyes, but I made it a point to go over and say hello. As we chatted, I wondered what he thought of my being there. I could tell he was uncomfortable, and I enjoyed the torture. I knew he'd be uneasy every time he saw me, and I wanted it to stay that way.

■ ■ ■

I was part of a three-member team of reporters assembled to cover City Hall and prepare for an upcoming election in which Mayor Barry was expected to receive several strong challenges. I was assigned to cover the D.C. city council. Another reporter, Rob Melton, covered the mayor. A third reporter, Michael Abramowitz, was sort of the general-assignment reporter on the team. Our editor, Eric Pianin, would coordinate the coverage. Our team, I learned, was put together to kill the competition.

I relished the challenge of learning a new city and figuring out the nuances of its politics, and I had no trouble figuring out the lay of the land at City Hall. But I discovered that it was not so easy dealing with my own newsroom, starting with Pianin, my editor. Soon after I arrived, I had trouble transmitting a story through the *Post*'s computer system. Pianin said over the phone, "Nathan, deadline is near. Just *send* the story!"

I didn't like the tone of his voice. Such impatience seemed unreasonable during my first few days on the job. I swallowed hard and remained calm, but the following day, when I went into the newsroom, I walked over to Pianin and told him I'd like to speak with him.

We went downstairs to the cafeteria for a cup of coffee and talked. I said, "I wanted to talk because it upset me a little when you raised your voice at me. I was wondering if there was something we needed to talk about so that it doesn't happen again."

He explained the computer system and deadlines. Fine. No problem. Cool. Not a great start, but that's O.K. I saw where I stood and what I faced with him. Pianin was a white guy from the Midwest. From the start, something about him had set off alarms. Some white people are whiter than others. They were raised in insulated, exclusively white settings, and have had little exposure to anything else. They have a worldview that sees whiteness as *the* standard and everything else as abnormal. I could spot such people in a stadium crowd. I could feel their overwhelming whiteness in my interactions with them. Pianin was that sort of guy.

In one of my first conversations with Pianin when I got to the *Post*, I asked him if other reporters knew about my prison record. He said yes and added that some had complained about the *Post*'s having hired an ex-con. I wondered if he was one of the complainers. I wondered even more when we started working together. I sensed his impatience with me, which contrasted sharply with how he treated Abramowitz. I knew what that was about. Smart-assed white boys. They think they're the only ones who can do the job, and anyone else who comes in and tries gets the cold shoulder, the white-boy double-bank. Consequently, every time I made a mistake, Pianin seemed to take it personally. Every time Abramowitz made a mistake, though, it was "Well, you know, he's a young go-getter." Seeing all that, I thought, *It never ends. You always have to fight them with your hands tied behind you.*

My relationship with my team partners was no more promising. Melton was a tall, mysterious white boy with a semi-pompous air. He was an excellent reporter, but his personality was as changeable as the wind. Not the kind of guy you go out for drinks or slap shoulders with. We seldom talked. Abramowitz was a twenty-four-year-old upstart trying to win a permanent spot on the political team. He reminded me of a bouncy but frumpy puppy. He was friendly but conspiratorial. Did a lot of whispering with Melton and Pianin. I noticed right off that he monitored my stories closely, as if he were keeping tabs on me.

It didn't take long for Abramowitz and me to butt heads. I noticed that whenever Melton and Abramowitz worked on stories together, Abramowitz fed information to Melton, who did the writing. But whenever Abramowitz and I worked together, there was a power struggle to see who would write the story. It was an irritating reminder of something I'd learned long ago: No matter how old or experienced you get, white boys are always going to assume that they're better and know more, even if they're right out of college, like Abramowitz was.

The first few times I felt tension from Abramowitz, I let him be the lead writer, to see if he'd extend the courtesy the next time around. Nothing doing. As long as I was willing to let him take the lead, he took it. He also tried to undermine me on stories. Whenever he was called upon to feed information to me, he didn't seem to hustle to get me the best quotes. When he fed info to Melton, he worked like a slave.

After several months of taking this, I went to Pianin and talked with him about Abramowitz's uncooperativeness. Pianin shrugged it off. "He's young and competitive," he said.

The atmosphere at the *Post* was fraught with competition that was so intense that there were always sparks flying everywhere. Whites, who understood and willingly played the game, seemed to have no problem elbowing and cutthroating to get their way. Like many blacks, though, I took conflicts personally and spent a lot of time trying to figure out what they meant. I wondered if Abramowitz was racist, merely competitive, or both. This whole situation brought home a problem that remains a constant source of irritation to me: Race relations in this country have become so complex and convoluted that it's hard nowadays to tell in interactions with whites what's racial and what's not.

When problems persisted, I went to the city editor and talked with her about it. Her response was similar to Pianin's. She said, "Oh, he's just a little insecure."

It pissed me off seeing everybody make excuses for the white boy. Nobody makes allowances for black folks anywhere.

Having done my part in trying to address these concerns, I called Abramowitz, looked him in the eye, and outlined the problems I had with him. He apologized, and we went our separate ways.

One day not long afterward, Abramowitz and I were working a story together. I completed my reporting and waited on him. Rather than pass along his information so that I could begin writing, though, he withheld it and busied himself with other things. I told him, "Mike, send me the info."

He stalled again. "All right," he said, "I've got a few more things to gather."

I left work that day furious. The deadline was nearing and we hadn't even started writing. The following morning, a Saturday, I was already at the office, waiting, when Abramowitz arrived. I'd decided it was time to talk—this time seriously. I had played by the rules and been ignored. I had heard all the excuses I wanted to hear. I said, "Mike, I need to talk to you."

We sat down. I got very close to him, glared into his eyes, and said, "I want to know what your problem is."

He looked sheepish. "There's no problem," he said.

"Yes there is. I notice that when you work with Melton, there are no conflicts, but every time you work with me, there *are* problems. That suggests to me that you've got a problem with *me,* and I want to know what it is."

I was mad as hell. I scooted even closer and put my finger in his face. "Now, I've asked you twice about this. I'm not going to ask you again. The next time you try to undermine me on a story, I'm gonna *fuck you up!* You understand?"

He nodded like a scolded child. Then his eyes moistened and tears began running down his cheeks—right there in the newsroom.

Just then, Pianin walked in. He came over to where we were sitting and asked, "Is the story ready?"

I said nothing. Abramowitz hung his head. Pianin looked at Abramowitz, then at me, then walked away and went to his desk. A minute later, Abramowitz's phone rang. He picked it up and began talking softly. I looked across the room at Pianin and saw that he, too, was on the phone. Abramowitz hung up and went directly to Pianin's desk, where they talked some more. I felt like I was in a boxing ring being double-banked by my opponent *and* the referee.

Somehow, we finished the story. I don't even recall what it was about. After that incident, I realized what was up with my editor and the rest of the team, and I accepted the relationships for what they were. I realized that we weren't going to kill the competition after all. The competition was me.

■ ■ ■

I was at home the night Mayor Marion Barry was taped on camera and busted for smoking crack at the Vista Hotel. Somebody from the newsroom called and told me. I felt a mixture of emotions. Mostly, I was shocked that he could be so stupid. He *had* to know that the FBI and the media, particularly the *Post,* were watching him closely in light of the rumors about his drug abuse. I concluded that if Barry allowed himself to be snared, knowing he was being watched, then in all likelihood he'd lost control of himself and really *did* have a drug problem.

Barry's arrest affected me like many other disappointments involving blacks: Every time somebody black did some highly publicized evil or stupid thing, I cringed because I knew that, in white folks' eyes, it reflected badly on the whole race. Every time I heard news accounts of some drug bust, carjacking, robbery, or rape, I'd close my eyes and think, *I hope it wasn't a black person who did it.*

No matter how hard I fought, it was always there, that tendency to see us through the accusing eyes of whites. After Barry was caught, I saw indications that other blacks at the *Post* were also hypersensitive about our racial image. Some blacks in the newsroom got seriously uptight when they saw whites celebrating Barry's downfall with obvious glee.

■ ■ ■

My domestic problems didn't end when I moved to Washington. In fact, they seemed to get worse. I went back and forth to court in Atlanta so much that it felt sometimes like I'd never left.

When several months passed without me seeing my children, I got some time off, called Debbie, and arranged to visit them. When I reached town, I telephoned her and let her know what time I'd pick up the kids. I was excited at the prospect of seeing Ian and Maya, who were then seven and five years old. I planned to take them out for ice cream, and I thought about all that I wanted to talk with them about. Driving onto the street near the house, I passed a policeman who appeared to be patrolling the neighborhood. I pulled up to my old house, parked, and rang the doorbell. Strangely, the house was dark. I had talked to Debbie less than an hour before.

Then I heard footsteps behind me and turned around. A policeman—the same one I'd passed moments earlier—rushed across the yard. Clutching his revolver, he yelled, "Freeze! Don't move!"

I stood still, wondering what the hell was going on. The cop said, "Put your hands against the wall."

I said, "What's the problem?"

"Just do as I say and be quiet."

I turned, raised my hands high, and spread my legs. He reached into my back pocket, took out my wallet, then slapped on handcuffs and led me to the patrol car. When he shoved me into the backseat, that old familiar feeling came over me. I glanced at the mesh-wire shield between the front and rear seats and felt once again the pain of trying to balance myself with my hands cuffed behind my back.

I was sure it was all some mistake. *Maybe,* I thought, *the lawman took me to be a prowler.* It would be straightened out as soon as Debbie came out and told him she was expecting me. But she never showed. I glanced up at the house and spotted a shadow peeping through parted curtains in the living room.

I asked the cop, "Can you tell me what this is about?"

"There's been a felony warrant issued for your arrest."

I couldn't believe it. "A warrant? For what?"

"Nonpayment of child support and abandonment."

I almost shouted, "I haven't abandoned anybody! I'm legally divorced!"

The cop shrugged. All he knew, he said, was that the warrant was taken out by my ex-wife.

Then everything crystallized. Debbie set me up to go to jail! I thought, *Damn. I can't believe she'd go this far. But then, why shouldn't I believe it after all she's done?* True, I had fallen behind on my $1,200-a-month combined child-support and mortgage payment, but I'd gotten loans from my parents and put my car up for sale to try to catch up. I'd tried to get someone—anyone—in the court system to understand that I was doing my best to comply with the law. But no one cared. When I told my attorney I was constantly falling behind, he looked at me, shrugged, and asked for another payment on the amount I owed him. Every time I tried to catch up on my payments to him, I fell further behind on payments to Debbie, and vice versa. I couldn't return to court to have the child-support order modified. That would cost thousands more in legal fees. And my financial problems were compounded because D.C. is a much more expensive place to live than Atlanta.

The system. Instead of resolving problems, it created more. I was trying my damnedest to play by the rules, but too often the rules made no sense to me. Thinking about all that while sitting in the cop car, I slumped in my seat, refusing to accept what was happening to me.

Before taking me in, the lawman made one more stop. He drove to a remote building and picked up another man, who was being detained by a second cop. The man, a tall, black guy with handcuffs on, was shoved into the backseat beside me. We exchanged knowing glances and remained quiet.

We got to the Fulton County jail complex, where we were taken through electronic gates and ushered into a bull pen. I flopped down on one of three steel benches lining a concrete wall. The tall guy, who appeared to be in his late forties, stretched out on a bench across the room. There was one other inmate already there. Each of us chilled on his own bench and stared emptily into space. I wondered again why this was happening to me. *It must be my karma. It must be God's way of repaying me for all the brutal stuff I've done to other people.*

It had been twelve years since I'd been in a jail. I'd always feared some strange, freak incident would bring me back. As the years had passed, I'd begun to think I might be one of the lucky few who beat the odds and never returned. But the cycle of prison had caught up with me. The only difference between me and all the others I knew who had gone back to prison was that I'd fought harder and lasted longer than most of them.

I thought about the implications of my arrest. The *Journal-Constitution*, I was sure, would pick up on it. Maybe even my bosses at *The Washington Post* would find out. I could hear the newsroom gossip: "Did you hear, the guy with the criminal record got arrested again?" I doubted my bosses would be so forgiving this time.

At that moment, it seemed irrelevant whether or not the charges against me would stick. I was going to return to prison anyway. I made up my mind right then and there that I was going to murder my ex-wife. I was fed up with her hassling me. I thought, *Now it's my turn to retaliate.*

During the alloted telephone call, I called my homeboy Claxton, who set about the task of contacting my parents and trying to raise bail. When I returned to the cellblock, a fourth guy had been added to our den. He was a friendly, chatty, toothless dude who clearly was no stranger to the place.

The guards came and passed out ugly, dry bologna sandwiches. I gave mine away. The guy who had been the first in the cellblock, a younger man, went and stood over Mr. Friendly. "What if I take one of those sandwiches from you?"

Mr. Friendly said, "Naw, man. You can't have my sammich."

Youngblood said, "I'll take the shit." Then he hauled off and punched Mr. Friendly in the face. *Whack!*

I propped one foot on the bench and watched nonchalantly and considered the silliness of two fools coming to blows over a stale bologna sandwich. The guy who had ridden to jail with me stretched out and watched also. Neither of us moved to break up the fight.

The two guys punched and wrestled in the center of the cellblock, then Mr. Friendly shot Youngblood's cuffs. He lifted him off the ground and slammed him into the steel bench with such force that I thought he'd broken the young guy's back. He pinned him between the bench and the floor and punched his face, rapid-fire, until guards, alerted by the ruckus, rushed into the cellblock and tore them apart.

Mr. Friendly explained how the fight got started. Youngblood stood there, silent and no doubt embarrassed to have lost a rumble he had started. He was removed from the cellblock.

The brawl was a quick reminder to me that I was back in the jungle. I would have to dust off some old instincts and play it by ear.

The jailers finished processing us around 3 A.M. Then it was time to get us bedded down for the night. A group of us was herded to a shower area and ordered to strip naked. One guard lined us along a wall while another sprayed our pubic hair and underarms with stuff that looked and smelled like insecticide—they were spraying for lice. Afterward, we were issued ill-fitting uniforms and taken to cells.

I don't recall how I slept that night or whether I slept at all. All I remember is the muddy, tasteless food served for breakfast the next morning and the horrible feeling of being confined, the feeling that I'd lost control of my life again.

Later in the day, I was taken along with other new arrivals to a dormitory cellblock. The Fulton County jail was so overcrowded that there weren't enough beds to go around. Inmates slept on the walkways of tiers. It was a familiar scene that brought back memories of the Norfolk jail: brothers huddled around a picnic table, playing cards and talking trash; others watching television or lying lazily on their bunks. I scanned the room and thought about how every jail seemed to sound, smell, and look the same: bars, concrete, and shiny floors. All eyes fixed on me and the few other newcomers. I felt a perverted comfort in knowing I was an old pro at doing time. I felt none of the jitters that first-timers feel. I staked out a spot on the floor and threw my mattress down against a wall.

After getting settled, I ventured into the dayroom and spotted a chess match in progress. I asked, "Who's up next?"

One of the players looked up from the board and said, "Nobody."

"I'm next," I said. When my turn came around, I sat down, got engrossed in a game, and momentarily forgot about my cares.

By midday, I felt like an inmate again. I pinpointed the thinkers in the cellblock and chatted with them—about my case, about their cases, about rules and procedures governing such important matters as use of the jail canteen.

When lunchtime rolled around, the food tasted so bad that it inspired me to fast. I used my food to barter for toothpaste and other necessities. My corn bread got me a new toothbrush. For a carton of milk I got a ballpoint pen. A piece of chicken bought me a legal pad. And so on. After bartering through three meals, I had nearly everything I needed, including a few luxury items such as a comb and a brush.

I spent that second night in jail fantasizing about killing Debbie. *Maybe I could pay somebody to cancel her out. A single gunshot to the head would do.*

The next day, I made phone calls: to my homeboys, to my mother, to anybody who could help me raise the two thousand dollars needed to get me out. I played chess, read, fasted, and pondered life.

By the third day, the spirit of the fast had kicked in. It had been a long while since I'd fasted. Getting in touch with my spirit again helped me regain perspective. As I moved about the cellblock and learned the terrible circumstances most other inmates faced, my own troubles seemed less severe. Some of those dudes faced serious charges that would get them big time. Others had sat in jail for months because they were too poor to make a hundred dollars' bail. I realized that no matter what happened to me, I could bounce back if I drew again on my inner reserves.

I was released early on the morning of the fourth day. My parents and friends scraped up the money to get me out. By then, I'd abandoned all those crazy thoughts about killing my ex-wife. The spiritual fast had helped me see something that I'd lost sight of: Human beings are far too complex to be labeled completely good or totally bad. Debbie was a good mother to my children. She was angry at me, and definitely vengeful, but not a bad person by any stretch of the imagination.

When the guard came to the cellblock and called my name, I left my belongings for inmates to split, bid farewell to my chess partners, and wished them all well. I strolled outdoors and thanked the Creator. Once again, I was free.

Chapter 43 CYCLES

My arrival in D.C. was more than just a good career move. It put me closer to a ghost of the past I needed to confront. Her name was Carolyn, and even though I hadn't seen or talked with her since I was eighteen, she'd haunted me for years. Back during the days when the fellas and I were running trains and raising hell, I met Carolyn at a local amusement park. We rapped and got together one night when my parents were out of town. For me, it was supposed to be a quick hit-and-forget, a slam-bam-thank-you-ma'am. I picked her up on a designated corner, took her to my house, and got over. A month later, Carolyn told me she was pregnant.

"No way," I told her. We'd only been together that once. I figured that given the ease with which I'd gotten her into bed, other dudes had likely done the same. When she insisted she was pregnant by me, I thought up a scheme to duck the blame: The fellas and I would run a train, to try to create confusion about paternity. Naively, we figured that if a number of guys said they had trained a girl, she couldn't possibly know who was the father of her child.

One night, I had Carolyn meet me at the Zeus Club in Douglas Park. Using my stepfather's car, I took her for a cruise, with my friend Greg riding shotgun. A group of the fellas followed inconspicuously in a different car. On the way to the lake, where we planned to run the train, Carolyn noticed the other car. She got hysterical and began to scream. "Nathan, stop the car and let me out!"

I said, "Be cool, girl. It'll be all right."

"Nathan, if you don't stop the car, I'm gonna jump."

I tried to scare her by accelerating. But the next thing I knew, Carolyn, who was sitting in the front passenger seat, opened the door, jumped from the car, and landed in the street, smashing her head against the pavement. The car behind us swerved sharply and barely avoided running over her. I pulled to the side of the road and ran back to where Carolyn lay motionless. The impact had knocked her unconscious. She went into convulsions, spewing foam from her mouth and trembling, like she was having a seizure.

Of course the guys in the other car split. After helping us load Carolyn into the backseat of my stepfather's car, they left Greg and me to handle it alone. We drove her back crosstown near her sister's house, parked in a wooded area, and tried unsuccessfully to bring her to. She really needed medical care. Greg said, "We better take her to the hospital."

I was too scared. "We can't, man. If we take her to the hospital, they gonna call the fuzz."

You never know what you're capable of doing until confronted with that kind of irrational, crazy fear. Several times before, fear had driven me to do foolish things with potential consequences far severer than the fate I was trying to avoid. That night, I concluded we had no option left except the most desperate. I told Greg, "If anybody finds out what happened to her, we goin' to jail. We gotta kill her, man. We ain't got no choice. . . . We can throw her in those bushes over there."

Years later, Greg told me he'd had no intention of going through with my idea, but that night he looked like he was willing. All I know is, I'd decided it was something I *had* to do and I was feeling desperate enough to carry it out.

As we talked, an elderly woman walked up from nowhere and passed the car. Noticing Carolyn lying motionless in the backseat, she stopped and asked, "Is anything wrong?" Moving closer to the car, she spoke again, pointing to the backseat. "Wha's the matter wit dat chile?"

"Uh, nothin's wrong, ma'am. She just had a little too much to drink and we were trying to help her get herself together before we took her home."

"You sure she all right?" The woman was still peering into the car, straining in the pitch dark to get a better look.

"Yeah, she'll be all right. She just needs some fresh air. That's all. . . . We gonna take her home."

"All right. If ya'll need help with anything, come and knock on my door." She pointed toward a lone house set off from the road, back in the woods. It was strange: I hadn't noticed that house when we first parked out there.

After the woman left, it was clear that killing Carolyn was out of the question. The woman had seen our faces. She saw our car. Greg looked at Carolyn and said, "We gotta take her home now."

I said, "I ain't taking her. I don't want her people to see me."

Greg left me on a corner and took her alone, rang the doorbell, and told Carolyn's sister she'd had too much to drink. Then he returned and picked me up.

A few days later, my folks got a telephone call from Carolyn's parents. She had been hospitalized. Her father said she had told them she'd been out with me. He wanted an explanation and hinted he might call the cops. With my mother and stepfather, I went to their house to explain. Sitting in the living room with the four stern-faced adults, I made up an account of what went down. They listened calmly, then talked among themselves. Carolyn's parents seemed disinclined to drag the police into it. They were decent, hardworking people, much like my own parents. They asked me to leave the room. I don't know what was said. All I knew or cared about was that I got off the hook.

Some months later, Carolyn delivered a baby girl. I never saw the child before I was sent to the joint. After I got out of prison, Carolyn moved to Washington, and we lost contact.

But not entirely. Toward the end of my stay in Atlanta, I learned my mother had been in touch with Carolyn from time to time in those intervening years. My mother and my stepfather had taken diapers and other supplies to Carolyn when the child was very young. Carolyn had written letters to me and sent them to my mother's address. Mama never showed them to me. She kept the letters until she got one just as I was about to leave Atlanta. She sent it to me.

■　■　■

After I got settled in D.C., I did what I'd thought of doing for years. I got in touch with Carolyn and made arrangements to see her and her daughter in their place in northeast Washington. By then, her daughter was about eighteen, two years older than Monroe.

It was a trip seeing Carolyn after all those years. Short, petite, and coffee-brown, she looked the same, right down to the gold tooth that sparkled in her mouth. She was warm and cordial. I wondered how she could bring herself to forgive me for what I'd done to her. She never said anything about it, though, and acted like it had never happened.

Carolyn introduced me to Cheryl, her daughter, and I didn't know whether to hug her, kiss her, or shake her hand. She seemed reticent, too. I sensed she wanted to reach out but was afraid to take the risk. As we talked, I searched her face for traces of myself. There were none. She had her mother's wide nose and thick eyebrows, and she was darker-complexioned than either of us.

Looking at her, I wondered, *How could I have gone so long without trying to resolve this matter?* Even as I asked myself that question, I half knew the answer: I was afraid to face the guilt it would bring if it turned out that I'd had other fatherhood responsibilities I'd neglected to face. It would force me to accept the fact that despite all my efforts to be different from my blood father, J.L., I was more like him than I realized.

Cheryl and I got together a few times after that first visit. I told her about my life and what I had been like when I met her mother. I was up-front with her. I told her I was unsure if she was mine, but that I intended to find out. "As soon as we get some blood tests done, we'll take it from there."

I sought advice from friends and family, and even talked with a counselor about it. All of them told me, "Leave it alone. There's little you can do for her now, at her age."

But I'd resolved to try to do what was right if the tests proved positive. Maybe I'd let her come live with me and make a new start. She'd dropped out of school in the ninth or tenth grade and wasn't doing much more with her life than hanging out and fighting. I talked to her about returning to school. It was evident from her blank expression and one-word responses that her concept of the value of an education was as vague as mine had once been. Thinking about my own past, I told her, "Anybody can rise above their station in life."

We didn't get a chance to see what she could do if given a shot at improving her life. Cheryl, who went back and forth to Portsmouth in impulsive fits, got pregnant by an unemployed hometown boy. She insisted on having the baby and making it on her own.

She gave birth to a baby girl in Washington. I went to the hospital after work one day to visit her. A nurse stopped me at the entrance to the maternity ward and said, "The baby can only have visits from its parents and grandparents. Who are you?"

I said, "My name is Nathan McCall."

"Oh, you're the grandfather?"

"Well, uh, uh . . . yeah."

"Go on in." She walked away.

I stood there a second, stunned. *Grandfather? I'm only thirty-six.*

I entered the room, where Cheryl was in bed, cradling her newborn baby like it was a play doll. Carolyn was there, along with a few other women I didn't know. The baby's father was nowhere to be found. The women chatted gaily about the sweetness of motherhood.

I remained quiet the entire time. I kept thinking about that nurse calling me a grandfather. I thought about the blood tests that we needed to take. I thought about something else that was bugging me: It seemed I was still investing a lot of energy trying to straighten out all the crazy things I'd done in the past.

When it was my turn to hold the baby, I couldn't pretend to share the joy the others felt. I kept looking into that baby's innocent eyes and thinking about the hell in store for her. *Another fatherless black child*, I thought. *These cycles. These cycles keep repeating themselves.*

■ ■ ■

One day, while I was sitting at my desk at work, a letter arrived from the Lorton prison, just outside of D.C. It was from an inmate who said he'd seen my byline in the newspaper. He wanted to know if I was the same Nathan McCall who once did time with him at Southampton. I recognized the name right off. It was Mahdee, a homeboy from Portsmouth who was once part of the group of prison intellectuals I hung with at Southampton.

I took the letter home, reread it a few times, and considered what to do. It was clear that Mahdee's letter was a plea for contact and support. I wrote him back, then went to see him.

The prison was comprised of several institutions that warehoused a total of nearly ten thousand inmates—about 96 percent of them black. Lorton made Southampton look like kindergarten. The place was so massive it looked like a small rural town. They even had street names within the complex. It broke my heart to see all that black talent and energy wasting away.

A few minutes after I got into the visiting room, Mahdee walked in, grinned broadly, and rushed over to the table to shake my hand. "Good to see you, my man. Thanks for comin' all the way out here to visit me."

It had been about ten years since I'd seen Mahdee. Tall and lean, he looked basically the same, but I couldn't help noticing that something about him was different. Of course, he was older—about thirty-five now—but age was not the only factor in the change. The stress lines on his face indicated that this latest prison bid was rougher on him than the one before. Of course, there was the added strain of doing time so far away from home. That meant he seldom got visits from friends and family, and had to make do on the prison yard without protection from homeboys to watch his back.

We talked for a good while. He said he'd served nine years on a forty-year sentence and was due for parole in one more year. "I've gotten a trade in brick masonry and plan to get a job workin' with a construction company when I get out. All I need is a union card and I'm on my way."

He went on. "I'm thinkin' 'bout relocatin' to D.C. I been writin' the sister of an inmate who lives in my dorm, and she wants me to come live with her and her four kids when I get out. I figure it shouldn't take me long to get on my feet. . . . I'm goin' straight this time, man. I can't afford to take another fall."

I sat there, listening quietly and thinking all the while, *Cycles. I've heard all this before.* My old buddy from Southampton, Jim, and I talked about the cycles all the time. We'd get on the phone and talk long-distance about the brothers we knew who had gotten out, been killed, or sent back to the joint. At least two of the guys who were at Southampton with us had since committed other crimes and been sent to the electric chair. I was sure that many of those cats had every intention of doing what they said they would when they were released. But once they got out and confronted the harsh realities of the streets, they were overwhelmed, sucked back into cycles they seemed unable to fend off.

That's what had happened to Mahdee. He was sharp at Southampton. An understudy of Jim's, he'd gotten involved in Islam and become well-read and disciplined. I think he had a near photographic memory. Once, I gave him a philosophical essay to read so he could join us in the next day's discussion on the prison yard. He came back and ran it down almost verbatim. The cat really had it together—when he was locked up.

When Jim and I got out, we'd continued going back to the joint to visit Mahdee to help him get through the rest of his bid. But after he got out, he began to change. He crept gradually back into the fast lane. At Southampton, he'd looked healthy and his skin was clear, but after he got back into drugs and hustling on the street his skin looked greasy and his face was gaunt. He even tossed aside his Muslim name and went back to using his old street name, Li'l Willie.

One night in 1982, Mahdee came with some friends to my house in Portsmouth. They were flying high as kites and talking pure trash. They stayed awhile, then I told them I had things to do. When I walked them to the door, I pulled Mahdee aside and said, "Slow down, man. You movin' kinda fast."

He looked at me through reddened eyes and said, "Don't worry, Nate. I got it under control."

A short time later, Jim called and told me the news. Mahdee and another guy had gotten busted. They drove from Portsmouth to D.C., stuck up somebody, and were caught. I thought, *All that promise gone down the drain—again.*

I thought about all that as I sat there in 1991 listening to Mahdee run down his plans. I thought about his life—how he'd spent most of it in and out of the joint. I thought about how he'd blown several opportunities to straighten himself out. After about an hour, I left.

I wrote him once or twice after that visit, but I never went back. I couldn't bring myself to look Mahdee in the eye and tell him I no longer believed he'd do what he said he would. When Jim asked me why I hadn't been back to see my homeboy, I told him that I no longer held out much hope for Mahdee. "I'm not sure he's as committed as he says he is."

Several months after that visit, we lost contact. Mahdee was transferred to another institution farther away from D.C., then he eventually made parole again.

I often reflected on what made the difference between Mahdee and me. We were similar in many ways. Although we both had done bad things, we were basically well-intentioned dudes trying to find our way in the world. I concluded that the distinction between us came down to some things that were simple and, at the same time, very complex:

Mahdee and his siblings had been raised by their mother in the Jeffry Wilson projects, a neighborhood of mostly single mothers and shiftless men who hung around. Life there hadn't convinced Mahdee that there was another way. None of the grand assertions that people make about human potential were ever concrete to him. Whenever he got out of prison, he went back to Jeffry Wilson and hung out, even after his family finally moved away. I think he felt unwelcome anywhere else—the world outside his neighborhood had never opened its doors to let him see what he could really be and do.

But I'd come from a stronger, intact family and a neighborhood where there were lots of hardworking, right-doing black men and women whose lives demonstrated that there were many alternatives to life in the streets. There had always been some older person—a teacher, a neighbor, a relative—to encourage me when I'd faltered or fallen down. Even when I chose the gutter, I'd always had a frame of reference for a better life.

That had made all the difference in the world.

■ ■ ■

It made a difference, too, when it came time for me to pass along the kind of support that had been given me. A few months after I moved to D.C., Liz called from California. "I'm sending Monroe to you."

I said nothing, waiting to hear more. Actually, I'd been expecting that phone call for some time. Once before when Liz had called, she'd sounded frustrated. Monroe had gotten into trouble. He and some other boys tried to steal some things from a record shop and got caught.

There had been other, more subtle signs of trouble in the previous year: Monroe was becoming more defiant toward Liz and aloof toward his stepfather and two half brothers. He was behaving in a way that nobody understood. But I understood, and I knew it was time for him to come to me.

Every time I mentioned it to Liz, she'd go off: "You must be crazy. You didn't do anything for him when he was very young, now you're trying to say you want to get custody of him?!"

She was right. But her refusal to hand him over was based on her judgment of the guy she'd known in the past. She hadn't seen much of me in the eleven years since I'd gotten out of prison, and she had no idea how much I'd changed.

But Monroe wanted to see more of me, just like I'd hungered for my old man when I was a boy. It was hard strengthening the bond when we lived two thousand miles apart. Our relationship was restricted largely to the telephone. That drove me up the wall sometimes and made me feel helpless and inept.

I was sure that if I had him with me I could compete with the pressures he'd get from school and neighborhood peers. But with little say in the matter, I resigned myself to do what I could during the summers, when he visited me in Atlanta. We did the usual things that fathers and sons do. We played basketball and went to the movies. But we also talked, shared, and hugged. We talked a lot about the streets so he wouldn't get a glorified perspective from uninformed peers. I'd take him bike-riding through the streets and point out drug dealers and prostitutes. I told him everything about my past, including the experience with doing time. I even drove him to Southampton a few times and ran down, in graphic detail, the horrors of prison. Of course, we talked a lot about racial matters, too. One summer, when he was about fifteen, I took Monroe to apply for a job at the Six Flags Over Georgia amusement park. It reminded me of my frustrating times job-hunting when I was a teen. All the white kids his age were working in air-conditioned buildings, and the black kids were given outdoor jobs cleaning up the amusement park. I told him, "You may as well get ready. This is what you're going to have to contend with *all your life*."

In July 1989, after Monroe had spent another summer vacation with me, he asked if he could live with me instead of returning home. I sensed a desperation in him that I hadn't seen before. When I talked with Liz about it again, her response was the same: "No way."

I didn't want to start another war with her, yet I didn't want Monroe to think I had turned my back on him. When it was time for him to return to California, we struck a deal. I told him to give it another try. "If it isn't working out for you by the midsemester mark, call me and I'll send you a ticket." I had no idea how soon I'd see him again.

When Liz called a few months later, she said she'd found a letter that Monroe was composing to her. In the letter, he explained why he wanted to live with me. "He said he feared that if he didn't live with you before graduating from school, he might never get a chance to get to know you well," Liz said. "That's what convinced me to let him come to you."

I resisted the temptation to gloat. Her voice was already shaky. Monroe was her firstborn, and she felt she was losing him.

By December, Monroe was standing in a terminal at Washington National Airport, waiting for his luggage. Right away, he entered the eleventh grade, starting his new life and settling into my tiny one-bedroom apartment, where he slept on the living-room couch.

Suddenly, my life was no longer my own. I had a teenage son, and three immediate goals: to help him prepare for his future, whatever he chose; to keep him away from macho pressures to hang in the streets; and to keep him alive in a city where young black males treat each other like targets on a shooting range.

I was really concerned because of our schedules. Monroe got out of school at three in the afternoon. I got off work at seven—on a good day. Most days, I worked until nine or ten and, if I could get a cab, got home by eleven. I was uneasy with all the time Monroe would spend alone.

At work, I constantly got visions of some gang member approaching my son, asking for money or his clothing, then pointing a gun to his head and firing, just for the hell of it. I came up with strategies to minimize the risks: I made sure he came nowhere near to being sharply dressed in school. No expensive sneakers or flashy clothes that might entice jealous dudes to go after him. I drilled him on ways to handle different street scenarios and coached him on how to respond if approached by hoods. "If somebody asks you for your coat, don't put up a fuss. Just take it off and hand it to them without a word. We can always get you another coat," I said.

Although I schooled him on practically every potential situation that came to mind, it still wasn't enough to calm my nerves. Every time I read a news story about some teenage boy being gunned down over some senseless shit, I got visions of my son in subway encounters or neighborhood brawls.

My fears about his safety forced me to come to grips with a troubling reality: As much as I ranted about white folks' messing with us, I felt more threatened—physically—by my own people and the powerful self-hatred driving them.

Eventually, I took a final precaution to ease my mind. I got Monroe out of the path of the urban storm and moved to Arlington, just across the river, where the violence seemed less intense.

I still worried about him and sensed that the cultural pull of pseudo-macho hip-hop fads was even more powerful than the things that once influenced me. I began to see signs of that after he met and started hanging with some cats at a local basketball court: He bopped with a more pronounced pimp and started letting his baggy jeans fall lower on his behind; he suddenly became resistant to doing household chores and took on that arrogant body language that teenagers use as their coded way of telling their parents to go to hell.

Finally, when things started getting out of hand, I had to yoke him, Cavalier Manor–style, break down the macho facade so he'd be real clear on what manhood was and was *not* about. It didn't take a whole lot more to bring him around. I think it helped that Liz and his stepfather had instilled in him a foundation of decency.

After that, we talked a lot about serious things, including girls, sex, and other matters of the heart. I learned from those rap sessions that little had changed on the streets since I was there. He came into my bedroom late one night and asked, "Is it all right to take it from a girl if you take her out and she won't give it up?"

I guessed it was something he'd heard in bathroom rap with other dudes, and I flashed back to those street-corner discussions that had shaped my views. After he posed the question, I paused a long while before I said anything. I wondered, *What can I say to him now? How can I tell him not to do things that I have done?*

Finally, I told him about the things we did to girls while growing up and explained how much I regretted it now. I couldn't bring myself to preach to him, but I presented the issue in a way that hit close to home. Monroe was always paranoid about guys hungrily eyeing Liz in public. So I used her as an example of the danger in viewing other females—girls *and* women—as pieces of meat. I asked him, "How would you feel if somebody decided that they could rape your mother just because she won't give it up?"

He paused. "I'd be mad."

"Then think about it that way with other girls."

He said he understood.

That's how we got through everything: talking, communicating, doing something my parents' generation hadn't been taught to do. I often wondered during those talks with Monroe how I might have turned out if I'd had somebody I could talk to about everything.

When Monroe graduated from high school in 1991, my parents drove up from Portsmouth and Liz flew in from California to see him march. He walked down the aisle, got his diploma, and became my parents' first grandchild to graduate from high school. We threw a cookout and invited his friends. As I watched them playing music, laughing, and jonin', I saw a cycle that brought back memories. I wondered if Monroe was as fearful of facing the hostile white world as I'd been on my graduation day. Watching him, I felt a lot of things. Mostly, though, I felt glad that Monroe was not in trouble and was college-bound. I felt proud and confident that he'd skip the rite of passage to prison that I went through.

Chapter 44 CHOICES

It makes me wanna holler
and throw up both my hands . . .
        —From "Inner City Blues," by Marvin Gaye

∎ ∎ ∎

I wish there were more successes like Monroe to point to. I wish that somehow, brothers everywhere would reach down deep and summon the will to defy the inner hatred driving them to self-destruct. But everywhere I see them giving in, and I am reminded of it especially when I go home.

Sure, there are some among the old crew who are doing all right: Greg kicked his drug habit, got married, and is living clean. Ton, the high school football great and heavyweight thumper, is a Navy chaplain now. Shell Shock works at the shipyard. My brother Dwight got married and settled down. Turkey is hanging: Once he was hustling; now he's got a real job. Nutbrain got married and is giving it a real shot on the straight side. "Nate," he said in a recent phone call, "I been working for a year. Ain't that *strange*?" And me, I'm just a tourist in the white mainstream.

But ours are the quiet triumphs you seldom hear about, the ones overshadowed by the ugly, depressing things.

These days, my visits home have become occasions for mourning, soul-searching, and anger. On one visit, I saw a story splashed across the top of the newspaper about the police busting up a twenty-million-dollar narcotics ring. Listed in the article were several people I've known most of my life. I sighed. It wasn't the first time that day I'd been hit with negative news about the neighborhood. And it wasn't the last. Before that day ended, family members and people I met on the streets told me tale after tale of homeboys, young black men like me, living lives mired in lunacy.

Every day in D.C., I read dismal accounts of blacks murdered over trivia—drugs, a coat, a pair of sneakers, pocket change. The people in these stories are faceless to me. I peruse the accounts with detached sadness, then turn the page.

But in my hometown, the names conjure images of real people who lived down the street, around the corner, on the next block. My trips to Cavalier Manor provide a distressingly close-up view of black America's running tragedy. When I'm there, it dawns on me over and over again that this "endangered species" thing is no empty phrase.

Most of the dudes I grew up with are either in prison, dead, drug zombies, or nickel-and-dime hustlers. Some are racing full-throttle toward self-destruction. Others have already plunged into the abyss: Kenny Banks got life for dealing drugs, Frog got shot in Lincoln Park, Lep just got sprung from a three-year bid, and Shane was recently sent to prison. He shot a man several times, execution-style. He got life.

Of the ten families living on my street when I was growing up that had young males in their households, four—including my own—have had one or more of those young men serve time.

Often, when I go home, I prepare with a pep talk to myself and a pledge to focus on the positive—to spend time with family and old friends who are doing well, and to seek out opportunities to lend a compassionate ear to those not so well off. I know I will see former buddies, old hoods, hanging on the same corners where I left them years ago. I see in them how far I've come. I'm not sure what they see in me. In exchanges that are sometimes awkward, they recount their hard knocks. I say little about my establishment job or the new life I've found. What should I say? Get a job? Go to college? Adopt my middle-class success strategies? The fact is, I know what they've been through. And I understand what they face. I took the plunge myself, many times.

Many people are puzzled about the culture of violence pervading black communities; it's so foreign to them. Some wonder if there is something innately wrong with black males. And when all else fails, they reach for the easy responses: Broken homes. Misplaced values. Impoverished backgrounds.

I can answer with certainty only about myself. My background and those of my running partners don't fit all the convenient theories, and the problems among us are more complex than something we can throw jobs, social programs, or more policemen at.

Shane and I and the others in our loosely knit gang started out like most other kids. Yet somewhere between adolescence and adulthood, something inside us changed. Our hearts hardened, and many of us went on to share the same fates as the so-called disadvantaged.

I'm not exactly sure why, but I've got a good idea. A psychologist friend once explained that our fates are linked partly to how we perceive our choices in life. Looking back, I see that the reality may well have been that possibilities for us were abundant. But in Cavalier Manor, we perceived our choices as being somewhat limited.

When I read about shootings in urban areas and at home, I often flash back to scenes in which I played a part. It's hard for me now to believe I was once very much a part of that world, and harder still sometimes for me to adapt to the one I crossed over into. My new life is still a struggle, harsher in some ways than the one I left. At times I feel suspended in a kind of netherworld, belonging fully neither to the streets nor to the establishment.

I have come to believe two things that might seem contradictory: Some of our worst childhood fears *were* true—the establishment *is* teeming with racism. Yet I also believe whites are as befuddled about race as we are, and they're as scared of us as we are of them. Many of them are seeking solutions, just like us.

I am torn by a different kind of anger now. I resent suggestions that blacks enjoy being "righteous victims." And when people ask, "What is wrong with black men?," it makes me want to lash out. When I hear that question, I am reminded of something Malcolm X once said: "I have no mercy or compassion in me for a society that will crush people and then penalize them for not being able to stand up under the weight."

Sometimes I wonder how I endured when so many others were crushed. I was not special. And when I hear the numbing statistics about black men, I often think of guys I grew up with who were smarter and more talented than me, but who will never realize their potential. Nutbrain, a mastermind in the ways of the streets, had the kind of raw intellect that probably could not be gauged in achievement tests. Shane, who often breezed effortlessly through tests in school, could have done anything he wanted with his life had he known what to do. Now he has *no* choices.

When Shane was caught in a police manhunt several years ago, I considered volunteering as a character witness but dismissed the notion because I knew there was no way to tell his jury what I had been unable to articulate to a judge at my own trial. How could I explain our anger and alienation from the rest of the world? Where was our common language?

Most people, I'm sure, would regard Shane's fate with the same detachment I feel when reading crime reports about people I don't know. But I hurt for Shane, who will likely spend the rest of his days behind bars and who must live with the agony of having taken a life. I hurt more for Shane's mother, who has now seen two of her four sons go to prison. A divorcee, she now delivers newspapers in Cavalier Manor.

I saw her recently after she tossed a paper onto my parents' doorstep. Her hair had grayed considerably. We hugged and chatted. She seemed proud that I had turned my life around, but I felt guilty and wondered again why I got a second chance and her sons did not. After an awkward silence, I got Shane's prison address from her and said good-bye. I wrote to him and he wrote me back. I broke down and cried when I read the letter:

> Yo Nate,
> I am sorry that I didn't get back with you before now. I am fine and everything is going well with me. I know that you are still doing well. I am proud of you, Nate. . . .
>   Now I have my mind in the right frame of thinking with this long-term bid of mine. But I did what I had to do. (There was more to it than appeared in the papers.) Anyway I will keep in touch with you from now on. I am really heavy in the Qur'an now. And I am truly a warrior from the spirit within me. I know what and where my life will lead me from here on. Peace be with you, Brother.
>   Later,
>   Shane

For those who'd like answers, I have no pithy social formulas to end black-on-black violence. But I do know that I see a younger, meaner generation out there now—more lost and alienated than we were, and placing even less value on life. We were at least touched by role models; this new bunch is totally estranged from the black mainstream. Crack has taken the drug game to a more lethal level and given young blacks far more economic incentive to opt for the streets.

I've come to fear that of the many things a black man can die from, the first may be rage—his own or someone else's. For that reason, I seldom stick around when I stop on the block. One day not long ago, I spotted a few familiar faces hanging out at the old haunt, the

7-Eleven. I wheeled into the parking lot, strode over, and high-fived the guys I knew. Within moments, I sensed that I was in danger. I felt hostile stares from those I didn't know.

I was frightened by these younger guys, who now controlled my former turf. I eased back to my car and left, because I knew this: that if they saw the world as I once did, they believed they had nothing to lose, including life itself.

It made me wanna holler and throw up both my hands.

ACKNOWLEDGMENTS

There's no way I could have written this book without the help and gentle encouragement of some key people at crucial times. To them I say, Thanks for helping me get some of this rage and pain off my chest, and thanks for being there in all phases of this project, from start to finish: Jean Fox-Alston, Donna Britt, Katie Davis, Debra Dennis, Carl Faison, Algenia Freeman, Joel Garreau, Ann Godoff, Deb Heard, Matthew Johnson, Danielle Lynch, Peter Perl, Rafe Sagalyn, Kay Shaw, Lucila Woodard, and especially my main man, Jeff Frank, who pushed, prodded, pleaded, and provided the editing spark for me to kick in that final lap.

ALL GOD'S CHILDREN NEED TRAVELING SHOES
by Maya Angelou

By the acclaimed poet and memoirist—*All God's Children Need Traveling Shoes* is a lyrical and acutely perceptive exploration of what it means to be an African-American on the mother continent, where color no longer matters but where the American-ness keeps asserting itself in ways both puzzling and heartbreaking.

Autobiography/0-679-73404-X

ALL STORIES ARE TRUE
by John Edgar Wideman

Set mainly in the Pittsburgh district of Homewood, these ten luminous stories by "one of America's premier writers of fiction" (*The New York Times*) depict African-Americans from all walks of life—ancestors, family, and lovers caught in the vortex of American history and haunted by their own particular demons.

Fiction/Literature/0-679-73752-9

BEST INTENTIONS
The Education and Killing of Edmund Perry
by Robert Sam Anson

Anson explores the racial attitudes of America, as illumined by the case of Edmund Perry: a seventeen-year-old black honors student from Harlem who, soon after being graduated from Phillips Exeter Academy, was killed by a plainclothes policeman whom he and a companion allegedly tried to mug.

True Crime/Sociology/0-394-75707-6

THE FIRE NEXT TIME
by James Baldwin

At once a powerful evocation of Baldwin's early life in Harlem and a disturbing examination of the consequences of racial injustice—to both the individual and the body politic—*The Fire Next Time* stands as one of the essential works of our literature.

Literature/African-American Studies/0-679-74472-X

IN MY PLACE
by Charlayne Hunter-Gault

The powerful memoir of how, in 1961, nineteen-year-old Charlayne Hunter walked calmly into history as she passed through a gauntlet of jeering whites to become the first black woman to attend the University of Georgia.

Autobiography/African-American Studies/Women's Studies/0-679-74818-0

INVISIBLE MAN
by Ralph Ellison

"The greatest American novel in the second half of the twentieth century . . . the classic representation of American black experience."
—R. W. B. Lewis

Winner of the National Book Award, *Invisible Man* is the searing portrait of a black man's search for personal identity in modern American society.

Fiction/Literature/0-679-73276-4

NATIVE STRANGER
A Black American's Journey Into the Heart of Africa
by Eddy L. Harris

Native Stranger is both a marvel of travel writing and a masterpiece of conscience and compassion, conveying at once Harris's sense of being a wanderer in a foreign land and a prodigal son who has finally found his way home.

Travel/African-American Studies/0-679-74232-8

SELECTED POEMS
by Langston Hughes

The poems in this collection, chosen by Hughes himself shortly before his death in 1967, celebrate the experience of invisible men and women—portraying that experience in a voice that blends the spoken with the sung, that turns poetic lines into the phrases of jazz and blues.

Poetry/Literature/0-679-73659-X

Available at your local bookstore, or call toll-free to order:
1-800-793-2665 (credit cards only).